BY MAN SHALL HIS BLOOD BE SHED

EDWARD FESER

JOSEPH M. BESSETTE

By Man Shall His Blood Be Shed

A Catholic Defense of Capital Punishment

IGNATIUS PRESS   SAN FRANCISCO

Cover image:
Lady Justice
Robert Wilson / us.fotolia.com

Cover design by Carl E. Olson

© 2017 by Ignatius Press, San Francisco
All rights reserved
ISBN 978-1-62164-126-1
Library of Congress Control Number 2016934525
Printed in the United States of America ∞

CONTENTS

Preface   7

Introduction   9

1: Natural Law and Capital Punishment   17

2: Church Teaching and Capital Punishment   97

3: Serving Justice in This World and Salvation in the Next   213

4: The American Bishops' Campaign against the Death Penalty   279

Conclusion   375

Bibliography   385

Index   401

PREFACE

We launched this project several years ago, not long after we first met. One of us (Feser), trained in philosophy and theology, had defended capital punishment from a Catholic and natural law perspective in several articles. The other (Bessette), trained in political science and with nine years of full-time experience in criminal justice, regularly taught the death-penalty debate in the classroom (mostly from a secular perspective) and was working on a large empirical study of the death penalty in the United States. Both of us strongly supported the death penalty and were deeply troubled by the growing opposition to it among Catholics—and by the ignorance among many Catholics of what the Church has traditionally taught on this subject. We agreed that there was an urgent need for a full-length defense of capital punishment, written from a Catholic point of view, that treated in detail every aspect of the question—philosophical, theological, and social scientific. A collaboration naturally suggested itself, and the result is this book.

Though we are equal contributors to what follows, Feser was primarily responsible for chapters 1 and 2 and Bessette for chapters 3 and 4. Despite this broad division of labor, each individual chapter benefited from our very close collaboration.

We would like to thank the following individuals who read one or more chapters of the draft and provided helpful comments, insights, suggestions, and corrections: Barry Latzer, Steven Long, Fr. Gerald Murray, and Edward Peters. We also thank the tutors of Thomas Aquinas College in Santa Paula, California, for their feedback during a presentation on our project given at the college during the summer of 2013 and the participants at two workshops on criminal justice and capital punishment hosted by the Salvatori Center at Claremont McKenna College in 2013. Any errors of fact or interpretation remain our sole responsibility.

Feser would also like to thank David Oderberg, for the insights he offered during a long discussion of the traditional natural law defense of capital punishment; Christopher Tollefsen, for the vigorous criticisms he has put forward during several public exchanges with Feser on the subject of capital punishment; and audience members at a lecture Feser gave on the natural law case for capital punishment in the spring of 2013 at the California State University at San Bernardino.

Bessette would like to thank the students at Claremont McKenna College for their insights in his crime class for the past twenty-five years; the dedicated staff at the Bureau of Justice Statistics, where Bessette worked as deputy director and acting director from 1985 to 1990, who have been compiling data on capital punishment for half a century; and the felony prosecutors in the Cook County, Illinois, State's Attorney's Office from whom he learned the realities of murder and its punishment in the United States while serving on State's Attorney Richard M. Daley's staff from 1981 to 1984. He also thanks his friend and colleague Eric Helland for reviewing some of the data and interpretations of chapter 4, and he gratefully acknowledges the research assistance of Jennifer Lee, a student at Scripps College, Dan Carpenter, then a student at the Claremont Graduate University, and Hugh O'Donnell of St. Monica Academy in Montrose, California.

INTRODUCTION

Whoever sheds the blood of man, by man shall his blood be shed;
for God made man in his own image.

—Genesis 9:6

If a Catholic were to be at odds with the Holy Father on the
application of capital punishment ... he would not for that rea-
son be considered unworthy to present himself to receive Holy
Communion. While the Church exhorts civil authorities ... to
exercise discretion and mercy in imposing punishment on crim-
inals, it may still be permissible ... to have recourse to capital
punishment. There may be a legitimate diversity of opinion even
among Catholics about ... applying the death penalty.

—Cardinal Joseph Ratzinger,
"Worthiness to Receive Holy Communion:
General Principles" (2004)

Between 1796 and 1865, Giovanni Battista Bugatti executed 516 condemned criminals, more than four-fifths for murder. Some of them were hanged, some guillotined, some decapitated with an ax. In the case of especially heinous crimes, the methods of execution were harsher. Some criminals had their heads crushed with a mallet, after which their throats were cut. Some were drawn and quartered.

Who was Bugatti? He was the official executioner of the Papal States, a devout Catholic who carried out his work as a loyal servant of the Holy Father.[1] Indeed, the popes and the Church were active participants in the process of execution, which was highly ritualized and freighted with spiritual significance. On the morning of the execution the pope would say a special prayer for the condemned. A

---

[1] The Papal States were a swath of territory in central Italy over which the popes had exercised both religious and political authority for more than a millennium. Six popes reigned during Bugatti's long career: Pius VI, Pius VII, Leo XII, Pius VIII, Gregory XVI, and Pius IX.

priest would hear Bugatti's confession and administer Holy Communion to him in advance of the event. In the hours before the execution, a special order of monks would cater to the spiritual needs of the
criminal, urging confession and repentance while there was still time
and offering the sacraments. They would then lead him to the site of
execution in a solemn procession. Notices in local churches would
request that the faithful pray for his soul. As the sentence was carried
out, the monks would hold the crucifix up to the condemned, so that
it would be the last thing he saw. Everything was done to ensure both
that the criminal received his just deserts and that the salvation of his
soul might be secured.[2] When asked in 1868 to stay an execution,
Blessed Pope Pius IX, though he certainly had the *legal* power to do
so, apparently thought he *morally* ought not to, replying: "I cannot,
and I do not want to."[3]

Many contemporary Catholic readers will find all of this surprising. They are used to hearing churchmen—including popes, most
famously Pope John Paul II—call for the *abolition* of the death penalty; and they are used to hearing this abolitionist position defended
precisely on moral and theological grounds. Capital punishment, they
are told, does not sit well with man's dignity as a creature made in
God's image. Yet Pius IX and his many predecessors who authorized
executions in the Papal States were no less Catholic, no less devout,
no less infallible than John Paul II. Moreover, in defense of capital punishment Pius IX could call upon a vast wealth of arguments
that no faithful Catholic can take lightly—arguments from natural
law, from Scripture, from the Fathers and Doctors of the Church,
and from the consistent teaching of previous popes. For example, he
could appeal to Genesis 9:6, quoted above, which sanctions the execution of murderers *precisely in the name of the victim's dignity as a creature made in God's image.* He could also appeal to the fact that previous
popes taught that Catholics *must, on pain of heterodoxy,* acknowledge
that the state has a right to inflict capital punishment on those guilty
of grave offenses. So what is going on here?

---

[2] For an account of Bugatti's career and the details surrounding executions in the Papal
States in the nineteenth century, see John L. Allen Jr., "He Executed Justice", *National Catholic Reporter*, September 14, 2001.

[3] Fr. George W. Rutler, "Hanging Concentrates the Mind", *Crisis*, February 8, 2013,
http://www.crisismagazine.com/2013/hanging-concentrates-the-mind.

What is going on, as we will demonstrate in this book, is that capital punishment is, and in the nature of the case must always be, an issue about which faithful Catholics may, within certain limits, legitimately disagree. The Church has certainly never taught that the state *must* in all cases execute those guilty of the most serious crimes. She has never *insisted* on applying the death penalty. But she has with equal certainty always taught that the state *may* in some cases legitimately execute those guilty of the most serious crimes. She has insisted that no Catholic is permitted to deny that the state has this right, at least in principle. On the question of whether resort to capital punishment is in practice appropriate under specific, concrete historical and cultural circumstances, she has left things to the free discussion of Catholics, and different attitudes have tended to prevail at different times. For most of the history of the Church, from about the fourth century until the 1970s, the attitude of churchmen and other Catholics toward the use of capital punishment tended to be positive. In the earliest centuries of Christian history, when the Church was subject to severe persecution by the state, the attitude of churchmen and other Catholics toward the use of capital punishment tended to be more negative, as it has in more recent decades.

Some Catholics believe that Pope John Paul II altered Catholic teaching on this subject at the level of principle. As we will also demonstrate, that is simply not the case. Pope Pius IX's *positive* attitude toward the use of the death penalty was what theologians call a *prudential* application of moral and theological principle to concrete circumstances, something Catholics must respectfully consider but with which they are not obliged to agree. Pope John Paul II's *hostile* attitude toward the use of the death penalty also reflected a prudential judgment that Catholics must respectfully consider but with which they need not agree. That is why Cardinal Joseph Ratzinger—then the head of the Congregation for the Doctrine of the Faith under Pope John Paul II, and later Pope Benedict XVI—could say, in the passage quoted above, that "there may be a legitimate diversity of opinion even among Catholics about ... applying the death penalty" and that a faithful Catholic could even be "at odds with the Holy Father on the application of capital punishment".

We will show in this book, we think conclusively, that it is the irreformable teaching of the Catholic Church not only that capital punishment can in *principle* be legitimate, but that it can in *principle* be legitimate for purposes such as securing retributive justice and deterring serious crime, and not merely to protect the lives of others in those rare and extreme cases in which an offender poses a clear and present danger. We fully acknowledge that faithful Catholics may nevertheless argue that in *practice* the death penalty ought not to be applied under modern circumstances, and we certainly would not defend the harsher methods of execution employed in the nineteenth century. We will show, however, that in fact there are no good arguments for abolishing capital punishment under modern circumstances and that many of the arguments commonly deployed are difficult or even impossible to reconcile with Scripture and Catholic Tradition. We will also show that there are very powerful arguments for preserving capital punishment and applying it with some regularity. At the very least we will show that the pendulum has swung too far in the direction of abolishing capital punishment and that the good both of society and of the Church requires that the traditional Catholic case for capital punishment be given much more serious consideration than many contemporary Catholics, including many churchmen, have afforded it.

The plan of the book is as follows. In chapter 1 we set out the traditional natural law justification for capital punishment and answer all the main objections to that justification. We do so at some length, for traditional Catholic teaching on this subject, as on other moral issues, is by no means grounded merely in an appeal to the Bible or Tradition, but also in human nature and in reason. The *rationale* of the teaching of Scripture, of the Fathers and Doctors of the Church, and of the popes simply cannot be understood except in light of this natural law approach to moral reasoning—an approach that has its philosophical foundations in the thought of Plato and Aristotle, which was brought to perfection by Catholic thinkers such as Saint Thomas Aquinas and which the Church has made her own.

Yet traditional natural law reasoning is simply not widely understood today even among most Catholics. Moral thinking about capital punishment, even among Catholics, is often guided instead by what amounts to little more than platitudes lacking any clear content or rational foundation or by ethical theories that are incompatible with Catholic teaching. Hence the philosophical foundations of traditional natural law reasoning and its implications for questions about rights and justice, political authority, and punishment in general must be set out with some care if contemporary readers are to understand the natural law justification of capital punishment specifically. The deficiencies of rival systems of ethics must also be exposed. We aim to do all of this in chapter 1.

In chapter 2, we examine in detail what Scripture, the Fathers and Doctors of the Church, and the popes have said about capital punishment. We show that the consistent teaching of all of these sources is that capital punishment is legitimate in principle, and for purposes other than defense against an imminent threat that an offender may pose to others—for example, for retributive justice and for deterrence. We show that the Church cannot possibly reverse this teaching consistent with the infallibility of Scripture or with her own indefectibility. We show that, contrary to what some have claimed, the teaching of Pope John Paul II did not constitute either a reversal or a development of doctrine on this subject. Along the way we discuss in some depth what the Church teaches about the authority of Scripture and of the Fathers and Doctors of the Church, and the different degrees of authority enjoyed by various types of magisterial statements. We argue that recent papal statements opposing capital punishment cannot plausibly be interpreted as anything other than prudential judgments of the sort with which faithful Catholics (including citizens and public officials) are permitted by the Church to disagree.

Many Catholics believe that even if they are only prudential judgments, the statements of recent popes and other churchmen to the effect that capital punishment ought to be abolished in modern times are well-founded. In chapters 3 and 4 we respectfully argue that this is not the case. In particular, in chapter 3 we argue that when the crimes of the very worst offenders are examined dispassionately and in detail, it cannot reasonably be denied that no punishment less than death could possibly be proportionate to the offense or capable of upholding the basic justice of the social order. We also argue in this chapter that there is powerful evidence that, far from removing the possibility of reform, the penalty of death actually tends to contribute to the repentance of many offenders (as Saint Thomas Aquinas held that it does). We consider in some detail many specific examples of crimes for which offenders have in recent years been executed in the United States, the situations of the families of the victims, and the state of mind of those on death row. We do this not to play on the reader's emotions but, on the contrary, precisely to dissipate the fog of naïve sentimentality that too often prevails in contemporary discussions of capital punishment.

In chapter 4 we address the arguments that the U.S. Catholic bishops have in recent decades raised against capital punishment. We show that some of the bishops' statements imply that these are arguments with which faithful Catholics can disagree, and we respectfully do disagree with them. We demonstrate that the theological arguments deployed by the bishops are surprisingly poor, in several respects. First, they tend to rest on little more than vague platitudes and lack the conceptual precision and careful reasoning that have historically been characteristic of Catholic moral theology and of magisterial documents. Second, they ignore crucial scriptural and magisterial statements that tend to undermine their case. Third, where they do appeal to Scripture, they sometimes deploy novel interpretations that cannot be reconciled with the traditional Catholic understanding of the relevant texts.

The bishops also argue that the administration of capital punishment in the United States is so "deeply flawed" that it should be rejected if only for this reason alone. Yet, we show that the bishops uncritically accept social-scientific arguments that seem to support capital punishment's abolition while they ignore powerful contrary evidence. For example, the bishops sometimes flatly assert that there is no evidence that capital punishment deters crime. That is simply false. The most a critic of capital punishment is entitled to say is that the studies are inconclusive. But in fact, as we also show, one can make a powerful case for the conclusion that capital punishment does indeed deter. The bishops also maintain that capital punishment in the United States is applied in a way that discriminates against racial minorities and the poor and that it poses a significant risk of the mistaken execution of innocent people. We show that none of these claims holds up to scrutiny.

In putting forward these criticisms, we are exercising the right (and indeed the duty) that the Church herself recognizes in her *Code of Canon Law*, which at canon 212 states:

The Christian faithful are free to make known to the pastors of the Church their needs, especially spiritual ones, and their desires.

According to the knowledge, competence, and prestige which they possess, they have the right and even at times the duty to manifest to the sacred pastors their opinion on matters which pertain to the good of the Church and to make their opinion known to the rest of the Christian faithful, without prejudice to the integrity of faith and morals, with reverence toward their pastors, and attentive to common advantage and the dignity of persons.

We will demonstrate in this book, then, that no Catholic may condemn capital punishment as intrinsically unjust, though a Catholic may still oppose the use of the death penalty on prudential grounds. But we will also show that there are no good prudential grounds for opposing it and that there are powerful prudential grounds not only for maintaining it but for applying it with some regularity. Many Catholics today glibly assert that capital punishment is incompatible with promoting a "culture of life". This makes about as much sense as saying that fining thieves is incompatible with promoting a culture that respects property, or that imprisoning kidnappers is incompatible with promoting a culture that respects individual liberty. It is simple-minded sloganeering, not serious thinking.

In fact, of course, fining thieves *itself* actually promotes respect for property, and imprisoning kidnappers promotes respect for individual liberty—both by deterring potential thieves and kidnappers and, via the infliction on the offender of the proportionate penalty he deserves, by reinforcing society's understanding of the evil of theft and of kidnapping. In the same way, and as we will show in this book, capital punishment *in fact promotes* a culture of life. For that reason too, then—in addition to the mountain of other moral, scriptural, and magisterial considerations in its favor—capital punishment is something we believe Catholics ought to support.

Natural Law and Capital Punishment

Natural law in Catholic moral theology

The *natural law*, according to a typical definition, consists of

> the universal, practical obligatory judgments of reason, knowable by all men as binding them to do good and avoid evil, and discovered by right reason from the nature of man adequately considered.[1]

What reason can know of good and evil from "the nature of man" it knows, specifically, from the *ends* or *final causes* toward which we are naturally directed. In this way, the precepts of natural law "reflect the *natural* structure of human *teleology*".[2] The classic expression of this idea is provided by Saint Thomas Aquinas:

> Since ... good has the nature of an end, and evil, the nature of a contrary, hence it is that all those things to which man has a natural inclination, are naturally apprehended by reason as being good, and consequently as objects of pursuit, and their contraries as evil, and objects of avoidance.[3]

The natural law is "natural" both in the sense that it is not man-made, having "a binding force flowing from the very nature of things prior

---

[1] Bernard Wuellner, *Dictionary of Scholastic Philosophy* (Milwaukee: Bruce, 1956), pp. 68–69.

[2] John W. Carlson, *Words of Wisdom: A Philosophical Dictionary for the Perennial Tradition* (Notre Dame, Ind.: University of Notre Dame Press, 2012), p. 183.

[3] *Summa theologica* (hereafter cited as *ST*) I–II, 94, 2. All quotations from Aquinas' *Summa theologica* are from Thomas Aquinas, *Summa Theologica*, 5 vols., trans. Fathers of the English Dominican Province (New York: Benziger Brothers, 1948). Numerical references are to part, question, and article, respectively. For example, the quotation above is from *Summa theologica*, the first part of the second part, question 94, article 2.

to any knowledge or determination by a human legislator"[4]; and in the sense that it is not *supernatural* but is distinct from the order of grace and knowable in principle apart from special divine revelation.

That is by no means to say that God is irrelevant to natural law. On the contrary, as Aquinas writes, law in general "is nothing else than an ordinance of reason for the common good, made by him who has care of the community, and promulgated"; and in the case of the natural law, it "is promulgated by the very fact that God instilled it into man's mind so as to be known by him naturally".[5] The knowledge of God and of his nature and operations presupposed by natural law need not, however, derive from Scripture, Tradition, or ecclesiastical teaching. Rather, it is the sort enshrined in the purely philosophical arguments of natural theology. Hence an understanding not only of natural law but also of its theological preconditions was achieved, albeit imperfectly, by pagan thinkers such as Plato and Aristotle.

Saint Paul famously affirmed the possibility of natural theology and natural law in his Letter to the Romans. Of those Gentiles who knew nothing of the revelation recorded in the Old Testament, Paul wrote:

> For what can be known about God is plain to them, because God has shown it to them. Ever since the creation of the world his invisible nature, namely, his eternal power and deity, has been clearly perceived in the things that have been made. (Rom 1:19–20)

Similarly, though these same Gentiles lacked the Law of Moses, Paul says that they are by no means devoid of moral knowledge:

> When Gentiles who have not the law do instinctively what the law requires, these, are a law to themselves, even though they do not have the law. They show that what the law requires is written on their hearts, while their conscience also bears witness. (Rom 2:14–15)

The official teaching of the Catholic Church also strongly affirms natural law and natural theology. On the latter subject, the Church

---

[4] Francesco Cardinal Roberti and Pietro Palazzini, eds., *Dictionary of Moral Theology* (London: Burns and Oates, 1962), p. 697.

[5] *ST* I–II, 90, 4.

has spoken especially forcefully. The First Vatican Council (1869–1970) declared:

> The same Holy mother Church holds and teaches that God, the source and end of all things, can be known with certainty from the consideration of created things, by the natural power of human reason....
>
> If anyone says that the one, true God, our creator and lord, cannot be known with certainty from the things that have been made, by the natural light of human reason: let him be anathema.[6]

Pope Leo XIII, in his encyclical *Libertas Praestantissimum* (1888), taught that

> the *natural law* ... is written and engraved in the mind of every man; and this is nothing but our reason, commanding us to do right and forbidding sin. Nevertheless, all prescriptions of human reason can have force of law only inasmuch as they are the voice and the interpreters of some higher power on which our reason and liberty necessarily depend. (no. 8)

Pope Pius XI, in *Casti Connubii* (1930), tied natural law to respect for "natural ends" and "natural functions" (no. 71). Pope Pius XII, in *Humani Generis* (1950), taught that despite its practical limitations,

> absolutely speaking, human reason by its own natural force and light can arrive at a true and certain knowledge of the one personal God, Who by His providence watches over and governs the world, and also of the natural law, which the Creator has written in our hearts. (no. 2)

Pius XII also, in the same encyclical, affirmed the principle of finality—the thesis that every natural thing is ordered toward some end—as among the "unshakable metaphysical principles" of that "sound philosophy" that has been "acknowledged and accepted by the Church" (no. 29). Pope Paul VI, in *Humanae Vitae* (1968), stated that "the natural law, too, declares the will of God, and its faithful observance is necessary for men's eternal salvation" (no. 4),

---

[6] See Norman Tanner, ed., "First Vatican Council (1869–1870)", *Decrees*, sess. 3, chap. 2, par. 1 and can. 2, par. 1, https://www.ewtn.com/library/COUNCILS/V1.HTM.

and he connected natural law to the teleology of our natural faculties, speaking of "the reverence due to the whole human organism and its natural functions" (no. 17; cf. no. 10).

Pope Saint John Paul II, in *Veritatis Splendor* (1993), noted that "the Church has often made reference to the Thomistic doctrine of natural law, including it in her own teaching on morality" (no. 44).[7] He also affirmed the foundation of natural law in human nature and its teleological features as ordained by God:

> Only God can answer the question about the good, because he is the Good. But God has already given an answer to this question: he did so *by creating man and ordering him* with wisdom and love to his final end, through the law which is inscribed in his heart (cf. *Rom* 2:15), the "natural law". (no. 12)
>
> It is in the light of the dignity of the human person—a dignity which must be affirmed for its own sake—that reason grasps the specific moral value of certain goods towards which the person is naturally inclined. (no. 48)
>
> The true meaning of the natural law ... refers to man's proper and primordial nature, the "nature of the human person", which is *the person himself in the unity of soul and body*, in the unity of his spiritual and biological inclinations and of all the other specific characteristics necessary for the pursuit of his end. (no. 50)
>
> Consequently the moral life has an essential *"teleological" character*, since it consists in the deliberate ordering of human acts to God, the supreme good and ultimate end (*telos*) of man. (no. 73)

Traditional natural law theory

Metaphysics of the good

In recent Catholic moral theology there has been enormous controversy over both the value of natural law and the question of how to articulate it philosophically. We will address these controversies below. First, we provide a sketch of *traditional natural law theory*,

---

[7] A Thomistic doctrine is one associated with Thomism, the school of thought originating with Saint Thomas Aquinas.

which is grounded in the metaphysics of Aristotle and Aquinas and is, accordingly, identified by its proponents with what John Paul II calls "the Thomistic doctrine of natural law" historically favored by the Church. We will also see how this theory approaches punishment in general and capital punishment in particular before looking at how its rivals approach those issues.[8]

In line with the characterization of natural law given above, traditional natural law theory is committed to an *essentialist* metaphysics insofar as it holds that every natural substance has an essence, nature, or substantial form that is immanent to it and is neither the invention of the human mind nor a mere artifact of human language; and it is *teleological* insofar as it holds that natural substances have final causes or ends toward which they are directed inherently, by virtue of their essences, natures, or forms. This commitment to formal and final causes (to use the jargon of Aristotelian-Thomistic philosophy) differentiates the traditional natural law theorist's conception of goodness and badness from that of modern philosophers who take for granted the broadly "mechanistic" conception of nature. This conception, which supplanted Aristotelian natural philosophy in the seventeenth century, denies that there are any formal causes or irreducible teleology in the natural world.

Hence, the early modern philosopher David Hume famously argued that conclusions about what *ought* to be the case (statements about *value*) cannot validly be inferred from premises concerning what *is* the case (statements of *fact*). To assume otherwise, it is claimed, is to commit a "naturalistic fallacy", and this Humean line has been pressed against Aquinas and other traditional natural law theorists by its secular critics. From the traditional natural law theorist's point of view, however, there is no fact-value dichotomy in the first place. More precisely, there is no such thing as a purely factual description of reality utterly divorced from value, for value is built into the structure of the facts from the start. A gap between fact and value could

---

[8] For recent defenses of traditional natural law theory, see Fulvio Di Blasi, *God and the Natural Law* (South Bend, Ind.: Saint Augustine's Press, 2006); Edward Feser, *Aquinas* (Oxford: Oneworld Publications, 2009), chap. 5; Anthony J. Lisska, *Aquinas's Theory of Natural Law* (Oxford: Clarendon Press, 1996); Ralph McInerny, *Ethica Thomistica*, rev. ed. (Washington, D.C.: Catholic University of America Press, 1997); and David S. Oderberg, *Moral Theory: A Non-Consequentialist Approach* (Oxford: Blackwell, 2000).

exist only given a mechanistic understanding of nature, on which the world is devoid of any immanent essences or teleology. No such gap, and thus no "fallacy" of inferring normative conclusions from "purely factual" premises, can exist given the Aristotelian-Thomistic essentialist and teleological conception of the world. "Value" is a highly misleading term in any case and subtly begs the question against critics of the fact-value dichotomy by insinuating that judgments about good and bad are purely subjective, insofar as "value" seems to presuppose someone doing the valuing. Traditional natural law theorists tend to speak, not of value, but of the good, which on their account is entirely objective.

To see how, consider a simple example. It is of the essence or nature of a Euclidean triangle to be a closed plane figure with three straight sides, and anything with this essence must have a number of properties, such as having angles that add up to 180 degrees. These are objective facts that we discover rather than invent; certainly it is notoriously difficult to make the opposite opinion at all plausible. Nevertheless, there are obviously triangles that fail to live up to this definition. A triangle drawn hastily during a bumpy bus ride might fail to be completely closed or to have perfectly straight sides, and thus its angles will add up to something other than 180 degrees. Even a triangle drawn slowly and carefully on paper with an art pen and a ruler will contain subtle flaws. Still, the latter will far more closely approximate the essence of triangularity than the former will. It will accordingly be a *better* triangle than the former. Indeed, we would naturally describe the latter as a *good* triangle and the former as a *bad* one. This judgment would be completely objective; it would be silly to suggest that we were merely expressing a personal preference for straightness or for angles that add up to 180 degrees. The judgment simply follows from the objective facts about the nature of triangles. This example illustrates how an entity can count as an instance of a certain type of thing even if it fails perfectly to instantiate the essence of that type of thing; a badly drawn triangle is not a nontriangle but rather a defective triangle. And it illustrates at the same time how there can be a completely objective, factual standard of goodness and badness, better and worse. To be sure, the standard in question in this example is not a *moral* standard. But from the traditional natural law theorist's point of view, it illustrates a general notion of goodness of which moral goodness is a special case.

Now consider an example that brings us closer to a specifically moral notion of goodness. The neo-Aristotelian philosopher Philippa Foot notes that living things are properly described in terms of general statements of the form *S's are F*, where *S* refers to a species and *F* to some feature attributed to the species.[9] To cite Foot's examples, "Rabbits are herbivores", "Cats are four-legged", and "Men have thirty-two teeth" would be instances of this general form. Now, saying, "Cats are four-legged", for example, is not saying, "There are some cats that are four-legged"; it is obviously meant instead as a statement about cats in general. But neither is it saying, "Everything that is a cat is in fact four-legged", since the occasional cat may be missing a leg due to injury or genetic defect.[10] Rather, statements of this form convey a *norm*, much like the description of what counts as a triangle does. If a particular *S* happens not to be *F*—if, for example, a cat is missing a leg—that does not show that *S's* are not *F* after all, but rather that this particular *S* is a *defective* instance of an *S*.

In living things the sort of norm in question is, as Foot tells us, inextricably tied to the notion of teleology. There are certain *ends* that any organism must realize in order to flourish as an organism of its kind, ends concerning activities such as development, self-maintenance, reproduction, the rearing of young, and so forth; and these ends entail a standard of goodness. Hence (again to cite Foot's examples) an oak that develops long and deep roots is to that extent a good oak, and one that develops weak roots is to that extent bad and defective; a lioness that nurtures her young is to that extent a good lioness, and one that fails to do so is to that extent bad or defective; and so on. As with our triangle example, it would be silly to pretend that these judgments are in any way subjective or reflective of human preferences, or that the inferences leading to them commit

---

[9] Philippa Foot, *Natural Goodness* (Oxford: Clarendon Press, 2001), chap. 2. The philosopher Michael Thompson labels statements of this form "Aristotelian categoricals". See Michael Thompson, "The Representation of Life", in Rosalind Hursthouse, Gavin Lawrence, and Warren Quinn, eds., *Virtues and Reasons: Philippa Foot and Moral Theory* (Oxford: Clarendon Press, 1995).

[10] Thus statements of this form cannot adequately be represented as either existential or universal propositions, as these are understood by modern logicians.

a "naturalistic fallacy". They simply follow from the objective facts about what counts as a flourishing or sickly instance of the biological kind or nature in question, and in particular with an organism's realization or failure to realize the ends set for it by its nature. The facts in question are, as it were, *inherently laden* with value from the start. Or, to use Foot's more traditional (and less misleading) language, the goodness that a flourishing instance of a natural kind exhibits is "natural goodness"—goodness *in the nature of things*, not in our subjective value judgments about them.

What is true of animals in general is true of men. Like nonrational animals, we have various ends to which we are directed by nature, and these determine what is good for us. In particular, as Aquinas says in the passage quoted above, "all those things to which man has a natural inclination, are naturally apprehended by reason as being good, and consequently as objects of pursuit, and their contraries as evil, and objects of avoidance."[11] It is important not to misunderstand the force of the expression "natural inclination" here. By "inclination" Aquinas does not necessarily mean something consciously desired, and by "natural" he does not mean something psychologically deep-seated, or even necessarily something genetically determined. What he has in mind are rather the *final causes* or *natural teleology* of our various capacities. For this reason, Anthony Lisska has suggested translating Aquinas' *inclinatio* as "disposition".[12] Though this has its advantages, even it fails to make clear that Aquinas is not interested in just any dispositions we might contingently happen to have, but rather in those that reflect nature's purposes for us.

Of course, there is often a close correlation between what nature intends and what we desire. Nature wants us to eat so that we will stay alive, and, sure enough, we tend to want to eat. Given that we are social animals, nature intends for us to avoid harming others, and, for the most part, we do want to avoid this. At the same time, there are people (such as anorexics and bulimics) who form very strong desires not to eat what they need to eat in order to survive and thrive; and at the other extreme there are people whose desire for food is excessive. Some people are not only occasionally prone to harm others,

---

[11] *ST* I-II, 94, 2.
[12] Lisska, *Aquinas's Theory of Natural Law*, p. 104.

but are positively misanthropic or sociopathic. Desires are nature's way of prodding us to do what is good for us, but like everything else in the natural order, they are subject to various imperfections and distortions. Hence, although, in general and for the most part, our desires match up with nature's purposes, this is not true in every single case. Habituated vice, peer pressure, irrationality, mental illness, and the like can often deform our subjective desires so that they turn us away from what nature intends, and thus from what is good for us. Genetic defect might do the same; just as it causes deformities such as clubfoot and polydactyly, so too might it generate psychological and behavioral deformities.

In general, for the traditional natural law theorist "natural" does not mean merely "statistically common", "in accordance with the laws of physics", "having a genetic basis", or any other of the readings that a mechanistic, nonteleological, and nonessentialist view of nature might suggest. It has instead to do with the final causes inherent in a thing by virtue of its essence, and which it possesses whether or not it ever realizes them or consciously wants to realize them. A person might not want what is genuinely good for him. A child, for instance, might refuse to eat his vegetables, or an addict might be convinced that it would be bad to stop taking drugs. From the traditional natural law theorist's point of view, knowing what is truly good for us requires taking an external, objective, third-person view of ourselves rather than a subjective, first-person view; it is a matter of determining what fulfills our *nature*, not our contingent desires. The good in question has *moral* significance for us because, unlike other animals, we are capable of intellectually grasping the good and freely choosing whether to pursue it.

Aquinas identifies three general categories of goods inherent in our nature. First are those we share in common with all living things, such as the preservation of our existence. Second are those common to animals specifically, such as sexual intercourse and the child-rearing activities that naturally follow upon it. Third are those peculiar to us as *rational* animals, such as "to know the truth about God, and to live in society", "to shun ignorance", and "to avoid offending those among whom one has to live".[13] These goods are ordered in a hierarchy

---

[13] *ST* I–II, 94, 2.

corresponding to the traditional Aristotelian hierarchy of living things (i.e., those with merely vegetative powers such as growth and reproduction, those that add to the vegetative powers distinctively animal powers such as sensation and self-movement, and those that add to the vegetative and animal powers the rational powers distinctive of men). The higher goods presuppose the lower ones; for example, one cannot pursue truth if one is not able to conserve oneself in existence. But the lower goods are subordinate to the higher ones in the sense that they exist for the sake of the higher ones. The point of fulfilling the vegetative and animal aspects of our nature is ultimately to allow us to fulfill the defining rational aspect of our nature.

What specifically will fulfill that nature? In other words, in what does the good for us, and thus our well-being or happiness, ultimately consist? Aquinas addresses the question at length.[14] He argues that the highest good for us cannot be wealth, because wealth exists only for the sake of something else that we might acquire with it. It cannot be honor, because honor accrues to someone only as a consequence of realizing some good and thus cannot itself be an ultimate good. For similar reasons, it cannot be fame or glory either; these are, in any case, often achieved for things that are not really good in the first place. Nor can it be power, for power is a means rather than an end and might be used to bring about evil rather than genuine good. It cannot be pleasure, because pleasure is also a consequence of realizing a good rather than the realization of a good itself; even less likely is it to be bodily pleasure specifically (such as the pleasures of eating or sexual pleasure), since the body exists for the sake of the soul, which is immaterial. For the same reason, it cannot consist of any bodily good of any other sort (such as good health). But neither can it even be a good of the soul, since the soul, as a created thing, exists for the sake of something else. Obviously, then, it cannot be found in any created thing whatsoever; our *ultimate* end could only possibly be something "which lulls the appetite altogether", beyond which nothing more could be desired, and thus something absolutely *perfect*. And "this is to be found", Aquinas concludes, "not in any creature, but in God alone.... Wherefore God alone can satisfy the will of man.... God alone constitutes man's happiness."[15] That is not

[14] *ST* I–II, 2.
[15] *ST* I–II, 2, 8.

to deny that wealth, honor, fame, power, pleasure, and the goods of body and soul have their place; they cannot fail to do so, given that we are the kinds of creatures that we are. Aquinas' point is that it is impossible for them to be the *highest* or *ultimate* good for us, that to which every other good is subordinated. God alone can be that.

Moral obligation

It is but a few short steps from the account of the metaphysics of the good just summarized to the traditional natural law theorist's understanding of morality and of human action in general. Aquinas famously held that the fundamental principle of natural law is that "good is to be done and pursued, and evil is to be avoided" such that "all other precepts of the natural law are based upon this."[16] Now, that "good is to be done ..." might at first glance seem to be a difficult claim to justify, and certainly not a very promising candidate for a first principle. For is not the question "Why should I be good?" precisely (part of) what any moral theory ought to answer? And is not this question notoriously difficult to answer to the satisfaction of the moral skeptic?

Properly understood, however, Aquinas' principle is not only plausible, but might seem trivially true. Aquinas is not saying that it is self-evident that we ought to be morally good. He is saying rather that it is self-evident that, whenever we act, we pursue something that we take to be good *in some way* or avoid something that we take to be evil or bad *in some way*, or both. And that is clearly right. Even someone who does what he believes to be morally bad does so only because he is seeking something he takes to be good in the sense of being worth pursuing. Hence the mugger who admits that robbery is wrong nevertheless takes his victim's wallet because he thinks it would be good to have money to pay for his drugs; hence the drug addict who regards his habit as degrading nevertheless thinks it would be good to satisfy the craving and bad to suffer the unpleasantness of not satisfying it. Of course, these claims are true only on a very thin sense of "good" and "bad", but that is exactly the sense Aquinas intends.

Now, Aristotelian–Thomistic metaphysics is not essential to seeing that this first principle is correct; it is supposed to be self-evident.

---

[16] *ST* I–II, 94, 2.

But that metaphysics can help us to understand *why* it is correct. For like every other natural phenomenon, practical reason has a natural end or goal toward which it is ordered, and that end or goal is just whatever the intellect perceives to be good or worth pursuing. This brings us to the threshold of a conclusion that does have real moral significance. Given what has been said, human beings, like every-thing else, have various ends; the realization of those ends is good for them, and the frustrating of those ends is bad, as a matter of objective fact. A rational intellect apprised of the facts will therefore perceive that it is good to realize these ends and bad to frustrate them. It fol-lows, then, that a rational person will pursue the realization of these ends and avoid their frustration. In short, practical reason is directed by nature toward the pursuit of what the intellect *perceives* to be good; what is *in fact* good is the realization or fulfillment of the various ends inherent in human nature; and thus a correctly informed and rational person *will* perceive this and accordingly direct his actions toward the realization or fulfillment of those ends.

In this sense, good action is just that which is "in accord with rea-son",[17] and the moral skeptic's question "Why should I do what is good?" has an obvious answer: because to be rational *just is* (in part) to do what is good, to fulfill the ends set for us by nature. Traditional natural law ethics as a body of substantive moral theory is just the formulation of general moral principles on the basis of an analysis of the various human ends and the systematic working out of their implications. So, to take just one example, when we consider that human beings have intellects and that the natural end or function of the intellect is to grasp the truth about things, it follows that it is good for us—it fulfills our nature—to pursue truth and avoid error. Con-sequently, a rational person apprised of the facts about human nature will see that this is what is good for us and thus strive to attain truth and to avoid error. And likewise for other natural human capacities.

Now, things are bound to get more complicated than that sum-mary lets on. Various qualifications and complications would need to be spelled out as we examine the various natural human capacities and ends in detail, and not every principle of morality that follows from this analysis will necessarily be as simple and straightforward

---

[17] *ST* I–II, 21, 1.

as "Pursue truth and avoid error." But this much is enough to give us at least a general idea of how traditional natural law theory determines the specific content of our moral obligations. It also suffices to give us a sense of the *grounds* of moral obligation, that which makes it the case that moral imperatives have categorical (or *unconditional*), rather than merely hypothetical (or *conditional*), force. The hypothetical imperative *(A) If I want what is good for me, then I ought to pursue what realizes my natural ends and avoid what frustrates them* is something that follows from the Aristotelian-Thomistic metaphysics of the good. By itself, it does not give us a categorical or unconditional imperative, because the consequent will have force only for someone who accepts the antecedent. But *(B) I do want what is good for me* is something true of all of us by virtue of our nature as human beings and is in any case self-evident, being just a variation on Aquinas' fundamental principle of natural law. These premises yield the conclusion *(C) I ought to pursue what realizes my natural ends and avoid what frustrates them.* C has categorical force because B has categorical force, and B has categorical force because it cannot be otherwise, given our nature. Not only the content of our moral obligations but also their obligatory character are thus determined by the Aristotelian-Thomistic metaphysics of final causality or natural teleology. As the traditional natural law theorist Michael Cronin has written: "In the fullest sense of the word, then, moral duty is natural. For not only are certain objects natural means to man's final end, but our desire of that end is natural also, and, therefore, the necessity [or obligatory force] of the means is natural."[18]

Clearly, the "naturalness" of natural law can, for the traditional natural law theorist, be understood only in terms of the Aristotelian-Thomistic metaphysics of the good, sketched above. But it is also illuminating to compare the natural law to the three other kinds of law famously distinguished by Aquinas. Most fundamental is what he calls the *eternal law*, which is essentially the order of archetypes or ideas in the divine mind according to which God creates and providentially governs the world.[19] Once the world, including men,

[18] Michael Cronin, *The Science of Ethics*, vol. 1, *General Ethics* (Dublin: M. H. Gill and Son, 1939), p. 222.
[19] *ST* I–II, 91, 1.

is created in accordance with this law, the result is a natural order that men as rational animals can come to know and freely choose to act in line with, and "this participation of the eternal law in the rational creature is called the natural law."[20] The *natural law*, then, can also be understood in terms of its contrast with eternal law, as the manifestation of the latter within the natural order.

The natural law provides us with general principles by which individuals and societies ought to be governed, but there are many contingent and concrete details of human life that the natural law does not directly address. To take a standard example, the institution of private property is something we seem suited to, given our nature, but that institution might take many forms consistent with natural law.[21] This brings us to *human law*, which is the set of conventional or man-made principles that govern societies and which give (as Aquinas puts it) a "more particular determination" to the general requirements of the natural law as it is applied to concrete cultural and historical circumstances.[22] Human law, then, is unlike both eternal law and natural law in that it is "devised by human reason" and contingent rather than necessary and unchanging. Finally there is *divine law*, which is law given directly by God, such as the Mosaic Law.[23] This differs from the natural law in being knowable, not through an investigation of the natural order, but only via a special divine revelation (though it may incorporate elements of the natural law, as the Ten Commandments do). It is like human law in being sometimes suited to contingent historical circumstances and thus temporary (as those parts of the Old Law given through Moses that did not overlap with natural law were superseded by the New Law given through Christ) but is unlike human law in being infallible and, while in force, absolutely binding.

Now, because the natural law is distinct from eternal law and divine law, the content and obligatory force of morality is in principle knowable to a significant extent even to the atheist, just as scientific knowledge of the world God has created is available even to the atheist. As Cronin writes:

---

[20] *ST* I–II, 91, 2.
[21] See *ST* II–II, 66, 2.
[22] *ST* I–II, 91, 3.
[23] *ST* I–II, 91, 4–5.

The eternal law of God does not move the world directly and immediately, but mediately, *i.e.*, through the operation of secondary causes
or causes residing in nature itself; and therefore it is not to be expected
that in the moral world the eternal law will be operative without some
such intermediate natural principle.[24]

Hence just as, in chemistry, botany, and physiology, knowledge
can be acquired merely by studying the natures of chemical, botan-
ical, and physiological phenomena, so too can moral knowledge be
acquired just by studying human nature. We can know that murder,
stealing, and adultery are bad for us and thus to be avoided whether
or not we know that God exists, just as we can know the causal powers of sulfuric acid, or the growth patterns of roots, or the function of
eyeballs whether or not we know that God exists.

With ethics as with natural phenomena, however, it by no means
follows that reference to God is *absolutely* unnecessary. On the contrary, arguments such as Aquinas' famous Five Ways of demonstrating the existence of God show that the order of natural secondary
causes, though the details of its operation can be studied without
continual allusion to God, nevertheless presupposes a divine First
Cause if it is to exist and operate at all.[25] Determining that sulfuric
acid has *specifically this* kind of effect rather than that requires no
reference to God; but that sulfuric acid and anything else have *any
causal power at all* in the first place, even for an instant, is unintelligible without God as Uncaused Cause. That roots develop in *this specific* way rather than that can be known without reference to God;
but that *any change occurs in the world at all* is unintelligible without
God as Unmoved Mover. It requires no theological knowledge to
realize that eyes are directed at seeing, specifically, as their natural
end; but that *anything is directed to any natural end at all*, even for
an instant, is unintelligible without God as Supreme Intelligence.
Similarly, we can know the goods toward which our capacities are
directed or ordered, and we can know also that the will is directed
toward pursuit of those goods, just by studying human nature; but
since nothing could be directed or ordered toward anything at all

[24] Cronin, *Science of Ethics*, 1:213.
[25] Cf. Feser, *Aquinas*, chap. 3.

in the first place in the absence of God, moral knowledge, like scientific knowledge, *ultimately* presupposes a divine director, orderer, or lawgiver.

Hence, while there is what Cronin calls "a *proximate* ground of duty residing in nature itself"—insofar as the will is fixed by nature on the pursuit of the good as its natural end or final cause—the "*ultimate* ground" of moral obligation is "the eternal law of the Supreme Lawgiver".[26] Since, for the Aristotelian-Thomistic metaphysician, things are *fully* intelligible only when traced back to the creative will of God, the necessity or obligatory nature of our moral obligations too can be *fully* intelligible only when traced back to him. A rational agent will act only in accordance with what reason and nature command, and precisely because reason and nature command it. But reason and nature command what they do only because God has ordered them that way. Hence a rational agent cognizant of the ultimate source of things will act only in accordance with what the divine will commands, and precisely because the divine will commands it. As Aquinas writes:

> In this way God Himself is the measure of all beings.... Hence His intellect is the measure of all knowledge; His goodness, of all goodness; and, to speak more to the point, His good will, of every good will. Every good will is therefore good by reason of its being conformed to the divine good will. Accordingly, since everyone is obliged to have a good will, he is likewise obliged to have a will conformed to the divine will.[27]

Natural rights

We are rationally obliged, then, to pursue what is good for us and to avoid what is bad, where "good" and "bad" have, again, the senses described in our discussion of the metaphysical foundations of traditional natural law theory. Hence we are obliged (for example) to pursue the truth and avoid error, to sustain our lives and our health and

---

[26] Cronin, *Science of Ethics*, 1:213, emphasis added.

[27] *Quaestiones disputatae de veritate* 23, 7, in Thomas Aquinas, *Truth*, trans. Robert W. Mulligan, James V. McGlynn, and Robert W. Schmidt, vol. 3 (Indianapolis: Hackett, 1994), pp. 123–24.

to avoid what is damaging to them, and so forth (ignoring as irrelevant to our present purposes the various complications and qualifications a fully developed natural law theory would have to spell out). The force and content of these obligations derive from our nature as human beings.

Now, it is part of that nature that we are *social* animals, as Aristotle famously noted. That is to say, we naturally live in communities with other human beings and depend on them for our well-being in various ways, both negative (such as our need not to be harmed by others) and positive (such as our need for various kinds of assistance from them). Most obviously, we are related to others by virtue of being either parents or children, siblings, grandparents or grandchildren, cousins, and so forth. Within the larger societies to which collections of families give rise, other kinds of relationships form, such as that of being a friend, an employee or an employer, a citizen, and so forth. To the extent that some of these relationships are natural to us, their flourishing is part of what is naturally good for us.

For example, as Philippa Foot writes, "Like lionesses, human parents are defective if they do not teach their young the skills that they need to survive."[28] It is part of our *nature* to become parents, and part of our *nature* that while we are children we depend on our own parents. Accordingly, it is simply an objective fact that it is good for us to be good parents to our children and bad for us to be bad parents, just as it is (even more obviously) an objective fact that it is good for children to be taken care of by their parents. Now, if it is good for a parent to provide for his children, then, given that we are obliged to do what is good for us, it follows that a parent has an obligation to provide for his children. Similarly, since, given their need for instruction, discipline, and the like, it is good for children to obey and respect their parents, it follows that they have an obligation to obey and respect them. But an obligation on the part of a person A toward a person B entails a right on the part of B against A. It follows in turn, then, that children have a *right* to be provided for by their parents, and parents have a *right* to be obeyed and respected by their children. And since the obligations that generate the rights in question are obligations under *natural* law (rather than positive law), it

---

[28] Foot, *Natural Goodness*, p. 15.

follows that they are *natural* rights, grounded not in human convention but in human nature.

Other obligations we have under natural law toward various other people will similarly generate various other natural rights. At the most general level, we are all obliged to refrain from interfering with others' attempts to fulfill the various moral obligations placed on them by the natural law. For as traditional natural law theorist Austin Fagothey puts it, "Man cannot have such obligations unless he has a right to fulfill them, and a consequent right to prevent others from interfering with his fulfillment of them."[29] The most *basic* natural right is the right to do what we are obligated to do by the natural law. Hence everyone necessarily has a natural right not to be coerced into doing evil. There are also many things that are naturally good for us even if we are not strictly obligated to pursue them, such as having children. This particular example is, according to classical natural law theory, the foundation for the natural right to marry. And, of course, we cannot pursue any good or fulfill any obligation at all if our very lives could be taken from us by others as they saw fit, so that the natural law entails that every person—or at least every *innocent* person— has a right not to be killed.

If traditional natural law theory entails the existence of natural rights, it also entails that there are very definite limits on those rights. To be sure, a right to a significant measure of personal liberty is clearly implied by the natural law, given that the natural differences between individuals in terms of their interests, talents, upbringing, and other personal circumstances, and in general the complexities inherent in the human condition, entail that there are myriad ways in which people might concretely realize the capacities and potentials inherent in their common nature, and each person will need to be free to discover for himself which way is best for him. But this freedom cannot possibly be absolute, for while there is much that the natural law allows, there is also much that it forbids as absolutely contrary to the human good, and rights exist only to allow us to fulfill the human good. Thus, as one traditional natural law theorist has put it, "the rights of all men are limited by the *end* for which the rights were

---

[29] Austin Fagothey, *Right and Reason*, 2nd ed. (St. Louis: C. V. Mosby, 1959), p. 250. Cf. Oderberg, *Moral Theory*, pp. 53–63.

given";[30] and therefore, to cite another, "there can never be a right to that which is immoral. For the moral law cannot grant that which is destructive of itself."[31] Natural rights have a *teleological* foundation and cannot exist except where they further the purposes they serve.

It is important to emphasize that this does not entail the institution of a totalitarian "morality police". As Aquinas emphasized, that the natural law *morally* prohibits something does not suffice to show that governments should *legally* prohibit it.[32] The point is rather that no one can coherently justify his indulgence of some vice on the grounds that he has a *natural right* to indulge in it, or that it would be *intrinsically* unjust to prevent him from doing so. The idea of a "natural right to do wrong" is an oxymoron. But there still might be many reasons of a prudential or even moral sort for government to tolerate certain vices; for instance, enforcing laws against them may be practically impossible or may inadvertently do more harm than good.

It is instructive to compare this account of the foundations and limits of natural rights with the account that would be given by the early modern political philosopher Thomas Hobbes and his followers, who reject the Aristotelian-Thomistic metaphysics of essences and natural teleology that grounds traditional natural law theory. In the Hobbesian "state of nature", everyone has a "right" to do anything he wants without any limitations whatsoever, including harming others. That is precisely because Hobbesians do not see us as *naturally* having "rights" in the *moral* sense at all, morality being the result of a kind of contract between rationally self-interested individuals. The rights we have in the state of nature are really a kind of license. Even when the social contract is made, though, the rights that result inevitably have very little in the way of restrictions upon them, at least in the thinking of contemporary contractarian moral theorists inspired by Hobbes.[33] The reason is that on a contractarian account, our rights are meant to further not any *objective* natural end but rather whatever

---

[30] Celestine N. Bittle, *Man and Morals: Ethics* (Milwaukee: Bruce, 1950), p. 293, emphasis added.

[31] Thomas J. Higgins, *Man as Man: The Science and Art of Ethics*, rev. ed. (Milwaukee: Bruce, 1958), p. 231.

[32] *ST* I–II, 96, 2.

[33] See David Gauthier, *Morals by Agreement* (Oxford: Oxford University Press, 1986), and Jan Narveson, *The Libertarian Idea* (Philadelphia: Temple University Press, 1988).

subjective desires or preferences we happen to have, whether or not these desires or preferences are in line with any purported natural ends. The contract that rationally self-interested individuals would agree to is essentially a nonaggression pact, each party granting the others the "right" to be left alone to do whatever they want, so long as they are willing to reciprocate. If such a right has very little in the way of restrictions on it, that is precisely because it is not natural but conventional, the invention of self-interested parties seeking to maximize their freedom to follow whatever desires they happen to have.

Of course, Hobbesian contractarians would not regard either the conventional status of rights or the lack of restrictions as a problem for their position. But contractarian theories also famously face the problems of explaining why we should attribute even conventional rights to the weakest members of society (who have nothing to offer the stronger parties to the proposed "contract" in return for being left alone) and why we should suppose that even every rationally self-interested individual would sincerely agree to such a contract in the first place (since some might prefer to take their chances in a Hobbesian war of all against all or opt for the life of a free rider who benefits from others' abiding by the contract while he secretly violates it whenever he knows he can get away with doing so). Contractarians have offered various responses to these difficulties, which typically involve inventive appeals to various less obvious ways in which the strong might benefit from leaving the weak alone, or in which even a rational misanthrope might benefit from sincerely abiding by the terms of the contract. At the end of the day, however, the contractarian can give no *rational* criticism of someone who fully understands the benefits that would accrue to him by agreeing to the social contract and treating others as if they had rights but nevertheless refuses to do so. The most the contractarian can say is that we need to be wary of such an individual, for he might do the rest of us harm. But he does not do *himself* harm on a contractarian analysis, and in denying others their rights, he does not deny them anything they really had objectively in the first place.

For the traditional natural law theorist, by contrast, such a sociopath *does* do himself harm and also fails to perceive the objective facts about others. As Foot puts it, "Free-riding individuals of a species whose members work together are just as *defective* as those who have defective hearing, sight, or powers of locomotion."[34] If we look at the evident facts of human experience through the lens of an Aristotelian-Thomistic essentialist and teleological metaphysics, we can see that a certain measure of fellow feeling is, like bipedalism or language, natural to human beings and thus objectively good for every person simply by virtue of being human, whether or not certain specific individuals fail, for whatever reason, to realize this.

Punishment

The goodness of punishment

To understand how punishment enters the picture, it is necessary to say something about the roles that pleasure and pain play in human life according to traditional natural law theory. As we have seen, for Aquinas it is an error to *identify* happiness with pleasure or unhappiness with pain. Happiness instead essentially has to do with the realization of the ends toward which we are directed by nature, and unhappiness with the failure to realize those ends. Nevertheless, pleasure and pain have key roles to play in our happiness or unhappiness. It would, after all, be absurd to suggest that, having realized the ends inherent in our nature, we would be perfectly happy even if we were in constant pain; or that having failed to realize those ends, we would be perfectly unhappy, even if we felt nothing but pleasure.

Nature has attached pleasure to certain goods precisely so that we will pursue them and has attached pain to certain evils precisely so that we will avoid them. That is why vicious behavior (such as immoderate indulgence of our appetites) so often results in "unhappiness" in the popular sense that associates it with mental and physical pain, and why virtuous behavior (such as moderation in indulgence of the appetites) results in "happiness" in the popular sense that associates it with a feeling of mental and physical well-being. Of course, the match is by no means always perfect, and particular vicious acts may bring pleasure, while particular virtuous acts may be painful. This is in part a consequence of the fact that what is good for a person is to

---

[34] Foot, *Natural Goodness*, p. 16.

be understood in terms of his overall character and the realization of his natural ends in the *long* term, and what brings pain at the moment may be part of a larger pattern of actions that will bring pleasure in the long run. It is also in part a consequence of the fact that, here as elsewhere, there are defects and aberrations in nature. Human beings who take pleasure in what is bad are in this sense like tree roots that grow in deformed patterns or like the lioness that kills rather than nurtures her cubs. But in general and in the long run, and when things are functioning properly, the realization of the ends toward which nature has directed us results in pleasure, and the failure to realize them brings pain.

Hence, though happiness is not the same as pleasure, pleasure is nevertheless what Aquinas calls a "proper accident" of happiness.[35] A proper accident of a thing is not part of its essence but nevertheless flows or follows from its essence. For example, the capacity for humor is not part of our essence—our essence is rather to be rational animals—but such a capacity follows *from* our essence as rational animals. Similarly, pleasure is not the same as happiness, but it naturally flows from happiness (i.e., from the realization of the ends nature has directed us toward), not in the sense that it always in fact follows from it, but that it tends in the long run to follow from it and will do so unless prevented. And since we are rational animals, and rationality is for Aquinas a spiritual rather than a bodily power, pleasure in spiritual things (rather than bodily pleasure) is for him the proper accident of our perfect happiness.

We might say, then, that just as a fully healthy specimen of a tree will grow thick roots and just as a fully healthy specimen of a lion will hunt and will possess a thick mane, so too will human happiness, in the sense of the realization of the ends that nature has set for us, be associated with pleasure. And just as a tree with weak roots or a lion disinclined to hunt will typically grow sickly, so too will a failure to realize the ends that nature has set for us be associated with pain. There is in the order of the world a *natural association* between, on the one hand, pleasure and the realization of the ends that follow from our essence and, on the other hand, pain and the failure to realize these ends. The connection is not without exceptions, any more than

---

[35] *ST* I–II, 2, 6.

every single tree has healthy roots or every single lioness nurtures her cubs. But like these latter examples, it is the *norm*, the way things tend to go when everything is functioning as it should.

The relevance to punishment should be obvious. An evildoer has deliberately acted in a way contrary to the ends toward which his nature has directed him. And he has done so in order to secure some pleasure that such action will afford him (even if, when considered from the point of view of the big picture, the action is detrimental to his happiness). Punishment is a matter of restoring the natural connection between pain and acting contrary to nature's ends—somewhat, you might say, as the gardener or horticulturalist who treats a disease of the roots or leaves is restoring a tree to its natural state. As one natural law theorist puts it:

> That is what crime and sin are—the inordinate indulging of our own will or the inordinate securing of pleasure at the expense of the law or of the order required by reason. The restoration of the right order of pleasures by the infliction of a proportionate pain is what we mean by retributive punishment.[36]

Now, as this passage indicates, the moral evil of wrongdoing is a consequence of its following from the *will*—something the tree or the lion does not have, which is why their failures to realize the ends that nature has set for them do not count as moral failures. The offender, Aquinas says, "has been too indulgent to his will" and thus rightly "suffers, either willingly or unwillingly, something contrary to what he would wish" for the sake of the "restoration of the equality of justice".[37] Hence punishment should, in Aquinas' view, involve "depriving a man of what he loves most", which includes "life, bodily safety, his own freedom, and external goods such as riches, his country and his good name".[38] Which of these punishments is appropriate will depend on the nature of the crime, but the "equality of justice" will be restored by answering an offender's overindulgence of his will with the infliction of something that is contrary to his will.

[36] Cronin, *Science of Ethics*, 1:588.
[37] *ST* I–II, 87, 6.
[38] *ST* II–II, 108, 3.

So, punishment is *inherently* good or fitting in the traditional natural law theorist's view—good in itself and not just for the sake of practical benefits such as deterrence and rehabilitation (though those ends are good too)—since it restores a natural balance that has been disrupted by the offender's overindulgent will. And no less good, in Aquinas' view, is our *inclination to inflict* punishment on wrongdoers, for this is a *natural* inclination in the sense described above.[39] Aquinas writes:

> Wherefore we find that the natural inclination of man is to repress those who rise up against him.... Consequently, whatever rises up against an order, is put down by that order or by the principle thereof. And because sin is an inordinate act, it is evident that whoever sins, commits an offense against an order: wherefore he is put down, in consequence, by that same order, which repression is punishment.[40]

Moreover, since it arises from a natural inclination, the tendency to punish is a virtue, so long as it is motivated by justice, say, rather than hatred.[41] Aquinas writes:

> Wherefore to every definite natural inclination there corresponds a special virtue. Now there is a special inclination of nature to remove harm, for which reason animals have the irascible power distinct from the concupiscible. Man resists harm by defending himself against wrongs, lest they be inflicted on him, or he avenges those which have already been inflicted on him, with the intention, not of harming, but of removing the harm done. And this belongs to vengeance.... Therefore vengeance is a special virtue.[42]

It might sound odd to contemporary ears to call vengeance a virtue, given that words such as "vengeance", "revenge", and "vindictiveness" have an entirely negative connotation these days. But from

---

[39] Cf. Peter Karl Koritansky, *Thomas Aquinas and the Philosophy of Punishment* (Washington, D.C.: Catholic University of America Press, 2012), chap. 3.

[40] *ST* I–II, 87, 1. Families (in which parents punish children for misbehavior) and states (in which governments punish criminals) would be examples of "orders" of the sort Aquinas has in mind.

[41] *ST* II–II, 108, 1.

[42] *ST* II–II, 108, 2.

the perspective of traditional natural law, this reflects a tendency to confuse the *abuse* of vengeance with vengeance itself. As Aquinas writes:

> Vengeance is not essentially evil and unlawful....
>
> Vengeance consists in the infliction of a penal evil on one who has sinned. Accordingly, in the matter of vengeance, we must consider the mind of the avenger. For if his intention is directed chiefly to the evil of the person on whom he takes vengeance and rests there, then his vengeance is altogether unlawful: because to take pleasure in another's evil belongs to hatred, which is contrary to the charity whereby we are bound to love all men....
>
> If, however, the avenger's intention be directed chiefly to some good, to be obtained by means of the punishment of the person who has sinned (for instance that the sinner may amend, or at least that he may be restrained and others be not disturbed, that justice may be upheld, and God honored), then vengeance may be lawful, provided other due circumstances be observed.[43]

Older manuals of moral theology reflected this distinction between vengeance or revenge, on the one hand, and their abuse on the other. For instance, Prümmer's *Handbook of Moral Theology* classifies "revenge" as among the "virtues related to justice" while condemning "cruelty or savagery" as vices of excess and warning that "under the pretext of obtaining justice there may lurk excessive love of self or even hatred of the neighbor."[44] Similarly, McHugh and Callan's

---

[43] *ST* II–II, 108, 1. As T.C. O'Brien writes when commenting on this passage in the Blackfriars edition of the *Summa Theologiae*: "'Vengeance' does not have the ring of virtue about it, yet in exact usage it is the best word here. *Vindicatio* comes from Cicero's list of virtues.... As a juridical term it meant laying legal claim to a thing; as a virtue Cicero intends it as a kind of self-defence from injuries and a way of redress. *Vindicta*, originally referring to the rod laid on a slave about to be freed in the ceremony of manumission, came to signify the means taken to avenge a wrong, a punishment. In English, 'vindicate' and 'vindication' have all but lost the meaning of avenging, and refer to clearing a claim, demonstrating a point, etc. (The usage 'vindictive' or 'vindicative justice' survives, connoting justice as retributive.) 'Vengeance' has the meaning of both the act of avenging and the object of the act, the punishment exacted. It should be noted that 'to avenge' has the connotation of a just retribution for an injury." Thomas Aquinas, *Summa Theologiae*, vol. 41, trans. T.C. O'Brien (Cambridge: Cambridge University Press, 1972), pp. 114–15.

[44] Dominic M. Prümmer, *Handbook of Moral Theology* (New York: P.J. Kenedy and Sons, 1957), pp. 215–16.

Moral Theology devotes a section to "the virtue of vengeance" while praising mercy, urging "moderation", and condemning "excess".[45] Apparently recognizing the modern change in usage, Roberti and Palazzini's *Dictionary of Moral Theology*, in its entry on "vengeance", tells us, on the one hand, that:

> In a general sense, the infliction of physical punishment upon someone as retribution for injury caused to another is called vengeance. If done for good and just motives, e.g., love of justice, or preservation of the juridico-social order, or the correction of an evildoer, by a competent authority, according to laws, vindication, of itself, is a good act.[46]

On the other hand, we are then told:

> However, if punishment for an evil deed is inflicted out of an ill-feeling toward the one who has offended, ill-treated, or caused suffering to another, or simply to satisfy one's ill feeling toward his enemy, or for the pleasure of payment in kind, vengeance is an evil act, opposed to that precept of charity which prescribes that Christians love their neighbor even if an enemy. The latter form of vindication is properly called vengeance.
>
> Vengeance is a sin, and opposed to the precept of the Divine Master to love everyone, even enemies, and to pardon sincerely any offense or injury. One of the main characteristics of vengeance is punishment of an offender beyond proper limits, with disregard of the laws which prohibit acts of vindictive justice by private individuals.

So, according to Roberti and Palazzini's *Dictionary*, in the "general" sense of the term—that is to say, when used to refer to the sort of thing Aquinas, Prümmer, and McHugh and Callan have in mind—an act of vengeance is "of itself, a good act". But what is "properly" called "vengeance" is the *abuse* of what Aquinas, Prümmer, and McHugh and Callan have in mind—namely, retribution that is carried out in a spirit of hatred, or is excessively harsh, or is carried out by those without authority to punish. Here the *Dictionary*

---

[45] John A. McHugh and Charles J. Callan, *Moral Theology*, vol. 2, rev. ed. (New York: Joseph F. Wagner, 1958), pp. 432, 434.

[46] Roberti and Palazzini, *Dictionary of Moral Theology*, p. 1268.

seems to give a nod to contemporary usage while agreeing in substance with the earlier authors.

However we use words such as "revenge" and "vengeance", the substantive point is that traditional natural law theory entails both the goodness or fittingness of punishment in itself and the virtuousness of following our natural inclination to inflict it. It is worth noting that the second thesis also provides a distinct, indirect natural law argument for the first, insofar as nature would not direct us toward an end—in this case, punishing evildoers—unless that end were good, given the Aristotelian-Thomistic principle that nature does nothing in vain.

The principle of proportionality

But what sorts of punishments ought to be inflicted? Thomistic natural law theorists appeal to the *principle of proportionality*, according to which a punishment ought to be *proportional* to the offense. Aquinas writes:

> Since divine justice requires, for the preservation of equality in things, that punishments be assigned for faults and rewards for good acts, then, if there are degrees in virtuous acts and in sins, as we showed, there must also be degrees among rewards and punishments. Otherwise, equality would not be preserved, that is, if a greater punishment were not given to one who sins more, or a greater reward to one who acts better. Indeed, the same reasoning seems to require different retribution on the basis of the diversity of good and evil, and on the basis of the difference between the good and the better, or between the bad and the worse.[47]

And again:

> Punishment should proportionally correspond to the fault, as we said above....
> Besides, if a man makes inordinate use of a means to the end, he may not only be deprived of the end, but may also incur some other injury....

[47] Thomas Aquinas, *Summa Contra Gentiles* III, trans. Anton C. Pegis et al. (South Bend, Ind.: University of Notre Dame Press, 1975), 142.

Moreover, as good things are owed to those who act rightly, so bad things are due to those who act perversely. But those who act rightly, at the end intended by them, receive perfection and joy. So, on the contrary, this punishment is due to sinners, that from those things in which they set their end they receive affliction and injury.[48]

Notice that in the first of these two passages from the *Summa Contra Gentiles*, Aquinas says that "the same reasoning seems to require *different* retribution on the basis of the *diversity* of good and evil." This indicates that proportionality in punishment is not merely a *quantitative*, but also a *qualitative* matter. That is to say, to satisfy Aquinas' principle of proportionality, it is not necessarily sufficient to inflict more of a certain sort of punishment on worse crimes than on lesser ones—for instance, larger fines for bank robbery than for petty theft, and larger fines still for murder, but where the punishment consists of a fine in each case.[49] The *character* of the punishment should somehow fit the character of the offense. Notice also that in the second passage, Aquinas says that it is in the nature of some offenses that their punishment can merit not merely the loss of a good that the offender should have pursued but a positive injury as well. Hence with some offenses it is not sufficient that the offender merely be deprived of some pleasure or benefit that he otherwise would have gotten. The active infliction on him of some pain or harm is called for. "Punishment", Aquinas writes, "is proportionate to sin in point of *severity*, both in Divine and in human judgments."[50]

The principle of proportionality is essentially just an extension of the idea that there is—in the long run and when things are functioning properly—a natural correlation between goodness and pleasure, on the one hand, and evil and pain on the other. The natural correlation is, specifically, between *degrees* of goodness and pleasure, on the one hand, and *degrees* of evil and pain on the other. Hence the natural order of things is—again, in the long run and when things are functioning properly—for greater goodness to be associated with

---

[48] *Summa Contra Gentiles* III, 145.

[49] This *might* be sufficient on the very different notion of proportionality criticized by Stephen Nathanson, *An Eye for an Eye? The Immorality of Punishing by Death*, 2nd ed. (New York: Rowman and Littlefield, 2001), pp. 76–77.

[50] *ST* I–II, 87, 3, emphasis added.

greater pleasure and less goodness with less pleasure, and for greater evil to be associated with greater pain and less evil with less pain. This seems to be the force of Aquinas' argument that "*since* divine justice requires, *for the preservation of equality in things*, that punishments be assigned for faults and rewards for good acts, *then*, if there are *degrees* in virtuous acts and in sins, as we showed, there must also be *degrees* among rewards and punishments."[51] And the correlation is, again, *qualitative* as well as quantitative.

This natural correlation, made intelligible by Aristotelian-Thomistic essentialism and immanent teleology, is for the natural law theorist the deep metaphysical reality that we grasp in an intuitive way when we judge that someone has received or failed to receive his "just deserts". We cannot help but regard it as *fitting* when things go well for good people and badly for bad people, and as *unfair* when the reverse occurs. For the traditional natural law theorist, this is not the mere expression of some noncognitive affective state but rather the inchoate apprehension of the objective order of things—of the fact that, given our nature, our good acts inherently "point to" or are "directed toward" happiness and our bad acts inherently "point to" or are "directed toward" unhappiness. When things do not work out this way, we rightly perceive this as a kind of disorder, just as we rightly perceive bodily or psychological abnormalities as instances of disorder. Rewards and punishments are, like medical and psychological treatment, essentially attempts to restore the proper order of things.

It must be emphasized, though, that while the natural law theorist's position is *consistent with* and indeed *explains* our moral intuitions about punishment, it is not *grounded in* an appeal to intuition. The natural law theorist is not saying: "This metaphysical account of punishment fits our intuitions; therefore it is true." Rather, he is saying: "We know on grounds independent of our intuitions that this metaphysical account of punishment is true, and it also happens to account for why we have the intuitions we have." Because they have abandoned the metaphysics that underlies traditional natural law theory, contemporary philosophers who defend aspects of common-sense morality often ground their arguments in an appeal to intuition,

---

[51] *Summa Contra Gentiles* III, 142, emphasis added.

and that is as true with regard to punishment as it is with regard to other moral issues. Unsurprisingly, their critics have little difficulty exposing the weaknesses in such appeals.[52] The traditional natural law account is not open to such criticism.

The purposes of punishment

The restoration of what Aquinas calls "the equality of justice" by inflicting on the offender a harm proportionate to his offense is known as *retribution*, and it is one of three traditional purposes of punishment, the others being *correction* or rehabilitation of the offender and the *deterrence* of those tempted to commit the same crimes as the offender has.[53] Other purposes identified by writers on the subject are the *incapacitation* of the offender, lest he commit further crimes, and *restitution* or compensation to the victims of his crime.

In modern secular society, retribution is the most controversial of these ends of punishment and is sometimes thought to be something we not only may dispense with but ought to dispense with. Psychiatrist Karl Menninger famously held that "the prevalent punitive attitude of the public toward criminals is self-destructive, and hence itself a crime" and that "we must renounce the philosophy of punishment, the obsolete, vengeful penal attitude."[54] Ramsey Clark, attorney general under President Lyndon Johnson, wrote that "punishment as an end in itself is itself a crime in our times."[55]

But as our discussion to this point indicates, for the natural law theorist, retribution is not only *a* legitimate end of punishment; it is the *fundamental* end. For one thing, the intelligibility and goodness both of retribution in itself and of our inclination to exact it follow straightforwardly from the metaphysics of the good sketched above, and this account of retribution is the very foundation of the traditional natural law theorist's account of punishment in general.

[52] See, e.g., David Boonin, *The Problem of Punishment* (Cambridge: Cambridge University Press, 2008), chap. 3, for a critique of attempts to justify retribution by appeal to intuition.

[53] See Fagothey, *Right and Reason*, pp. 418–22; David S. Oderberg, *Applied Ethics: A Non-Consequentialist Approach* (Oxford: Blackwell, 2000), pp. 146–56.

[54] Karl Menninger, *The Crime of Punishment* (New York: Viking Press, 1968), p. 156.

[55] Ramsey Clark, *Crime in America* (New York: Simon and Schuster, 1970), p. 219. Cf. Austin Sarat, *When the State Kills: Capital Punishment and the American Condition* (Princeton, N.J.: Princeton University Press, 2002).

It is not surprising that modern secular thinkers would find retribution mysterious in the absence of this metaphysical foundation, but goodness and badness *themselves* as objective features of the world, and thus morality *as such* (never mind the morality of punishment specifically), become problematic in the absence of that metaphysical foundation. *All* of our inclinations—not just to punish, but also to reward, to love, and indeed even to feel outrage at the very idea of retribution—become mere subjective preferences if there are no formal and final causes, no essences or teleology immanent to the world. Now, the natural law theorist has *arguments* for the metaphysics of the good that underlies his position and for the moral conclusions he derives from it. He has given an account of why retribution is both intelligible and good and not a mere relic of a less rational and less humane era. The burden of proof is therefore not on the traditional natural law theorist, but rather on his critic, not only to refute the Aristotelian-Thomistic metaphysics of the good but also to show how morality, including any moral criticism of retribution, is possible in the absence of that metaphysics.

This burden is a very great one, because the other functions of punishment themselves become problematic in the absence of retribution. If we need not give someone his just deserts, then there can be no objection *in principle* to realizing the corrective and deterrent functions of punishment by meting out extremely mild punishments for major crimes or extremely harsh punishments for minor crimes. Perhaps certain murderers could be deterred or persuaded to change their ways by a moderate fine, and perhaps minor thefts could be virtually eliminated by the threat of summary execution. There might be *practical* problems implementing such policies, but there could be no *moral* objection if there is no objective fact of the matter about whether an offender deserves a punishment proportionate to his offense.

If we *do* object morally to such disproportionate punishments, though, we must rationally justify this objection, and this cannot plausibly be done unless we acknowledge that there is such a thing as desert. As C. S. Lewis puts the point:

> The concept of Desert is the only connecting link between punishment and justice. It is only as deserved or undeserved that a sentence can be just or unjust. I do not here contend that the question "Is it

deserved?" is the only one we can reasonably ask about a punishment.
We may very properly ask whether it is likely to deter others and
to reform the criminal. But neither of these two last questions is a
question about justice.... When we cease to consider what the criminal deserves and consider only what will cure him or deter others,
we have tacitly removed him from the sphere of justice altogether;
instead of a person, a subject of rights, we now have a mere object, a
patient, a "case".[56]

Nor is disproportion between a particular offense and a particular
act of punishment the only problem. As Lewis goes on to note, if
we consider only correction and deterrence in the absence of desert,
then someone guilty even of a minor and nonviolent offense could in
principle be taken into custody indefinitely, for as long as we think it
will take us to cure him. Or we might inflict a punishment on someone who has committed no offense at all, if others believe he committed an offense and we judge such punishment to have sufficiently
high value as a deterrent to them.

Hence, while retribution is not the only end we might consider
when inflicting a punishment, it must always be *one* of the ends,
and indeed the fundamental end, if punishment is to be just. For, all
things being equal, we *may* punish even if we will thereby achieve no
end other than retribution; but we *may not* punish if retribution is not
at least one of the ends aimed at. The (updated 1997 edition of the)
Catechism of the Catholic Church endorses the primacy of retribution:

> Legitimate public authority has the right and duty to inflict punish-
> ment *proportionate to the gravity of the offense. Punishment has the primary
> aim of redressing the disorder introduced by the offense.* When it is willingly
> accepted by the guilty party, it assumes the value of expiation. Punish-
> ment then, in addition to defending public order and protecting peo-
> ple's safety, has a medicinal purpose: as far as possible, it must contribute
> to the correction of the guilty party.[57] (*CCC* 2266, emphasis added)

"Redressing the disorder" by inflicting a "proportionate" punishment is just the "restoration of the equality of justice" spoken of
by Aquinas.

---

[56] C.S. Lewis, "The Humanitarian Theory of Punishment", in *God in the Dock* (Grand
Rapids, Mich.: William B. Eerdmans, 1970), p. 288.
[57] Cf. Lk 23:40–43.

Public authority

Given that a wrongdoer merits a punishment proportionate to his offense, there is still the question of who is to inflict this punishment. Aquinas answers as follows:

> It has passed from natural things to human affairs that whenever one thing rises up against another, it suffers some detriment therefrom.... Wherefore we find that the natural inclination of man is to repress those who rise up against him. Now it is evident that all things contained in an order, are, in a manner, one, in relation to the principle of that order. Consequently, whatever rises up against an order, is put down by that order or by the principle thereof. And because sin is an inordinate act, it is evident that whoever sins, commits an offense against an order: wherefore he is put down, in consequence, by that same order, which repression is punishment.
>
> Accordingly, man can be punished with a threefold punishment corresponding to the three orders to which the human will is subject. In the first place a man's nature is subjected to the order of his own reason; secondly, it is subjected to the order of another man who governs him either in spiritual or in temporal matters, as a member either of the state or of the household; thirdly, it is subjected to the universal order of the Divine government. Now each of these orders is disturbed by sin, for the sinner acts against his reason, and against human and Divine law. Wherefore he incurs a threefold punishment; one, inflicted by himself, viz. remorse of conscience; another, inflicted by man; and a third, inflicted by God.[58]

So, since an offense is an offense against an order of things, it is the head of that order that has the primary responsibility for repairing that order by inflicting punishment. In the case of immoral actions that affect only the offender himself, his intellect, which governs the rest of his nature, will punish him via a troubled conscience. In the case of offenses against divine law, God will punish him. Writes Aquinas, "If man were by nature a solitary animal, this twofold order would suffice. But since man is naturally a civic and social animal ... a third order is necessary, whereby man is directed in relation to other men among whom he has to dwell."[59] Hence it is the head of

[58] *ST* I–II, 87, 1.
[59] *ST* I–II, 72, 4.

this third, social sort of order that has the primary responsibility for punishing offenses against it.

Now, in the family, the responsibility lies with parents. In the political order, "the care of the common good is entrusted to persons of rank having public authority."[60] Of the need for these governmental authorities, Aquinas writes:

> Since some people pay little attention to the punishments inflicted by God, because they are devoted to the objects of sense and care only for the things that are seen, it has been ordered accordingly by divine providence that there be men in various countries whose duty it is to compel these people, by means of sensible and present punishments, to respect justice.... Now, it is just for the wicked to be punished, since by punishment the fault is restored to order.[61]

As the reference to divine providence here indicates, Aquinas ties governmental authority to divine authority.[62] He regards the former as derivative from the latter, governmental authorities being instruments, as it were, of divine authority. Hence, following the passage just quoted, he writes:

> Again, in various countries, the men who are put in positions over other men are like executors of divine providence; indeed, God through the order of His providence directs lower beings by means of higher ones, as is evident from what we said before. But no one sins by the fact that he follows the order of divine providence. Now, this order of divine providence requires the good to be rewarded and the evil to be punished, as is shown by our earlier remarks. Therefore, men who are in authority over others do no wrong when they reward the good and punish the evil.[63]

Aquinas' position is thus very different from that of modern political philosophers such as Hobbes and Locke, who take political authority to derive entirely from the consent of the governed rather than from God—only "from below", as it were, rather than also "from above".

---

[60] *ST* II–II, 64, 3.

[61] *Summa Contra Gentiles* III, 146, 1.

[62] See Koritansky, *Philosophy of Punishment*, chap. 5; Steven A. Long, *The Teleological Grammar of the Moral Act* (Naples, Fla.: Sapientia Press, 2007), pp. 58–62.

[63] *Summa Contra Gentiles* III, 146, 2.

To be sure, Aquinas' view by no means entails a "divine right of kings" doctrine or the rejection of democratic institutions. Aquinas' natural law position is compatible with the view that popular elections are better than hereditary monarchies and the like as a means of determining who will *fill* a political office. The point is rather that the authority that attaches *to the office itself* is *ultimately* delegated by God rather than by the people.[64]

Here natural law theory once again dovetails with the teaching of Scripture and of the popes. Saint Paul writes, in the Letter to the Romans:

> Let every person be subject to the governing authorities. For there is no authority except from God, and those authorities that exist have been instituted by God. Therefore he who resists the authorities resists what God has appointed, and those who resist will incur judgment. (Rom 13:1–2)

In his encyclical *Immortale Dei* (1885), Pope Leo XIII teaches:

> As no society can hold together unless some one be over all, directing all to strive earnestly for the common good, every body politic must have a ruling authority, and this authority, no less than society itself, has its source in nature, and has, consequently, God for its Author. Hence, it follows that all public power must proceed from God. (no. 3)

And in *Diuturnum* (1881), while affirming that "those who may be placed over the State may in certain cases be chosen by the will and decision of the multitude", Leo insists that, in such cases, while the *ruler* is designated by the people, "the rights of ruling are not thereby conferred. Nor is the authority delegated to him, but the person by whom it is to be exercised is determined upon" (no. 6). He also says, contra the sort of view associated with Hobbes and Locke:

> Very many men of more recent times, walking in the footsteps of those who in a former age assumed to themselves the name of philosophers, say that all power comes from the people.... But from these,

[64] Compare the defense of popular consent developed by Scholastic thinkers such as Saint Robert Bellarmine and Francisco Suarez, who argue that authority derives from God but is transferred to the ruler through the people.

Catholics dissent, who affirm that the right to rule is from God, as from a natural and necessary principle. (no. 5)

Capital punishment

The death penalty and retributive justice

With this background in place, the basic natural law argument for the legitimacy in principle of capital punishment is very straightforward. It can be summarized as follows:

1. Wrongdoers deserve punishment.
2. The graver the wrongdoing, the severer is the punishment deserved.
3. Some crimes are so grave that no punishment less than death would be proportionate in its severity.
4. Therefore, wrongdoers guilty of such crimes deserve death.
5. Public authorities have the right, in principle, to inflict on wrongdoers the punishments they deserve.
6. Therefore, public authorities have the right, in principle, to inflict the death penalty on those guilty of the gravest offenses.

Conclusions 4 and 6 clearly follow from the premises of this argument. The reasons for premises 1, 2, and 5 have been given in the sections above on the goodness of punishment, the principle of proportionality, and public authority, respectively.

Premise 3 is, we think, obviously true, but perhaps further comment is appropriate. If wrongdoers deserve punishment, and if punishment ought to be proportionate to the gravity of the crime, then it seems absurd to deny that there is *some* level of criminality for which nothing less than capital punishment would be proportionate. For on the principle of proportionality, there is no such thing as deserving a punishment merely *of some severity or other*, any more than there is such a thing as being of *some height or other*. It makes no sense to say that it is an objective fact that rape, for example, merits punishment but that there is no fact about whether it merits a punishment as mild as a fifty-cent fine or as harsh as scourging, any more than it makes sense to say that it is an objective fact that John has height but that there is no fact about whether he is five feet tall, or six feet tall, or any other particular height. To have height is to have *some specific* height, and to deserve punishment is to deserve a punishment of *some specific severity.*[65] It is to deserve a punishment *as severe as the offense is grave.* Proportionality, then, is built into the notion of desert, and thus is built into the notion of punishment. (To be sure, we might not always be able, in *practice*, to determine exactly how severe is the punishment some offense merits, but that does not mean that there is no such specific severity, any more than the fact that some object might be too small or too large for us to measure entails that it does not have a specific height.)

Now, since there are crimes as grave as death or even graver, so too must there be crimes for which nothing less than death would be a sufficiently severe penalty. Even if it were claimed that a single murder would not be such a crime, it is not difficult to imagine a crime that would be. Mass murder? Genocide? Genocide coupled with the rape and torture of the victims? To claim that there is *no* crime for which death would be a proportionate punishment— to claim, for instance, that a cold-blooded genocidal rapist can never *even in principle* merit a greater punishment than the lifelong imprisonment that might be inflicted on, say, a recidivist bank robber—is implicitly to give up the principle of proportionality. For to agree that genocide is a far worse offense than bank robbery while maintaining that genocide cannot in principle merit a punishment worse than the punishment for bank robbery is implicitly to deny that a punishment ought to be proportionate to the offense.

Now, if, as we have argued, the legitimacy of punishment entails desert, and desert in turn entails proportionality, then to deny proportionality is implicitly to deny desert, and thus implicitly to deny the legitimacy of punishment. But proportionality entails the legitimacy in principle of capital punishment. Hence to deny the legitimacy in principle of capital punishment is implicitly to deny proportionality,

---

[65] Keep in mind that for the natural law theorist, to "fit" the crime, punishments should be proportionate in their *quality* and not merely their *quantity*. If we fined rapists a dime for one rape and a dollar for ten rapes, it would be absurd to suggest that we are respecting the principle that punishments be proportionate to the offense.

and thus desert, and thus the legitimacy of punishment itself. In short, the legitimacy of *punishment in general* and the legitimacy in principle of *capital* punishment in particular *stand or fall together*. And as with the fittingness of punishment in general, here too common sense tracks the conclusions of traditional natural law theory. As one Catholic natural law theorist writes:

> There is in every human breast a strong sense of what the learned call *lex talionis*, and children *tit for tat*. "If a man has done to him what he has done to others, that is the straight course of justice;" so says the canon of Rhadamanthus, quoted by Aristotle. (*Eth.*, V., v., 3.).... It appears in the divine direction given to Noe: "Whoso sheddeth man's blood, his blood shall be shed." (Gen. ix. 6.) It appears in that popular sentiment, which in some parts of America displays itself in the lynching of murderers, who have unduly escaped the hands of the law; and which, under a similar paralysis of law in Corsica, broke out in blood-feuds, whereby the nearest relative of the deceased went about to slay the murderer. [Though such] taking of justice into private hands is morally unlawful ... [it] is a violent outburst of a natural and reasonable sentiment deprived of its legitimate vent. Unquestionably then there is an apparent and commonly recognized fairness of retribution in the infliction of capital punishment for murder. Thus the first condition of appropriate punishment is satisfied, that it be *manifestly proportioned to the crime*.[66]

Now, sometimes inflicting a proportionate punishment is impossible—for example, a mass murderer cannot be executed multiple times—but the practical difficulties involved in implementing a principle do not per se cast doubt on a principle itself. After all, restitution is also often practically impossible, but that does not entail that we should not at least try to approximate it. Furthermore, when the other aims of punishment (correction, deterrence, etc.) are taken into account, we may have reason to give an offender some punishment other than what he strictly deserves. And, of course, there are cases in which considerations of mercy might lead us to inflict a much lesser punishment or no punishment at all. Then there is the fact that moral hazards entailed by certain punishments ought to make us wary of

---

[66] Joseph Rickaby, *Moral Philosophy*, 4th ed. (London: Longmans, Green, 1919), pp. 346–47.

inflicting them. For instance, a murderer whose preferred method is to stab his victims multiple times may deserve the same treatment; but given the psychological damage the infliction of such grisly punishments would do to executioners, we ought to confine ourselves to the more antiseptic methods of execution typical of modern times.

In short, the principle of proportionality does not require that we *must* always in fact inflict on a wrongdoer a punishment that is exactly proportionate to his offense. Rather, it provides us with a presumption that can be overridden, a baseline from which we will often have practical and moral reasons to deviate.

It might be objected, however, that certain punishments are morally problematic in a way that poses a fatal dilemma for our position. For example, capital punishment opponent Christopher Tollefsen notes that rape is "intrinsically wrong" and thus "not available as an option for punishment, regardless of its feasibility or the proportion of goods to bads it might bring about".[67] So if we were to claim, on the basis of the principle of proportionality, that a rapist could at least in *principle* be punished with rape, our position would entail a falsehood. Yet if we acknowledge instead (as we do) that the principle of proportionality cannot justify rape, even in principle, as a legitimate punishment, then (Tollefsen seems to conclude) we should agree that it also cannot, by itself, justify capital punishment, even in principle.

This argument breaks down, however, because there is a crucial disanalogy between rape and the taking of someone's life. To take a life is, essentially, to inflict a single harm—namely, the taking of the life. (Of course, other harms might follow from this—one's children might be orphaned, one's spouse widowed, and so forth—but the taking of a life would still be a harm, even if such other harms did not follow.) Rape, however, essentially involves *several* harms: not only the humiliation and bodily harm inflicted on the victim but also the sexual perversion and sadism by which the rapist harms his own character. Now, to indulge in such sexual perversion and sadism is intrinsically immoral; and therefore rape is intrinsically immoral, even

[67] Christopher O. Tollefsen, "Capital Punishment, Dignity, and Authority: A Response to Ed Feser", *Public Discourse*, September 30, 2011, http://www.thepublicdiscourse.com/2011/09/4045/. Cf. Nathanson, *An Eye for an Eye?*, p. 74, and Boonin, *The Problem of Punishment*, p. 110.

if carried out as a punishment. And the principle of proportionality does not imply otherwise. Rather, it implies, at most, only that a rapist deserves the humiliation and bodily harm he has inflicted on others—just as it implies that a murderer deserves to suffer the same harm *he* has inflicted on others—but it does not imply that anyone, including those with authority to punish wrongdoers, can even in principle legitimately indulge in the sexual perversion and sadism that are involved in rape.

Natural law proponent David Oderberg, in his defense of capital punishment, takes the view that there is such a thing as the worst possible crime and also such a thing as the worst possible punishment.[68] He argues that given the principle of proportionality, whatever the worst possible crime is would have to merit the worst possible punishment. Now death, as he also argues, is the worst possible punishment. Therefore, whatever the worst possible crime happens to be—and he allows that it might turn out that there is a class of crimes that are equally bad, but where there are no crimes that are worse than those in this class—will be one for which a penalty of death is merited.

The argument is interesting, but in our view the basic argument for the legitimacy in principle of capital punishment does not require that there be a worst possible crime or a worst possible punishment. All that is required is the principle of proportionality itself. Though there are, as we have allowed, cases where it might be difficult to apply the principle in practice, there are also obvious paradigms of proportionality. A large fine is proportionate to the crime of destroying someone's home or car in a way that a literal slap on the wrist would not be; incarceration is proportionate to the crime of kidnapping in a way that a small fine would not be; death is proportionate to the crime of murder in a way that a brief incarceration would not be; and so forth. The question of whether there is a worst possible crime and a worst possible punishment seems irrelevant to the plausibility of these illustrations of proportionality.

The death penalty and the other purposes of punishment

As we have seen, according to traditional natural law theory, retribution is the primary aim of punishment insofar as we must always

---

[68] Oderberg, *Applied Ethics*, chap. 4.

have retribution in view when punishing, even if we have other aims in view as well. Purposes of correction, deterrence, and the like are never *by themselves* sufficient to justify punishment, since it is never legitimate to inflict a punishment on someone unless he *deserves* it. But if retribution is a necessary aim of punishment, is it also sufficient? Can we inflict a punishment *merely* to secure retributive justice? Some traditional natural law theorists think not. Aquinas writes:

> The punishments of this life are medicinal rather than retributive.[69] For retribution is reserved to the Divine judgment which is pronounced against sinners.... Wherefore, according to the judgment of the present life the death punishment is inflicted, not for every mortal sin, but only for such as inflict an irreparable harm, or again for such as contain some horrible deformity. Hence according to the present judgment the pain of death is not inflicted for theft which does not inflict an irreparable harm, except when it is aggravated by some grave circumstance, as in the case of sacrilege which is the theft of a sacred thing, of peculation, which is theft of common property ... and of kidnaping which is stealing a man, for which the pain of death is inflicted.[70]

As his examples indicate, Aquinas nevertheless thinks that recourse to the death penalty is justified by the other aims of punishment (even for offenses less serious than those that most contemporary defenders of capital punishment have in view). For example, it is in his view justifiable for purposes of deterrence:

> The punishment that is inflicted according to human laws, is not always intended as a medicine for the one who is punished, but sometimes only for others: thus when a thief is hanged, this is not for his own amendment, but for the sake of others, that at least they may be deterred from crime through fear of the punishment.[71]

Emphasizing man's social nature, Aquinas stresses especially the value of capital punishment in incapacitating those members of society

---

[69] Richard Regan translates this, more accurately, as: "The punishments of this life are more medicinal than retributive." Thomas Aquinas, *On Law, Morality, and Politics*, 2nd ed., trans. Richard J. Regan (Indianapolis: Hackett, 2002), p. 139. Aquinas is not denying that punishments are *in part* retributive.

[70] *ST* II–II, 66, 6.

[71] *ST* I–II, 87, 3.

who pose a danger to the whole.[72] Aquinas also holds that there is a
sense in which the death penalty can even benefit the offender himself:

> Moreover the death inflicted by the judge profits the sinner, if he be
> converted, unto the expiation of his crime; and, if he be not con-
> verted, it profits so as to put an end to the sin, because the sinner is
> thus deprived of the power to sin any more.[73]

It is important to emphasize that, contrary to the impression given
by some commentators, there is nothing in these passages that implies
that Aquinas regards deterrence, protection of the community, and
the like as sufficient *in themselves* to justify capital punishment, independent of retributive justice. Indeed, that cannot be what Aquinas
thinks, given that, as we have seen above, he is committed to the
principle that a punishment should be proportionate to the offense.
Obviously, Aquinas would not say that we might justly execute
someone to deter others even if such a punishment were out of proportion to what he actually deserves. Rather, in these passages, it is
simply taken for granted that the offenders in question already deserve
death as a matter of retributive justice. What Aquinas is addressing is
the question of why we should sometimes inflict on them what they
deserve given that "the punishments of this life are more medicinal
than retributive."

Once again emphasizing our social nature, Aquinas is clear that the
death penalty can be inflicted only by those with special responsibility
for the political order and never by private individuals:

> It is lawful to kill an evildoer in so far as it is directed to the welfare
> of the whole community, so that it belongs to him alone who has
> charge of the community's welfare.... Now the care of the common
> good is entrusted to persons of rank having public authority: where-
> fore they alone, and not private individuals, can lawfully put evildoers
> to death.[74]

This reflects the traditional natural law position that the social and
political order is natural rather than the product of a "social contract"

---

[72] *ST* II–II, 64, 2 and *Summa Contra Gentiles* III, 4–5.
[73] *ST* II–II, 25, 6.
[74] *ST* II–II, 64, 3.

among self-interested individuals, and that authority comes from God rather than man, "from above" rather than merely "from below".

Now, a further benefit of capital punishment is that, precisely because of its supreme gravity, it can uniquely reinforce our sense of the transcendent source of the political order that inflicts it, and thus our respect for that order. As the late Walter Berns wrote:

> Capital punishment ... serves to remind us of the majesty of the moral order that is embodied in our law and of the terrible consequences of its breach. The law must not be understood to be merely statute that we enact or repeal at our will and obey or disobey at our convenience, especially not the criminal law. Wherever law is regarded as merely statutory, men will soon enough disobey it, and will learn how to do so without any inconvenience to themselves. The criminal law must possess a dignity far beyond that possessed by mere statutory enactment or utilitarian and self-interested calculations; the most powerful means we have to give it that dignity is to authorize it to impose the ultimate penalty. The criminal law must be made awful, by which I mean, awe-inspiring, or commanding "profound respect or reverential fear." It must remind us of the moral order by which alone we can live as *human* beings, and in our day the only punishment that can do this is capital punishment.[75]

As Berns goes on to say, "Only a relatively few executions are required to enhance the dignity of the criminal law, and that number is considerably smaller than the number of murderers and rapists."[76] (We put off for now the question of how often the death penalty should be used so as best to serve the public good.)

That government's *power* legitimately to inflict capital punishment must always, as it were, lurk in the background, even if it is seldom exercised, is a point emphasized by Fr. Joseph Rickaby, who writes:

> Capital punishment is moreover expedient, nay, necessary to the State. The right to inflict it is one of the essential prerogatives of government.... No Government can renounce it. The abolition of capital punishment by law only makes the power of inflicting it *latent* in

---

[75] Walter Berns, *For Capital Punishment: Crime and the Morality of the Death Penalty* (New York: Basic Books, 1979), pp. 172–73.

[76] Ibid., p. 183.

the State. . . . It does not and cannot wholly take the power away. You ask: Is there not hope, that if humanity goes on improving as it has done, capital punishment will become wholly unnecessary? I answer that—waiving the question of the prospect of improvement—in a State mainly consisting of God-fearing, conscientious men, the *infliction* of capital punishment would rarely be necessary, but the *power to inflict it* could never be dispensed with. . . . All States need this dread figure of the Sword-bearer standing at the elbow of the Sovereign.[77]

As Rickaby points out, capital punishment also serves the function of counteracting the attraction some men feel toward certain heinous crimes. To "excite horror" of such crimes and "disenchant" those tempted to them, "there is nothing goes to the heart like death. Death is the most striking of terrors."[78] Related to this is a point emphasized by David Gelernter, to the effect that capital punishment is uniquely able to reinforce within society a horror of especially heinous crimes and confidence in the reality of an objective moral order:

> In fact, we execute murderers in order to make a communal proclamation: that murder is intolerable. A deliberate murderer embodies evil so terrible that it defiles the community. . . .
>
> When a murder takes place, the community is obliged, whether it feels like it or not, to clear its throat and step up to the microphone. Every murder demands a communal response. Among possible responses, the death penalty is uniquely powerful because it is permanent and can never be retracted or overturned. An execution forces the community to assume forever the burden of moral certainty; it is a form of absolute speech that allows no waffling or equivocation.[79]

We will, in later chapters, have much more to say by way of development and defense of the thesis that capital punishment furthers some of the aims of punishment other than retribution. But some preliminary points can be made in the context of discussion of how the traditional natural law theorist would respond to the stock objections to capital punishment.

---

[77] Rickaby, *Moral Philosophy*, pp. 347–49.

[78] Ibid., p. 348.

[79] David Gelernter, "What Do Murderers Deserve?" *Commentary* (April 1998): 21–24, https://www.commentarymagazine.com/articles/what-do-murderers-deserve/.

Replies to some common objections

1. "Capital punishment violates the right to life."

It is often suggested that proponents of capital punishment contradict themselves by advocating the death penalty for murderers. If we say that it is wrong for murderers to kill their victims, then (so the argument goes) to be consistent we ought also to say that it is wrong to kill murderers. As a popular bumper sticker puts it: "Why do we kill people who kill people to show that killing people is wrong?"

That this is not a serious objection should be obvious from the fact that those who put it forward would not object to fining thieves or incarcerating kidnappers. No one would think it clever to display a bumper sticker asking: "Why do we take money from people who take people's money in order to show that taking people's money is wrong?" or: "Why do we hold people involuntarily when they hold people involuntarily in order to show that holding people involuntarily is wrong?" The reason, of course, is that there is a crucial moral difference between forcibly taking money from an innocent person and forcibly taking it from a guilty person, and between forcibly taking custody of an innocent person and forcibly taking custody of a guilty person. The advocate of capital punishment maintains that there is an equally crucial moral difference between killing an innocent person and killing a guilty person. And the advocate of capital punishment does not hold in the first place that it is wrong to kill, period; he holds that it is wrong to kill *an innocent person*. So, the objection in question is simply aimed at a straw man, and the advocate of capital punishment cannot justly be charged with so blatant an inconsistency.

Still, it might seem that the critic could plausibly accuse the advocate of the death penalty of a more subtle inconsistency. As we have seen, traditional natural law theory affirms that we have rights that derive from the natural law itself and are thus grounded in human nature rather than in convention. This includes the right to life. But if the right to life is grounded in human nature, then surely (so the argument might go) *guilty* human beings have it no less than innocent human beings do. And in that case, while the difference between guilt and innocence is, of course, important, it is not a difference that makes a difference in this particular case. Though the advocate of capital punishment does indeed hold only that it is wrong to kill the innocent, he *should* hold also that it is wrong to kill the guilty, because the considerations that lead him to attribute a right to life to the innocent should, if he is consistent, lead him to attribute it also to the guilty.

But that there is something wrong with this argument should be obvious when we consider that those who put it forward would also typically hold that we have a right to a significant degree of liberty of action, but would allow that this liberty can legitimately be taken away from criminals guilty of serious crimes, which is why it is not wrong to imprison them. And if the difference between the innocent and the guilty is relevant to whether we can take away a person's liberty, why is it not also relevant to whether we can take his life?

Recall that for the advocate of traditional natural law, rights have a teleological foundation. Their function is to safeguard our ability to fulfill our obligations under natural law. For that reason there are, as we have seen, definite limitations on our rights so that those rights cannot defeat the purpose for which they exist. For instance, we cannot have a natural right to do what is intrinsically immoral. Now, the legitimacy of inflicting on a wrongdoer a punishment that is proportional to his offense is itself part of the natural law. Therefore, our rights cannot be so strong that they would prevent our inflicting such punishments. That is why we can legitimately take away a criminal's liberty. His right to liberty is not so strong that it could prevent us from legitimately punishing him in this manner. But the same thing is true of his right to life, which is why his having a right to life does not entail that he cannot legitimately be executed if guilty of a sufficiently heinous offense.

In short, the same natural law that entails that you have a right to X (whether X is liberty of action, life, or whatever) also entails that you may nevertheless legitimately be deprived of X if depriving you of X is a proportionate punishment for some crime you have committed.[80]

---

[80] Furthermore, by punishing a person for his offense, the rights of others are made more secure. As we have seen, for the natural law theorist, having a natural right to X does not entail that the exercise of that right might not be limited in ways that facilitate the realization of the end for which the right exists. For example, the natural right to a significant degree of personal liberty includes the right to travel, but governments justly regulate exercise of the right to travel (e.g., by requiring that we drive only on one side of the street and that we stop at red lights) so as to maximize the safe exercise of that right.

A natural way to express the idea is by saying that a wrongdoer *forfeits* his right not to be treated in certain ways.[81] Pope Pius XII gave expression to this idea when he stated:

> Even when it is a question of the execution of a man condemned to death, the State does not dispose of the individual's right to live. It is reserved rather to the public authority to deprive the criminal of the benefit of life when already, by his crime, *he has deprived himself of the right to live.*[82]

2. "Capital punishment is an affront to human dignity."

This claim is often put forward as if it were obvious, but in our view it is not obvious at all and there are no remotely plausible arguments for it. *How* exactly is capital punishment an affront to human dignity? One way to cash out this claim would be to say that capital punishment violates a person's right to life, but we have already explained why that is not a good objection. Alternatively, it might be argued, along Kantian lines, that capital punishment treats an offender purely as a means rather than as an end in himself insofar as it involves interfering with his freedom as a rational agent. But imprisonment and other punishments also involve interfering with a rational agent's freedom. If such interference does not entail that *these* punishments involve using a person as a means or affronting his dignity, then neither does it entail that capital punishment involves this. Indeed, like other defenders of the death penalty, we would argue that it actually *affirms* human dignity precisely because, in inflicting on the offender a punishment proportionate to his offense, it treats him as a free and rational agent who is fully responsible for his behavior, rather than as a mere animal or a robot.[83] It also affirms the dignity of the *victims* of the gravest crimes, insofar as nothing less than a penalty of death would reflect the gravity of what has been done to them. (As we will see in the next chapter, Genesis 9:6

---

[81] Oderberg, *Moral Theory*, pp. 149–50; Oderberg, *Applied Ethics*, pp. 175–77.

[82] Quoted in John F. McDonald, *Capital Punishment* (London: Catholic Truth Society, 1964), http://www.ecatholic2000.com/cts/untitled-71.shtml, emphasis added. Cf. E. Christian Brugger, *Capital Punishment and Roman Catholic Moral Tradition* (Notre Dame, Ind.: University of Notre Dame Press, 2003), p. 130.

[83] See John Cottingham, "Punishment and Respect for Persons", in M. A. Stewart, ed., *Law, Morality, and Rights* (Dordrecht: Reidel, 1983).

sanctions capital punishment for murderers precisely in the name of the dignity of those who have been murdered.) It is hardly irrelevant to note that Kant himself, who staunchly supported capital punishment, would have agreed with these judgments and would have vehemently rejected the abolitionist claims now made in the name of a Kantian respect for persons.

So, Kantian concerns about the dignity of persons could just as well (and indeed, we think more plausibly) be said to tell in *favor* of capital punishment. On the other hand, one could also argue that the offender loses his dignity precisely because of his offense. Aquinas is often taken to give such an argument in the following passage:

> By sinning man departs from the order of reason, and consequently falls away from the dignity of his manhood, in so far as he is naturally free, and exists for himself, and he falls into the slavish state of the beasts, by being disposed of according as he is useful to others.... Hence, although it be evil in itself to kill a man so long as he preserve his dignity, yet it may be good to kill a man who has sinned, even as it is to kill a beast. For a bad man is worse than a beast, and is more harmful.[84]

However, as some commentators have pointed out, Aquinas need not be taken as claiming that offenders lose their human dignity without qualification.[85] As Steven Long argues, what Aquinas is talking about here is an offender's loss not of his "substantive dignity" as a human being but rather of his "acquired dignity" as an innocent citizen immune from molestation by the state.[86] (It also cannot be emphasized too strongly that, contrary to what some commentators suppose, Aquinas' defense of capital punishment simply does not *require* the premise that an offender loses his dignity. As we have seen, Aquinas' commitment to the principle of proportionality, together with considerations about such secondary ends of punishment as

---

[84] *ST* II–II, 64, 2.

[85] Lawrence Dewan, "Thomas Aquinas, Gerard Bradley, and the Death Penalty", in *Wisdom, Law, and Virtue: Essays in Thomistic Ethics* (New York: Fordham University Press, 2007); Koritansky, *Philosophy of Punishment*, p. 189.

[86] Steven A. Long, "Fundamental Errors of the New Natural Law Theory", *National Catholic Bioethics Quarterly* 13 (2013): 118.

deterrence and protection of the community, suffice to give him grounds to affirm capital punishment.)

As Louis Pojman points out, that the defender of capital punishment need not deny the dignity of the offender puts the opponent of capital punishment in a dilemma.[87] Either a murderer has inherent dignity as a free being or he does not. If he does, then because he is responsible for his crime, he can legitimately have inflicted upon him a penalty proportionate to his offense, which would be death. If he does not, then he is no better than a beast, and beasts can legitimately be put to death. Either way, the penalty of death is legitimate. And either way, there is no affront to human dignity.

3. "Capital punishment erodes respect for human life."

The opponent of capital punishment might acknowledge that the murderer has forfeited his right to life but argue that even if murderers deserve to die, we only perpetuate the "cycle of violence" if we kill them. Once again, though, if this were a good objection to capital punishment, it would be a good objection to any other punishment. It is like saying that imprisoning kidnappers further erodes respect for human freedom, or that fining thieves perpetuates the cycle of theft. Of course, no one speaks of a "cycle of theft" or a "cycle of kidnapping", precisely because everyone knows there is a crucial moral difference between the innocent and the guilty, and thus a crucial moral difference between the way criminals treat the innocent and the way public authorities treat the guilty. When we punish, we simply are *not*, from a moral point of view, doing the same thing to offenders that they did to their victims and thus are not furthering any morally problematic "cycle". But this is as true of the penalty of death as it is of any other punishment. Talk of a "cycle of violence" papers over the crucial moral difference between the innocent and the guilty and thereby falsely insinuates that execution is morally on a par with murder. In fact, just as incarcerating kidnappers *affirms* the value of human freedom and fining thieves *affirms* the value of property rights, so too does executing murderers *affirm* the value of human life.

---

[87] Louis P. Pojman and Jeffrey Reiman, *The Death Penalty: For and Against* (New York: Rowman and Littlefield, 1998), p. 35.

4. "Capital punishment is motivated by vengeance."

We have already indicated what is wrong with this objection. Words such as "vengeance", "revenge", and so forth are ambiguous. If these words are meant in the older sense in which Aquinas and other natural law theorists would use them, then it is true that capital punishment is motivated by vengeance, but so is every other punishment. For vengeance in *this* sense is just the carrying out of retributive justice by inflicting a punishment proportional to the offense, and as the traditional natural law theorist has argued, this is a good thing. If instead "vengeance" is taken to mean punishment that is motivated by hatred, then it is false to say that capital punishment is necessarily motivated by vengeance, just as it would be false to say that a desire to imprison or fine criminals is necessarily motivated by vengeance in the sense of hatred. As with imprisonment and fines, it is perfectly possible to favor capital punishment simply because one sincerely believes on the basis of rational arguments that it is a just punishment. Alternatively, if those who accuse proponents of capital punishment of being motivated by "vengeance" mean by that that the punishment is excessive, then they are simply begging the question, since defenders of capital punishment argue that the death penalty is both deserved and sometimes necessary, and therefore *not* excessive.

Given our argument above to the effect that the legitimacy of punishment in general and the legitimacy of capital punishment in particular stand or fall together, it is perhaps not surprising that opponents of capital punishment tend rather indiscriminately to condemn "vengeance" without carefully distinguishing the different senses of the word. "Vengeance" in the sense of inflicting punishment as a matter of retributive justice and "vengeance" of the sort that reflects excess or mere hatred for the offender are bound to blur together in the minds of these opponents. As the Catholic philosopher Ralph McInerny noted concerning those of his students who opposed the death penalty:

What I detected, rightly or wrongly, was an animus against punishment as such. When I gingerly introduced the subject of Hell, those who had spontaneously rejected capital punishment and then had some second thoughts about life imprisonment when looked at in itself and not as an alternative to the death penalty seemed inclined toward a creative interpretation of eternal punishment.[88]

Yet to condemn as per se immoral our inclination to exact retribution would, from the point of view of natural law theory, simply be untrue to human nature and thus untrue to the moral facts. As traditional natural law theorist Joseph Rickaby says:

> If punishment is never *retributive*, the human race in all countries and ages has been the sport of a strange illusion.... No one will deny that the idea, and to some extent the desire, of vengeance, of retaliation, of retrospective infliction of suffering in retribution for evil done, of what we learn to call in the nursery *tit for tat*, is natural to mankind. It is found in all men....
>
> A thing is essentially evil, when there is no possible use of it which is not an abuse. Not far different is the conception of a thing positively evil, evil, that is, not by reason of any deficiency, or by what it is not, but evil by what it is in itself. Such an essential, positive evil in human nature would vengeance be, a natural thing for which there was no natural use, unless punishment may in some measure be retributive. We cannot admit such a flaw in nature. All healthy philosophy goes on the principle, that what is natural is so far forth good. Otherwise we lapse into Manicheism, pessimism, scepticism, abysses beyond the reach of argument. Vengeance undoubtedly prompts to many crimes, but so does the passion of love. Both are natural impulses.... It is the abuse in each case, not the use, that leads to sin. If the matrimonial union were wicked and detestable, as the Manicheans taught, then would the passion of love be an abomination connatural to man. Such another enormity would be the affection of vengeance, if punishment could never rightly be retributive.[89]

Now, a powerful natural impulse needs an outlet. If we condemn the impulse as evil and deny it a lawful and constructive outlet, it will simply find a lawless and destructive one instead. This is well understood in the case of our sexual appetites. To condemn sexual desire

---

[88] Ralph McInerny, "Opposition to the Death Penalty", *Catholic Dossier* 4 (1998), http://www.catholiceducation.org/en/religion-and-philosophy/social-justice/opposition-to-the-death-penalty.html.

[89] Rickaby, *Moral Philosophy*, pp. 169–71.

as per se immoral would be a recipe for misery and social chaos and would lead to greater sexual immorality rather than less. The correct way to prevent such immorality is to acknowledge the goodness of the sexual appetite and to insist that it be indulged only in marriage. But what is true of sexual desire is also true of our natural desire to see retributive justice done. It too needs to be acknowledged as good in itself and given a proper outlet. Now, as James Fitzjames Stephen noted, "The criminal law stands to the passion for revenge in much the same relation as marriage to the sexual appetite."[90] That is to say, public authority's infliction of punishments proportional to the gravity of the offense provides a lawful outlet for the public's natural desire to see retributive justice done. When public authority fails to inflict such punishments, social order is threatened, just as it is when the institution of marriage is weakened. As Louis Pojman writes:

> Failure to punish would no more lessen our sense of vengeance than the elimination of marriage would lessen our sexual appetite. When a society fails to punish criminals in a way thought to be proportionate to the gravity of the crime, the public is likely to take the law into its own hands, resulting in vigilante justice, lynch mobs, and private acts of retribution. The outcome is likely to be an anarchistic, insecure state of injustice.[91]

Nor is it merely the *citizenry's* natural retributive impulse for which capital punishment provides a lawful outlet. The state exists for the sake of suppressing evildoing, and as we have argued, this will in principle always include the right to inflict death on the worst evil-doers if this is necessary to maintain social order. But as with the citizenry, the state too must have an outlet by means of which it can kill *lawfully*, as opposed to arbitrarily or in excess. To eliminate this outlet will, given the realities of human life, be to eliminate not the killing itself, but only the lawfulness of it. As John Lamont has argued:

> States or state-like organisations are necessary for human society, and ... such organisations have to be ready to inflict violence to the point

---

[90] James Fitzjames Stephen, *A General View of the Criminal Law in England* (London: Macmillan, 1863), p. 99.

[91] Pojman and Reiman, *The Death Penalty*, p. 21.

of death if they are to be able to survive and function. This means that deliberate killing by the state cannot be eliminated; it is inevitable that it will happen. [An anti–capital punishment] position ... cannot therefore have the effect of preventing state killing. All it will do, if accepted, is to remove any foundation for moral and legal restraints on such killing. People who see that killing by the state is deliberate, and accept [the capital punishment opponent's] view about the evil of acting against the good of life, will end up concluding that doing evil is unavoidable. They will in consequence become liable to commit any atrocity that seems to promise some advantage. Developments of this sort are most noticeable in war.[92]

As the reference to war suggests, Lamont's point is related to Catholic philosopher Elizabeth Anscombe's critique of pacifism. Anscombe argued that the prevalence of pacifism actually *exacerbates* the evils associated with war rather than mitigates them:

Now pacifism teaches people to make no distinction between the shedding of innocent blood and the shedding of any human blood. And in this way pacifism has corrupted enormous numbers of people who will not act according to its tenets. They become convinced that a number of things are wicked which are not; hence seeing no way of avoiding wickedness, they set no limits to it.[93]

In other words, if the state accepts the principle that *all* killing is wrong—including capital punishment and war, and whether the person killed is innocent or guilty—but nevertheless finds that in practice it cannot avoid killing, then inevitably it will decide which killing it will engage in on grounds of *utility* rather than on grounds of morality. As a result, the state will be more open to the possibility of killing innocent people if it regards the beneficial consequences of doing so to be sufficiently great.

Hence, we would argue that blanket condemnations of "vengeance", "revenge", and the like, which fail carefully to distinguish the different senses attached to these words and to acknowledge the

---

[92] John Lamont, "Finnis and Aquinas on the Good of Life", *New Blackfriars* 83 (2002): 377–78.

[93] G. E. M. Anscombe, "War and Murder", in *Ethics, Religion, and Politics* (Oxford: Basil Blackwell, 1981), p. 57.

naturalness, goodness, and ineradicability of some of the impulses named by them, are not merely unjust and uncharitable when directed at defenders of capital punishment. Such condemnations also reflect a gravely deficient understanding of human nature and political life and are seriously harmful to a just and stable social order.

5. "Capital punishment does not deter."

We will address the empirical issues surrounding the question of deterrence in detail in a later chapter. For the moment, some general points of a more philosophical nature are in order. The first is that those who deny that capital punishment deters often presuppose too crude a model of deterrence. As sociologist Steven Goldberg has written:

> *[It is incorrectly assumed that since] many murders result from emotional impulse (e.g., the angry husband who kills his wife), the death penalty could have, at best, only the slightest deterrent effect.* [But if] the death penalty deters, it is likely that it does so through society's saying that certain acts are so unacceptable that society will kill one who commits them; the individual internalizes the association of the act and the penalty throughout his life, constantly increasing his resistance to committing the act. There is no *a priori* reason for assuming that this process is less relevant to emotional acts than rational acts....
>
> Note that there is no implication here that the potential murderer consciously weighs the alternatives and decides that the crime is worth life in prison but not death.... No serious theory of deterrence claims that such rational calculation of punishment (as opposed to no rational calculation or calculation only of the probability of getting caught ...) plays an important role. Thus, the issue of rational calculation of severity of punishment is irrelevant to the central question of deterrence. If the death penalty deters, it is, in all likelihood, primarily because it instills a psychological resistance to the act, not because it offers a rational argument against committing the act at the time that the decision is being made whether or not to commit the act.[94]

Here Goldberg is restating a point more famously and pithily made by James Fitzjames Stephen:

---

[94] Steven Goldberg, "Does the Death Penalty Deter?", in *When Wish Replaces Thought* (Buffalo, N.Y.: Prometheus Books, 1991), pp. 26–27, emphasis in original.

Some men, probably, abstain from murder because they fear that if they committed murder they would be hanged. Hundreds of thousands abstain from it because they regard it with horror. One great reason why they regard it with horror is that murderers are hanged with the hearty approbation of all reasonable men. Men are so constituted that the energy of their moral sentiments is greatly increased by the fact that they are embodied in a concrete form.[95]

This is not to say that the question of rational calculation has no significance at all, only that it is not *fundamental*. The *fundamental* question where deterrence is concerned is not what will deter those who are willing to consider murder, but rather what will prevent people from being willing to consider murder in the first place. This, as Goldberg and Stephen emphasize, has to do with the very idea of murder being so appalling to a person that he is not even tempted to commit it, not even in the heat of passion. Social opprobrium is necessary to reinforce this horror of murder, and capital punishment makes this opprobrium *palpable* in a way no other punishment can. The point dovetails with those made by Berns, Gelernter, and Rickaby in arguing that capital punishment functions to uphold the majesty of the law, the reality of the moral order, and a horror of crime.

A second point that must be emphasized is that those who deny that the death penalty deters overestimate the significance of statistical evidence. That is by no means either to deny that such evidence is important or to concede that it supports the opponent of capital punishment. Again, we will address that evidence in detail in a later chapter. The point is rather that there is, in addition to the statistical evidence, what Pojman calls "commonsense or anecdotal evidence" and Goldberg calls "informal evidence", which only an unjustifiable scientism could lead us to regard as less important than the statistical evidence.[96] Goldberg argues:

We have an enormous amount of both informal and formal evidence— from everyday experience of socializing children and limiting adult behavior and from such "experiments" as increasing the fees for parking violations—that, as a general rule, the greater a punishment, the

---

[95] Stephen, *Criminal Law in England*, pp. 99–100.

[96] Pojman and Reiman, *The Death Penalty*, p. 45; Goldberg, "Does the Death Penalty Deter?", p. 27.

fewer people will behave in the punished way. Thus, it is perfectly reasonable to expect that the death penalty would have a more dissuasive effect than would life imprisonment and there is no *a priori* reason to believe that the increase from the threat of life imprisonment to that of death fails to dissuade anyone from committing murder.[97]

Goldberg goes on to allow that "it certainly is possible that the relationship between penalty and behavior breaks down at some point." But the point is that the commonsense or informal evidence gives us significant reason to think that the death penalty deters, and this evidence must be weighed alongside the statistical evidence.

Now, if it turned out that the statistical evidence is inconclusive—and as we will argue, that is the most the opponent of capital punishment can plausibly maintain—then, we argue, the commonsense or informal evidence would still tell in favor of capital punishment's having deterrence value. Moreover, the inconclusiveness of the statistical evidence can plausibly be attributed to such factors as protracted appeals processes and other obstacles to carrying out executions, which dilute the deterrent effects of the death penalty, and for which opponents of capital punishment are themselves largely responsible.

A third general consideration is Ernest van den Haag's "best bet" argument.[98] Even if we do not know whether the death penalty deters, we should still "bet" that it does. For if it does deter and we fail to make use of it, then this failure will result in the deaths of innocent people, whose murderers we would have deterred had we made use of capital punishment. If, however, we make use of capital punishment and it does not deter, then those who are executed will still have deserved death. Since it is not wrong to execute those deserving of death but it is wrong to fail to prevent the murder of the innocent when we can do so, we should act on the assumption that the death penalty deters.

So there are, we maintain, good a priori reasons to think both that the death penalty deters and that we should in any event act on the

[97] Goldberg, "Does the Death Penalty Deter?", p. 27; cf. Pojman and Reiman, *The Death Penalty*, p. 45.

[98] Ernest van den Haag, "On Deterrence and the Death Penalty", in Robert M. Baird and Stuart E. Rosenbaum, eds., *Punishment and the Death Penalty: The Current Debate* (Amherst, N.Y.: Prometheus Books, 1995).

assumption that it deters, even if it were to turn out that the statistical evidence does not support its deterrence value.

6. "Capital punishment removes the possibility of reform."

This objection is often regarded as especially powerful by Catholic opponents of the death penalty. But Aquinas regarded it as "frivolous", and although that may seem a harsh judgment, he was in our view correct to be skeptical. He argues as follows:

> The fact that the evil, as long as they live, can be corrected from their errors does not prohibit the fact that they may be justly executed, for the danger which threatens from their way of life is greater and more certain than the good which may be expected from their improvement. They also have at the critical point of death the opportunity to be converted to God through repentance. And if they are so stubborn that even at the point of death their heart does not draw back from evil, it is possible to make a highly probable judgment that they would never come away from evil to the right use of their powers.[99]

Aquinas makes two points here. The first is that the good that might be afforded the offender if he is not executed has to be balanced against the evil that others might suffer if he is not executed. He *might* repent of his evil in the time remaining to him and thereby attain the salvation of his soul, but, of course, he might not. Many criminals are, after all, only *hardened* in evildoing by their time in prison with other criminals. Furthermore, there are various ways in which others might be harmed if the offender is not executed. He might himself contribute to the hardening in evil of the other criminals around him in prison. He might kill one of them. And if (as we have argued) it is reasonable to think that the death penalty has deterrence value, then if we abolish capital punishment, this will lead to the deaths of innocent people whose murderers might otherwise have been deterred; and some of those innocent people will thereby lose their *own* chance to repent of their (lesser) sins and thereby attain salvation. So, it is too glib to pretend that we risk serious harm only if we execute. We also risk it if we do *not* execute, and it is by no

---

[99] *Summa Contra Gentiles* III, 146.

means obvious that the harm risked is greater in the first case than in the second.

Aquinas' second point is that the prospect of imminent execution can actually *facilitate* an evildoer's repentance. It is a commonplace that many people who otherwise ignore the state of their souls turn to God when they face the prospect of death. A person who would have died in a state of mortal sin if he had been hit by the proverbial bus will die in the state of grace when he asks for confession and anointing after learning that he has a fatal disease. Why is a condemned prisoner any less likely to be moved to repentance *precisely because* he knows he will soon die? As Samuel Johnson famously put it: "Depend upon it, sir, when a man knows he is to be hanged in a fortnight, it concentrates his mind wonderfully." By contrast, if he is spared execution, he may put off the reform of his soul until it is too late, dying unexpectedly in prison by violence or natural causes before he can repent. And as Aquinas says, if a person is so hardened in evil that the prospect of imminent death will not move him to repent, how likely is he to repent given more time?

There are further considerations. A wrongdoer cannot truly be rehabilitated until he comes to acknowledge the gravity of his offense. But the gravity of an offense is more manifest when the punishments for that offense reflect its gravity—that is to say, when the principle of proportionality is respected. In a society in which armed robbery was regularly punished with at most a small fine, armed robbers would have greater difficulty coming to see the seriousness of their crimes, and they would for that reason be less likely to be rehabilitated. Similarly, in a society in which even the most cold-blooded murderers were given the same punishments as bank robbers, cold-blooded murderers will have greater difficulty in coming to see the seriousness of *their* crimes and thus will be less likely to be rehabilitated. Knowing that he has done something so awful that it is *worthy of death*, an offender is more likely to repent. In that way too, the existence of capital punishment can actually promote the reform of an offender's soul.

Finally, if a potential murderer is deterred by the prospect of capital punishment from committing a horrendous crime in the first place, then we have, as it were, preemptively "reformed" him. His soul may never in the first place get into the state of corruption that characterizes the worst offenders.

So, it simply is not correct to say, flatly, that "capital punishment removes the possibility of reform." With the time from capital sentence to execution now averaging more than fifteen years in the United States, murderers have ample opportunity to reform.[100] Even if we could reduce this excessive delay by two-thirds, surely five years would be enough time for an offender to come to grips with the evil of his acts and to seek reconciliation with his Maker. Indeed, among convicted murderers, there may be some who would not reform *unless* they faced the prospect of execution. It is also worth pointing out that a willingness to accept a penalty of death is itself a powerful indication of true contrition.[101] That serial killer Jeffrey Dahmer's repentance was genuine is indicated in part precisely by the fact that he believed that he ought to have been executed.[102]

7. "Who are we to think we have the authority to take someone's life?"

Christopher Tollefsen, a Catholic philosopher, "New Natural Law" theorist, and opponent of capital punishment, writes:

> Perhaps some human beings *do* deserve death; that need not be enough to warrant the permissibility for anyone of *killing* that human being. It could well be that no human being has the authority to warrant intentional killing, even of the guilty.[103]

Others have made similar objections. But why, if this were a good objection at all, would it not also be a good objection to imprisoning or fining offenders? If authority to punish is a problem in this case, why

[100] Bureau of Justice Statistics, *Capital Punishment, 2013—Statistical Tables*, Tracy L. Snell (December 2014, NCJ 248448), table 10, p. 14, http://www.bjs.gov/content/pub/pdf/cp13st.pdf.

[101] Pojman and Reiman, *The Death Penalty*, p. 34.

[102] Roy Ratcliff, the minister who baptized Dahmer in prison and who is convinced that Dahmer's conversion to Christianity was genuine, reports that Dahmer told him: "I feel very, very bad about the crimes I've committed. In fact, I think I should have been put to death by the state for what I did." Greg Taylor, "Jeffrey Dahmer's Story of Faith", *Christianity Today* (September 1, 2006), http://www.christianitytoday.com/ct/2006/september/34.125.html. See Roy Ratcliff with Lindy Adams, *Dark Journey Deep Grace: Jeffrey Dahmer's Story of Faith* (Abilene, Tex.: Leafwood Publishers, 2006).

[103] Christopher O. Tollefsen, "Capital Punishment, Sanctity of Life, and Human Dignity", *Public Discourse*, September 16, 2011, http://www.thepublicdiscourse.com/2011/09/3985/.

do we not also ask: "Who are we to think we have the authority to take away someone's freedom?" or "Who are we to think we have the authority to take away someone's property?" But if the state does, given the principle of proportionality, have the authority to take away an offender's liberty and property, what non-question-begging reason is there for denying that it also has the authority to take away an offender's life?

This is, in any event, an odd objection for a Catholic natural law theorist to raise. As we have seen, for the traditional natural law theorist, the state's authority to inflict punishment—*any* punishment at all, not just capital punishment—derives from God. Now, God certainly has the right to take the life of an offender, and given the principle of proportionality and the purposes of punishment, there is no reason whatsoever to think that the power to inflict the penalty of death is any less delegated to the state by God than is the power to inflict lesser punishments. Scripture and papal teaching agree with traditional natural law theory about the divine source of the state's authority, and Saint Paul even ties the power of "the sword" to the state's divinely delegated authority. Hence we maintain that reason and revelation alike agree that the state does have the authority to inflict capital punishment.

In his highly influential 1764 treatise *On Crimes and Punishments*, Italian reformer Cesare Beccaria denied that the state could legitimately take a citizen's life, on the grounds that no party to a social contract would agree to hand such power over to the state.[104] Now, Beccaria's conclusion does not necessarily follow even if one accepts his view about the source of authority. Immanuel Kant, who also embraced a version of social-contract theory, argued, against Beccaria, that while qua criminal I might not will to be executed, "the pure juridical legislative reason (*homo noumenon*) in me" nevertheless wills a system of laws and punishments that includes capital punishment.[105] But we need not adjudicate this dispute between social-contract theorists. For from a traditional natural law perspective, Beccaria's argument is a nonstarter, because it is simply mistaken about the source

---

[104] See Cesare Beccaria, *On Crimes and Punishments*, trans. Henry Paolucci (Indianapolis: Bobbs-Merrill, 1963).

[105] Immanuel Kant, *The Metaphysical Elements of Justice*, trans. John Ladd (New York: Macmillan, 1965), p. 105.

of political power. For the natural law theorist, authority ultimately comes "from above" rather than merely "from below", from God rather than from a humanly devised social contract.

8. "An innocent person wrongly executed cannot get his life back."

There are several problems with this objection. The first is that it obviously has no force in cases where there is no room for doubt about guilt, as when a murderer against whom there is already a mountain of evidence confesses (as in the case of Jeffrey Dahmer). Second, a similar objection could be raised against other harsh punishments. Someone wrongly convicted of a crime who spends thirty years in prison cannot get back those years or be compensated for all the good things (family, friendships, job, etc.) that he has missed out on because of his imprisonment. If that is not a good objection to long imprisonments as a punishment, then neither is the possibility of error a good objection to capital punishment. Third, if the death penalty has deterrence value, then we also risk the lives of innocent people if we do *not* have capital punishment.

Now, we tolerate the risk to innocent lives of other practices because of the benefits they afford us. For example, we know that many innocent people will die every year from traffic accidents, but no one thinks that is a good reason to make it illegal to drive a car. We arm police in the United States even though police officers occasionally misuse their weapons, or offenders wrest control of them to harm the officers or others; yet few argue that this risk outweighs the public benefits of arming police. We vaccinate millions of children against dangerous diseases despite the knowledge that a few may react badly and die. Similarly, we argue that capital punishment serves a larger social good that outweighs the exceedingly small risk of executing the innocent. Not only does the death penalty satisfy the demands of retributive justice, which is a real good, but it can also foster recognition of respect for the objective moral order and the majesty of the law, promote repentance, and deter at least some potential murderers. If our legal institutions are set up so that the chances of executing an innocent person are reduced to a minimum, then it is simply unreasonable to demand that the benefits of capital punishment be forsaken because of the very small risk that remains, just as it would be unreasonable to outlaw the driving of automobiles, the arming of police, or the use of vaccines. (And as we will see in a later chapter, there is no compelling evidence that a single innocent person has been executed in the United States among the more than 1,300 who have been subjected to the death penalty during the past four decades.)

Again, we will consider some of these objections at greater length in later chapters and will deal there also with other objections to which the empirical evidence is more crucial (such as the claim that there is racial bias in the implementation of capital punishment). But we believe it should be clear already that, given the traditional natural law theory that the Church has favored historically, the case for capital punishment is very strong and the case against it very weak.

Rival ethical theories

Some further objections to the traditional natural law defense of capital punishment might be grounded in alternative general approaches to moral philosophy. This is not the place for an extended treatment of these rival ethical theories, and most of them would in any case be unacceptable from the point of view of a Catholic who is faithful to the Magisterium of the Church. After briefly addressing the views of Immanuel Kant and contemporary consequentialists, we will address at greater length the most influential alternative to our views within modern Catholic thought, the New Natural Law theory.

Kant on capital punishment

From the point of view of Immanuel Kant, the traditional natural law position might, if anything, seem too lenient. He famously wrote:

> If [someone] has committed a murder, he must die. In this case, there is no substitute that will satisfy the requirements of legal justice. There is no sameness of kind between death and remaining alive even under the most miserable conditions, and consequently there is also no equality between the crime and the retribution unless the criminal is judicially condemned and put to death.... Even if a civil society were to dissolve itself by common agreement of all its members (for

example, if the people inhabiting an island decided to separate and disperse themselves around the world), the last murderer remaining in prison must first be executed, so that everyone will duly receive what his actions are worth and so that the bloodguilt thereof will not be fixed on the people because they failed to insist on carrying out the punishment; for if they fail to do so, they may be regarded as accomplices in this public violation of legal justice.[106]

There is nothing in the traditional natural law theorist's position that entails that we *must* execute offenders who deserve death. Natural law entails that we *may* do so, all things being equal. It may even be said to entail that there is a presumption in favor of doing so. But it is a presumption that can be overridden if circumstances dictate that leniency would better serve the other ends of punishment or the furtherance of other moral goals. If a follower of Kant wanted to show otherwise, he would have to appeal to specifically Kantian philosophical premises that the traditional natural law theorist would not accept in the first place. Nor, in our view, could a hard-line Kantian position be reconciled with Catholic teaching, which, as we will see, certainly *allows*, but with equal certainty does not *require*, recourse to capital punishment.

Consequentialism and proportionalism

No one denies that the consequences of our actions are important. But consequentialism holds that consequences are the *only* thing that matters where morality is concerned. It is typically contrasted with views according to which there are certain acts that are *absolutely* required of us or forbidden to us, regardless of the consequences. The utilitarian theories of Jeremy Bentham and John Stuart Mill are well-known examples of consequentialist theories.

Consequentialist arguments could be given and have been given both for capital punishment and against it. Bentham was against it; Mill supported it. But since what matters for the consequentialist are consequences alone, the question of what the offender *deserves* is not what is key for consequentialism. Retributive justice is "backward-looking" in the sense that it is concerned with what *has already*

---

[106] Ibid., p. 102.

happened, whereas consequentialism is "forward-looking" in the sense that it is concerned with what *will* happen. Thus, questions of deterrence, rehabilitation, and the like are all that matter for consequentialist arguments concerning capital punishment.

Though consequentialist writers have tried to build into their position various safeguards against its otherwise unsavory implications, the fact remains that, as we saw C. S. Lewis argue above, if we ignore the question of what a person deserves and focus only on consequences, there is no limit *in principle* to what we might do either to the guilty or to the innocent. Again, we might punish the innocent, or take indefinite custody of someone guilty of only a minor offense, or let the guilty off scot-free, if we judge that this would have the best chances of facilitating deterrence, rehabilitation, and the like.

Catholic moral teaching, which insists on moral absolutes, is flatly incompatible with consequentialist moral theory. Yet in recent decades, some Catholic moralists have adopted a view known as proportionalism, according to which the morality of an action is determined by the proportion of benefits and harms it is likely to bring about. The right action, according to this view, is the one with the greater proportion of benefits to harms. This is essentially a variation on consequentialism and has been criticized by the Magisterium. In *Veritatis Splendor*, Pope John Paul II spoke of "the unacceptability of ... 'consequentialist' and 'proportionalist' ethical theories" (no. 90), and wrote:

> [P]roportionalism [and] consequentialism ... while acknowledging that moral values are indicated by reason and by Revelation, maintain that it is never possible to formulate an absolute prohibition of particular kinds of behaviour which would be in conflict, in every circumstance and in every culture, with those values....
>
> Such theories however are not faithful to the Church's teaching, when they believe they can justify, as morally good, deliberate choices of kinds of behaviour contrary to the commandments of the divine and natural law. These theories cannot claim to be grounded in the Catholic moral tradition. (nos. 75 and 76)

The "New Natural Law" theory

The so-called New Natural Law theory (NNLT) poses a more significant challenge to our position, since its proponents do seek to be faithful to the Magisterium of the Church. This theory was first developed in the 1960s by Germain Grisez and has been further developed and defended by John Finnis, Joseph Boyle, William May, Robert P. George, Christopher Tollefsen, and others.[107]

The NNLT differs from traditional natural law theory in several crucial respects. As we have seen, for the traditional natural law theorist, what is good for us is grounded in human nature, where "nature" is understood in terms of the Aristotelian-Thomistic metaphysics of formal and final causes. Given formal and final causality, "value" is built into the very structure of the "facts", and there is no metaphysical space between them by which David Hume and his positivist followers might pry them apart. NNLT proponents, by contrast, tend to *endorse* the Humean fact-value dichotomy. Like Hume, they insist that an "ought" cannot be derived from an "is". Thus, like Hume, they deny that morality can be grounded in a metaphysical analysis of human nature.

The NNLT, however, does not endorse Hume's verdict in his *Treatise of Human Nature* that "the rules of morality ... are not conclusions of our reason." Yet what rational foundation can morality have if not in human nature? Like Kant, the NNLT tries to solve this problem by recourse to a theory of practical reason. In particular, on the NNLT account:

> Practical reason, that is, ... reason oriented towards action, grasps as *self-evidently* desirable a number of basic goods. These goods, which are described as constitutive aspects of genuine human flourishing, include life and health; knowledge and aesthetic experience; skilled work and play; friendship; marriage; harmony with God, and harmony among a person's judgments, choices, feelings, and behavior. As grasped by practical reason, the basic goods give foundational reasons for action to human agents.[108]

As David Oderberg describes the difference between the views, traditional natural law theory is "world-centered", whereas the

---

[107] See John Finnis, *Natural Law and Natural Rights* (Oxford: Clarendon Press, 1980); Robert P. George, *In Defense of Natural Law* (Oxford: Oxford University Press, 1999); Germain Grisez, *The Way of the Lord Jesus*, vol. 1, *Christian Moral Principles* (Chicago: Franciscan Herald Press, 1983); and, for a useful brief overview, Christopher Tollefsen, "The New Natural Law Theory", *Lyceum* 10 (2008): 1–18.

[108] Tollefsen, "New Natural Law Theory", p. 2, emphasis added.

NNLT is "agent-centered".[109] For the traditional natural law theorist, an agent knows the good by taking an objective, or "third-
person", view of himself. He asks what sorts of ends human beings
have, given the kind of creatures they are, and thereby knows what is
good for *him* qua human since he is one instance of that kind among
others. According to the NNLT, the agent knows the good from
the subjective, or "first-person", point of view. Considering what
reasons he has for acting this way or that, he asks what sorts of goods
are *self-evidently* desirable and for whose sake he might pursue other
goods. That is by no means to say that his judgments are, according
to the NNLT, "subjective" in the sense of being arbitrary or idiosyncratic. They are taken by the NNLT to reflect human practical reason
as such, not merely the practical reason of this or that agent, and are
thus in *that* sense "objective". But they are "subjective" in the sense
that it is from the agent's introspection of his own practical reason in
operation, rather than from mind-independent facts of a philosophically informed anthropology, that he finds a guide to action.

What the NNLT calls "basic goods" are taken by the theory to be
basic in several respects:

> (i) Their goodness is self-evident and cannot be demonstrated; (ii) they
> provide basic reasons for action, in the sense that an action undertaken
> for the sake of achieving one of them is not also undertaken for the
> sake of some further good; (iii) no one of them is a form of any of
> the others; (iv) together they exhaust all the ultimate motivations that
> humans can have for rational action.[110]

These goods are taken to be "incommensurable" in the sense that
there is nothing deeper in reference to which their relative importance might be weighed. They are equally fundamental rather than
ordered in a hierarchy. Thus, "integral human fulfillment" requires
pursuit of all of them. One implication of this is that what Tollefsen
calls the good of "harmony with God" cannot be regarded as higher
than other basic goods such as "friendship", "aesthetic experience",

---

[109] David S. Oderberg, "The Metaphysical Foundations of Natural Law," in H. Zaborowski,
ed., *Natural Moral Law in Contemporary Society* (Washington, D.C.: Catholic University of
America Press, 2010), p. 46.
[110] Lamont, "Finnis and Aquinas", p. 366.

and "play". This is another radical departure from the traditional natural law theory, according to which God is, as Pope John Paul II put it, "the supreme good and ultimate end (*telos*) of man" (*Veritatis Splendor*, no. 73).

As we have seen, traditional natural law theory also holds that while there is in the natural orientation of the will toward the good a "proximate" ground of obligation, its "ultimate" ground is the eternal law of the Supreme Lawgiver. Thus does Aquinas hold that:

> Every good will is therefore good by reason of its being conformed to the divine good will. Accordingly, since everyone is obliged to have a good will, he is likewise obliged to have a will conformed to the divine will.[111]

By contrast, NNLT proponent John Finnis, while by no means dismissive of natural theology, purports to offer "a theory of natural law without needing to advert to the question of God's existence or nature or will" and "positively decline[s] to explain obligation in terms of conformity to superior will".[112]

Given its eschewal of formal and final causes, the NNLT has no resources by which to provide an objective or third-person description of the nature and characteristic effects of an action. The moral evaluation of an action thus depends for the NNLT entirely on how it is characterized from the agent's first-person point of view. Some of the implications of this approach have been highly controversial:

> From this perspective, certain consequences that might, in a more "objective" or third-personal account of action appear intended, will not in fact be so. Thus Grisez, Boyle and Finnis have argued that craniotomy, in which a fetus's head is crushed to facilitate removal from the mother, need not involve an intention to kill the child. The intention rather can be "to change the dimensions of the child's skull to facilitate removal."[113]

To be sure, NNLT writers emphasize that such actions will often still be immoral. They are staunch opponents of direct abortion and

---

[111] *Quaestiones disputatae de veritate* 23, 7, in Aquinas, *Truth*.

[112] Finnis, *Natural Law*, pp. 49, 403.

[113] Tollefsen, "New Natural Law Theory", p. 9.

of most indirect abortion (i.e., a procedure that does not aim at the death of the unborn child, but has death as a byproduct), and they would condemn indirect abortion via craniotomy if not performed for a proportionate reason. But their position does in principle allow for indirect abortion if the reason is proportionate, with the death of the fetus interpreted as an unintended side effect allowed by the principle of double effect.[114] As Matthew O'Brien and Robert Koons write:

> In spite of Grisez and Boyle's manifest opposition to "proportion-alism" in philosophical and theological ethics, therefore, their own version of natural law theory includes a structurally significant realign-ment that gives proportionality a prominence it never had in the traditional Aristotelian-Thomistic moral theory that they wished to revise.[115]

Whereas traditional natural law theory regards the political common good as something transcending the sum of the private interests of individual citizens, NNLT proponent John Finnis regards the political order as having only "instrumental" value, serving to promote the private good of families and individuals.[116] On Finnis' account of punishment, since "the exercise of freedom of choice [is] in itself a great human good", the offender "gains a certain sort of advantage over those who have restrained themselves".[117] Punishment restores the proper distribution of advantages and disadvantages

[114] According to the principle of double effect, an action that is in itself good or at least permissible but is foreseen to have bad effects as well as good ones may be justifiable if the bad effects are unintended and if they are outweighed by a proportionate good that would also follow from the act, which is intended and to which the bad effects are not the means. For exposition and defense, see Oderberg, *Moral Theory*, pp. 88–126.

[115] Matthew B. O'Brien and Robert C. Koons, "Objects of Intention: A Hylomorphic Critique of the New Natural Law Theory", *American Catholic Philosophical Quarterly* 86 (2012): 657–58.

[116] John Finnis, "Is Natural Law Theory Compatible with Limited Government?", in Robert P. George, ed., *Natural Law, Liberalism, and Morality* (Oxford: Oxford University Press, 1996). For discussion of the difference between Finnis' and Aquinas' positions, see Lawrence Dewan, "St. Thomas, John Finnis, and the Political Good", *Thomist* 64 (2000): 337–74; Koritansky, *Philosophy of Punishment*, pp. 86–98; and John Goyette, "On the Transcendence of the Political Common Good: Aquinas versus the New Natural Law Theory", *National Catholic Bioethics Quarterly* 13 (2013): 133–55.

[117] Finnis, *Natural Law*, p. 263.

between criminals and law-abiding citizens. This contrasts sharply with Aquinas' view that, far from benefiting himself, the offender *harms* himself by acting unjustly, precisely because he is by nature a social and political animal and is thus acting contrary to what is good for him by nature.[118]

Most important for present purposes is the difference between traditional natural law theory and the NNLT over capital punishment. According to the NNLT, an agent must respect all of the "basic goods" in every act. One must therefore never act *directly* against a basic good in any act. Whereas it is not intrinsically wrong to act against a nonbasic good or to act indirectly against a basic good, acting directly against a basic good is wrong intrinsically, and thus under all circumstances. Now, the intentional killing of a person involves acting directly against the basic good of life. Since acting directly against a basic good is always and inherently wrong, the intentional killing of a person is always and inherently wrong. Since capital punishment involves such intentional killing, it is always and inherently wrong.[119]

The NNLT has been severely criticized by traditional natural law theorists and others.[120] Among the charges raised against it are the following:

---

[118] Koritansky, *Philosophy of Punishment*, pp. 143–57.

[119] Germain Grisez, "Toward a Consistent Natural-Law Ethics of Killing", *American Journal of Jurisprudence* 15 (1970): 64–96; Gerard V. Bradley, "No Intentional Killing Whatsoever: The Case of Capital Punishment", in Robert P. George, ed., *Natural Law and Moral Inquiry: Ethics, Metaphysics, and Politics in the Work of Germain Grisez* (Washington, D.C.: Georgetown University Press, 1998); Brugger, *Capital Punishment*; Tollefsen, "Capital Punishment, Sanctity of Life, and Human Dignity".

[120] See Nigel Biggar and Rufus Black, eds., *The Revival of Natural Law: Philosophical, Theological and Ethical Responses to the Finnis-Grisez School* (Aldershot: Ashgate, 2000); Di Blasi, *God and the Natural Law*; Russell Hittinger, *A Critique of the New Natural Law Theory* (South Bend, Ind.: University of Notre Dame Press, 1987); Lisska, *Aquinas's Theory of Natural Law*; Steven A. Long, "Natural Law or Autonomous Practical Reason: Problems for the New Natural Law Theory", in John Goyette, Mark S. Latkovic, and Richard S. Myers, eds., *Saint Thomas Aquinas and the Natural Law Tradition: Contemporary Perspectives* (Washington, D.C.: Catholic University of America Press, 2004); Ralph McInerny, "The Principles of Natural Law", *American Journal of Jurisprudence* 25 (1980): 1–15; O'Brien and Koons, "Objects of Intention"; Oderberg, "Metaphysical Foundations"; and Henry Veatch, "Natural Law and the 'Is-Ought' Question: Queries to Finnis and Grisez", in *Swimming against the Current in Contemporary Philosophy* (Washington, D.C.: Catholic University of America Press, 1990). The spring 2013 issue of *National Catholic Bioethics Quarterly* is devoted to the theme "Critiques of the New Natural Law Theory".

First, it is essentially an attempt to reformulate natural law without either *nature* or *law* and is therefore not really a "natural law" theory at all. For since it denies that the good can be grounded in the natures of things in general or human nature in particular, there is nothing "natural" about it; and since it denies that our obligation to pursue the good has anything essentially to do with conforming ourselves to the will of the divine lawgiver, its imperatives lack the character of true "law".

Second, the endorsement of Hume's fact-value dichotomy is a dangerously radical concession to the philosophical naturalism, positivism, and scientism that are fundamentally at odds not only with the systems of philosophy historically favored by the Church, but with Catholicism itself. This concession is also completely unnecessary, since the Aristotelian-Thomistic metaphysical foundations of the traditional natural law theory's account of the good are entirely defensible,[121] and since the fact-value dichotomy has in contemporary philosophy been severely criticized, not only by writers sympathetic to the natural law tradition[122] but by others as well.[123]

Third, the approach to political philosophy taken by some NNLT writers also involves dangerous concessions to modern philosophy, owing more to the liberalism and individualism of Hobbes, Locke, and Kant than to the natural law political tradition of Aristotle and Aquinas.

Fourth, the NNLT account of intention is excessively subjectivist and has implications that are simply bizarre from the point of view of traditional Catholic moral theology. As the craniotomy example shows, what would historically have been regarded as an absolutely forbidden direct abortion becomes, on the NNLT, a kind of indirect abortion that is permissible in principle. Meanwhile, because any war appears obviously to involve intentional killing, the very idea of a

---

[121] Edward Feser, *Scholastic Metaphysics: A Contemporary Introduction* (Heusenstamm: Editiones Scholasticae/Transaction Books, 2014); Edward Feser, "Being, the Good, and the Guise of the Good", in Daniel D. Novotny and Lukas Novak, eds., *Neo-Aristotelian Perspectives in Metaphysics* (London: Routledge, 2014); and David S. Oderberg, *Real Essentialism* (London: Routlege, 2007).

[122] Christopher Martin, "The Fact/Value Distinction", in David S. Oderberg and Timothy Chappell, eds., *Human Values: New Essays on Ethics and Natural Law* (New York: Palgrave Macmillan, 2004); Oderberg, *Moral Theory*, pp. 9–15.

[123] Hilary Putnam, *The Collapse of the Fact/Value Dichotomy and Other Essays* (Cambridge, Mass.: Harvard University Press, 2002).

just war becomes highly problematic. The problem can be dealt with only via implausible and convoluted reasoning to the effect that the deaths of enemy soldiers are not intended but rather a foreseen but unintended side effect of combat.

Fifth, the NNLT list of basic goods (which varies somewhat from writer to writer) is arbitrary and ad hoc, formulated precisely so as to guarantee that certain desired conclusions will be reached and certain undesirable conclusions will be ruled out. The NNLT's eschewal of philosophical anthropology deprives it of a way of providing an objective criterion by which to determine which goods are really basic, and its appeal instead to the "self-evidence" of some goods and not others seems merely dogmatic.

We agree with these criticisms of the NNLT, and we believe that they are reason enough to reject the theory and its critique of capital punishment. But since this is not the place for a general treatment of the dispute between traditional natural law theory and the NNLT, we will focus on three problems with the NNLT's objection to capital punishment, specifically, (1) whether it really entails that capital punishment is intrinsically immoral, (2) whether its approach is coherent, and (3) whether it is compatible with Catholic teaching.

1. Does the NNLT in fact entail that capital punishment is intrinsically immoral?

The first problem is that even if we were to accept the NNLT, it is not clear that a condemnation of capital punishment as inherently immoral really does follow from it. Indeed, Finnis at one time *defended* capital punishment against Grisez's objection.[124] He wrote:

> A person who violates the order of fairness, which can be described as a system of rights, forfeits certain of his own rights. That is to say, he loses the right that all others should respect in his person all the basic aspects of human well-being. For those persons (and only those) whose responsibility it is to maintain the order of justice are now entitled to deprive him of certain of those basic goods, in order to restore the order of justice he disrupted. This act of deprivation will be, in one

[124]John Finnis, *Fundamentals of Ethics* (Washington, D.C.: Georgetown University Press, 1983), pp. 130, 135.

sense, an intentional attack on or suppression of basic human goods. But ... the deprivation or suppression will be intended neither for its own sake nor as a means to any further good state of affairs. Rather, it is intended precisely as itself a good, namely the good of restoring the order of justice, a restoration that cannot (logically cannot) consist in anything other than such an act of deprivation or suppression.

This reasoning ... shows why even capital punishment need not be regarded as doing evil that good may come of it, nor as treating the criminal as a mere means, nor as a choice which must be characterized as either wholly or primarily an attack (however well motivated) on a basic good.[125]

This passage implies that, with the NNLT account of the good as with the traditional natural law account, when desert and the principle of proportionality are factored in, the legitimacy of depriving an offender of a good (including the good of life) follows as a matter of retributive justice. The differences between the NNLT and traditional natural law theory would seem to drop out as irrelevant.

2. Is the NNLT approach to capital punishment coherent?

But suppose the NNLT advocate rejects this argument for reconciling capital punishment and the NNLT, as Finnis later did.[126] This merely makes the overall NNLT position on punishment incoherent. For as we have argued, the principles of desert and proportionality entail the legitimacy in principle of capital punishment. Hence, if the NNLT advocate accepts these principles, he has to accept the legitimacy in principle of capital punishment. If the NNLT account of the basic goods entails the *illegitimacy* in principle of capital punishment, then this just shows that to restore coherence to his position, the NNLT advocate will either have to reject the principles of desert or of proportionality, or both, so as to preserve his opposition to capital punishment, or will have to modify his account of the basic goods and return to Finnis' earlier position, on which capital punishment is, after all, reconcilable with the NNLT. Since the former option—rejecting desert or proportionality, or both—would land the NNLT

---

[125] Ibid., pp. 129–30.
[126] John Finnis, *Aquinas* (Oxford: Oxford University Press, 1998), p. 293.

in precisely the sort of consequentialist position vis-à-vis punishment that the NNLT rejects as much as the traditional natural law theorist does, we would recommend taking the latter course instead and dropping opposition in principle to capital punishment.

In response to this sort of objection, NNLT advocate Christopher Tollefsen has argued that while "instrumental goods" such as "liberty and money" may be taken away from an offender as a proportionate punishment for an offense, a "basic or intrinsic" good such as human life cannot be.[127] "As a basic, or intrinsic, human good," Tollefsen claims, "human life, just in itself, gives us only reasons for its pursuit, promotion, and protection, and no reason for its damage or destruction." But from the claim that "*life, just in itself*, gives us no reason ever to destroy life but only reason to protect it", it does not follow that *there is no* reason ever to destroy life, but only reason to protect it. For there may be reasons derived from something *other* than "life, just in itself", to destroy life in some cases rather than protect it. Indeed, the principle of proportionality gives us just such a reason. While Tollefsen evidently does not think it is a good reason, he does not offer any non-question-begging grounds for that opinion.

In attempting to ground his opinion, Tollefsen asserts that "human beings have intrinsic dignity", which gives even the life of a mass murderer a "sacred or inviolable quality". This is *mere* assertion, however, not argument. The NNLT advocate must explain *why* human dignity—which, as we have noted, defenders of capital punishment typically affirm no less than its critics do—forbids ever taking life. After all, life *by itself* cannot be what gives human beings their dignity; plants and nonhuman animals also have life, and yet the NNLT does not deny that it is legitimate to kill them. What is it, then, that makes human beings different from plants and other animals? The traditional answer is that human beings have reason and free will. Unlike other animals, we can *understand* what various possible courses of action entail and can *choose* how to act in light of this understanding. That is why our behavior is uniquely subject to moral evaluation; we alone possess the liberty of choice and action that makes moral life possible. It is why, unlike plants, animals, and inanimate objects, we cannot be

---

[127] Tollefsen, "Capital Punishment, Dignity, and Authority".

treated merely as means to others' ends and is thus why kidnapping, slavery, and the like are grave evils.

Now, though our liberty flows from the rationality and free choice that are unique to us, and that are surely the source of our special dignity, even the NNLT advocate agrees that a criminal can justly be deprived of this liberty. Indeed, the very possibility of punishment presupposes this, since even the mildest punishment typically involves inflicting a harm on the offender to which he does not consent. So, if life is *not* unique to us and thus cannot be what gives us our special dignity, how can depriving an offender of his life be intrinsically wrong? And if life is a "basic, intrinsic good", then why should liberty of choice and action—which flows from the rationality and freedom that *are* unique to us and *do* give us our special dignity—not also be regarded as a "basic, intrinsic good"? Yet Tollefsen regards this liberty as a "merely instrumental" good, the taking away of which is not contrary to human dignity!

If there is any principled reason for mapping this moral territory in such a peculiar fashion, Tollefsen does not make clear what it is. Given that it is our capacity for rationality and free choice that affords us our special dignity, liberty of action would seem to be no less basic and intrinsic a good than life is. In that case, the NNLT advocate is faced with a dilemma: he can either say that neither life nor liberty can ever legitimately be taken from a wrongdoer—which would be absurd and would undermine the very possibility of punishment—or he can say that a wrongdoer can be deprived of his liberty, even though it is a basic, intrinsic good—in which case he will have to admit that the status of life as a basic, intrinsic good does not entail that capital punishment is inherently immoral.[128]

---

[128] In an attempt to defend the NNLT critique of capital punishment against these objections, Tollefsen has developed an additional line of argument. (See Christopher O. Tollefsen, "Punishment: Political, Not Metaphysical", *Public Discourse*, October 14, 2011, http://www.thepublicdiscourse.com/2011/10/4135/.) In response to the question of how the NNLT can consistently allow an offender to be deprived of liberty but not of life, Tollefsen distinguishes between "the *capacity* for freedom" and "the *exercise* of freedom". The former, he says, may never legitimately be taken away, but the latter may be, and that is, he thinks, sufficient to explain why a wrongdoer's freedom can be taken away while his life can never be, and thus to save the NNLT position from the arbitrariness of which we accuse it.

But there are two problems with this move. First, it has implications we suspect NNLT advocates would not be happy with. Suppose it were suggested that instead of executing

In a further line of defense of the NNLT approach to capital punishment, Tollefsen appeals to considerations about the purpose of punishment in general. Echoing liberal political philosopher John Rawls' conception of justice as "political, not metaphysical",[129] Tollefsen insists that just *punishment*, in particular, ought to be

---

murderers, we put them into suspended animation (as in the science-fiction movie *Demolition Man*). Neither their lives nor their capacity for free action would be destroyed. It is merely their *exercise* of that capacity that would be taken from them. Or suppose we kept them in solitary confinement in a small space for the entirety of their lives—again, thereby preserving both their lives and their *capacity* for freedom, and taking away (at least to a very great extent) only the exercise of the latter. NNLT advocates would presumably regard such harsh punishments as intrinsically wrong and contrary to human dignity. But if so, it is hard to see how they could defend such a claim, given that it is only the capacity for freedom, and not its exercise, that we can never in principle destroy.

Nor would it do for Tollefsen to suggest that such punishments would be intrinsically wrong insofar as they frustrated the pursuit of other "basic goods", such as skilled work, play, aesthetic experience, and the like. For one thing, ordinary imprisonment frustrates the pursuit of these goods to a great extent, but the NNLT is not opposed to ordinary imprisonment. For another, even though (unlike ordinary imprisonment) suspended animation or solitary confinement in a small space would completely or very largely prevent the pursuit of these goods, it is still only their *pursuit* and not the *capacity* for their pursuit that is taken away. And if preserving a capacity while frustrating its exercise is not intrinsically wrong in the case of free action, it is hard to see why it would be intrinsically wrong in the case of work, play, aesthetic experience, etc.

A second problem is that Tollefsen's distinction between the capacity for freedom and its exercise does not seem to sit well with other NNLT arguments. For example, NNLT writers, like traditional natural law theorists, argue that masturbation, fornication, homosexual acts, etc. are intrinsically wrong. For the NNLT, this is because such acts are contrary to the "basic good of marriage", as that is defined by the NNLT. But if Tollefsen is right, it seems that we could distinguish between the *capacity* for the basic good of marriage and the *exercise* of that capacity. And while acts of the sort in question are contrary to the exercise of this capacity, they leave the capacity itself intact—in which case, by analogy with what Tollefsen says about freedom, they would not be *intrinsically* wrong after all (or at least not intrinsically wrong by virtue of acting against a basic good).

Now, Tollefsen might reply that such acts indirectly damage the capacity itself insofar as they make it psychologically more difficult to exercise it. Our capacity to realize the "basic good of marriage", he might say, will be damaged by indulgence in acts of the sort in question. But something similar could be said of taking away a criminal's exercise of freedom, insofar as imprisonment can make one less capable of independent action. Because he is directed by and dependent on others, the prisoner's capacity for self-direction will at least be blunted, in some cases seriously. Yet Tollefsen does not deny that imprisonment is legitimate.

In short, it seems the capacity-exercise distinction can help Tollefsen get out of the difficulty that freedom of action poses for the NNLT critique of capital punishment only by leading him into problems elsewhere in the NNLT program.

[129] John Rawls, "Justice as Fairness: Political, Not Metaphysical", *Philosophy and Public Affairs* 14 (1985): 223–51.

construed as political rather than metaphysical. That is to say, it is a means of "restor[ing] a kind of equality between citizens that the criminal's overly self-assertive act(s) of will had disrupted", and not a matter of inflicting on criminals something that they "deserve ... in some absolute sense".[130] The trouble with the traditional natural law position we defend, in Tollefsen's view, is that it *is* metaphysical, a matter of looking at justice "from the point of view of the universe, not of the state". Writes Tollefsen:

> A political conception of retributive punishment makes somewhat softer claims about merit and proportionality than Feser does. Merit is ... necessary in this sense: punishment should only be done to those who are guilty of the assertion of will that punishment redresses. Hence, if not deserved (merited), punishment should not be inflicted. Proportionality, too, is somewhat softened by contrast with Feser's account. Feser supposes there is a precise, or specific, amount of punishment that is merited by the criminal and that ought, barring practical considerations and considerations of mercy, to be exacted. The cosmic scales are finely tuned.
>
> But political scales—not so much. The degree to and way in which a criminal's will ought to be restricted does not seem, even in principle, subject to such a fine-grained assessment.[131]

Now, this gives the impression that the difference between Tollefsen's position and ours is this: our position (so Tollefsen implies) claims that the state should strive to realize cosmic justice, which is why we defend capital punishment. Murderers and the like deserve death in an absolute, metaphysical sense; the state is supposed to inflict on offenders what they deserve in this sense; so the state ought to execute murderers and the like. Tollefsen, by contrast, regards punishment as a means of upholding what he calls "a political community" that is "constituted by an ordering of the wills of the community's members".[132] Since it has a merely political, this-worldly end, punishment is for Tollefsen not concerned with inflicting on wrongdoers what they deserve in some absolute metaphysical sense, but

---

[130] Tollefsen, "Punishment: Political, Not Metaphysical."
[131] Ibid.
[132] Tollefsen, "Capital Punishment, Dignity, and Authority".

merely with restoring the order of the political community. And capital punishment (so the implied argument seems to go) is not necessary in order to realize this political end.

Now, we do indeed deeply disagree with Tollefsen over matters of general political philosophy. Following traditional natural law theory, we regard the state as a natural institution rather than as something "constituted" by "the wills of the community's members". (Tollefsen, like Finnis, here makes what, from the point of view of traditional natural law theory, is an unnecessary and unwise accommodation to the liberal political tradition of Hobbes, Locke, and Kant.) But settling these matters is not in fact essential to the dispute between us, as the rest of Tollefsen's discussion makes evident.

Consider first that Tollefsen distorts the traditional natural law position on punishment. Like Aquinas, we do not claim that the state ought, in general, to try to realize cosmic justice. Nor do we deny that there are aspects of the law that ought to be determined by "custom, prior commitment, or other considerations".[133] Our position is rather that what Tollefsen calls "metaphysical" justice is a *necessary* condition for just punishment, even if it is not a *sufficient* condition. The state cannot perfectly realize cosmic justice and should not try to; all the same, the state should not inflict a punishment on a wrong-doer unless in some cosmic or metaphysical sense he deserves it.

Hence, consider, on the one hand, a murderer, and, on the other hand, someone who routinely lies to his spouse and his friends. Both of them deserve punishment in an absolute sense. Now, the state obviously has a reason to punish murderers (whether or not one thinks they should be punished with death) because murder is destructive of the very possibility of a political order. But the state has no business punishing ordinary liars as such (except in cases of perjury and the like, where what is against the law is not lying per se but a specific kind of lying), because doing so is not necessary to maintaining political order and would even undermine it, given how draconian enforcement would have to be. So, desert in an absolute sense is not a sufficient condition for the state's punishing someone. But it is a necessary condition—the state may punish a murderer only because he deserves punishment, even if considerations additional

---

[133] Contrary to the impression Tollefsen gives in "Punishment: Political, Not Metaphysical".

to desert also play a role. Now Tollefsen, it seems, essentially agrees with this. For he goes on to write:

> Of course, such determinations [of what punishments are allowable] must be made within the scope of what is otherwise morally permissible, what the natural law *requires*; and if the natural law, as a matter of deduction, and not determination, *requires* that one never intentionally kill, then that choice is ruled out of the range of determinations one might make regarding punishment.[134]

The real reason Tollefsen objects to capital punishment, then, is not that it plays no role in a purely political conception of justice. It is rather that he thinks it is wrong in an *absolute* sense (indeed, a *cosmic* sense). Tollefsen believes, no less than we do, that questions of politics and punishment must be settled within boundaries set by natural law, even if we disagree about the grounds and content of natural law. The notion that punishment is "political, not metaphysical" thus drops out as irrelevant.

The question on the table, though, is *how* the NNLT can consistently regard capital punishment as wrong in an absolute, cosmic sense while adhering to the principles of desert and proportionality. In our view, neither Tollefsen nor any other NNLT advocate has satisfactorily resolved this problem.

3. Is the NNLT position on capital punishment compatible with Catholic teaching?

Our main concern in this book is with the relationship of capital punishment to Catholic moral teaching, and it is with respect to this concern that the NNLT position faces its gravest difficulty. NNLT writers claim that capital punishment is immoral not merely under certain circumstances, but *intrinsically* immoral, *always and in principle* immoral. Yet Scripture, Tradition, and the popes not only have never taught this, but have consistently denied it. Indeed, as we will argue in the next chapter, the claim that capital punishment is always and intrinsically immoral is flatly incompatible with Catholic orthodoxy. Hence, *if* the NNLT really does entail that capital punishment is

---

[134] Tollefsen, "Punishment: Political, Not Metaphysical".

always and intrinsically immoral, then the NNLT is (notwithstanding the good intentions of its proponents) incompatible with Catholic orthodoxy. That is all the more reason for NNLT writers to reconsider their extreme position on the issue and return to Finnis' more moderate earlier position.

2

Church Teaching and Capital Punishment

Capital punishment in Scripture

The authority of Scripture

To set the stage properly for a consideration of scriptural teaching on capital punishment, it is crucial to call to mind the extremely high authority the Catholic Church attributes to Scripture. The Church has consistently maintained that Scripture is divinely inspired and inerrant. The First Vatican Council (1869–1970) teaches:

> The complete books of the old and the new Testament with all their parts, as they are listed in the decree of the ... Council [of Trent] and as they are found in the old Latin Vulgate edition, are to be received as sacred and canonical.
>
> These books the Church holds to be sacred and canonical not because she subsequently approved them by her authority after they had been composed by unaided human skill, nor simply because they contain revelation without error, but because, being written under the inspiration of the Holy Spirit, they have God as their author, and were as such committed to the Church....
>
> In matters of faith and morals, belonging as they do to the establishing of Christian doctrine, that meaning of Holy Scripture must be held to be the true one, which Holy mother Church held and holds, since it is her right to judge of the true meaning and interpretation of Holy Scripture.
>
> In consequence, it is not permissible for anyone to interpret Holy Scripture in a sense contrary to this, or indeed against the unanimous consent of the fathers....

If anyone does not receive as sacred and canonical the complete books of Sacred Scripture with all their parts, as the holy Council of Trent listed them, or denies that they were divinely inspired: let him be anathema.[1]

The Second Vatican Council teaches in *Dei Verbum* (1965) that

since everything asserted by the inspired authors or sacred writers must be held to be asserted by the Holy Spirit, it follows that the books of Scripture must be acknowledged as teaching solidly, faithfully and without error that truth which God wanted put into sacred writings for the sake of salvation. (no. 11)

And in a footnote, reference is made to Leo XIII's *Providentissimus Deus* and Pius XII's *Divino Afflante Spiritu*. The *Catechism of the Catholic Church* (no. 107) in turn quotes approvingly from this passage in *Dei Verbum*.

The Church has been especially concerned to rebut the claim that Scripture is inerrant merely where matters of faith and morals are concerned. What matters for our purposes, though, is that for that very reason it cannot possibly be denied that the Church teaches that Scripture is inerrant *at least* where matters of faith and morals are concerned (something even the modernist theologians whose views the popes were condemning did not dare to deny). It is equally undeniable that the Church teaches, in the words of the First Vatican Council, that "it is not permissible for anyone to interpret Holy Scripture in a sense contrary to" the meaning "which Holy mother Church held and holds" or which is "against the unanimous consent of the fathers".

Now, the question of whether capital punishment is ever permissible is clearly a matter of faith and morals. It follows that if Scripture, understood as the Fathers of the Church and the Church herself have always understood it, teaches that capital punishment is in principle morally legitimate, then any faithful Catholic must maintain that this teaching is inerrant and indeed divinely inspired. But it is manifest

---

[1] See Norman Tanner, ed., *Decrees of the Ecumenical Councils*, 2 vols. (Washington, D.C.: Georgetown University Press, 1990). Tanner's text for the "First Vatican Council (1869–1870)", *Decrees*, is available at https://www.ewtn.com/library/COUNCILS/V1.HTM. See Session 3, chap. 2, par. 6–9 and can. 2, par. 4.

that this is what Scripture does in fact teach, and that this is what the Church has always understood it to teach.

The Old Testament

"In the history of Christian theological legitimation of the death penalty", writes James Megivern, the following passage from Genesis "has probably been cited more frequently than any other text as basic proof of the propriety of humans executing fellow human malefactors":[2]

> And God blessed Noah and his sons, and said to them,... "For your lifeblood I will surely require a reckoning; of every beast I will require it and of man; of every man's brother I will require the life of man. Whoever sheds the blood of man, by man shall his blood be shed; for God made man in his own image." (9:1, 5–6)

An especially striking aspect of this passage is the way it affirms the penalty of death precisely in the name of man's dignity as made in God's image—in sharp contrast to those modern abolitionists (including Catholic ones) who *reject* the death penalty in the name of human dignity. As J. Budziszewski writes in commenting on this passage:

> Someone may object that the murderer, too, is made in God's image, and so he is. But this does not lighten the horror of his deed. On the contrary, it heightens it, because it makes him a morally accountable being....
>
> Genesis says murderers deserve death *because* life is precious; man is made in the image of God. How convincing is our reverence for life if its mockers are suffered to live?[3]

Nevertheless, Megivern alleges that the traditional understanding of this passage from Genesis is "unwarranted".[4] For one thing, he

[2] James J. Megivern, *The Death Penalty: An Historical and Theological Survey* (New York: Paulist Press, 1997), p. 15.

[3] J. Budziszewski, "Capital Punishment: The Case for Justice", *First Things* 145 (2004): 39, 43.

[4] Megivern, *The Death Penalty*, p. 16; cf. Michael L. Westmoreland-White and Glen H. Stassen, "Biblical Perspectives on the Death Penalty", in Erik C. Owens, John D. Carlson, and Eric P. Elshtain, eds., *Religion and the Death Penalty: A Call for Reckoning* (Grand Rapids, Mich.: William B. Eerdmans, 2004), pp. 126–28.

says, there is no distinction made in the passage between accidental and willful homicide, no distinction between a crime of passion and a murder that is planned maliciously, and no reference to state executions as opposed to private vengeance. Hence, Megivern concludes, the passage cannot be used to justify modern state executions for first-degree murder. For another thing, the passage is, in his view, probably best read in a "proverbial" way rather than as a divine command. It is not advocating capital punishment but merely noting that murderers will tend, as a matter of fact, to suffer the repercussion of being killed themselves.

But Megivern's arguments have no force. First of all, the "proverbial" reading of the passage is simply not true to the text. God does not merely observe that a murderer will tend in the course of things to be killed himself; he says, "*I will surely require* a reckoning", and "*I will require* the life of man." These words are immediately preceded by another command, namely: "*You shall not* eat flesh with its life, that is, its blood*" (Gn 9:4, emphasis added); and they are immediately followed by yet another: "*And you, be fruitful and multiply*, bring forth abundantly on the earth and multiply in it" (Gn 9:7, emphasis added). It is absurd to deny that the words "Whoever sheds the blood of man, by man shall his blood be shed" are, given this context, intended precisely as a divine *sanction* of the penalty of death.

Moreover, the clause "for God made man in his own image" would make little sense on Megivern's reading. The passage gives the fact that murder victims are made in God's image as the *reason why* their murderers will be killed by other men. That is to say, it not only tells us that murderers will themselves tend to be killed, but it identifies the motive for killing them as a distinctively *moral* motive. This hardly squares with the suggestion that the passage has merely "proverbial" rather than moral significance.

Nor is it relevant that the passage does not distinguish between various kinds of homicide or make reference to the institution of state executions. When Christ commands his followers to "give to him who begs from you, and do not refuse him who would borrow from you" (Mt 5:42), it would be ridiculous to argue: "No distinction is made in this passage between those who are truly in need and those who would take advantage of our generosity, or between private charities and governmental assistance; nor are we told whether we are supposed to give to the poor even at the expense of our own well-being or that of our family members; therefore this passage cannot be used as a proof-text to show that almsgiving is required of us." Obviously, the passage from Matthew *does* teach the general principle that almsgiving is required of us, even if it does not address every question we might have about how to apply that principle in various concrete circumstances. Similarly, it is absurd to deny that Genesis 9:5–6 affirms the legitimacy in principle of capital punishment, even though it does not address every question about how *that* principle is to be applied in concrete circumstances.

Then there is the problem that Megivern's proposed interpretation of the passage from Genesis is, by virtue of its very novelty, difficult to square with the principle that "it is not permissible for anyone to interpret Holy Scripture in a sense contrary to" the meaning "which Holy mother Church held and holds". For by Megivern's own admission, to regard the passage as a divine sanction of capital punishment is "the 'traditional' use of Genesis 9:6", which held "for centuries".[5]

Even E. Christian Brugger, a Catholic New Natural Law theorist opposed in principle to the death penalty and willing (as we will see below) to consider reinterpreting biblical passages traditionally understood as sanctioning that penalty, concedes that such a reinterpretation is hard to defend in the case of Genesis 9:6. Writes Brugger:

> The passage in Genesis 9:6 seems to affirm that human agents have a mediating role in the justice of God which includes as a consequence, in some cases, the infliction of death. The passage seems to me to warrant at least a provisional conclusion that the biblical author *intended* to refer to a role belonging to humans as such by reason of the relationship of human authority to divine authority.[6]

Hence Brugger acknowledges that the passage is a "problem" for the abolitionist position that is "left standing" despite existing attempts at reinterpretation.

It is, in any event, uncontroversial that the law given to Israel by God through Moses not only sanctions capital punishment but, in the

---

[5] Megivern, *The Death Penalty*, pp. 15–16.

[6] E. Christian Brugger, *Capital Punishment and Roman Catholic Moral Tradition* (Notre Dame, Ind.: University of Notre Dame Press, 2003), p. 73.

famous *lex talionis*, endorses a straightforward version of the principle of proportionality. Some key passages are the following:

> Whoever strikes a man so that he dies shall be put to death. But if he did not lie in wait for him, but God let him fall into his hand, then I will appoint for you a place to which he may flee. But if a man willfully attacks another to kill him treacherously, you shall take him from my altar, that he may die....
>
> When men strive together, and hurt a woman with child, so that there is a miscarriage, and yet no harm follows, the one who hurt her shall be fined, according as the woman's husband shall lay upon him; and he shall pay as the judges determine. If any harm follows, then you shall give life for life, eye for eye, tooth for tooth, hand for hand, foot for foot, burn for burn, wound for wound, stripe for stripe. (Ex 21:12–14, 22–25)

> He who kills a man shall be put to death.... When a man causes a disfigurement in his neighbor, as he has done it shall be done to him, fracture for fracture, eye for eye, tooth for tooth; as he has disfigured a man, he shall be disfigured. (Lev 24:17, 19–20)
>
> But if any man hates his neighbor, and lies in wait for him, and attacks him, and wounds him mortally so that he dies, and the man flees into one of these cities, then the elders of his city shall send and fetch him from there, and hand him over to the avenger of blood, so that he may die. Your eye shall not pity him, but you shall purge the guilt of innocent blood from Israel, so that it may be well with you. (Deut 19:11–13)

In Numbers, God declares that "blood pollutes the land, and no expiation can be made for the land, for the blood that is shed in it, except by the blood of him who shed it" (35:33). The parallel with Genesis 9:6 is obvious, and a "proverbial" reading is even less plausible here. The passage does not say merely that a murderer will tend, given human vindictiveness, to be killed himself. It says that the murderer's death provides "expiation" or reparation for his crime, and that *only* his death can do so.

There are also in the Mosaic Law many crimes other than murder for which the death penalty might be inflicted, including false witness (Deut 19:18–21), idolatry (Deut 13:6–10), adultery (Deut

22:22; Lev 20:10), homosexual acts (Lev 20:13), bestiality (Ex 22:19; Lev 20:15–16), incest (Lev 20:11–12), kidnapping (Ex 21:16), and striking one's parents (Ex 21:15). Unlike the sanction in Genesis 9:6 of the death penalty for murder, which is presented as having application to the human race in general and predates the Mosaic Law, capital punishment for these other offenses reflects the special circumstances of ancient Israel and is no longer in force after the Mosaic Law was abrogated. But that it was in force even temporarily reinforces the point that Scripture regards the death penalty as in principle legitimate.

In the Psalms, David writes: "Morning by morning I will destroy all the wicked in the land, cutting off all the evildoers from the city of the LORD" (Ps 101:8). The *Roman Catechism* (which we discuss below) cites this passage in defense of capital punishment.

The New Testament

It is sometimes supposed that Christ repudiated the lex talionis when he taught, in the Sermon on the Mount:

> You have heard that it was said, "An eye for an eye and a tooth for a tooth." But I say to you, Do not resist one who is evil. But if any one strikes you on the right cheek, turn to him the other also; and if any one would sue you and take your coat, let him have your cloak as well; and if any one forces you to go one mile, go with him two miles. (Mt 5:38–41)

Christ said in the very same sermon, however, that he had come "not to abolish the law and the prophets ... but to fulfil them" (Mt 5:17). The way in which the passage in question fulfills rather than abolishes the Mosaic Law is explained by Saint Augustine in *Contra Faustum*:

> Nor, again, is there any opposition between that which was said by them of old time, "An eye for an eye, a tooth for a tooth," and what the Lord says.... The old precept as well as the new is intended to check the vehemence of hatred, and to curb the impetuosity of angry passion.... To put a restraint upon a revenge so unjust from its excess, the law established the principle of compensation, that the penalty should correspond to the injury inflicted. So the precept, "an eye for

an eye, a tooth for a tooth," instead of being a brand to kindle a fire that was quenched, was rather a covering to prevent the fire already kindled from spreading. For there is a just revenge due to the injured person from his assailant; so that when we pardon, we give up what we might justly claim.... There is no injustice in asking back a debt, though there is kindness in forgiving it.... Though there is no sin in wishing for revenge within the limits of justice, the man who wishes for no revenge at all is further from the sin of an unjust revenge.[7]

As Augustine's reading indicates, Christ's teaching does not *reject* the principle that an offender deserves a punishment proportionate to his offense, but *presupposes* it. The lex talionis principle was intended to ensure that offenders were given a penalty they deserved, as opposed to a penalty that was *harsher* than what they deserved. Jesus is not denying that this is good. Rather, he is saying that it is even better to forgive an offender altogether. In that way the Mosaic Law, which required just deserts but nothing more, is perfected by Christ, who commends mercy rather than mere justice. But forgiveness and mercy presuppose that the offender *really does deserve* the punishment we refrain from inflicting.

All the same, Christ's teaching does *not* imply that capital punishment (which is not even mentioned in the passage) ought never to be inflicted. To suppose that it does, one would, to be consistent, also have to suppose that Christ would condemn arresting and imprisoning kidnappers, fining thieves, returning fire when bank robbers or invading armies are shooting at us, and so forth. Yet even most opponents of capital punishment who cite the Sermon on the Mount would not advocate pacifism or the abolition of the criminal justice system. In fact, Christ is not directly addressing questions of government and criminal justice in this passage in the first place, but is speaking of the attitude that the individual Christian ought to strive to take toward the injustices he suffers. And that is how the passage has traditionally been understood by Catholic theologians. As we read in Fr. George Haydock's once widely used edition of the Douay-Rheims Bible, which quotes the earlier Catholic biblical scholars Robert Witham and Richard Challoner:

---

[7] Augustine, *Contra Faustum* 19, 25.

These are to be understood as admonitions to Christians, to forgive every one, and to bear patiently all manner of private injuries. But we must not from hence conclude it unlawful for any one to have recourse to the laws, when a man is injured, and cannot have justice by any other means [quoted from Witham].... What is here commanded, is a Christian patience under injuries and affronts, and to be willing even to suffer still more, rather than to indulge the desire of revenge; but what is further added does not strictly oblige according to the letter, for neither did Christ, nor S. Paul, turn the other cheek. S. John xviii. and Acts xxiii [quoted from Challoner].[8]

There are additional problems with the view that Christ intended in this passage from the Sermon on the Mount to condemn capital punishment. Earlier in the Sermon, Christ explicitly addresses the sin of murder and says:

You have heard that it was said to the men of old, "You shall not kill; and whoever kills shall be liable to judgment." But I say to you that every one who is angry with his brother shall be liable to judgment; whoever insults his brother shall be liable to the council, and whoever says, "You fool!" shall be liable to the hell of fire. (Mt 5:21-22)

Christ's point is that merely refraining from murdering a person is not good enough and that the moral demands he makes on us are *more stringent* than his listeners might have expected. It is hard to see in that a reason for giving murderers a *less severe* punishment than his listeners might have expected. Nor can anyone who threatens "the hell of fire" plausibly be taken to oppose harsh punishments! Furthermore, when Christ cites the lex talionis in Matthew 5:38, he does not quote any complete formulation from the Pentateuch. In particular, he does not make reference to taking "life for life". He refers only to taking "an eye for an eye and a tooth for a tooth". This, together with the fact that he discussed murder earlier in the Sermon, indicates that he is not talking here about how one should deal with murderers. Rather, he is discussing the attitude that victims

[8] George Leo Haydock, *Haydock's Catholic Family Bible and Commentary* (New York: Edward Dunigan and Brother, 1859), p. 1256.

of less serious offenses should take toward those who have victimized them.[9]

It is also sometimes suggested that the account of the woman caught
in adultery and brought forward for stoning (Jn 8:1–11), wherein
Jesus says that he who is without sin should cast the first stone, is evidence that he opposed capital punishment. Here too, though, such an
inference is unwarranted. Why not conclude instead that Christ was
merely condemning the death penalty as a punishment for adultery,
but not for other offenses? Or why not conclude that he was against
punishment of any sort, since he does not assign a lesser punishment
to the woman caught in adultery? In fact, as with the Sermon on
the Mount, the passage is not concerned with questions about criminal justice per se in the first place. Nor does Jesus even deny that
the particular punishment in this case was just. He merely indicates
that those who brought the woman forward for stoning were guilty
of hypocrisy.[10]

---

[9] It is worth noting what one ancient Christian writer commenting on this passage has to
say about anger: "Therefore everyone who is angry with cause will not be guilty. For if there
is no anger, neither does doctrine profit, nor do judgments stand, nor are offenses restrained.
A just anger is the mother of discipline. Consequently, not only do they who get angry
with cause not sin, but contrariwise, unless they become angry they sin; they sin because an
unreasonable patience sows vices, nourishes negligence and invites not only evil people, but
even good people, to evil, because an evil person is not corrected, to be sure, even if he is
not reproved, but a good person perishes unless he is reproved because evil prevails more in
the body than good does. The anger that is with cause is not anger but judgment." *Incomplete Commentary on Matthew* (Opus imperfectum), Ancient Christian Texts, trans. James A.
Kellerman, ed. Thomas C. Oden (Downers Grove, Ill.: InterVarsity Press, 2010), 1:96. Of
the author of this passage, the translator tells us: "The work is also incomplete because the
author is unknown. Or, to speak more accurately, it was wrongly ascribed for centuries to
John Chrysostom. Under closer analysis, however, Chrysostom cannot have been the author"
(for reasons having to do with style, reference to apocryphal books, the use of Latin, etc.).

[10] There are yet other possible interpretations of this passage: (1) Adultery was a capital
crime under the Mosaic Law for men as well as for women. Now, if the woman was caught
in the act, so too was the man with whom she was committing adultery. Yet we hear nothing
about him. Perhaps the point of the story is that it is unfair to punish the woman for this
offense without punishing the man. (2) We do not know whether the woman was given a
trial. Perhaps the story is about the denial of due process. (3) Roman law prohibited Jews
from executing anyone (which is why Christ had to be condemned by Pilate). For Christ's
interlocutors to get him to endorse the stoning of the woman would have given them a way
to represent him as endorsing disobedience to Roman law. The main point of the story may
merely be to relate how Christ evaded this attempt to trap him. Again, there is simply no good
reason to think that the point of the passage is to criticize capital punishment per se.

Other passages in the New Testament not only do not condemn capital punishment but clearly take for granted its legitimacy. At the Crucifixion, the good thief affirms that, unlike Jesus, he and his fellow criminal are being executed "justly" and receiving their "due reward" (Lk 23:41). Christ does not suggest that this remark is somehow contrary to a respect for human dignity or insufficiently merciful, nor does he in any other way criticize it. (Nor is it plausible that Luke would have reported the good thief's words had he believed capital punishment to be contrary to Christ's teaching.) In defending himself before Festus, Saint Paul says: "If then I am a wrongdoer, and have committed anything for which I deserve to die, I do not seek to escape death" (Acts 25:11). He implies here that there are offenses worthy of death, although he denies that he has justly been accused of any such offense.

Then there is Romans 13:1–4, traditionally understood as a straightforward affirmation of the right of the state to execute criminals:

> Let every person be subject to the governing authorities. For there is no authority except from God, and those that exist have been instituted by God. Therefore he who resists the authorities resists what God has appointed, and those who resist will incur judgment. For rulers are not a terror to good conduct, but to bad. Would you have no fear of him who is in authority? Then do what is good, and you will receive his approval, for he is God's servant for your good. But if you do wrong, be afraid, for he does not bear the sword in vain; he is the servant of God to execute his wrath on the wrongdoer.[11]

Even Tertullian, commonly understood to have opposed capital punishment, seems to have acknowledged that Romans 13 allows for it in principle.[12] Origen cites it too as evidence of the state's authority to inflict the death penalty.[13] Saint Ambrose, though recommending mercy rather than the infliction of capital punishment, acknowledges

---

[11] Note that just a few sentences before, in Romans 12:19, Paul had written: "Beloved, never avenge yourselves, but leave it to the wrath of God; for it is written, 'Vengeance is mine, I will repay, says the Lord.'" It can hardly be clearer that for Paul, prohibition of *private* vengeance has nothing to do with whether *public authorities* may inflict punishments.

[12] Tertullian, *Treatise on the Soul* 33; see also *Scorpiace* 14.

[13] Origen, *Contra Celsum* 8, 65.

on the basis of Romans 13:4 that the death penalty has "the Apostle's authority" behind it.[14] Saint Augustine also implies that Romans 13 gives the state power over life and death.[15] Aquinas explicitly cites Romans 13:4 as scriptural warrant for capital punishment.[16] Indeed, as Brugger acknowledges (despite his own opposition to capital punishment), there was in the patristic and medieval eras a "consensus" to the effect that Romans 13 sanctions the death penalty.[17]

Nevertheless, Brugger suggests that the passage in question was not intended by Saint Paul as a timeless statement on the nature of state authority, but rather an ad hoc way of dealing with a local political problem facing the Christian community in Rome during the 50s.[18] Specifically, according to Brugger, Paul merely intended to encourage the Roman Christians to pay their taxes (as the Apostle goes on to do in Romans 13:6–7), so as to avoid the persecution they would face if they did not, given circumstances in the city at the time. The appeal to the divinely appointed power of the state was "a piece of cultural wisdom" intended merely to lend force to this exhortation.[19] Hence, we cannot derive from this passage any general lesson about the legitimacy of capital punishment.

But there are serious problems with Brugger's proposed reading. First, it is entirely speculative and evidently motivated by a desire to soften the tension that Brugger believes exists between biblical teaching and his claim that capital punishment is inherently immoral. Now, even in nontheological contexts, there is a presumption against such novel readings. Those who were closer in time and place to the author of a passage and the circumstances in which

---

[14] Ambrose, Letter 90 (to Studius), in *Letters*, trans. Sister Mary Melchior Beyenka, O.P. (Washington, D.C.: Catholic University of America Press, 1954), p. 492.

[15] Augustine, Letter 87 (to Emeritus), in *Letters*.

[16] *Summa Contra Gentiles* III, 146, 5–6. Elsewhere Aquinas writes: "For we are forbidden to return evil for evil when it is inspired by hatred or envy, so that we take pleasure in another's evil. But if in return for the evil of guilt which someone commits a judge pronounces an evil of punishment in a just way to compensate for malice, he does, indeed, return evil materially, but formally and in itself he returns a good. Hence, when a judge hangs a criminal for murder, he does not return evil for evil but good for evil." Thomas Aquinas, *Lectures on the Letter to the Romans*, trans. Fabian Larcher, O.P., ed. Jeremy Holmes (Ave Maria, Fla.: Aquinas Center for Theological Renewal, n.d.), chap. 12, lect. 3, 1008.

[17] Brugger, *Capital Punishment*, p. 112.

[18] Ibid., pp. 64–71.

[19] Ibid., p. 69.

it was written are, naturally, more likely to understand correctly what was meant than are those of us who are reading the passage centuries or even millennia later. Hence, when there is a conflict between the traditional understanding of a passage and some proposed novel reading, the traditional reading must get the benefit of the doubt (even if we were to concede, as we should not, that there is doubt about the traditional reading in the case of Romans 13). But we must be especially wary of novel readings where doctrinal matters are concerned, since, as we have seen, the Church teaches that "it is not permissible for anyone to interpret Holy Scripture in a sense contrary to" the meaning "which Holy mother Church held and holds" or which is "against the unanimous consent of the fathers". Now, Romans 13 has traditionally and consistently been understood as putting forward moral principles concerning state power in general and capital punishment in particular, not merely as an ad hoc response to a local set of problems concerning taxation. Hence, in the absence of some decisive argument against this traditional understanding of the passage, the traditional interpretation must stand as authoritative.

Brugger's argument is, in any event, not only less than decisive but extremely weak. By Brugger's own admission, the "piece of cultural wisdom" concerning the divine source of state power to which Saint Paul appeals is not merely reflective of human tradition or popular sentiment but has its source in *biblical* teaching. Brugger himself cites Proverbs 8:15–16, Proverbs 24:21–22, Wisdom 6:1–4, Jeremiah 29:7, Mark 12:14–17, and 1 Peter 2:13–14 as scriptural background for what Paul says about state power in Romans 13. Nor does Paul present his remarks about state power as a mere summary of the conventional wisdom. He says, peremptorily and without qualification, that "there is no authority except from God, and those that exist have been instituted by God", that the ruler "is the servant of God to execute his wrath on the wrongdoer", and so forth. He does not say: "You people *believe* the state to have divine backing, so make sure you act in a way that is consistent with that belief when the taxman comes around." The form of Paul's statements and the manner in which he makes them are precisely what one would expect of the assertion of general theological principles, but not of a mere allusion to contingent "cultural wisdom".

Furthermore, while Brugger spills much ink about the need carefully to consider Paul's "motive" and of what he "intend[ed] to assert",[20] the inference he draws from this exegetical desideratum is simply fallacious. Suppose that, to dissuade you from handing Socrates a cup of hemlock, I want to convince you that *Socrates is mortal*; and suppose that, in order to do that, I appeal to the premises that "All men are mortal" and that "Socrates is a man." It would be ridiculous to suggest that, since my motive is to save Socrates' life and since what I "intend to assert" is that *Socrates is mortal*, I must not really be asserting that *all men are mortal*, but am merely alluding to "a piece of cultural wisdom" when I say that all men are mortal. On the contrary, I *must* be taken to be asserting that *all men are mortal*, precisely because if I were not, then I could not expect you to agree that it gives us a reason to think that *Socrates is mortal*. Similarly, even if we agreed with Brugger (as we should not) that Saint Paul's motive in Romans 13 was merely to get the Roman Christians to pay their taxes, it simply would not follow that he was not *also* making a general statement about political authority. On the contrary, the specific assertion about taxes that Paul is making can be supported by his general remarks about the divine source of political authority only if we also take Paul to be making an assertion about political authority when he makes those remarks.

Indeed, after several pages of tortuous exegesis and heavy emphasis on the theme that Paul's intent in Romans 13 is to address a local tax issue rather than put forward a "timeless doctrine", even Brugger himself appears finally to concede that Saint Paul really does after all "intend to assert" in Romans 13 that "legitimate authority, including governmental authority, derives from God for purposes of maintaining the good order of communities"![21] So the relevance of most of Brugger's discussion to the topic of capital punishment is obscure. What appears to be doing most of the real work is a brief reference to the view of "contemporary biblical scholars" that Paul's expression "bear the sword" is a metaphor for the state's coercive power rather than a reference to capital punishment.[22] But Brugger himself

---

[20] Ibid., p. 70.
[21] Ibid.
[22] Ibid.

concedes that this reading may not be correct and that not all biblical scholars agree with it; and he concedes also that there was in the
patristic and medieval eras a "consensus" to the effect that Romans
13 sanctions capital punishment.[23] Since the novel and controversial
reading to which Brugger appeals would conflict with this traditional
understanding, we have, for the reasons given above, decisive reason
to reject that novel reading.

We conclude that the clear, consistent teaching of Scripture is that
capital punishment is in principle legitimate and that none of the arguments that attempt to show otherwise have any force. Since the Church
maintains that scriptural teaching on matters of faith and morals is
divinely inspired and inerrant, we conclude also that, for this reason
alone, the radical claim that capital punishment is always and in principle wrong simply cannot be made consistent with Catholic orthodoxy.
But this judgment is further reinforced by the consistent teaching of
the Fathers and Doctors of the Church, the popes, and authoritative
ecclesiastical documents.

The Fathers and Doctors of the Church on capital punishment

Once again making a significant concession, Catholic death-penalty
opponent E. Christian Brugger, in his study of the history of Catholic
teaching on capital punishment, writes:

> For the Fathers of the early Church, the authority of the state to kill
> malefactors is taken for granted. Opinions differed on whether Chris-
> tians should hold offices whose responsibilities include the judging and
> carrying out of capital punishments—pre-Constantinian authors said
> they should not, those writing after AD 313 said they should—but the
> principled legitimacy of the punishment itself is never questioned.[24]

The second-century apologist Athenagoras of Athens, while defending his fellow Christians against the charges leveled against them

---

[23] Ibid., p. 112.
[24] Ibid., p. 74.

by their persecutors, allows in *A Plea for the Christians* that the harshest penalties would be merited if the charges were true:

> If, indeed, any one can convict us of a crime, be it small or great, we do not ask to be excused from punishment, but are prepared to undergo the sharpest and most merciless inflictions. . . .
>   Three things are alleged against us: atheism, Thyestean feasts, Oedipodean intercourse. But if these charges are true, spare no class: proceed at once against our crimes; destroy us root and branch, with our wives and children, if any Christian is found to live like the brutes.[25]

To be sure, Athenagoras is not an enthusiastic supporter of the death penalty. Defending Christians against the charge of cannibalism, he writes: "When [our accusers] know that we cannot endure even to see a man put to death, though justly; who of them can accuse us of murder or cannibalism?"[26] But, as the word "justly" indicates, the legitimacy in principle of capital punishment is not denied.

Tertullian (d. ca. 220) and Lactantius (d. ca. 320) are often cited as Fathers who were opposed to the death penalty. Tertullian did indeed teach that a Christian ought not to participate in capital punishment,[27] and Lactantius wrote, in *The Divine Institutes*:

> For when God forbids us to kill, He not only prohibits us from open violence, which is not even allowed by the public laws, but He warns us against the commission of those things which are esteemed lawful among men. Thus it will be neither lawful for a just man to engage in warfare, since his warfare is justice itself, nor to accuse any one of a capital charge, because it makes no difference whether you put a man to death by word, or rather by the sword, since it is the act of putting to death itself which is prohibited. Therefore, with regard to this precept of God, there ought to be no exception at all; but that it is always unlawful to put to death a man, whom God willed to be a sacred animal.[28]

As even Brugger and Megivern acknowledge, however, these Church Fathers did not in fact regard capital punishment as immoral

---

[25] Athenagoras, *A Plea for the Christians* 2 and 3.
[26] Ibid., chap. 35.
[27] Tertullian, *De Idolatria* 19; *De Corona* 11, 2.
[28] Lactantius, *The Divine Institutes* 6, 20.

in principle.[29] For Tertullian also indicates, in *A Treatise on the Soul*, that a penalty of death can be just:

> Hence those souls must be accounted as passing an exile in Hades, which people are apt to regard as carried off by violence, especially by cruel tortures, such as those of the cross, and the axe, and the sword, and the lion; *but we do not account those to be violent deaths which justice awards*, that avenger of violence.[30]

Lactantius, in the very chapter cited above, allows that a man can be "justly condemned [to] be slain", and in his *Treatise on the Anger of God* writes:

> They are deceived by no slight error who defame all censure, whether human or divine, with the name of bitterness and malice, thinking that He ought to be called injurious who visits the injurious with punishment. But if this is so, it follows that we have injurious laws, which enact punishment for offenders, and injurious judges who inflict capital punishments on those convicted of crime. But if *the law is just* which awards to the transgressor his due, and if *the judge is called upright and good when he punishes crimes ... it follows* that God, when He opposes the evil, is not injurious.[31]

In other words, Lactantius is defending the justice of God's punishments precisely by comparing them to the justice of human punishments such as the death penalty. Brugger concludes that "the exceptionless prohibition against killing that Lactantius defends in the *Divine Institutes* clearly applies only to the members of the Christian community"[32] and does not reflect any judgment to the effect that capital punishment is per se wrong.

Other Church Fathers are much more explicit about the justice of capital punishment. Clement of Alexandria (d. ca. 215) writes:

> But when [the law] sees any one in such a condition as to appear incurable, posting to the last stage of wickedness, then in its solicitude

---

[29] Brugger, *Capital Punishment*, pp. 77, 84; Megivern, *The Death Penalty*, pp. 22, 26.

[30] Tertullian, *A Treatise on the Soul* 56, emphasis added.

[31] Lactantius, *A Treatise on the Anger of God* 17, emphasis added.

[32] Brugger, *Capital Punishment*, p. 84.

for the rest, that they may not be destroyed by it (just as if amputating a part from the whole body), it condemns such an one to death, as the course most conducive to health. . . .

When one falls into any incurable evil—when taken possession of, for example, by wrong or covetousness—it will be for his good if he is put to death.[33]

In his *Homilies on Leviticus*, Origen (d. ca. 254) teaches: "Death which is inflicted as the penalty of sin is a purification of the sin itself for which it was ordered to be inflicted. Therefore, sin is absolved through the penalty of death."[34] Cyprian of Carthage (d. ca. 258) also implies that death can be a legitimate penalty.[35] To be sure, like other Church Fathers in the pre-Constantinian period, Origen and Cyprian also teach that Christians should avoid bloodshed. But the right of the state to execute criminals is not denied. In holding Christians to a more rigorous standard than the (as yet unconverted) governing authorities, these Fathers do not claim that the latter's resort to capital punishment is inherently wrong.

After the time of Constantine, the view that even Christian governing authorities may resort to the death penalty becomes standard, though leniency is also often commended. Eusebius (d. ca. 340) affirmed that Constantine's execution of his rival Licinius was the just punishment of a tyrant.[36] In his *Homilies on the Statues*, Saint John Chrysostom (ca. 347–407) praises the emperor Theodosius for mercifully refraining from what would have been a "justifiable slaughter"[37] in punishment for the seditious actions of the citizens of Antioch and allows that "although you were to put to death; or whatever else you might do, you would never yet have taken on us the revenge we deserve."[38] Saint Gregory of Nazianzus (ca. 325–389), though also recommending mercy,[39] allows that evildoers can

---

[33] Clement of Alexandria, *The Stromata* I, 27.

[34] Origen, *Homilies on Leviticus*, trans. Gary Wayne Barkley (Washington, D.C.: Catholic University of America Press, 1990), Homily 14, p. 252.

[35] Cyprian of Carthage, *Ad Demetrianum* 13.

[36] Eusebius, *Life of Constantine* II, 18.

[37] John Chrysostom, *Homilies on the Statues*, trans. W. R. W. Stephens, in *Nicene and Post-Nicene Fathers*, 1st ser., vol. 9, ed. Philip Schaff (Buffalo, N.Y.: Christian Literature, 1889), Homily 6.

[38] Ibid., Homily 21.

[39] Gregory of Nazianzus, *Epistola* LXXVIII.

merit the death penalty.[40] Saint Ephraem of Syria (d. 373) holds that women who obtain abortions deserve death.[41] Saint Hilary (d. 368) held that it is lawful to kill if one is fulfilling the duty of a judge.[42]

As we noted above, Saint Ambrose of Milan (ca. 340–397) allowed, on the basis of Saint Paul's authority, that capital punishment was legitimate in principle.[43] He too recommends mercy, however, emphasizing that evildoers will have more time to find repentance if they are not executed.[44] Similarly, Saint Augustine (354–430), though he often strongly pleaded for mercy for those guilty of capital offenses,[45] also strongly affirmed the right of the state to inflict the penalty of death.[46] In his commentary *On the Sermon on the Mount*, Augustine writes:

> But great and holy men ... punished some sins with death, both because the living were struck with a salutary fear, and because it was not death itself that would injure those who were being punished with death, but sin, which might be increased if they continued to live. They did not judge rashly on whom God had bestowed such a power of judging. Hence it is that Elijah inflicted death on many, both with his own hand and by calling down fire from heaven; as was done also without rashness by many other great and godlike men, in the same spirit of concern for the good of humanity.[47]

And in *The City of God*, Augustine says:

> However, there are some exceptions made by the divine authority to its own law, that men may not be put to death.... They who have waged war in obedience to the divine command, or in conformity with His laws, have represented in their persons the public justice or the wisdom of government, and in this capacity have put to death

[40] Gregory of Nazianzus, *Oratio* XVII, 6.
[41] Ephraem of Syria, *De Timore Dei* X.
[42] Cited in Robert Bellarmine, *De Laicis, or The Treatise on Civil Government*, ed. Kathleen E. Murphy (New York: Fordham University Press, 1928), p. 55.
[43] Letter 90 (to Studius), in Ambrose, *Letters*.
[44] Ambrose, *On Cain and Abel* 2.
[45] Augustine, Letters 100, 104, 133, 134, 139, and 153 in *Letters*.
[46] Augustine, Letters 137 and 153 in *Letters*.
[47] Augustine, *On the Sermon on the Mount* I, 20, 64.

wicked men; such persons have by no means violated the commandment, "You shall not kill."[48]

Saint Optatus, bishop of Milevus in the fourth century, writes in
book 3 of *Against the Donatists*:

> As if no-one ever deserved to die for the vindication of God!...
> Whatever [the executed] may possibly have suffered, if it be an evil to
> be killed, they are the cause of their own evil.... Accuse first Moses,
> the lawgiver himself, who, when he descended from Mount Sinai,
> almost before the tables of the law had been put forward, in which it
> was written, *Thou shall not kill*, ordered the killing of three thousand
> people in a single moment.[49]

Saint Jerome (ca. 347–420), in book 4 of his *Commentary on Jeremiah*,
remarking on the verse that says, "Do not shed innocent blood in this
place", says that "to punish murderers, the sacrilegious, and poisoners
is not the shedding of blood, but the duty of the laws."[50] He also says,
in his *Commentariorum in Isaiam Prophetam*, that "He who slays cruel
men is not cruel."[51]

Thus does even Brugger speak of a "Patristic consensus" on the
legitimacy in principle of capital punishment[52]—a legitimacy the
Fathers regarded as grounded in Scripture and which they upheld
despite the very strong emphasis some of them put on mercifully
refraining from inflicting death on those who deserved it. Now, the
Fathers, especially when there is a consensus among them, have a
very high degree of authority in Catholic theology. As G. Van Noort
notes, the standard position among orthodox Catholic theologians
is that "the unanimous agreement of the fathers on a doctrine as
revealed is a sure argument for divine Tradition."[53] As Van Noort

---

[48] Augustine, *The City of God* I, 21.

[49] Optatus, *Against the Donatists*, trans. Mark Edwards (Liverpool: Liverpool University Press, 1997), pp. 72–73.

[50] Quoted in Brugger, *Capital Punishment*, p. 213n87.

[51] Quoted in Patrick M. Laurence, "He Beareth Not the Sword in Vain: The Church, the Courts, and Capital Punishment", *Ave Maria Law Review* 1 (2003): 222.

[52] Brugger, *Capital Punishment*, p. 95.

[53] G. Van Noort, *Dogmatic Theology*, vol. 3, *The Sources of Revelation and Divine Faith*, trans. and rev. John J. Castelot and William R. Murphy (Westminster, Md.: Newman Press, 1961), p. 172. Cf. George Agius, *Tradition and the Church* (Boston: Stratford, 1928), chap. 10; and A. Tanquerey, *A Manual of Dogmatic Theology*, vol. 1, trans. John J. Byrnes (New York: Desclée, 1959), pp. 178–80.

goes on to say, "This proposition is *certain* and, in fact, is partially defined by the Councils of Trent and of the Vatican in what they have to say about the interpretation of Scripture."[54] The Council of Trent teaches:

> In order to curb impudent clever persons, the synod decrees that no one who relies on his own judgment in matters of faith and morals, which pertain to the building up of Christian doctrine, and that no one who distorts the Sacred Scripture according to his own opinions, shall dare to interpret the said Sacred Scripture contrary to that sense which is held by holy mother Church, whose duty it is to judge regarding the true sense and interpretation of holy Scriptures, *or even contrary to the unanimous consent of the Fathers.*[55]

And as we have already seen, the First Vatican Council decreed that

> in matters of faith and morals, belonging as they do to the establishing of Christian doctrine, that meaning of Holy Scripture must be held to be the true one, which Holy mother Church held and holds, since it is her right to judge of the true meaning and interpretation of Holy Scripture.
>
> In consequence, it is not permissible for anyone to interpret Holy Scripture in a sense contrary to this, or *indeed against the unanimous consent of the fathers.* (emphasis added)

Van Noort adds two further considerations.[56] First, the Fathers reflected the authoritative ecclesiastical Magisterium of their day. Some held positions of Church authority, and others wrote with the approval of Church authority. Second, in the history of the Church since the days of the Fathers, the Magisterium has consistently consulted them when deciding matters of doctrinal controversy. Nor can it be emphasized too strongly that "their writings enable us to render a better account of our Faith because they were closer to the fountain of truth."[57] Their historical proximity to Jesus and the apostles is a powerful argument for the certainty of any teaching on faith and

---

[54] Van Noort, *Dogmatic Theology*, 3:173.

[55] Henry Denzinger, *The Sources of Catholic Dogma*, trans. Roy J. Deferrari (St. Louis: B. Herder, 1957), §786, emphasis added.

[56] Van Noort, *Dogmatic Theology*, 3:173.

[57] Agius, *Tradition and the Church*, pp. 230–31.

morals about which they are agreed. Scheeben, Wilhelm, and Scannell's once widely used manual of theology sums up the authority of the Fathers as follows:

> When ... all the Fathers agree, their authority attains its perfection. The consent of the Fathers has always been looked upon as of equal authority with the teaching of the whole Church, or the definitions of the Popes and Councils.... The Consent of the Fathers does not always prove the Catholic character of a doctrine in the same way. If they distinctly state that a doctrine is a public dogma of the Church, the doctrine must be at once accepted. If they merely state that the doctrine is true and taught by the Church, without formally attributing to it the character of a dogma, this testimony has by no means the same weight. The doctrine thus attested cannot, on that account, be treated as a dogma. Nevertheless *it is at least a Catholic truth and morally certain, and the denial of it would deserve the censure of temerity or error.*
>
> The authority of the Fathers is held in high esteem by the Church in the interpretation of Scripture.... *The consent of the Fathers is a positive and not an exclusive rule, i.e. the interpretation must be in accordance with it where it exists,* but where it does not exist we may lawfully interpret even in opposition to the opinions of some of the Fathers.[58]

Now, as we have seen, even those among the Fathers who were largely or wholly opposed *in practice* to capital punishment—and who thus had every incentive to try to find in Scripture or Tradition a warrant for an absolute condemnation of the practice—affirmed that capital punishment is *in principle* morally legitimate, and often did so precisely on the grounds that Scripture forbids such an absolute condemnation. It is inconceivable that they could have been mistaken about this matter of moral principle, given the authority the Church has always attributed to them, especially where the proper understanding of Scripture is concerned. We conclude that the consensus of the Fathers provides further compelling evidence that any claim to the effect that capital punishment is *intrinsically* immoral is simply irreconcilable with Catholic orthodoxy.

---

[58] Joseph Wilhelm and Thomas B. Scannell, *A Manual of Catholic Theology Based on Scheeben's "Dogmatik"*, vol. 1, 4th ed. (New York: Benziger Brothers, 1909), pp. 80–81, emphasis added.

The testimony of the Doctors of the Church reinforces this judgment. As Cardinal Avery Dulles writes, "The official title 'Doctor of the Church' has been bestowed on certain canonized saints who have been singled out by popes or councils for their eminence in learning and soundness of doctrine."[59] There are thirty-five such Doctors, and they include not only Fathers such as Ephraem, Ambrose, Jerome, and Augustine, but also later thinkers such as Saint Anselm (1033–1109), Saint Albert the Great (1206–1280), Saint Bonaventure (1221–1274), Saint Thomas Aquinas (1225–1274), Saint Peter Canisius (1521–1597), Saint Robert Bellarmine (1542–1621), and Saint Alphonsus Liguori (1696–1787). The Doctors have, historically, had a very high level of authority in Catholic theology. As Scheeben, Wilhelm, and Scannell write:

> The Church herself has bestowed the title of "Doctor Ecclesiae," by which it honours the most illustrious Fathers in the Liturgy, upon many saints of later date, and has thereby put them on the same level. We may even say that the canonization of a theological writer raises him to some extent to the dignity of a "Father."[60]

Given the saintliness, learning, and orthodoxy of the Doctors and the exemplary status officially conferred on them by the Church, it is simply not plausible to suppose that they could all be wrong on some matter of faith and morals about which they agree—especially where they agree also with Scripture and the Fathers—consistent with the indefectibility of the Church. As Scheeben, Wilhelm, and Scannell argue:

> If ... [theologians] agree in declaring that a doctrine is sufficiently certain and demonstrated, their consent is not indeed a formal proof of the Catholic character of the doctrine, nevertheless the existence of the consent shows that the doctrine belongs to the mind of the Church (catholicus intellectus), and that consequently its denial would incur the censure of rashness.
>
> These principles on the authority of Theologians were strongly insisted on by Pius IX in the brief, Gravissimas inter (cf. infra, § 29), and

---

[59] Avery Dulles, Magisterium: Teacher and Guardian of the Faith (Naples, Fla.: Sapientia Press, 2007), p. 44.

[60] Wilhelm and Scannell, Manual of Catholic Theology, 1:79.

they are evident consequences of the Catholic doctrine of Tradition. Although the assistance of the Holy Ghost is not directly promised to Theologians, *nevertheless the assistance promised to the Church requires that He should prevent them as a body from falling into error; otherwise the Faithful who follow them would all be led astray. The consent of Theologians implies the consent of the Episcopate, according to Saint Augustine's dictum: "Not to resist an error is to approve of it—not to defend a truth is to reject it."*...

The Church holds the mediaeval Doctors in almost the same esteem as the Fathers. The substance of the teaching of the Schoolmen and their method of treatment have both been strongly approved of by the Church.[61]

Now, those Doctors who comment on the subject of capital punishment are in agreement about its legitimacy in principle. We have, in chapter 1, already quoted several passages from Aquinas in which he strongly upholds capital punishment both in theory and in practice, and we have just seen how those Doctors who are also Fathers of the Church affirm the legitimacy in principle of the death penalty. Other Doctors make similar statements. When addressing the question of how Scripture teaches that voluntary homicide is to be vindicated, the catechism of Saint Peter Canisius answers by quoting passages such as Genesis 9:6 ("Whoever sheds the blood of man, by man shall his blood be shed") and Psalm 54:24 (55:23), which states that "men of blood and treachery shall not live out half their days."[62] In his *Theologia Moralis*, Saint Alphonsus Liguori, patron saint of moral theologians, upholds the penalty of death "if it is necessary for the defense of the republic" or "in order to preserve the order of law".[63] Saint Robert Bellarmine, in chapter 13 of his *Treatise on Civil Government*, argues:

It is lawful for a Christian magistrate to punish with death disturbers of the public peace. It is proved, first, from the Scriptures, for in the law of nature, of Moses, and of the Gospels, we have precepts and examples

---

[61] Ibid., pp. 83–84, emphasis added. Cf. Tanquerey, *Manual of Dogmatic Theology*, 1:180, and Van Noort, *Dogmatic Theology*, 3:176–78.

[62] Cf. Brugger, *Capital Punishment*, p. 225n34, and Laurence, "He Beareth Not the Sword", pp. 223, 227–28.

[63] Alphonsus Liguori, *Theologia Moralis* III, 4, 1, quoted in Brugger, *Capital Punishment*, pp. 124–25.

of this. For God says, "Whosoever shall shed man's blood, his blood shall be shed." These words cannot utter a prophecy, since a prophecy of this sort would often be false, but a decree and a precept. . . .

Secondly, it is proved from the testimony of the Fathers. . . .

Lastly, it is proved from reason; for it is the duty of a good ruler, to whom has been entrusted the care of the common good, to prevent those members which exist for the sake of the whole from injuring it, and therefore if he cannot preserve all the members in unity, he ought rather to cut off one than to allow the common good to be destroyed; just as the farmer cuts off branches and twigs which are injuring the vine or the tree, and a doctor amputates limbs which might injure the whole body.[64]

(Note how Bellarmine considers and rejects the "proverbial" interpretation of Genesis 9:6 and takes the passage to be "a decree and a precept.")

Given this uniform testimony of the Fathers and Doctors of the Church, it is no surprise that the most eminent Catholic theologians from the Middle Ages to the present day have also affirmed the legitimacy of capital punishment. These include Blessed John Duns Scotus (1266–1308), Cardinal Cajetan (1469–1534), Francisco de Vitoria (1492–1546), Francisco Suarez (1548–1617), Juan de Lugo (1583–1660), Charles-Rene Billuart (1685–1757), and the authors of numerous widely used and ecclesiastically approved manuals of moral theology in the nineteenth and twentieth centuries.[65] If capital punishment really were, after all, always and intrinsically immoral, this would entail a massive breakdown in the ordinary Magisterium of the Church for two millennia and therefore cast doubt on its general reliability. Such a breakdown is in the view of eminent and influential Catholic theologians such as Melchior Cano (1509–1560) therefore not possible, consistent with the Church's indefectibility. Summarizing Cano's position, Avery Dulles writes:

By exception, individual Fathers can err, but, according to Cano, it is impossible for all the Fathers to err in matters of faith. As for the

---

[64] Bellarmine, *De Laicis*, pp. 54–55.

[65] See Brugger, *Capital Punishment*, pp. 111–12, 114–17, 120–24, 125–27, for summaries of these various sources.

Scholastic theologians, it would be close to heresy (*haeresi proximum*), he states, to contradict their unanimous opinion on a matter of faith and morals.[66]

The danger of dissenting from the common teaching of the Scholastic theologians was emphasized by Pope Pius IX, who in *Tuas Libenter*, an 1863 letter to the archbishop of Munich-Freising, taught that such dissent deserves at least "theological censure" and indeed that, in some cases, the common teaching must be accepted by an act of "divine faith":

> That subjection which is to be manifested by an act of divine faith ... would not have to be limited to those matters which have been defined by express decrees of the ecumenical Councils, or of the Roman Pontiffs and of this See, but would have to be extended also to those matters which are handed down as divinely revealed by the ordinary teaching power of the whole Church spread throughout the world, *and therefore, by universal and common consent are held by Catholic theologians to belong to faith.*
>
> It is not sufficient for learned Catholics to accept and revere the aforesaid dogmas of the Church, but ... it is also necessary to subject themselves ... *to those forms of doctrine which are held by the common and constant consent of Catholics as theological truths and conclusions, so certain that opinions opposed to these same forms of doctrine, although they cannot be called heretical, nevertheless deserve some theological censure.*[67]

We conclude that the consensus among the Doctors of the Church and the great Scholastic theologians on the legitimacy in principle of capital punishment provides further grounds for regarding affirmation of its legitimacy as a requirement of Catholic orthodoxy.

Capital punishment in papal and other ecclesiastical teaching prior to Pope Saint John Paul II

The judgment that it would be "close to heresy" to deny that capital punishment can at least in principle be legitimate might seem harsh,

---

[66] Dulles, *Magisterium*, p. 43.
[67] Denzinger, *Sources of Catholic Dogma*, §§1683, 1684, emphasis added.

yet it is hardly implausible in light of the uniform teaching of Scripture and of the Fathers and Doctors of the Church. The plausibility of such a judgment is only further reinforced by the unbroken teaching of the Magisterium of the Church from her beginning to the present day, including the teaching of several popes. To be sure, there have been popes who have urged rulers not to inflict the death penalty, such as Pope Saint John Paul II and, in an earlier age of Church history, Pope Saint Nicholas I (d. 867).[68] But no pope has condemned capital punishment as in principle immoral, and several have explicitly affirmed its legitimacy.

In 405, Pope Saint Innocent I wrote to the bishop of Toulouse, addressing a query concerning civil authorities who, after becoming Christians, continue to inflict the penalty of death:

> About these things we read nothing definitive from the forefathers. For they had remembered that these powers had been granted by God and that for the sake of punishing harm-doers the sword had been allowed; in this way a minister of God, an avenger, has been given. How therefore would they criticize something which they see to have been granted through the authority of God? About these matters therefore, we hold to what has been observed hitherto, lest we may seem either to overturn sound order or to go against the authority of the Lord.[69]

Note that what the pope is alluding to here is the traditional understanding of the teaching of Romans 13 (as Brugger acknowledges).[70] The pope is saying that to deny the legitimacy of capital punishment would be to go against *biblical* authority, indeed "*the authority of the Lord*" himself.

In 1210, Pope Innocent III required adherents of the Waldensian heresy, as a condition for their reconciliation with the Church, to affirm a number of doctrinal points that included the following:

> We declare that the secular power can without mortal sin impose a judgment of blood provided the punishment is carried out not in

---

[68] See the latter's Epistula XCVII, quoted in Laurence, "He Beareth Not the Sword", p. 229.

[69] Innocent I, Epistle VI (to Exsuperium), quoted in Brugger, *Capital Punishment*, p. 89.

[70] Brugger, *Capital Punishment*, p. 147.

hatred but with good judgment, not inconsiderately but after mature deliberation.[71]

The significance of this passage is difficult to overstate. The context—again, a set of demands made to a *heretical* group as a condition for reconciliation—makes it clear that the pope held affirmation of the legitimacy in principle of capital punishment to be *a matter of Catholic orthodoxy*.

New Natural Law theorist Germain Grisez suggests that the affirmation required of the Waldensians "concerns only the subjective morality of the act of capital punishment" and thus requires merely that it be acknowledged that "officials need not commit a *mortal sin* when they carry out a death sentence."[72] This leaves open, in Grisez's view, whether capital punishment might be objectively evil while officials might not realize this, so that one of the conditions of *mortal* sin would be absent. However, Grisez's reading is strained and idiosyncratic, finds no support in the text itself, and appears to have no motivation other than providing a way to reconcile Grisez's opposition in principle to capital punishment with Catholic teaching. One could say of *any* objectively sinful act—adultery, abortion, theft, and so forth—that it is possible for it not to be a mortal sin if the offender is not aware of its objective sinfulness. It is absurd to suppose that what Innocent III was concerned to uphold was merely that one of the conditions for a sin to be mortal—namely, subjective culpability—might be lacking in the case of capital punishment. There is no reason to think that the Waldensians would have denied that in the first place. Their misgivings about capital punishment were instead evidently motivated by their general commitment to nonviolence. Moreover, in an earlier letter to a Waldensian leader, Innocent wrote:

Let none of you presume to assert the following: that the secular power cannot carry out a judgment of blood without mortal sin. This is an error because the law, not the judge, puts to death so long as the punishment is imposed, not in hatred, nor rashly, but with deliberation.[73]

---

[71] Quoted in ibid., p. 104; cf. Denzinger, *Sources of Catholic Dogma*, §425.

[72] Germain Grisez, *The Way of the Lord Jesus*, vol. 2, *Living a Christian Life* (Quincy, Ill.: Franciscan Press, 1993), p. 893.

[73] Quoted in Brugger, *Capital Punishment*, p. 104.

The pope does not say that the reason the Waldensian position is wrong is that the condition of subjective culpability might be absent, but rather that "the law" requires the death penalty. In light of this earlier passage, even Brugger admits that "it seems probable that Innocent's [later] developed statement should be understood ... as asserting the limited uprightness of the death penalty. That is, Innocent should be understood as asserting the proposition that under the prescribed conditions, choosing to impose the death penalty is itself not always wrong."[74]

In his 1520 bull *Exsurge Domine*, Pope Leo X condemned a number of propositions associated with Martin Luther. Of these propositions, he wrote:

> [They are] either heretical, scandalous, false, offensive to pious ears or seductive of simple minds, and against Catholic truth. By listing them, we decree and declare that all the faithful of both sexes must regard them as condemned, reprobated, and rejected.... We restrain all in the virtue of holy obedience and under the penalty of an automatic major excommunication.

Among the condemned propositions is the following: "That heretics be burned is against the will of the Spirit." Obviously what was at issue here is not whether heresy is a bad thing (even if, equally obviously, Luther would disagree with the pope about what *constitutes* heresy). What was at issue is whether heretics could legitimately be *executed*. Pope Leo is clearly implying that it can at least *in principle* be legitimate to resort to capital punishment in order to suppress heresy. Certainly he is teaching that the faithful must not deny this, on pain of "excommunication". But that entails that it cannot be denied by the faithful that in at least some cases capital punishment can in principle be legitimate.

In 1566, at the order of the Council of Trent, Pope Saint Pius V promulgated the *Roman Catechism*, also known as the *Catechism of the Council of Trent*. As the *Catholic Encyclopedia* says, this catechism, the work of leading theologians, "enjoy[ed] an authority equalled by no other catechism" and was "intended ... to be the Church's official manual ... to give a fixed and stable scheme of instruction to the faithful". The *Encyclopedia* elaborates as follows:

---

[74] Ibid., p. 107.

The Catechism has not of course the authority of conciliary definitions or other primary symbols of faith.... Yet it possesses high
authority as an exposition of Catholic doctrine. It was composed
by order of a council, issued and approved by the pope; its use has
been prescribed by numerous synods throughout the whole Church;
Leo XIII, in a letter to the French bishops (8 Sept., 1899), recommended the study of the *Roman Catechism* to all seminarians, and the
reigning pontiff, Pius X, has signified his desire that preachers should
expound it to the faithful.[75]

Unlike the statements from Innocent I, Innocent III, and Leo X, the
teaching of the *Roman Catechism* was not formulated in response to a
specific problem or aimed at a particular audience but was intended
to be a completely general statement of Catholic teaching that would
give sound guidance for the faithful as a whole for generations. On
the subject of capital punishment, the *Catechism* teaches:

> Another kind of lawful slaying belongs to the civil authorities, to
> whom is entrusted power of life and death, by the legal and judicious
> exercise of which they punish the guilty and protect the innocent.
> The just use of this power, far from involving the crime of murder,
> is an act of paramount obedience to this Commandment which pro-
> hibits murder. The end of the Commandment is the preservation and
> security of human life. Now the punishments inflicted by the civil
> authority, which is the legitimate avenger of crime, naturally tend
> to this end, since they give security to life by repressing outrage and
> violence. Hence these words of David: *In the morning I put to death all
> the wicked of the land, that I might cut off all the workers of iniquity from the
> city of the Lord.*[76]

The *Catechism* goes on to say:

> It is easy to see ... how many are guilty of murder, if not in fact, at
> least in desire. As, then, the Sacred Scriptures prescribe remedies for
> so dangerous a disease, the pastor should spare no pains in making

---

[75] Joseph Wilhelm, "Roman Catechism", in *Catholic Encyclopedia*, vol. 13 (New York:
Robert Appleton, 1912).

[76] *Catechism of the Council of Trent*, trans. John A. McHugh and Charles J. Callan (Rockford,
Ill.: TAN Books, 1982), p. 421, emphasis in original.

them known to the faithful. Of these remedies the most efficacious is to form a just conception of the wickedness of murder. The enormity of this sin is manifest from many and weighty passages of Holy Scripture. So much does God abominate homicide that He declares in Holy Writ that of the very beast of the field He will exact vengeance for the life of man, commanding the beast that injures man to be put to death. And if (the Almighty) commanded man to have a horror of blood, He did so for no other reason than to impress on his mind the obligation of entirely refraining, both in act and desire, from the enormity of homicide. The murderer is the worst enemy of his species, and consequently of nature.[77]

Note that the *Catechism* teaches that the death penalty is legitimate not only in order to "protect the innocent" but also to "punish the guilty" and "avenge ... crime"—that is to say, as a matter of retributive justice. There is also an implication to the effect that the state's "exact[ing] vengeance" by means of capital punishment helps the citizenry to "form a just conception of the wickedness of murder" and is thus a "remedy" to temptations to violate the Fifth Commandment.

The legitimacy and even the need for capital punishment were presupposed by the practice of the popes when they exercised temporal authority. As Avery Dulles notes:

In the Papal States the death penalty was imposed for a variety of offenses.... The Vatican City State from 1929 until 1969 had a penal code that included the death penalty for anyone who might attempt to assassinate the pope.[78]

One writer summarizes nineteenth-century practice as follows:

The Papacy ... engaged during this time in a voluminous series of its own executions stemming from its role as civil authority. From 1815, when the Pope regained political control of Rome from Napoleon, until 1870, the Popes ordered the executions of hundreds of malefactors.

---

[77] Ibid., pp. 425–26.
[78] Avery Dulles, "Catholicism and Capital Punishment", *First Things* 112 (2001): 31.

One man, Giovanni Battista Bugatti, carried out 516 executions as
the "Pope's Executioner" between 1796 and 1865. The executioner
used one of three methods: guillotine (after 1816), smashing the head
with a mallet and cutting the throat of the condemned, or drawing
and quartering.[79]

Another writer adds:

> Pope Pius IX, ... beatified by John Paul II in 2000, was unflinching
> in the importance with which he invested public executions as an
> "encouragement" to others.... When Blessed Pius IX was asked to
> grant a stay of execution for those condemned in 1868, the Pope
> firmly replied, "I cannot, and I do not want to."[80]

In his 1891 encyclical *Pastoralis Officii*, Pope Leo XIII notes
that Scripture forbids killing a human being except for either "self
defense" or "public cause" (no. 2). The 1912 *Catechism of Christian
Doctrine* issued by Pope Saint Pius X (also known as the *Catechism of
Saint Pius X*), says in the context of discussion of the Fifth Commandment: "It is lawful to kill ... when carrying out by order of the
Supreme Authority a sentence of death in punishment of a crime."
In his 1930 encyclical *Casti Connubii*, Pope Pius XI says that "the
public authority['s] ... right of taking away life ... has regard only to
the guilty" (no. 64). None of these documents is primarily concerned
with capital punishment, but all of them clearly regard it as legitimate.

Pope Pius XII addressed the topic of punishment in considerable
detail in several public speeches. It is worthwhile quoting him at
length, because his teaching is highly systematic and illuminating, yet
not nearly as well known as it should be. In an address to the Catholic
jurists of Italy on December 5, 1954, Pius put forward an account of
retributive justice that is essentially the same as the Thomistic natural
law position we expounded in chapter 1:

> Connected with the concept of the criminal act, is the concept that
> the author of the act becomes deserving of punishment.... The

[79] Michael A. Norko, "The Death Penalty in Catholic Teaching and Medicine: Intersections and Places for Dialogue", *Journal of the American Academy of Psychiatry and the Law* 36
(2008): 470–81.

[80] Fr. George Rutler, "Hanging Concentrates the Mind", *Crisis*, February 8, 2013, http://
www.crisismagazine.com/2013/hanging-concentrates-the-mind.

punishment is the reaction, required by law and justice, to the crime: they are like a blow and a counter-blow. The order violated by the criminal act demands the restoration and re-establishment of the equilibrium which has been disturbed. It is the proper task of law and justice to guard and preserve the harmony between duty, on the one hand, and the law, on the other, and to re-establish this harmony, if it has been injured.... Punishment properly so-called cannot therefore have any other meaning and purpose than that just mentioned: to bring back again into the order of duty the violator of the law, who had withdrawn from it. This order of duty is necessarily an expression of the order of being, of the order of the true and the good, which alone has the right of existence, in opposition to error and evil, which stand for that which should not exist. Punishment accomplishes its purpose in its own way, in so far as it compels the criminal, because of the act performed, to suffer, that is, it deprives him of a good and imposes upon him an evil.[81]

He notes also that: "The law of retaliation would inflict a *proportionate* evil on the culprit."[82]

Pius emphasized that punishment of its nature is not merely a response to a criminal *offense* but involves the infliction of a harm on *the offender himself* on the basis of an abiding state of guilt that persists even after the offense is committed:

We add that the criminal has brought about, by his act, a *state which does not automatically cease when the act itself is completed*. He remains the man who has consciously and deliberately violated a law which binds him ... and simultaneously he is involved in the penalty.... Thus there is brought about an enduring state of guilt and punishment, which indicates a definite condition of the guilty party in the eyes of the authority offended, and of this authority with respect to the guilty party.[83]

The natural complement of inflicting punishment is that it be carried out on the understanding that it is the effective privation of a good, or the positive imposition of an evil, established by competent

[81] Pope Pius XII, "Discourse to the Catholic Jurists of Italy", in *Catholic Documents*, vol. 17 (1955), p. 15, http://www.apropos.org.uk/documents/Punishment-PiusXII-speechtoItalianJurists5thDec1954.pdf.

[82] Ibid., p. 25, emphasis added.

[83] Ibid., p. 15, emphasis added.

Authority as a reaction to the criminal action. It is a weight placed to restore balance in the disturbed juridical order, *and not aimed immediately at the fault as such.*[84]

The clear implication is that punishment is not to be thought of as a defensive or protective reaction either to an act in progress or to an act that might be committed in the future, but is rather properly inflicted on the offender *after* the act is committed and *whether or not* he is likely to commit a further offense, precisely because he is in a state of guilt either way.

As this indicates, Pius XII would reject any suggestion that the retributive aspect of punishment could ever be entirely dispensed with in favor of other purposes, such as the medicinal and protective ends of punishment. In the same address to Italian jurists, he says:

> Many, though not all, reject vindictive punishment, even if it is proposed to be accompanied by medicinal penalties.... [But] it would not be just to reject completely, and as a matter of principle, the function of vindictive punishment. As long as man is on earth, such punishment can and should help toward his definitive rehabilitation.... This, as We already pointed out, is an essential element of punishment.[85]
>
> Many, perhaps the majority, of civil jurists reject vindictive punishment.... However ... the Church in her theory and practice has maintained this double type of penalty (medicinal and vindictive), and ... this is more in agreement with what the sources of revelation and traditional doctrine teach regarding the coercive power of legitimate human authority. It is not a sufficient reply to this assertion to say that the aforementioned sources contain only thoughts which correspond to the historic circumstances and to the culture of the time, and that a general and abiding validity cannot therefore be attributed to them.[86]

Note that the pope here explicitly rejects the suggestion that retribution can be written off as a historically relative aspect of the teaching of Scripture and Catholic Tradition.

[84] Ibid., p. 19, emphasis added.
[85] Ibid.
[86] Ibid., p. 30.

Similarly, in a 1953 address to the Sixth International Congress of Penal Law, Pius XII taught that retribution is essential to upholding respect for the law and explicitly rejected the suggestion that the retributive or "expiatory" function of punishment could be discarded in favor of the protective function:

> Most modern theories of penal law explain punishment and justify it in the last resort as a protective measure, that is, a defense of the community against crimes being attempted, and at the same time, as an effort to lead the culprit back to observance of the law. In these theories, punishment may indeed include sanctions in the form of a diminution of certain advantages guaranteed by the law, in order to teach the culprit to live honestly; but they fail to consider *expiation of the crime committed*, which itself is a sanction on the violation of the law, *as the most important function of the punishment.* . . .
>
> The protection of the community against crimes and criminals must be ensured, but *the final purpose of punishment must be sought on a higher plane.*[87] This more profound understanding of punishment gives no less importance to the function of protection, stressed today, but it goes more to the heart of the matter. For it is concerned, not immediately with protecting the goods ensured by the law, but the very law itself. There is nothing more necessary for the national or international community than respect for the majesty of the law and the salutary thought that the law is also sacred and protected, so that whoever breaks it is punishable and will be punished.[88]

Pius teaches that the retributive function of punishment is grounded in Scripture and is presupposed by the Christian doctrine of the Last Judgment:

> These reflections help to a better appreciation of another age, which some regard as outmoded, which distinguished between medicinal punishment . . . and vindicative punishment. . . . In vindicative punishment the function of expiation is to the fore. . . . Canon law, as you know, still maintains the distinction. . . . Only it gives full meaning to

---

[87] Pius XII, "An International Code for the Punishment of War Crimes", *Saint John's Law Review* 28 (December 1953): 15–16, emphasis added. PDF available online at http://scholarship.law.stjohns.edu/cgi/viewcontent.cgi?article=4716&context=lawreview.

[88] Ibid., p. 17.

the well known word of the Apostle in the Epistle to the Romans ...
"It is not for nothing that he bears the Sword: he is God's minister
still, to inflict punishment on the wrong-doer." Here it is expiation
which is brought out. Finally, it is only the expiatory function which
gives the key to the last judgment of the Creator Himself.... The
function of protection disappears completely in the afterlife.... But
the supreme Judge, in His last judgment, applies uniquely the principle of retribution. This, then, must be of great importance.[89]

In several places, Pope Pius XII also spoke of what sorts of penalties are appropriate for various offenses. In the 1953 address, while
condemning excessively harsh punishments for minor offenses, he
also insists that punishments not go to the opposite extreme of excessive leniency:

> It is possible to punish in a way that would hold the penal law up to
> ridicule.... In the case where human life is made the object of a crim-
> inal gamble, where hundreds and thousands are reduced to extreme
> want and driven to distress, *a mere privation of civil rights would be an
> insult to justice*.... The fixing of the penalties in penal law and their
> adaptation to the individual case should correspond to the gravity of
> the crimes.[90]

In the 1954 address, he adds:

> Up to a certain point it may be true that imprisonment and isolation,
> properly applied, is the penalty most likely to effect a return of the
> criminal to right order and social life. But it does not follow that it is
> the only just and effective one. What We said in Our discourse on
> international penal law, on 3rd October, 1953, referring to the theory
> of retribution ... is to the point here.[91]

The clear implication of these remarks is that capital punishment
is sometimes called for, and indeed Pius explicitly said that it can be
legitimate. In a 1957 address to Italian jurists, he said:

[89] Ibid.
[90] Ibid., pp. 6–7, emphasis added.
[91] Pope Pius XII, "Discourse to Jurists", pp. 18–19.

The penal justice of the past, ... that of the present to a certain degree, and—if it is true that history often teaches us what to expect in the future—that of tomorrow as well, makes use of punishments involving physical pain ... and capital punishment in various forms.[92]

Earlier, in his February 23, 1944, "Allocution to Lenten Preachers", Pius had said:

> But even in such matters the key to every solution is given by faith in a personal God, Who is fount of justice and has reserved to Himself the right over life and death. Nothing else but this faith can confer the moral force to observe the proper limits in the face of all insidious temptations to overstep them; keeping in mind that, excepting in cases of legitimate defense, of just war fought with just means, and of capital punishment inflicted by the public authority for well-determined and proven gravest crimes, human life is intangible.[93]

And in a 1952 address to the first International Congress of the Histopathology of the Nervous System, Pius made what is perhaps his best-known statement on the subject:

> Even when it is a question of the execution of a man condemned to death, the State does not dispose of the individual's right to live. It is reserved rather to the public authority to deprive the criminal of the benefit of life when already, by his crime, *he has deprived himself of the right to live.*[94]

Pope Pius XII's teaching is noteworthy in several respects. First, he appears to have said much more on the subject of crime and punishment than any other pope has before or since. Second, he offers a general and systematic treatment of the subject rather than merely an ad hoc response to local or historical circumstances. Third, he puts forward arguments and analysis rather than merely laying down

---

[92] Quoted in John F. McDonald, *Capital Punishment* (London: Catholic Truth Society, 1964), p. 15; and Brugger, *Capital Punishment*, pp. 129–30.

[93] Michael Chinigo, ed., *The Pope Speaks: The Teachings of Pope Pius XII* (New York: Pantheon Books, 1957), pp. 227–28.

[94] Quoted in McDonald, *Capital Punishment*, emphasis added. Cf. Brugger, *Capital Punishment*, p. 130.

authoritative dicta. Fourth, the arguments are in no way idiosyncratic or novel but are deeply rooted in Scripture, Tradition, and the kind of natural law theory and moral theology hammered out by the Doctors of the Church and generations of ecclesiastically approved theologians. Fifth, as a consequence, what he says "hangs together" in such a way that it is at least not obvious how one could reject one part of it consistently with accepting the rest. It constitutes a systematization of the tradition he inherited. Sixth, he does all this not as a private theologian but precisely in his office as pope. And, of course, much of what he has to say is a reaffirmation of previous papal teaching. So, though the various addresses from which we have quoted do not per se enjoy the status that ex cathedra statements or even encyclicals do, they nevertheless have considerable weight.

In 1976, under Pope Paul VI, the Pontifical Commission for Justice and Peace issued a document titled "The Church and the Death Penalty". Overall, the document takes a negative view of capital punishment. It affirms, however, that "the traditional doctrine is that the death penalty is not contrary to divine law nor demanded by divine law but depends on the circumstances, the gravity of the crime, etc."; allows that "[the fact] that the state has the right to enforce the death penalty has been ceded by the church for centuries"; and acknowledges that "the church has never condemned its use by the state" and indeed that "the church *has* condemned the *denial* of that right" to the state.[95] As we will see in the next section, notwithstanding his well-known criticisms of capital punishment, Pope Saint John Paul II did not deny that it can be legitimate in principle and explicitly reaffirmed the Church's traditional teaching that it can be. Nor have the popes since his time denied its legitimacy in principle.

We will address the teaching of John Paul II and his successors on the application of capital punishment in *practice* in the next section. What needs to be emphasized for the moment is that, as we have seen, not only has no pope denied the legitimacy in principle of capital punishment, but some popes have explicitly affirmed that legitimacy, have held that affirming that legitimacy is a matter of upholding Catholic orthodoxy and fidelity to divine revelation, and have done so in magisterial acts of a very high degree of authority.

[95] Quoted in Brugger, *Capital Punishment*, pp. 136–37, emphasis added.

This alone would justify the conclusion that it is not open to any Catholic to hold that capital punishment is always and intrinsically immoral. When the clear and consistent teaching of the popes is added to the clear and consistent teaching of Scripture and of the Fathers and Doctors of the Church, that conclusion is beyond any reasonable doubt. To be sure, as Fr. John F. McDonald has written:

> A Catholic is entitled to argue ... that in the present state of our civilization the use of the death penalty is not a practical necessity, and to that extent ... may give his support to any movement for its abolition which is inspired by humanitarian motives.[96]

And indeed, recent popes have taken just such a position. However, we also strongly concur with the judgment of Fr. McDonald when he writes:

> In any discussion about the abolition of the death penalty, a distinction must be made between the right of the State to inflict capital punishment and the use of this right. A Catholic may not deny that the State has the right and therefore he may not give his support to any movement for the abolition of the death penalty if such a movement is an expression of the denial that the State has the right to inflict it.... It must always be understood ... that even if the use of the death penalty were to be abolished, the State would still have the right, and in a particular case even the duty, to reintroduce the death penalty, if it were to be considered necessary in the circumstances for the security and adequate protection of society.[97]

Brugger on infallibility

There is, then, conclusive evidence that affirmation of the legitimacy in principle of capital punishment is required by Catholic orthodoxy. But it seems that not all Catholics loyal to the Magisterium would agree. For as we saw in chapter 1, despite their reputation for orthodoxy, Germain Grisez, John Finnis, Robert P. George, and other Catholic thinkers associated with the "new natural law theory" have

[96] McDonald, *Capital Punishment*, p. 16.
[97] Ibid.

taken the position that capital punishment is *always and inherently*
immoral. How can such a view possibly be reconciled with Catholic
teaching? By far the most detailed attempt to reconcile the new natural
law view with Catholic orthodoxy is that of E. Christian Brugger.[98]
Among the remarkable aspects of Brugger's position is how much he
concedes to those who would maintain that his radically abolitionist
position is incompatible with Catholicism. As we have seen, while
he proposes some novel (and utterly unconvincing) reinterpretations
of some biblical passages, Brugger concedes that his interpretation of
Romans 13 is controversial and that no one who denies the legitimacy in principle of capital punishment has found a way to explain
away Genesis 9:6 convincingly. Nor does he deny that most of the
many scriptural passages that have always been understood as affir-
mations of capital punishment really do affirm it. In effect, Brugger
concedes that Scripture teaches the legitimacy of capital punishment.
He also concedes that there is a "consensus" among the Fathers of the
Church about the legitimacy of capital punishment, that that consensus was grounded in a shared understanding of scriptural passages
such as Romans 13, and that the popes, including John Paul II, have
all affirmed the legitimacy in principle of capital punishment, in some
cases on scriptural grounds.

Brugger primarily rests his case not on reinterpretations of Scripture, Tradition, or magisterial statements of the past but on two crucial claims. The first is that, while Pope Saint John Paul II did not
explicitly teach that capital punishment is intrinsically immoral, and
indeed explicitly taught that it is *not* intrinsically immoral, nevertheless (argues Brugger) the conclusion that it is intrinsically immoral
is *implicit* in John Paul II's teaching. We will respond to this claim
in the next section. Brugger's second crucial claim is that although
the legitimacy in principle of capital punishment has indeed always
been taught by the Church, it has (so Brugger argues) never been
taught *infallibly*.

Brugger's reasoning is as follows.[99] Vatican II, in section 25 of
Lumen Gentium, taught that the Church teaches infallibly when (1) the

---

[98] Brugger, *Capital Punishment*. A second edition of Brugger's book was published by the
University of Notre Dame Press in 2014.
[99] Brugger, *Capital Punishment*, pp. 142–52.

pope speaks ex cathedra, or (2) the bishops gathered together with the pope (at an ecumenical council, say) definitively put forward some teaching about faith and morals, or (3) the bishops dispersed throughout the world but united in communion with each other and with the pope definitively put forward some teaching about faith and morals. Now, none of the papal pronouncements cited above amounts to an ex cathedra definition of doctrine, nor has any ecumenical council or the like put forward a definitive statement on capital punishment. So that leaves possibility 3, which, Brugger says, can be fulfilled in the present case only on four conditions:

1. The bishops must have been in communion with each other and the pope in regard to the question of capital punishment.
2. They must have authoritatively taught on the morality of capital punishment.
3. They must have agreed in their judgment with respect to its morality.
4. They must have intended that judgment to be *definitively held*.

Brugger allows that, in light of the kind of evidence that has been summarized above, conditions 1, 2, and 3 have been met. In particular, the evidence shows that among the bishops there has been widespread agreement on, and no dissent from, the judgment that the state has in principle the right to inflict capital punishment and that this right is scripturally grounded. Condition 4, however, has not been met, says Brugger. To be sure, Brugger acknowledges that examples such as Pope Innocent I's letter to the bishop of Toulouse and the oath Pope Innocent III required of the Waldensian heretics *are* plausibly cases of a bishop (the pope, in these examples) teaching something as to be *definitively held*. What is not plausible, Brugger argues, is that the bishops dispersed throughout the world have *together* intended that a judgment that capital punishment is legitimate be *definitively* held. Hence the legitimacy in principle of capital punishment is not, Brugger concludes, an infallible teaching of the Church.

In our estimation Brugger's argument is without force, and indeed is manifestly fallacious. There are three main problems with it. To take the least serious problem first, Brugger's way of applying the criteria to which he appeals makes it highly doubtful that condition 4 has not been satisfied. For Brugger tells us that one of the reasons we know that conditions 1, 2, and 3 have been met is that the bishops dispersed throughout the world have agreed that the legitimacy in principle of capital punishment is grounded in *Scripture*. In other words, the bishops have regarded the legitimacy in principle of capital punishment as *divinely revealed*. So, in order to believe (as Brugger does) that conditions 1, 2, and 3 have been met while 4 has not, you have to believe that the bishops have regarded the legitimacy in principle of capital punishment to be both *divinely revealed* and not *to be definitively held*. And that, needless to say, is absurd. It makes no sense to say of a proposition *both* that God has revealed it to be true *and* that it might nevertheless turn out to be false and thus need not be definitively held. Hence, by virtue of teaching the legitimacy of capital punishment as scripturally based and thus divinely revealed, the bishops *have implicitly* taught it to be definitively held. In which case condition 4 has been fulfilled, and thus *even by Brugger's own criteria* he must regard the legitimacy in principle of capital punishment as an infallible teaching.

An even more serious problem, though, is that Brugger's appeal to section 25 of *Lumen Gentium* commits the logical fallacy of confusing *sufficient* conditions with *necessary* conditions. *Lumen Gentium* does indeed say that a teaching is infallible if it is put forward ex cathedra by the pope or is taught definitively by the bishops and the pope either gathered together or dispersed but in communion. It does *not* say, however, that those are the *only* ways in which a teaching might be taught infallibly. The three scenarios discussed by Brugger are *sufficient* for infallibility, but they are not *necessary* for it. Now, as we have seen above, Pope Pius IX taught in *Tuas Libenter* that "divine faith"—the complete submission of the intellect and will to what has been divinely revealed (and is thus infallible and irreformable)—cannot be limited to what is taught ex cathedra or by ecumenical councils, but extends even "to those matters which are handed down as divinely revealed by the ordinary teaching power of the whole Church spread throughout the world, and therefore, by universal and common consent are held by Catholic theologians to belong to faith". But Brugger himself would admit that popes, bishops, and theologians have for two millennia consistently taught that the legitimacy in principle of capital punishment has a *scriptural basis*. Surely, then, the "ordinary teaching power of the whole Church" and the "universal and common consent ... [of] Catholic theologians" has been at least *implicitly* committed to the proposition that the legitimacy in principle of capital punishment has been "divinely revealed". And in that case, by Pius' criteria, it would count as something to which we owe "divine faith".

Then there is the First Vatican Council's teaching on the assent owed to Scripture. The Council declares that "by divine and Catholic faith all those things are to be believed which are contained in the word of God as found in Scripture"; and as we have seen, it also teaches that "it is not permissible for anyone to interpret Holy Scripture in a sense ... [that is] against the unanimous consent of the fathers [of the Church]." Now, Scripture clearly teaches the legitimacy of capital punishment, and by Brugger's own admission, the Fathers all regarded it as taught by Scripture. The obvious implication is that every Catholic must believe "by divine and Catholic faith" that capital punishment is legitimate at least in principle.

Consider also the "Profession of Faith" issued in 1989 by the Congregation for the Doctrine of the Faith, which includes the following two paragraphs:

> With firm faith, I also believe everything contained in the word of God, whether written or handed down in Tradition, which the Church, either by a solemn judgment or by the ordinary and universal Magisterium, sets forth to be believed as divinely revealed.
>
> I also firmly accept and hold each and everything definitively proposed by the Church regarding teaching on faith and morals.

Now, a commentary on the profession issued by Cardinal Joseph Ratzinger (then prefect of the Congregation) and Archbishop Tarcisio Bertone explains that doctrines covered by the first paragraph "require *the assent of theological faith* by all members of the faithful [and that] whoever obstinately places them in doubt or denies them falls under the censure of heresy".[100] They give, as examples of doctrines covered in the first paragraph, not only solemnly proclaimed

---

[100] Joseph Ratzinger and Tarcisio Bertone, "Commentary on the Profession of Faith's Concluding Paragraphs", *Origins* 28 (1998): 116–19 reprinted in Dulles, *Magisterium*, appendix H, p. 166.

doctrines such as "the various Christological dogmas and Marian dogmas", but also teachings that have not been solemnly proclaimed, such as "the doctrine on the grave immorality of direct and voluntary killing of an innocent human being". Those doctrines that fall under the second paragraph quoted above, explain Ratzinger and Bertone, *"are necessary for faithfully keeping and expounding the deposit of faith, even if they have not been proposed by the Magisterium of the Church as formally revealed"*. Catholics are "required to give *firm and definitive assent* to these truths", and "whoever denies these truths would be in a position of *rejecting a truth of Catholic doctrine and would therefore no longer be in full communion with the Catholic Church.*" Ratzinger and Bertone explain that examples of teachings covered in the second paragraph include even teachings not explicitly found in Scripture but only logically connected to what is explicitly taught there, such as "the doctrine on the illicitness of euthanasia".[101]

Now, if one must regard as divinely revealed even teachings not solemnly defined, such as "the doctrine on the grave immorality of direct and voluntary killing of an innocent human being", then how can one fail also to regard as divinely revealed the right of the state to inflict capital punishment, which is no less clearly grounded in Scripture? And if one must—on pain of "rejecting a truth of Catholic doctrine and ... therefore no longer [being] in full communion with the Catholic Church"—believe even teachings that are not explicitly found in Scripture, such as "the doctrine on the illicitness of euthanasia", then how much more must one believe that the state has a right to inflict capital punishment, which *is* explicitly found in Scripture?

A third problem for Brugger's position is that, even if the legitimacy in principle of capital punishment were not the irreformable teaching of the Church (as we have argued it is), it simply would not follow that Brugger or any other new natural law theorist has any right to dissent from the teaching. As Pope Pius IX taught in the passages from *Tuas Libenter* quoted above, it is "necessary [for Catholics] to subject themselves" not only to the dogmas of the Church, but even to "those forms of doctrine which are held by the common and constant consent of Catholics as theological truths and conclusions, so certain that opinions opposed to these same forms

---

[101] See Dulles, *Magisterium*, chap. 7.

of doctrine, although they cannot be called heretical, nevertheless deserve some theological censure". Pope Pius XII taught in *Humani Generis* that even when popes do not exercise "the supreme power of their Teaching Authority", nevertheless:

> if the Supreme Pontiffs in their official documents purposely pass judgment on a matter up to that time under dispute, it is obvious that that matter, according to the mind and will of the Pontiffs, cannot be any longer considered a question open to discussion among theologians. (no. 20)

Similarly, section 25 of *Lumen Gentium*, so emphasized by Brugger, teaches that "religious submission of mind and will must be shown in a special way to the authentic magisterium of the Roman Pontiff, even when he is not speaking *ex cathedra*." And the 1989 "Profession of Faith" includes a further paragraph that reads as follows:

> Moreover, I adhere with religious submission of will and intellect to the teachings which either the Roman Pontiff or the College of Bishops enunciate when they exercise their authentic Magisterium, even if they do not intend to proclaim these teachings by a definitive act.

Now, by Brugger's admission, the popes, including Pope Saint John Paul II, have consistently affirmed the right of the state to inflict capital punishment and have in some cases done so in documents of a high degree of authority intended to settle a question of doctrine. Brugger also would agree that the legitimacy in principle of capital punishment has at the very least been "held by the common and constant consent of Catholics as [a] theological [truth] and [conclusion]". So, given the criteria laid down by Pius IX, Pius XII, and *Lumen Gentium*, how could the legitimacy in principle of capital punishment possibly be "considered a question open to discussion among theologians"? Given that the "Profession of Faith" teaches that we must give "religious submission of will and intellect" even to authentic teachings that are *not* proclaimed definitively, how could dissent from the teaching that the state has the right to inflict capital punishment be justified on the grounds that the bishops have (as Brugger alleges) not taught that this is to be definitively held?

Brugger anticipates this objection and offers a surprisingly brief and weak response.[102] He says that "if the traditional teaching has [not] been proposed infallibly ... the question *in principle* remains open." Yet he also acknowledges that even if it turned out to be noninfallible, "its status in the tradition is such that a subsequent revision ... would have to provide a satisfactory demonstration of the insufficiency of the traditional view", and he says that providing such a demonstration is "beyond the scope" of his own work. Ultimately, he admits, it is what he takes to be *implicit* in Pope John Paul II's teaching that he thinks justifies his dissent from what the Church has always taught (where the traditional teaching that Brugger dissents from includes, it should be emphasized—though Brugger, unsurprisingly, does not emphasize it—*John Paul II's own explicit teaching* that capital punishment can be legitimate!).

This is simply not consistent with what the Church herself has taught regarding the duties of theologians vis-à-vis nonirreformable teaching. In *Donum Veritatis, On the Ecclesial Vocation of the Theologian,* issued in 1990, the Congregation for the Doctrine of the Faith taught:

> The willingness to submit loyally to the teaching of the Magisterium on matters *per se* not irreformable must be the rule. It can happen, however, that a theologian may, according to the case, raise questions regarding the timeliness, the form, or even the contents of magisterial interventions....
>
> Such a disagreement could not be justified if it were based solely upon the fact that the validity of the given teaching is not evident *or upon the opinion that the opposite position would be the more probable.* (nos. 24 and 28, emphasis added)

So, even if one has reason to think an opposite position *more probable* than some nonirreformable teaching, that would not by itself suffice to justify refraining from assenting to it. *Donum Veritatis* evidently requires a higher degree of certainty than that. As William May (himself a new natural law sympathizer) very plausibly suggests:

> Ordinarily ... theologians raise questions of this kind when they can appeal to other magisterial teachings that are more certainly and

---

[102] Brugger, *Capital Punishment,* p. 157.

definitively taught with which they think the teaching questioned is incompatible.[103]

Yet Brugger can hardly claim to have shown that his position is even *as* probable as the traditional teaching, much less certain or even *more* probable. For by his own admission, he has no satisfactory way of reconciling his position with Scripture, and by his own admission he has not "provide[d] a satisfactory demonstration of the insufficiency of the traditional view". By his own admission his position is in conflict with two millennia of papal teaching, with the teaching of the Fathers and Doctors of the Church, and with the traditional understanding of the relevant biblical passages. It is based entirely on his personal theological interpretation of the teaching of Pope Saint John Paul II, an interpretation that, by Brugger's admission, the pope himself did not give. It would be preposterous, then, to suggest that Brugger has come remotely close to overriding the presumption against dissent taught by *Donum Veritatis* even *if* the traditional teaching on the legitimacy in principle of capital punishment were not irreformable (which, as we have argued, it is).

We conclude that, despite their good intentions, Brugger's position and that of the new natural lawyers in general simply cannot be reconciled with Catholic orthodoxy. The judgment may seem harsh, especially in light of the well-earned reputation of these thinkers for fidelity to the Magisterium. Nevertheless, we believe that it is a judgment that is unavoidable in light of the evidence. Indeed, in our view it is surprising that the new natural law position on capital punishment has not generated more vigorous opposition among Catholics concerned with faithfulness to tradition and to the Magisterium. For if the new natural law position were correct, it would follow that the Church has been teaching grave moral error for two thousand years, and indeed that Scripture itself teaches grave moral error. Or, if the new natural lawyers could somehow find a way to reinterpret Scripture to fit their position—something even Brugger admits no one has yet successfully done—it would follow that the Church (including the Fathers and greatest Doctors of the Church) has been

---

[103] William E. May, *An Introduction to Moral Theology*, rev. ed. (Huntington, Ind.: Our Sunday Visitor, 1994), p. 242.

misunderstanding Scripture for two millennia. This seems to us to be a position that would destroy the very credibility of the Church's Magisterium. It is also self-undermining. If the Church could be that wrong for that long, then how confident could we be that anything she teaches in the future—including the novel and radically abolitionist teaching on capital punishment Brugger thinks the Church ought to move toward—would be correct?

Pope Saint John Paul II and his successors on capital punishment

Four categories of magisterial statement

Pope Saint John Paul II and his successors have made a number of statements about capital punishment, some of them well known. But these statements have had varying degrees of magisterial authority. Thus, before examining them, it will be useful to survey the different levels of authority enjoyed by different kinds of magisterial statement and the different degrees of assent required of such statements, especially since clarification on that subject was given by the Congregation for the Doctrine of the Faith under John Paul II himself and in various remarks by Cardinal Joseph Ratzinger, who was prefect of the Congregation during John Paul II's papacy and who went on to become Pope Benedict XVI.

The most important document on this subject is *Donum Veritatis*, from which we have already quoted. As Cardinal Avery Dulles has noted, paragraphs 23 and 24 of this document appear to distinguish four broad categories or grades of magisterial statement.[104] The first three of these have already been referred to and correspond to the three paragraphs from the "Profession of Faith" quoted above (which, as we noted, Cardinal Ratzinger and Archbishop Bertone

---

[104] Avery Dulles, "The Magisterium and Theological Dissent", in *The Craft of Theology: From Symbol to System*, expanded ed. (New York: Crossroad, 1995). Cf. Anthony J. Figueiredo, *The Magisterium-Theology Relationship: Contemporary Theological Conceptions in the Light of Universal Church Teaching since 1835 and the Pronouncements of the Bishops of the United States* (Rome: Gregorian University Press, 2001), pp. 262–65.

clarified in their 1998 commentary). Dulles summarizes all four of the categories as follows:

1. Statements that definitively set forth something that all Catholics are to accept as divinely revealed (such statements are dogmas in the strict sense)
2. Definitive declarations of nonrevealed truths closely connected with revelation and the Christian life
3. Nondefinitive but obligatory teaching of doctrine that contributes to the right understanding of revelation
4. Prudential admonitions or applications of Christian doctrine in a particular time or place[105]

Statements in category 1, says *Donum Veritatis*, are to be believed with "theological faith", or (as Dulles notes) with what is also called in Catholic theology "divine and Catholic faith". Examples given by Ratzinger and Bertone include the christological and Marian dogmas, papal infallibility, the doctrine of Original Sin, the grave immorality of directly and voluntarily killing an innocent person, and so forth. Statements in category 2 must be "firmly accepted and held". Examples from Ratzinger and Bertone include moral teachings such as the immorality of euthanasia and of fornication, and the teaching that priestly ordination is reserved to men.

Statements in category 3, *Donum Veritatis* says, call for "the religious submission of will and intellect ... [a] response [that] cannot be simply exterior or disciplinary but must be understood within the logic of faith and under the impulse of obedience to the faith" (no. 23). Here the 1998 commentary of Ratzinger and Bertone does not give examples, but speaks of:

teachings set forth by the authentic ordinary Magisterium in a nondefinitive way, which require degrees of adherence differentiated according to the mind and the will manifested; this is shown especially by the nature of the documents, by the frequent repetition of the same doctrine, or by the tenor of the verbal expression.

---

[105] Dulles, "The Magisterium and Theological Dissent", pp. 108–9.

Dulles suggests by way of example that "the teaching of Vatican II, which abstained from new doctrinal definitions, falls predominantly into this category."[106] As Dulles also notes,[107] while *Donum Veritatis* clearly says that assent to such teachings is the norm, it also acknowledges the possibility that a theologian might raise legitimate questions about a nondefinitive teaching. *Donum Veritatis* addresses this matter at some length:

> The willingness to submit loyally to the teaching of the Magisterium on matters *per se* not irreformable must be the rule. It can happen, however, that a theologian may, according to the case, raise questions regarding the timeliness, the form, or even the contents of magisterial interventions. Here the theologian will need, first of all, to assess accurately the authoritativeness of the interventions which becomes clear from the nature of the documents, the insistence with which a teaching is repeated, and the very way in which it is expressed....
>
> The possibility cannot be excluded that tensions may arise between the theologian and the Magisterium. The meaning attributed to such tensions and the spirit with which they are faced are not matters of indifference. If tensions do not spring from hostile and contrary feelings, they can become a dynamic factor, a stimulus to both the Magisterium and theologians to fulfill their respective roles while practicing dialogue....
>
> The preceding considerations have a particular application to the case of the theologian who might have serious difficulties, for reasons which appear to him wellfounded, in accepting a non-irreformable magisterial teaching.
>
> Such a disagreement could not be justified if it were based solely upon the fact that the validity of the given teaching is not evident or upon the opinion that the opposite position would be the more probable. Nor, furthermore, would the judgment of the subjective conscience of the theologian justify it because conscience does not constitute an autonomous and exclusive authority for deciding the truth of a doctrine.
>
> In any case there should never be a diminishment of that fundamental openness loyally to accept the teaching of the Magisterium as is fitting for every believer by reason of the obedience of faith.

---

[106] Ibid., p. 110.
[107] Ibid., pp. 110–11; Dulles, *Magisterium*, p. 93.

The theologian will strive then to understand this teaching in its contents, arguments, and purposes. This will mean an intense and patient reflection on his part and a readiness, if need be, to revise his own opinions and examine the objections which his colleagues might offer him.

If, despite a loyal effort on the theologian's part, the difficulties persist, the theologian has the duty to make known to the Magisterial authorities the problems raised by the teaching in itself, in the arguments proposed to justify it, or even in the manner in which it is presented. He should do this in an evangelical spirit and with a profound desire to resolve the difficulties. His objections could then contribute to real progress and provide a stimulus to the Magisterium to propose the teaching of the Church in greater depth and with a clearer presentation of the arguments....

It can also happen that at the conclusion of a serious study, undertaken with the desire to heed the Magisterium's teaching without hesitation, the theologian's difficulty remains because the arguments to the contrary seem more persuasive to him. Faced with a proposition to which he feels he cannot give his intellectual assent, the theologian nevertheless has the duty to remain open to a deeper examination of the question.

For a loyal spirit, animated by love for the Church, such a situation can certainly prove a difficult trial. It can be a call to suffer for the truth, in silence and prayer, but with the certainty, that if the truth really is at stake, it will ultimately prevail. (nos. 24, 25, 28–30, 31)

Clearly, while *Donum Veritatis* foresees the possibility in principle of justifiably refraining from assenting to a statement in category 3, it teaches not only that there is a presumption in favor of assent but also that, in the normal case, even a justifiably doubtful theologian's further investigations into the matter will eventually result in assent. The burden of proof is on the doubting theologian to justify his non-assent, and even a judgment to the effect that his position is "more probable" than the category-3 teaching in question cannot suffice to meet that burden. *Donum Veritatis* also emphasizes that such a theologian "should avoid turning to the 'mass media'" and "exert[ing] the pressure of public opinion" as a way of trying to get the Church to come around to his point of view (no. 30).

Evidently, though, this is not meant to exclude public scholarly discussion. As William May notes:

The Instruction obviously considers it proper for theologians to publish their "questions," for it speaks of their obligation to take seriously into account objections leveled against their views by other theologians and to revise their positions in the light of such criticism—and this is normally given only after a theologian has made his questions known by publishing them in professional theological journals.[108]

What is excluded is a polemical spirit, political pressure tactics, and doubting theologians' making of themselves a kind of "counter-Magisterium". *Donum Veritatis* even allows that it is possible that a doubting theologian's criticisms could "contribute to real progress and provide a stimulus to the Magisterium to propose the teaching of the Church in greater depth and with a clearer presentation of the arguments". This seems most likely to happen when, as May put it in the passage quoted above, it is precisely *other* "magisterial teachings that are more certainly and definitively taught" that give reason seriously to doubt the content or formulation of some magisterial statement in category 3.

That respectful criticisms of this sort are possible was affirmed in 1968 by the American Catholic bishops in their document *Human Life in Our Day*, which teaches that

> there exist in the Church a lawful freedom of inquiry and of thought and also general norms of licit dissent. This is particularly true in the area of legitimate theological speculation and research. When conclusions reached by such professional theological work prompt a scholar to dissent from non-infallible received teaching the norms of licit dissent come into play. They require of him careful respect for the consciences of those who lack his special competence or opportunity for judicious investigation. These norms also require setting forth his dissent with propriety and with regard for the gravity of the matter and the deference due the authority which has pronounced on it.
>
> The reverence due all sacred matters, particularly questions which touch on salvation, will not necessarily require the responsible scholar to relinquish his opinion but certainly to propose it with prudence born of intellectual grace and a Christian confidence that the truth is great and will prevail.

---

[108] May, *Introduction to Moral Theology*, pp. 241–42. Cf. Dulles, "The Magisterium and Theological Dissent", p. 115.

Unfortunately, in the years since this document was issued, the term "dissent" has come to have the connotation of a willful rejection of Catholic teaching of *any* sort—even of statements in categories 1 and 2, which, of course, is never permitted. What the U.S. bishops were talking about was respectful and cautious disagreement with teaching having a level of authority no higher than category-3 statements, and even then only when the disagreement is (as the document puts it) "serious and well-founded".

Cases of legitimate doubt are more likely with respect to statements in category 4, which *Donum Veritatis* calls "interventions in the prudential order" (no. 24) and Dulles calls "contingent prudential applications"[109] or "disciplinary interventions".[110] With respect to these statements, *Donum Veritatis* says:

> The Magisterium can intervene in questions under discussion which involve, in addition to solid principles, certain contingent and conjectural elements....
>
> When it comes to the question of interventions in the prudential order, it could happen that some Magisterial documents might not be free from all deficiencies. Bishops and their advisors have not always taken into immediate consideration every aspect or the entire complexity of a question. But it would be contrary to the truth, if, proceeding from some particular cases, one were to conclude that the Church's Magisterium can be habitually mistaken in its prudential judgments, or that it does not enjoy divine assistance in the integral exercise of its mission. (no. 24)

In a press conference on *Donum Veritatis*, Cardinal Ratzinger gave as examples of prudential interventions "the statements of the Popes during the last century on religious freedom as well as the antimodernistic decisions of the Biblical Commission of that time",[111] in which "the details of the determinations of their contents were later superseded once they had carried out their pastoral duty at a particular moment."[112] Dulles indicates that other examples from

---

[109] Dulles, "The Magisterium and Theological Dissent", p. 111.

[110] Dulles, *Magisterium*, p. 94.

[111] The reference here is to the Pontifical Biblical Commission, a Vatican committee with responsibility for setting guidelines for the proper interpretation of Scripture.

[112] Quoted in Dulles, "The Magisterium and Theological Dissent", p. 111.

the past of merely prudential interventions include the Church's "caution in admitting new scientific theories that seemed contrary to Scripture and longstanding Tradition" such as heliocentrism and the theory of evolution.[113] Of category-4, or prudential, statements, Dulles comments, "They require external conformity in behavior, but do not demand internal assent."[114] If even well-intentioned nonassent to category-3 magisterial statements can legitimately be expressed in public scholarly writings, though, it seems that this "external conformity" to category-4 statements, which have an even lower degree of certitude, is compatible with respectful disagreement in such public contexts.

Now, the examples of "prudential" interventions given by Cardinals Ratzinger and Dulles are all closely tied to matters of doctrine, and thus to matters concerning which the Church has special expertise. The Church made the prudential interventions she did vis-à-vis heliocentrism, evolution, and the decisions of the Biblical Commission because these issues are highly relevant to questions about the proper interpretation of Scripture, questions that have dramatic implications for the entire system of Catholic teaching. For instance, questions about evolution are obviously relevant to questions about how the first chapters of Genesis are to be interpreted, and those questions are in turn relevant to questions about how to understand the doctrine of Original Sin.

The expression "prudential judgment" has in Catholic circles in recent decades, however, come to be applied very broadly, to many issues that have no such dramatic theological implications and that involve issues concerning which the Church does not have special expertise. In particular, it is very commonly used to refer to the application of the general principles of Catholic moral theology to specific matters of public policy. For example, Catholic just-war doctrine lays down clear, binding general principles concerning when a war can justly be initiated and how it may justly be conducted. The harm caused by the aggression that is being responded to must be lasting, grave, and certain; alternative ways of responding to it must be known to be ineffective or impractical;

---

[113] Dulles, *Magisterium*, p. 94.
[114] Ibid.

the proposed military action must have a realistic prospect of success; and so forth. But whether these conditions are met in a particular case is not something about which the Church has special expertise. For example, the Church has no special expertise in discerning the motivations of the leaders of the belligerent nations in a particular conflict; or in determining how dangerous some aggressor nation's military is and how harmful its policies are likely to be; or in evaluating which military strategies are likely to succeed; and so on. Thus, after summarizing the principles of just-war doctrine, the *Catechism of the Catholic Church* states that "the evaluation of these conditions for moral legitimacy belongs to the prudential judgment of those who have responsibility for the common good" (no. 2309). That is to say, the application of the principles to concrete circumstances is the responsibility of those in positions of public authority rather than of the Church.

Similarly, Catholic social teaching lays out clear and binding general principles concerning economic affairs. She teaches, for example, that a just wage can in some cases diverge from the wage one is likely to be offered in the free market. But she does not pretend that it can easily be determined exactly what the just wage will amount to in a particular case. As Fr. John Ryan wrote:

> And wisely so; for, owing to the many distinct factors of distribution involved, the matter is exceedingly complicated and difficult. Chief among these factors are from the side of the employer, energy expended, risk undergone, and interest on his capital; from the side of the labourer, needs, productivity, efforts, sacrifices, and skill; and from the side of the consumer, fair prices. In any completely just system of compensation and distribution all these elements would be given weight; but in what proportion?[115]

Obviously, weighing these considerations in a particular case requires knowledge of concrete circumstances about which the Church has no special expertise. Thus did Pope Saint John Paul II write in *Centesimus Annus*, concerning matters of economics:

---

[115]John A. Ryan, "Compensation", in *Catholic Encyclopedia*, vol. 4 (New York: Robert Appleton, 1908).

The Church has no models to present; models that are real and truly effective can only arise within the framework of different historical situations, through the efforts of all those who responsibly confront concrete problems in all their social, economic, political and cultural aspects, as these interact with one another. (no. 43)

"Prudential judgments" concerning how to apply Catholic moral principles to matters of war, economics, and the like in specific concrete circumstances are, therefore, primarily the responsibility of the public officials and other laymen who have the relevant expertise and who must make and implement the decisions. Prudential judgments concerning these matters that are made by churchmen, although they should certainly be given serious and respectful consideration by any Catholic, are not within the Church's special competence and thus are not put forward as binding on the faithful. As Grisez writes of this particular kind of prudential judgment:

It is necessary to distinguish between teachings proposed as certainly true and "prudential judgments," which popes and other bishops sometimes propose as guidance for the faithful without asking for or expecting their religious assent. While in some cases the latter are clearly labeled, in other cases their tentative character is indicated by various signs. For example, a judgment not proposed as certainly true might be expressed only informally or communicated only to some public authority, rather than published in a document addressed to the Church's teachers and/or members as such; it might take a new and very specific position on a particular situation, rather than recall and apply a common and constant Church teaching; it might use language which is indirect or tentative rather than straightforward and unqualified.[116]

Nor, in the nature of the case, does it seem that the Church *could* command assent in such cases, precisely *because* the contingent circumstances in question are not something about which she has special competence. As the sixteenth-century Dominican theologian and bishop Melchior Cano wrote:

---

[116] Grisez, *The Way of the Lord Jesus*, 2:262.

The authority of the saints, be they few or many, when brought to bear on matters which fall within the province of natural reason, does not furnish certain proof, but is only as valid as the reasoning process on which it is based.[117]

What is true of the saints is surely no less true of living churchmen. The Church may command us to assent to the moral principle that in a just war there must be a realistic hope of success. But she may not command us to assent to a churchman's judgment to the effect that some particular proposed military strategy is either likely or unlikely to succeed. The Church may command us to assent to the moral principle that a just wage may be higher than what an employer may be willing to pay in a free market. But she may not command us to assent to a churchman's judgment to the effect that a particular proposed minimum-wage law will be likely to guarantee just wages, that it will not bring about unintended bad effects that outweigh any good done by the law, and so forth. A bishop's judgments concerning such matters outside the Church's special competence are binding only to the extent that one finds the "reasoning process" that is offered in support of those judgments to be cogent.

So, there seem to be two grades within category-4, or prudential, statements: (a) those that directly touch on theological matters about which the Church has special competence, and examples of which Cardinal Ratzinger gave at the press conference on *Donum Veritatis* (past decisions of the Biblical Commission, etc.); and (b) a lesser grade of prudential judgment about concrete contingent circumstances surrounding the application of moral principles within public policy, in which the primary responsibility for making such judgments lies with public officials and laymen and where churchmen merely offer nonbinding advice. Whereas prudential judgments of the former sort require, in Dulles' words, "external conformity in behavior, but do not demand internal assent"—for example, a biblical scholar, in his work, must conform to the decisions of the Biblical Commission even if he disagrees with them—prudential judgments of the latter sort evidently do not require anything more than respectful consideration.

---

[117] Melchior Cano, *De locis theologicis* VII, 3, quoted in Van Noort, *Dogmatic Theology*, 3:176.

Contemporary works of theology published with the nihil obstat and imprimatur and written by theologians loyal to the Magisterium often recognize this category of type-b prudential statements to which Catholics need not assent. For example, J. Michael Miller (currently the archbishop of Vancouver) writes:

> John Paul II's support for financial compensation equal to other kinds of work for mothers who stay at home to take care of their children, or his plea to cancel the debt of Third World nations as a way to alleviate massive poverty, fall into this category. Catholics are free to disagree with these papal guidelines as ways in which to secure justice. They can submit to debate alternative practical solutions, provided that they accept the moral principles which the pope propounds in his teaching.[118]

Germain Grisez suggests that there are five sorts of cases in which assent is not required.[119] These are cases in which popes and other churchmen:

1. Are not addressing matters of faith and morals
2. Are addressing matters of faith and morals but speaking merely as individual believers or private theologians rather than in an official capacity
3. Are teaching in an official capacity, but tentatively
4. Put forward nonbinding arguments for a teaching that is itself binding on Catholics
5. Put forward merely disciplinary directives with which a Catholic might legitimately disagree even if he has to follow them

Statements made by Cardinal Ratzinger during his tenure as prefect for the Congregation of the Doctrine of the Faith as well as by other bishops support the conclusion that some statements made even by the pope have only this lesser, nonbinding advisory status (i.e., that they are "prudential judgments" of type b). For example, when asked in a May 2, 2003, interview with *Zenit* about the U.S.-led

---

[118] J. Michael Miller, *The Shepherd and the Rock: Origins, Development, and Mission of the Papacy* (Huntington, Ind.: Our Sunday Visitor, 1995), p. 175.

[119] Grisez, *The Way of the Lord Jesus*, 2:49.

war in Iraq, which Pope Saint John Paul II strongly opposed, the cardinal said:

> The Pope expressed his thought with great clarity, not only as his individual thought but as the thought of a man who is knowledgeable in the highest functions of the Catholic Church. *Of course, he did not impose this position as doctrine of the Church* but as the appeal of a conscience enlightened by faith. (emphasis added)

And in an earlier, September 22, 2002, *Zenit* interview, the cardinal acknowledged, despite his own judgment that the war in Iraq did not meet the *Catechism*'s just-war criteria, that "one cannot simply say that the catechism does not legitimize the war", as if the *Catechism* by itself, and apart from prudential consideration of contingent circumstances, could be said either to favor or disfavor any particular war. Similarly, in a statement of March 19, 2003, on the eve of war in Iraq, Bishop Wilton Gregory, then president of the United States Conference of Catholic Bishops, expressed the Conference's regret that the war was proceeding but also said:

> While we have warned of the potential moral dangers of embarking on this war, we have also been clear that there are no easy answers. War has serious consequences, so could the failure to act. *People of good will may and do disagree on how to interpret just war teaching and how to apply just war norms to the controverted facts of this case.* We understand and respect the difficult moral choices that must be made by our President and others who bear the responsibility of making these grave decisions involving our nation's and the world's security. (emphasis added)

In a more official capacity, Cardinal Ratzinger wrote the following in a memorandum on the subject "Worthiness to Receive Holy Communion: General Principles", which was sent to Cardinal Theodore McCarrick, then archbishop of Washington, D.C., and made public in July 2004:

> Not all moral issues have the same moral weight as abortion and euthanasia. For example, *if a Catholic were to be at odds with the Holy Father on the application of capital punishment or on the decision to wage war, he would not for that reason be considered unworthy to present himself to*

receive Holy Communion. While the Church exhorts civil authorities to seek peace, not war, and to exercise discretion and mercy in imposing punishment on criminals, it may still be permissible to take up arms to repel an aggressor or to have recourse to capital punishment. *There may be a legitimate diversity of opinion even among Catholics about waging war and applying the death penalty,* but not however with regard to abortion and euthanasia. (emphasis added)[120]

Note that Cardinal Ratzinger goes so far as to say that a Catholic may be "at odds with" the pope on the application of capital punishment and the decision to wage war and still be worthy to receive Communion—something he could not have said if it were mortally sinful to disagree with the pope on those issues. It follows that there is no grave duty to assent to the pope's statements on those issues. The cardinal also says that "there may be a legitimate diversity of opinion even among Catholics about waging war and applying the death penalty", despite the fact that Pope John Paul II, under whom the cardinal was serving at the time, made very strong statements against capital punishment and the Iraq war. It follows that the pope's statements on those issues were not binding on Catholics even on pain of venial sin, for diversity of opinion could not be "legitimate" if it were even venially sinful to disagree with the pope on these matters. In the memorandum, Cardinal Ratzinger also explicitly says that Catholic voters and politicians must oppose laws permitting abortion and euthanasia, as well as abstain from Holy Communion if they formally cooperate with these evils. By contrast, he makes no requirement on the behavior (such as voting) of Catholics who disagree with the pope about the death penalty or the decision to wage war. So, papal statements on those subjects, unlike type-a category-4 statements, evidently do not require any sort of external obedience, much less assent. Catholics thus owe such statements serious and respectful consideration, but nothing more.

The language of the passage quoted from Cardinal Ratzinger's memorandum was incorporated almost verbatim into a 2004 document titled "Theological Reflections on Catholics in Political Life

---

[120]Joseph Cardinal Ratzinger to Theodore Cardinal McCarrick, memorandum, July 2004, "Worthiness to Receive Holy Communion: General Principles", par. 3, https://www.ewtn.com/library/CURIA/cdfworthycom.HTM.

and the Reception of Holy Communion", written by Archbishop William J. Levada (later made a cardinal and prefect of the Congregation for the Doctrine of the Faith under Pope Benedict XVI) and posted on the website of the United States Conference of Catholic Bishops.[121]

These various remarks by Cardinal Ratzinger and other bishops (in some cases, made in formal documents intended precisely to clarify what is required of the faithful), as well as the teaching of approved manuals of theology, thus imply that what we have been calling prudential judgments of type b in effect constitute a fifth, even less binding category of statement that might be added to Cardinal Dulles' list. Following Cardinal Ratzinger's language, we might formulate this category as follows:

> 5. Statements of a prudential sort on matters about which there may be a legitimate diversity of opinion among Catholics

As Cardinal Ratzinger's memorandum indicates, the distinctions we have drawn between different grades of magisterial statement are crucial to understanding Pope Saint John Paul II's teaching on capital punishment. Cardinal Ratzinger's remarks confirm what, as we shall argue, there is, in any case, ample independent reason to think— namely, that the late pope's criticisms of capital punishment constitute a category-5 statement (or prudential judgment of type b) with which Catholics are not obligated to agree. In fact, among his statements on capital punishment, the ones that have the most binding character are those that *reaffirm* aspects of traditional Catholic teaching.

---

[121] The relevant passage in Archbishop Levada's statement reads: "Not all moral issues have the same moral weight as abortion and euthanasia. For example, if a Catholic were to disagree with the Holy Father on the application of capital punishment or on the decision to wage war, he would not for that reason be considered unworthy to present himself to receive Holy Communion. While the Church exhorts civil authorities to seek peace, not war, and to exercise discretion and mercy in imposing punishment on criminals, it may still be permissible to take up arms to repel an aggressor or to have recourse to capital punishment. There may be a legitimate diversity of opinion even among Catholics about waging war and applying the death penalty, but not with regard to abortion and euthanasia" (Archbishop William J. Levada, "Theological Reflections on Catholics in Political Life and the Reception of Holy Communion", USCCB website, June 13, 2004, http://www.usccb.org/issues-and -action/faithful-citizenship/church-teaching/theological-reflections-tf-bishops-politicians -2004-06-13.cfm).

Pope Saint John Paul II's teaching on capital punishment

Sections 2266 and 2267 of the original edition of the *Catechism of the Catholic Church*, issued in 1992 (during John Paul II's papacy), teach the following on the subjects of punishment in general and the death penalty in particular:

> 2266 Preserving the common good of society requires rendering the aggressor unable to inflict harm. For this reason the traditional teaching of the Church has acknowledged as well-founded the right and duty of legitimate public authority to punish malefactors by means of penalties commensurate with the gravity of the crime, not excluding, in cases of extreme gravity, the death penalty. For analogous reasons those holding authority have the right to repel by armed force aggressors against the community in their charge.
>
> The primary effect of *punishment* is to redress the disorder caused by the offense. When his punishment is voluntarily accepted by the offender, it takes on the value of expiation. Moreover, punishment has the effect of preserving public order and the safety of persons. Finally punishment has a medicinal value; as far as possible it should contribute to the correction of the offender.[122]

> 2267 If bloodless means are sufficient to defend human lives against an aggressor and to protect public order and the safety of persons, public authority should limit itself to such means, because they better correspond to the concrete conditions of the common good and are more in conformity to the dignity of the human person.

Unsurprisingly, much attention has been focused on the turn in this passage toward a more negative overall attitude toward the use of the death penalty than was present in much traditional Catholic teaching. It cannot be emphasized too strongly, however, that the passage nevertheless clearly reaffirms the key aspects of past teaching. In particular, it affirms that the *primary* purpose of punishment is to "to redress the disorder caused by the offense" and that this can serve as expiation for the offense. This is an acknowledgment that punishment in general is *fundamentally retributive*. The passage also explicitly

---

[122] Cf. Lk 23:40–43.

affirms the principle of proportionality when it says that malefactors should be punished "by means of penalties *commensurate with the gravity of the crime*". And when the passage immediately goes on to say that such a penalty can include "in cases of *extreme* gravity, the death penalty", it is clearly implying that the death penalty can be merited *precisely because it is proportionate* to the most extreme offenses. In short, the 1992 edition of the *Catechism* clearly affirms the essentials of the basic natural law argument for the legitimacy in principle of capital punishment that we defended in chapter 1. It also seems to reaffirm most of the other traditional purposes of punishment—in particular, deterrence, incapacitation, and rehabilitation—when it speaks of "preserving public order and the safety of persons" and the "medicinal value" of punishment.

The reason the 1992 *Catechism* gives for preferring "bloodless" penalties where possible is that they "better correspond to the concrete conditions of the common good and are more in conformity to the dignity of the human person". No explanation is given of exactly *how* capital punishment is less conducive to the common good or a respect for human dignity. These claims are merely asserted. We will return below to the question of their doctrinal status.

In 1995, Pope Saint John Paul II issued the encyclical *Evangelium Vitae*. In sections 55–57 he addressed the topics of punishment and the death penalty:

> "Legitimate defence can be not only a right but a grave duty for someone responsible for another's life, the common good of the family or of the State".[123] Unfortunately it happens that the need to render the aggressor incapable of causing harm sometimes involves taking his life. In this case, the fatal outcome is attributable to the aggressor whose action brought it about, even though he may not be morally responsible because of a lack of the use of reason.
>
> This is the context in which to place the problem of the death penalty. On this matter there is a growing tendency, both in the Church and in civil society, to demand that it be applied in a very limited way or even that it be abolished completely. The problem must be viewed in the context of a system of penal justice ever more in line with human dignity and thus, in the end, with God's plan for man

[123] *CCC* 2265.

and society. The primary purpose of the punishment which society inflicts is "to redress the disorder caused by the offence".[124] Public authority must redress the violation of personal and social rights by imposing on the offender an adequate punishment for the crime, as a condition for the offender to regain the exercise of his or her freedom. In this way authority also fulfils the purpose of defending public order and ensuring people's safety, while at the same time offering the offender an incentive and help to change his or her behaviour and be rehabilitated.

It is clear that, for these purposes to be achieved, the nature and extent of the punishment must be carefully evaluated and decided upon, and ought not go to the extreme of executing the offender except in cases of absolute necessity: in other words, when it would not be possible otherwise to defend society. Today however, as a result of steady improvements in the organization of the penal system, such cases are very rare, if not practically non-existent.

In any event, the principle set forth in the new Catechism of the Catholic Church remains valid: "If bloodless means are sufficient to defend human lives against an aggressor and to protect public order and the safety of persons, public authority must limit itself to such means, because they better correspond to the concrete conditions of the common good and are more in conformity to the dignity of the human person".[125]

If such great care must be taken to respect every life, even that of criminals and unjust aggressors, the commandment "You shall not kill" has absolute value when it refers to the innocent person. And all the more so in the case of weak and defenceless human beings, who find their ultimate defence against the arrogance and caprice of others only in the absolute binding force of God's commandment.

In effect, the absolute inviolability of innocent human life is a moral truth clearly taught by Sacred Scripture, constantly upheld in the Church's Tradition and consistently proposed by her Magisterium....

Therefore, by the authority which Christ conferred upon Peter and his Successors, and in communion with the Bishops of the Catholic Church, I confirm that the direct and voluntary killing of an innocent human being is always gravely immoral.

Here also, much attention has been focused on the more negative overall attitude the pope took toward capital punishment than many

---

[124] CCC 2266.
[125] CCC 2267.

of his predecessors had.[126] But as with the 1992 *Catechism*, it is no less remarkable—though, strangely, it is not often remarked upon—how continuous with traditional teaching John Paul II's teaching here is. Reiterating the 1992 *Catechism*, the pope says that "the *primary* purpose of the punishment [is] ... to redress the disorder caused by the offence" and that this requires "an *adequate* punishment". He thereby reaffirms both the principle that punishment is primarily retributive and the principle of proportionality. He clearly teaches that a penalty of death can be justifiable, since he explicitly speaks of exceptions to the general policy that public authority should use bloodless means, albeit he thinks the exceptions are "very rare". He explicitly contrasts respect for the lives of "criminals and unjust aggressors" with the "*absolute* value" that "the commandment 'You shall not kill'" has "when it refers to the *innocent* person". Obviously, the implication is that the commandment does *not* have "absolute value" where the *guilty* are concerned. And the pope repeatedly makes it clear that it is *innocent* human beings, specifically, that he has in mind when he speaks of the grave immorality of taking life. The pope also cites some of the other traditional purposes of punishment—namely, "defending public order", "ensuring people's safety", and rehabilitation—and explicitly says that public authority should strive to achieve *all* of the *purposes* of punishment—he uses the plural—when deciding upon the punishment to be inflicted. Thus, contrary to the impression given by some commentators, the pope by no means ignores all but the defensive purposes of punishment, nor does he treat the lives of the guilty and the innocent as of equal value, nor does his teaching somehow subtly imply—indeed, it explicitly denies—that capital punishment is per se immoral. Though the tone and emphases are certainly very different from those of, say, the *Roman Catechism* or the teaching of Pope Pius XII, the fundamental principles of those older magisterial statements are all reaffirmed by Pope Saint John Paul II. (We consider claims to the contrary in more detail below.)

In 1997, the *editio typica* of the *Catechism* was issued, and the sections dealing with capital punishment were altered to reflect what

[126] It is worth noting that, for all the attention it has understandably gotten from Catholic opponents of capital punishment, very little of *Evangelium Vitae* is actually devoted to the death penalty. Indeed, John Paul II actually said relatively little about the subject during his papacy and certainly gave nothing like the lengthy and systematic treatment of the subject of punishment that Pius XII did.

the pope had said in *Evangelium Vitae*. The revised treatment reads
as follows:

> 2266 The efforts of the state to curb the spread of behavior harmful
> to people's rights and to the basic rules of civil society correspond to
> the requirement of safeguarding the common good. Legitimate public
> authority has the right and duty to inflict punishment proportion-
> ate to the gravity of the offense. Punishment has the primary aim of
> redressing the disorder introduced by the offense. When it is willingly
> accepted by the guilty party, it assumes the value of expiation. Pun-
> ishment then, in addition to defending public order and protecting
> people's safety, has a medicinal purpose: as far as possible, it must
> contribute to the correction of the guilty party.[127]

> 2267 Assuming that the guilty party's identity and responsibility have
> been fully determined, the traditional teaching of the Church does
> not exclude recourse to the death penalty, if this is the only possible
> way of effectively defending human lives against the unjust aggressor.
>   If, however, non-lethal means are sufficient to defend and protect
> people's safety from the aggressor, authority will limit itself to such
> means, as these are more in keeping with the concrete conditions of
> the common good and more in conformity with the dignity of the
> human person.
>   Today, in fact, as a consequence of the possibilities which the state
> has for effectively preventing crime, by rendering one who has com-
> mitted an offense incapable of doing harm—without definitively tak-
> ing away from him the possibility of redeeming himself—the cases in
> which the execution of the offender is an absolute necessity "are very
> rare, if not practically nonexistent."[128]

Once again both the thesis that punishment is primarily retributive and the principle of proportionality are explicitly reaffirmed, as
are the other traditional purposes of punishment. And once again
the legitimacy in principle of capital punishment is also explicitly
reaffirmed and characterized as part of "the traditional teaching of
the Church". The main alteration is that the 1997 edition of the
Catechism reflects the judgment of *Evangelium Vitae* that the cases in
which capital punishment is called for today are "very rare, if not

---

[127] Cf. Lk 23:40–43.
[128] John Paul II, *Evangelium Vitae*, no. 56.

practically nonexistent" and that the reasons have to do with the ability of the modern penal system to defend society without resorting to execution. Given the reaffirmation of traditional teaching together with the appeal to empirical claims about the modern penal system in justifying a restriction on the use of capital punishment, the mainly negative evaluation of the death penalty in *Evangelium Vitae* and the 1997 *Catechism* has the flavor of a category-5 magisterial statement (or type-b prudential judgment). Indeed, we hold that that is precisely what it is and that it cannot in principle be more than that. But some have claimed that there is much more going on here—a "development" or even reversal of doctrine.

Reversal, development, or prudential judgment?

Cardinal Avery Dulles has usefully identified three main schools of interpretation of Pope Saint John Paul II's teaching on capital punishment.[129] The first holds that nothing less than a *change or reversal* of traditional Catholic doctrine regarding capital punishment is implicit in the pope's teaching. This is Brugger's position. The second holds that the pope has not strictly reversed traditional doctrine but that his teaching nevertheless constitutes a significant *development* of doctrine in the direction of making the conditions under which the death penalty may be inflicted more restrictive in principle. This is the view of Charles Rice and Christopher Kaczor.[130] The third holds that the pope has neither reversed nor restricted the principles of traditional teaching, but rather has merely made a *prudential judgment* about how those principles are to be applied in contemporary circumstances. This is the position of Dulles himself and of Steven Long,[131] and it is our position.[132] Indeed, we think no other interpretation can

---

[129] Avery Dulles, "Catholic Teaching on the Death Penalty: Has It Changed?", in Erik C. Owens, John D. Carlson, and Eric P. Elshtain, eds., *Religion and the Death Penalty: A Call for Reckoning* (Grand Rapids, Mich.: William B. Eerdmans, 2004).

[130] Charles Rice, "Papal Teaching Deserves 'Submission'", *National Catholic Register*, March 24–31, 2002; Christopher Kaczor, "Capital Punishment and the Catholic Tradition: Contradiction, Circumstantial Application, or Development of Doctrine?", *Nova et Vetera*, English ed. 2 (2004): 279–304.

[131] Steven A. Long, "*Evangelium Vitae*, St. Thomas Aquinas, and the Death Penalty", *Thomist* 63 (1999): 511–52.

[132] See also Laurence, "He Beareth Not the Sword"; George Rutler, "Scalia's Right: Catechism's Problematic", *National Catholic Register*, March 24–31, 2002.

possibly be reconciled either with irreformable Catholic tradition or with the entirety of the evidence from Pope Saint John Paul II's own Magisterium.

Let's consider these three interpretations in turn. In arguing that the pope's teaching points to a reversal of tradition, Brugger puts heavy emphasis on the treatment of the death penalty in the 1997 *Catechism*.[133] To be sure, even Brugger acknowledges that what he calls the "plain-face interpretation" of the 1997 *Catechism* does not support the claim that there is even a *development* of doctrine here, much less a reversal.[134] He thinks, however, there is an *implicit* reversal. Brugger notes that the *Catechism* places its treatment of the death penalty in the larger context of a subsection entitled "Legitimate defense", that it denies in section 2263 that legitimate defense of oneself or others is an exception to the divine commandment against killing, and that in the same section it approvingly cites Aquinas' teaching that killing in self-defense is legitimate under the principle of double effect insofar as the death of the aggressor is foreseen but not intended. When read in light of these points, the *Catechism*'s teaching that the death penalty should be limited to cases where it "is the only possible way of effectively defending human lives against the unjust aggressor" can be seen, in Brugger's view, to imply that execution is really justifiable only as a kind of *self-defense*, and *not as punishment* per se.

Meanwhile, Pope Saint John Paul II's repeated emphasis in *Evangelium Vitae* on the "sacred" and "inviolable" character of human life at least implies, in Brugger's view, that it is inherently wrong intentionally to kill any person, even if the pope did not explicitly say this.[135] When we combine all these considerations, the picture that emerges, in Brugger's view, is this: it is always and inherently wrong *intentionally* to kill any person, including those guilty of the worst offenses. As Brugger expresses the view, "I cannot will the death of a human person, any human person, innocent or guilty, with a good will";[136] for even in the case of "perpetrators of certain reprehensible

[133] Brugger, *Capital Punishment*, pp. 12–23.
[134] Ibid., pp. 11–12.
[135] Ibid., pp. 25–27.
[136] Ibid., p. 34.

crimes [who might] *deserve* ... death ... the value of their human lives forbids us from ever choosing to destroy their lives".[137] Killing in self-defense is justifiable given the principle of double effect if the death of the aggressor is, while foreseen, *not* intended. Hence, if a criminal is executed for the sake of protecting others from him, this could be justified as a kind of self-defense allowable under double effect as long as the death of the criminal is not intended, even if foreseen. Executing a criminal for any other reason, however, would not be permissible even in principle. In particular, a criminal could not even in principle be executed for the sake of exacting retributive justice. Execution for self-defense would, strictly speaking, not be a matter of *punishment*. This is a reversal of the Church's traditional teaching that the death of a criminal can be intended as a form of retributive punishment. While Brugger admits that the pope did not explicitly teach such a reversal, he claims that the ingredients for it are there in what he did say and could be drawn out explicitly by the Church in the future.

There are a number of grave problems with Brugger's position. The first is that it presupposes that the traditional teaching is something that *could* be reversed, and as we have argued, that is simply not the case. Even if the pope had intended such a reversal (which, as we will argue, he most certainly did *not*), it is simply not within his power to contradict the uniform teaching of Scripture, the Fathers and Doctors of the Church, and the binding statements of previous popes, or to introduce novel teachings such as the one Brugger and other new natural law theorists would like the Church to promulgate. As the First Vatican Council taught:

> For the Holy Spirit was promised to the successors of Peter *not so that they might, by his revelation, make known some new doctrine*, but that, by his assistance, they might religiously guard and faithfully expound the revelation or deposit of faith transmitted by the apostles. (emphasis added)[138]

Nor, given other statements from the First Vatican Council cited earlier, does any pope have authority to reinterpret Scripture in a

---

[137] Ibid., pp. 33–34.
[138] Tanner, "First Vatican Council", *Decrees*, sess. 4, chap. 4, par. 6, https://www.ewtn.com/library/COUNCILS/V1.HTM.

way contrary to the meaning it is understood to have by the Fathers and past Magisterium of the Church—as Brugger's position would require a pope to do if he were to try to reconcile the new natural law position with Scripture. As the Second Vatican Council teaches in *Dei Verbum*:

> The task of authentically interpreting the word of God, whether written or handed on, has been entrusted exclusively to the living teaching office of the Church.... *This teaching office is not above the word of God, but serves it, teaching only what has been handed on.* (no. 10, emphasis added)

A second and related problem is that any pope who tried to reverse the traditional teaching on capital punishment would thereby undermine the Magisterium of the Church, including his own Magisterium and thus any confidence we could have in the act of reversal itself. Such a reversal would therefore be self-defeating. As Cardinal Dulles writes:

> The reversal of a doctrine as well established as the legitimacy of capital punishment would raise serious problems regarding the credibility of the magisterium. Consistency with Scripture and long-standing Catholic tradition is important for the grounding of many current teachings of the Catholic Church; for example, those regarding abortion, contraception, the permanence of marriage, and the ineligibility of women for priestly ordination. If the tradition on capital punishment had been reversed, serious questions would be raised regarding other doctrines....
>
> If, in fact, the previous teaching had been discarded, doubt would be cast on the current teaching as well. It too would have to be seen as reversible, and in that case, as having no firm hold on people's assent. The new doctrine, based on a recent insight, would be in competition with a magisterial teaching that has endured for two millennia—or even more, if one wishes to count the biblical testimonies. Would not some Catholics be justified in adhering to the earlier teaching on the ground that it has more solid warrant than the new? The faithful would be confronted with the dilemma of having to dissent either from past or from present magisterial teaching.[139]

---

[139] Dulles, "Catholic Teaching on the Death Penalty", p. 26.

A third problem is that Brugger's interpretation requires a selective reading of the relevant texts. The fact that the *Catechism*'s treatment of capital punishment occurs in the context of a discussion of "legitimate defense" is taken by Brugger to indicate that the pope's teaching implies that execution is justifiable *only* as a kind of self-defense *rather than* as a kind of punishment. Yet as we have seen, the *Catechism* also explicitly raises the issue of punishment when discussing the death penalty and reaffirms the primacy of retribution, the principle of proportionality, and the other traditional purposes of punishment. Moreover, in *Evangelium Vitae* the pope explicitly raises the issue of punishment when discussing the death penalty, reaffirms retribution and the other traditional purposes, and says that it is "for these *purposes* to be achieved" that he teaches what he does about capital punishment. Hence when *all* of the textual evidence is taken account of, it is clear that the pope did *not* intend to deny either that the death penalty was properly understood as a kind of punishment, or that the purposes of punishment other than self-defense were relevant to the question. And it would be sheer special pleading for Brugger to insist on the relevance of the references to self-defense in interpreting the pope's teaching while downplaying the relevance of the references to punishment.

Brugger also reads John Paul II selectively when discussing the pope's teaching on the sacredness of life. Brugger suggests that the pope's emphasis on the inviolability of human life implies, whether the pope intended this or not, that life cannot ever be taken intentionally.[140] Yet, as we have seen, the pope explicitly says in *Evangelium Vitae* that it is "*innocent* life", specifically, that has "*absolute* inviolability" and clearly indicates that the commandment against killing has "*absolute* value" with respect to the innocent *rather than* the guilty. The principle that John Paul II solemnly "confirms" with papal authority in *Evangelium Vitae* is formulated as the teaching that "the direct and voluntary killing of an *innocent* human being is always gravely immoral." As Cardinal Dulles remarks, "If [the pope] had wanted to teach the doctrine proposed by Professor Brugger, he would have omitted the word 'innocent' in that sentence."[141]

---

[140] Brugger, *Capital Punishment*, pp. 26–27.
[141] Dulles, "Catholic Teaching on the Death Penalty", p. 27.

Here too, then, the *total* textual evidence thus points *away from* Brugger's favored reading. (If anything, it seems to be the *rehabilitative* end of punishment, rather than life's sacredness per se, that lies behind the reluctance in *Evangelium Vitae* and the 1997 *Catechism* to apply capital punishment. *Evangelium Vitae* speaks of "offering the offender an incentive and help to change his or her behaviour and be rehabilitated",[142] and the *Catechism* speaks of not "definitively taking away from him the possibility of redeeming himself". See the discussion below of Pope Benedict XVI's teaching on the subject.)

A fourth problem with Brugger's position is that it presents us with a false alternative. Even if the pope were departing from traditional doctrine, it wouldn't follow that his teaching implies that execution is permissible *only* as self-defense *rather than* as punishment. One could instead take him to be teaching that execution is permissible as punishment, but only when it is *also* necessary for purposes of self-defense. Indeed, this is the view of those who interpret his teaching as a development of doctrine. And denying that punishment is at least part of the story would be problematic for reasons other than those already given. If the one executed does not deserve to be killed as a matter of retributive justice, then it would seem to follow that even those who are not guilty of serious crimes could justifiably be executed if this were necessary for self-defense—for example, those who are infected with highly contagious fatal diseases for which there is no cure. Indeed, it would seem to follow that abortion for the sake of saving a mother's life would be justifiable on grounds of self-defense. Obviously the pope would not have endorsed these conclusions, which is reason enough to conclude that he did not intend to deny that the death penalty had a punitive aspect (a conclusion that, as we have seen, is amply supported by the textual evidence in any event).

A fifth problem with Brugger's interpretation is that the legitimacy in principle of execution as punishment would follow from what the pope did teach *whether or not* he had explicitly drawn that conclusion. The 1992 edition of the *Catechism* spoke of "penalties commensurate with the gravity of the crime, not excluding, in cases of extreme gravity, the death penalty" (2266). Brugger makes much

---

[142] John Paul II, *Evangelium Vitae*, March 25, 1995, no. 56, http://w2.vatican.va/content/john-paul-ii/en/encyclicals/documents/hf_jp-ii_enc_25031995_evangelium-vitae.html.

of the fact that in the 1997 edition, the words "not excluding, in cases of extreme gravity, the death penalty" were omitted from the statement about proportionate punishments and the discussion of the death penalty moved to the next paragraph.[143] But this proves nothing. If I say, "All men are mortal, and Socrates is a man", the conclusion that "Socrates is mortal" follows necessarily, *whether or not* I explicitly draw that conclusion immediately, or a paragraph later, or not at all. Similarly, the principle that offenders deserve punishment and the principle that the punishment should be proportional to the gravity of the offense—principles affirmed by both *Evangelium Vitae* and the 1997 *Catechism*—together entail, as we have seen, that execution can in principle be legitimate as punishment. And it entails this *whether or not* someone committed to those principles explicitly draws that conclusion. So *Evangelium Vitae* and the 1997 *Catechism* would in fact teach that conclusion *implicitly*, whether or not they taught it explicitly. In any event, as we have also seen, they *do* teach it explicitly, since they teach that the death penalty can be legitimate *as punishment*, even if they also indicate that recourse to that punishment should be limited to cases where it is also necessary for self-defense.

A sixth problem with Brugger's position is that his overall approach to interpreting the pope's magisterial statements is seriously deficient, on two counts. First, as Steven Long has emphasized, "the interpretation of *Evangelium vitae* must take account of a basic principle: as a magisterial document, its meaning is constituted in relation to tradition."[144] And as Pope Benedict XVI emphasized, in general, Catholic theologians ought to apply a "hermeneutic of continuity" when interpreting magisterial statements. From the point of view of Catholic theology, it simply will not do to say that some of Pope Saint John Paul II's statements considered in isolation could be interpreted in a way that entails that intentional killing is always wrong, or that execution is justifiable only as self-defense and not as punishment. For we should not read those statements in isolation, but always in light of the tradition that preceded them. After all, some of Saint Paul's statements interpreted in isolation might seem to support Luther's understanding of nature and grace; some of Saint Augustine's statements

---

[143] Brugger, *Capital Punishment*, p. 22.
[144] Long, "*Evangelium Vitae*", p. 514.

interpreted in isolation might seem to support Calvin's view of pre-destination; various biblical passages interpreted in isolation might seem to support any number of heresies. But none of these statements should be interpreted apart from the tradition in the first place, and neither should the pope's statements. This is simply not a Catholic way to interpret authoritative documents.

Moreover, it is a basic exegetical mistake to fixate upon certain striking words and phrases in a papal document and try to wrest from them various portentous novel implications—as Brugger does with respect to the pope's use of words such as "sacred", "inviolable", and "inalienable" in *Evangelium Vitae*. As even very traditional theologians recognize, popes, like anyone else, can sometimes speak imprecisely or with rhetorical flourish, even in magisterial documents, and this must be taken account of when interpreting those documents. Fr. John Ford and Fr. Gerald Kelly, writing during the pontificate of Pius XII, give an apt example:

> The words themselves are not the ultimate criterion of the true sense of the papal pronouncement; they can be obscure and admit of re-formulation. This can be illustrated by the *acta* of both Pius XI and Pius XII relative to punitive sterilization....
>
> In the originally published text of *Casti connubii,* the words of Pius XI at least strongly implied that he was condemning punitive sterilization; but a *notandum* in the next fascicle of the *Acta apostolicae sedis* contained a rewording of the passage which showed that the Pope did not intend to commit himself on the controversy among theologians about the licitness of punitive sterilization. Ten years later the Holy Office, with the approval of Pius XII, condemned direct sterilization, without qualification, as being contrary to the natural law. That was in 1940. But in 1951, and again in 1953, Pope Pius XII, when referring to this condemnation, restricted it to the direct sterilization of the innocent. In both these instances the Popes apparently realized that, though perfectly apt for condemning the errors at which they were aimed, the formulas were broader than their own intention.
>
> The very fact that popes themselves have gone out of their way to clarify or restrict their moral pronouncements indicates that a theologian is not necessarily irreverent or disloyal in supposing that other such statements may need clarification or restriction or rephrasing.[145]

---

[145] John C. Ford and Gerald Kelly, *Contemporary Moral Theology*, vol. 1, *Questions in Fundamental Moral Theology* (Westminster, Md.: Newman Press, 1958), pp. 29–30.

A seventh problem with Brugger's position is that he greatly exaggerates the novelty of Pope Saint John Paul II's teaching. As we have seen, many Fathers of the Church affirmed the legitimacy of the death penalty on grounds of retributive justice and nevertheless tended to oppose its use in practice. This combination of views is not uncommon in Church history, and one can find it expressed even in works written in the decades before the Second Vatican Council, when there was in general a more positive attitude toward capital punishment in Catholic circles. For example, in his *Manual of Moral Theology*, Fr. Thomas Slater defends capital punishment on biblical and natural law grounds and also says that "if the time should ever come when the infliction of less severe penalties will suffice to punish crime and safeguard life and property, then capital punishment should be abolished, but that time does not seem to be at hand yet."[146] In his 1899 book *The Catechism Explained*, Fr. Francis Spirago, though defending capital punishment on biblical grounds and (like Aquinas) by comparing execution of the offender to removal of a diseased limb from the body, nevertheless goes so far as to say:

> The judge must not act arbitrarily; he must only sentence the criminal to death when the welfare of society demands it.... The Church does not like to see blood shed, she desires that every sinner should have time to amend. She permits, but does not approve capital punishment.[147]

Fr. Spirago even situates his treatment of capital punishment in the context of a section of his book devoted to the topic of self-defense. And even Aquinas emphasized the medicinal purposes of the punishments of this life over the retributive end. Brugger himself notes that writers such as Cajetan and Francisco de Vitoria emphasized the defensive end of capital punishment over the retributive end.[148]

As these examples show, John Paul II's teaching was by no means novel. It simply fell on one side of a spectrum of positions on capital punishment that has *always* existed within the Church. Now,

---

[146] Thomas Slater, *A Manual of Moral Theology*, vol. 1, 5th ed. (New York: Benziger Brothers, 1925), p. 196.

[147] Francis Spirago, *The Catechism Explained*, ed. Rev. Richard F. Clarke (Rockford, Ill.: TAN Books, 1993), pp. 388–89.

[148] Brugger, *Capital Punishment*, pp. 115–16.

much of the rhetorical force of Brugger's position derives from his emphasis on the purported novelty of the pope's statements. What the pope says is so unprecedented, in Brugger's view, that we must interpret his teaching as supporting, whatever his own intentions, nothing less than an outright reversal of the tradition. But this rhetoric collapses when we see that the pope's teaching was actually in no way unprecedented and can easily be fitted into the range of views that has existed historically, views that are perfectly compatible with the teaching that capital punishment is in principle legitimate and sanctioned by Scripture.

We conclude that Brugger simply has no serious grounds for attributing to Pope Saint John Paul II the extreme position that he does. Brugger claims that it is "irresponsible" to ignore what (according to his interpretation) the pope was teaching.[149] In our judgment, it is in fact the position taken by Brugger and other new natural law theorists that is irresponsible. As we have seen, that position contradicts the uniform teaching of Scripture, the Fathers and Doctors of the Church, and the popes, and threatens the very credibility of the Magisterium. Where they try to reconcile their position with past teaching, they rely on novel and implausible readings of scriptural and magisterial statements. In other cases Brugger flatly admits that it has not been shown how a reconciliation can be achieved. Their position seems to be primarily motivated by the desire to make the entire Catholic tradition conform itself to a novel view about the ethics of killing that was invented by Germain Grisez in 1970. We believe this gets things the wrong way around. It is the new natural lawyers who must conform themselves to the traditional teaching of the Church. If they cannot, so much the worse for the new natural law position.

Much more responsible, though in our view still seriously mistaken, is the view that Pope Saint John Paul II's teaching constitutes a *development* of doctrine rather than a reversal. The claim here is that whereas the pope has not reversed the traditional teaching that the death penalty is justifiable in principle as a means of achieving retributive justice and the other ends of punishment, he has nevertheless restricted its actual application to cases in which no other means are

---

[149] Ibid., p. 157.

available to defend society. On this interpretation, retributive justice, deterrence, and encouraging repentance may be *among* the ends pursued in executing an offender, but they may never be the *only* ends. Rather, they may be pursued only when such an execution is necessary to protect others against the offender's aggression. Charles Rice even claims that accepting this restriction is now nothing less than a requirement of Catholic orthodoxy, writing:

> When may that penalty be used? John Paul has given us a development of the teaching on that point....
>
> A Catholic can no longer argue for the use of the death penalty on grounds of retribution, deterrence of others from committing crimes or for any other reason unless the execution is "the only possible way" of protecting others from this criminal....
>
> Although that factual judgment must be made as to each penal system and each case, the new test according to which that judgment must be made is a universal criterion, binding in all places and in all cases. If the death penalty in that system is not an "absolute necessity," that is, "the only possible way" to protect others from this criminal, it is immoral to impose it.[150]

So, if Rice is correct, then Pope Saint John Paul II's teaching entails that the requirement that the death penalty be inflicted only where necessary for defense against an aggressor is a "universal criterion, binding in all places and in all cases", so that it would be "immoral" to execute an offender merely for retributive, deterrent, or rehabilitative purposes. Moreover, dissent from this judgment would "no longer" be open to a Catholic.

But this *cannot* be correct. For as Cardinal Dulles has noted, even this position really entails "a partial reversal" rather than a mere development of past teaching.[151] Scripture, the Fathers of the Church, and previous popes all explicitly affirm not only that capital punishment can in principle be legitimate but also that it can in principle be legitimate *for purposes other than defense.*

Consider the many passages from Scripture and the Fathers cited above. Genesis 9:6, Numbers 35:33, Deuteronomy 19:11–13, Luke

---

[150] Rice, "Papal Teaching Deserves 'Submission'".
[151] Dulles, "Catholic Teaching on the Death Penalty", p. 28.

23:41, Acts 25:11, and Romans 13 all clearly regard capital punishment as legitimate *precisely when carried out simply for the purpose of securing retributive justice.* The lex talionis of Exodus 21 and Leviticus 24 is also obviously a matter of exacting retribution for its own sake, and many of the offenses for which one could be executed under the Mosaic Law—such as false witness, idolatry, adultery, homosexual acts, bestiality, incest, kidnapping, and striking one's parents—clearly do not necessarily pose a danger to the physical safety of the community. No doubt the *deterrent* end of capital punishment was also at least partly in view here—Deuteronomy 19:20 talks of striking "fear" in potential offenders—and deterrence is clearly in view in Romans 13. Hence Scripture clearly teaches that capital punishment can in principle be legitimate for the sake of retributive justice or for purposes of deterrence. In fact, there does not seem to be any scriptural passage that clearly speaks of the defense of society even as *one of* the purposes of capital punishment, much less the crucial purpose—and this *despite* the fact that it was supposedly more difficult in biblical times to protect society against aggressors without recourse to execution!

The citations we have given above also indicate that among the Fathers of the Church, Athenagoras of Athens, Tertullian, Lactantius, Origen, Cyprian of Carthage, Eusebius, John Chrysostom, Ephraem of Syria, Optatus, and Jerome all regarded capital punishment as at least in principle justifiable as a means of exacting retribution, even if some of them also commend mercy. Gregory of Nazianzus and Augustine emphasize the deterrence value of capital punishment, and Augustine and Clement also speak of its medicinal value. Remarkably, and as with Scripture, none of the Fathers appear to refer to self-defense against an aggressor even as one of the purposes of capital punishment, let alone the overriding purpose.

Among the popes, Innocent I and Pius XII clearly appear to regard capital punishment as in principle legitimate when inflicted for the purpose of securing retributive justice, as does the *Roman Catechism,* issued under Pius V. Leo X appears to have held that capital punishment can in principle be a legitimate means of dealing with heretics, which clearly has nothing necessarily to do with the physical safety of society. Pius XII, as we have seen, also put forward a very detailed and systematic account of punishment grounded in Scripture and traditional natural law reasoning, according to which the retributive function is fundamental and can neither be discarded in favor of the protective function of punishment nor regarded as reflective merely of past historical circumstances.

We conclude that the claim that it is *in principle* immoral to execute an offender when he does not pose a danger to society simply cannot be reconciled with the teaching of Scripture, the Fathers, or previous popes. Hence, if John Paul II had really intended to teach this, he would be *reversing*, rather than merely developing, the teaching of Scripture, the Fathers, and previous popes.

Now, even if we were to ignore the evidence of Scripture and the Fathers, interpreting John Paul II's teaching as a partial reversal just of the teaching of previous popes would be seriously problematic. John Paul II certainly did not *clearly and explicitly* reverse the teaching of his predecessors, nor did he offer an analysis of retributive justice to match Pius XII's. In particular, he did not explain *why* it would not be justifiable, even in principle, to execute an offender when self-defense is not in view (*if* that were really what he had intended to teach). If the "development" interpretation of John Paul II's teaching were correct, we would be faced with a conflict between clear and systematic previous papal teaching and inexplicit and inchoate current papal teaching, and given the Catholic theological imperative of applying a "hermeneutic of continuity", the presumption would be against the novel teaching and in favor of the traditional teaching. When we factor in the teaching of Scripture and the Fathers—which no pope has the right to reverse, even if he could reverse the previous papal teaching in question—we have something much stronger than a presumption against novelty. We have a decisive reason to reject the novel teaching.

In any event, and as such theorists of the "development of doctrine" as Saint Vincent of Lerins and Cardinal John Henry Newman emphasized, a true development is precisely *not* a reversal of past teaching. A reversal would be what Newman, in his *Essay on the Development of Doctrine*, calls a "corruption" rather than a development. Hence, despite their intention to maintain continuity with past teaching, those who interpret John Paul II's teaching as a "development of doctrine" are really implicitly committed to something like Brugger's position, which they agree is unacceptable.

If the pope's teaching on capital punishment is neither a reversal nor a development of past teaching, the only remaining option is the one identified by Dulles—namely, that the pope was merely putting forward a prudential judgment. And there is ample reason even apart from the considerations just adduced to conclude that that is what his teaching amounts to. Recall that the 1992 edition of the *Catechism* had affirmed the traditional teaching that public authority has the right to "punish malefactors by means of penalties commensurate with the gravity of the crime, not excluding, in cases of extreme gravity, the death penalty" (2266). After *Evangelium Vitae* appeared, Cardinal Ratzinger, then prefect of the Congregation for the Doctrine of the Faith, indicated that the *Catechism* would be updated to reflect the teaching of the encyclical. Fr. Richard John Neuhaus wrote to the cardinal asking for clarification about the relationship between what the 1992 *Catechism* taught and the teaching of the encyclical. Cardinal Ratzinger responded:

> You ask about the correct interpretation of the teaching of the encyclical on the death penalty. Clearly, the Holy Father *has not altered* the doctrinal principles which pertain to this issue as they are presented in the Catechism, but has simply *deepened the application* of such principles in the context of present-day historical circumstances. Thus, where other means for the self-defense of society are possible and adequate, the death penalty may be permitted to disappear. Such a development, occurring within society and leading to the forgoing of this type of punishment, is something good and ought to be hoped for.
>
> In my statements during the presentation of the encyclical to the press, I sought to elucidate these elements, and noted the importance of taking such *circumstantial considerations* into account. It is in this sense that the Catechism may be rewritten, *naturally without any modification* of the relevant doctrinal principles.[152]

Cardinal Ratzinger—who, as the man chosen by the pope to safeguard doctrine, was in a position to know—explicitly denies that the relevant doctrinal principles were "altered" or "modified" by *Evangelium Vitae*, which rules out any reversal or development of doctrine.

---

[152] Quoted in Richard John Neuhaus, "That They May Be One", *First Things* 56 (October 1995): 83, emphasis added.

(Though the cardinal uses the word "development", he applies it not to *doctrine*, but to *social and legal* developments in the direction away from use of the death penalty.) The cardinal also explicitly cites "circumstantial considerations" and attention to "the context of present-day historical circumstances" as underlying the encyclical's teaching on capital punishment. Clearly all of this is indicative that the encyclical was presenting a category-5 magisterial statement (or type-b prudential judgment) rather than a reversal or doctrinal development. (It also indicates that the same can be said of the 1997 *Catechism*, since the cardinal explicitly says that it is "in [the] sense" of "taking such circumstantial considerations into account", and "without any modification of the relevant doctrinal principles", that the *Catechism* would be revised.)

As we have seen, Cardinal Ratzinger also stated, in a memorandum sent to Cardinal McCarrick in 2004:

> Not all moral issues have the same moral weight as abortion and euthanasia. For example, *if a Catholic were to be at odds with the Holy Father on the application of capital punishment . . . he would not for that reason be considered unworthy to present himself to receive Holy Communion.* While the Church exhorts civil authorities . . . to exercise discretion and mercy in imposing punishment on criminals, it may still be permissible . . . to have recourse to capital punishment. *There may be a legitimate diversity of opinion even among Catholics about . . . applying the death penalty,* but not however with regard to abortion and euthanasia. (emphasis added)[153]

If Rice's interpretation of the pope's teaching were correct, Cardinal Ratzinger could not have said this. For if the pope's teaching really were a development of doctrine and not merely a prudential judgment, then all Catholics would be obliged to accept it with religious assent. There could, in that case, be no "legitimate diversity of opinion" about the matter, and those who were "at odds" with the pope on this issue could not be considered worthy to present themselves for Holy Communion. The cardinal's remarks make perfect sense, though, if John Paul II's teaching were of a merely prudential character.

---

[153] Ratzinger, "Worthiness to Receive Holy Communion", par. 3.

What exactly *are* the considerations underlying the pope's prudential judgment to the effect that, in contemporary circumstances,
capital punishment should be restricted to cases where it is necessary
for the defense of society, which are "very rare, if not practically
non-existent"? Patrick Laurence plausibly suggests that John Paul II's
hope was that limiting the use of capital punishment would help to
promote respect for life in general and thereby counteract the *disrespect* for *innocent* life represented by practices such as abortion and
euthanasia and the mass murder practiced by totalitarian states during
the twentieth century:

> After his comments on the death penalty, John Paul II asserted that
> "If such great care must be taken to respect every life, even that
> of criminals and unjust aggressors, the commandment 'You shall
> not kill' has absolute value when it refers to the innocent person."
> John Paul II seemed to suggest that if society refrains from execut-
> ing even those who deserve death, it will underscore the sanctity of
> every human life, particularly those that do not deserve death. This
> argument is concerned with the didactic message of capital pun-
> ishment, or more properly, the medicinal value of refraining from
> capital punishment.[154]

Steven Long suggests that the basis of such a prudential judgment
might be the observation that "contemporary secular societies tend
to lack the basis for imposing the death penalty in a virtuous fashion,
and apparently no longer embody those moral norms by reference
to which such penalty is morally intelligible."[155] Similarly, Cardinal
Dulles suggests that a prudential reason for refraining from use of
the death penalty today is the absence in modern society of belief
in a "transcendental order of justice", so that capital punishment
is bound to reduce to the mere expression of the "collective anger
of the group" rather than a matter of divine judgment.[156] And, of
course, *Evangelium Vitae* and the 1997 edition of the *Catechism* suggest
that modern improvements in the penal system make it possible to
protect society without recourse to execution.

[154]Laurence, "He Beareth Not the Sword", p. 246.
[155]Long, "*Evangelium Vitae*", pp. 546–47.
[156]Dulles, "Catholicism and Capital Punishment", p. 33.

Christopher Kaczor, who favors the "development of doctrine" interpretation of John Paul II's teaching, notes that there are serious problems with such prudential arguments against capital punishment.[157] First, it is not plausible to say that modern penal systems have made dramatic advances in providing for the physical protection of society. "Ancient Greek and Romans could enslave entire peoples for life. In the middle ages, the *oubliette* [a type of dungeon] left prisoners to languish until the end of their lives. The Tower of London likewise contained many prisoners without parole. So, the ability of society to imprison for life does not seem to be a radical new development."[158] Second, given the number of murders that occur in prison, the ability of incarcerated mafia leaders to order hits from behind prison walls, and so forth, it is not plausible that executions for the sake of protecting society would be that rare. Third, many ancient societies, such as the pagan Roman Empire, also lacked respect for innocent life and a Christian understanding of the transcendent moral order. Yet this did not prevent Christians such as Saint Paul from defending the use of capital punishment even in the context of such societies.

We agree with Kaczor that the prudential arguments in question are not very good arguments. Indeed, we would add that the prudential argument to the effect that refraining from killing the guilty will increase respect for innocent life is not plausible either. For, in fact, there does not seem to be any significant correlation between opposition to capital punishment and respect for innocent life. On the contrary, it is well known that many people who strongly oppose capital punishment also strongly *support* abortion and euthanasia, whereas many people who strongly support capital punishment are *already* strongly opposed to abortion and euthanasia.

The weakness of these prudential arguments shows (contrary to what Kaczor suggests) not that the pope was not, after all, making a mere prudential judgment (we have shown that he must have been doing so) but that it is seriously doubtful that the prudential judgment he was making has a solid basis. Indeed, some of the arguments Kaczor rightly criticizes as weak are arguments that were made by *the pope himself*, rather than his interpreters. Kaczor's interpretation

---

[157] Kaczor, "Capital Punishment", pp. 293–99.
[158] Ibid., p. 294.

would thus entail that the pope was giving weak arguments for a *development of doctrine*, rather than merely giving weak arguments in favor of a prudential judgment. Surely that is a reason for *rejecting* the "development of doctrine" interpretation, not for accepting it!

There is a further problem with the "development of doctrine" interpretation inadvertently highlighted by Kaczor's discussion. Kaczor rightly takes Brugger to task for claiming that the pope assimilates the death penalty to self-defense. He writes:

> The treatment of the death penalty is itself within *Evangelium Vitae* and the *Catechism* explicitly put in the context of *punishment*, not within the treatment of killing in self-defense. Furthermore, in private self-defense, one may not kill an attacker who has been, at least for the moment, incapacitated. If someone attacks me and I knock him out and then tie him up, I would not be justified in going a step further and killing him. But virtually all forms of capital punishment (hanging, electric chair, guillotine, lethal injection) presuppose that the "aggressor" is not, at least for the time being, an aggressor. Thus, if capital punishment were simply a form of community self-defense governed by the same norms as private defense, then justified capital punishment should not be described in *Evangelium Vitae* as "rare, if not practically non-existent" but rather as *entirely non-existent*. Lethal private self-defense is not justified in cases where the aggressor is incapable of inflicting harm, but that is precisely the circumstance in which capital punishment is exercised.[159]

Now, this entails that by the pope's own criteria, when the 1997 *Catechism* says that recourse to capital punishment is justifiable when necessary in order to "defend and protect people's safety from the aggressor", it cannot mean that the aggressor must be an imminent threat. The death penalty could be justified even if the offender is a threat to society in some less immediate way. But then it is hard to see why the death penalty would not also be justifiable for purposes of deterrence, *if* there were grounds for thinking that execution might truly have a deterrent effect. For *if* it had such an effect, then an execution for the purposes of deterrence would "defend and protect people's safety" no less than an execution for the purpose of preventing a dangerous criminal from escaping would.

---

[159] Ibid., p. 291.

So, it seems arbitrary or even incoherent to say that capital punishment *could* be justifiable in principle for the purposes of preventing a dangerous criminal from escaping, but *not* justifiable *even in principle* for the purposes of deterring others from committing murder. Yet that is just the position that Charles Rice, who favors the "development of doctrine" interpretation, would by implication attribute to the *Catechism* when he claims that "a Catholic can no longer argue for the use of the death penalty on grounds of ... deterrence of others from committing crimes."[160] Surely it is much more plausible to hold that the *Catechism* was presenting a prudential judgment to the effect that deterrence could not justify capital punishment in contemporary circumstances, rather than a doctrinal development to the effect that deterrence could not justify capital punishment even in principle—given that the latter interpretation would require attributing an arbitrary or incoherent position to the *Catechism*.

That *Evangelium Vitae* and the 1997 *Catechism* have been subject to such divergent interpretations indicates that the teaching contained in these documents—though, as we have argued, it is entirely compatible with tradition and represents a prudential judgment rather than a reversal or development of doctrine—nevertheless was not expressed with adequate clarity. And as even Kaczor, who agrees with the teaching, implicitly admits, the arguments given for it are not all very plausible. In contexts without the magisterial authority of an encyclical or a catechism, Pope Saint John Paul II called outright for the abolition of the death penalty, in statements whose import was even less clear than some of those we have examined. For example, in a homily in Saint Louis, Missouri, on January 27, 1999, the pope characterized the death penalty as "cruel and unnecessary". We have seen why he thought it unnecessary in contemporary circumstances, but in what sense could it be "cruel", consistent with the teaching of Scripture and the Fathers that capital punishment can be justifiable simply because it is *deserved*? (Recall that Saint Jerome held that "he who slays cruel men is not cruel"!)

But as we have seen, *Donum Veritatis* acknowledges that "when it comes to the question of interventions in the prudential order, it could happen that some Magisterial documents might not be free from all deficiencies." As Ford and Kelly note, "a theologian is not

---

[160] Rice, "Papal Teaching Deserves 'Submission'".

necessarily irreverent or disloyal in supposing that [papal] statements may need clarification or restriction or rephrasing."[161] And as Cardinal Ratzinger indicated in his letter to Cardinal McCarrick, faithful Catholics may legitimately disagree with the pope's judgment about the use of capital punishment in modern circumstances. We respectfully do disagree with it. We will discuss what we regard as the difficulties with the pope's prudential judgment about capital punishment in more detail below.

Pope Benedict XVI and Pope Francis on capital punishment

The *Compendium of the Catechism of the Catholic Church* was issued in 2005, during the pontificate of Benedict XVI. Paragraphs 468–69 deal with punishment and the death penalty:

468. What is the purpose of punishment?

A punishment imposed by legitimate public authority has the aim of redressing the disorder introduced by the offense, of defending public order and people's safety, and contributing to the correction of the guilty party.

469. What kind of punishment may be imposed?

The punishment imposed must be proportionate to the gravity of the offense. Given the possibilities which the State now has for effectively preventing crime by rendering one who has committed an offense incapable of doing harm, the cases in which the execution of the offender is an absolute necessity "are very rare, if not practically non-existent" (*Evangelium Vitae*). When non-lethal means are sufficient, authority should limit itself to such means because they better correspond to the concrete conditions of the common good, are more in conformity with the dignity of the human person, and do not remove definitively from the guilty party the possibility of reforming himself.

Clearly the *Compendium* essentially reiterates the teaching of the 1997 edition of the *Catechism*. It reaffirms the retributive aspect of punishment, the principle of proportionality, and the permissibility

---

[161] Ford and Kelly, *Contemporary Moral Theology*, 1:30.

in principle of capital punishment, though also John Paul II's judgment that the cases in which capital punishment is called for are very rare. Brugger (of all commentators), however, sees a nod to continuity with tradition in the placement of the sentence about proportional punishments at the head of the paragraph about the death penalty in paragraph 469. In the 2014 second edition of his book, Brugger writes:

> It may very well ... be the case that the drafters of the *Compendium* wished to reduce the distance between retribution and the justification of capital punishment that the text of the [1997 edition of the *Catechism*] had introduced. ...
>
> In light of Cardinal Ratzinger's/Pope Benedict's efforts to accentuate marks of continuity between [*Evangelium Vitae* and the *Catechism*] and the tradition, it may be the case that Benedict was aware of and approved of the inclusion of [the] sentence ... into section no. 469.[162]

In general, Brugger judges that "Benedict's interventions ... indicate a reluctance to move his predecessor's doctrinal principles any further in the direction of abolition."[163] Brugger even admits that he "doubts" that Pope Benedict XVI would accept the condemnation of capital punishment as inherently immoral that Brugger thinks is implicit in John Paul II's teaching.[164]

Pope Francis, in a message to participants of the Fifth World Congress against the Death Penalty in Madrid on June 19, 2013, called for an abolition of the death penalty.[165] In an address to the International Association of Penal Law on October 23, 2014, the pope said:

> It is impossible to imagine that States today fail to employ means other than capital punishment to protect the lives of other people from the unjust aggressor.
>
> St John Paul II condemned the death penalty (cf. Encyclical Letter *Evangelium Vitae*, n. 56), as does also the *Catechism of the Catholic Church* (n. 2267). ...

---

[162] E. Christian Brugger, *Capital Punishment and Roman Catholic Moral Tradition*, 2nd ed. (Notre Dame, Ind.: University of Notre Dame Press, 2014), pp. xvii–xviii.

[163] Ibid., p. x.

[164] Ibid., p. xxiii.

[165] Ibid., p. xxivn4.

All Christians and men of good will are thus called today to fight not only for the abolition of the death penalty, whether legal or illegal, and in all its forms, but also in order to improve the prison conditions, with respect for the human dignity of the people deprived of their freedom. And I link this to life imprisonment. A short time ago the life sentence was taken out of the Vatican's Criminal Code. A life sentence is just a death penalty in disguise.[166]

Naturally this statement does not have the kind of magisterial authority that an encyclical or catechism does, and it is problematic in any case. For one thing, it is simply factually incorrect to say that Pope John Paul II condemned the death penalty either in *Evangelium Vitae* or in the *Catechism*. In fact, of course, both documents explicitly reaffirm as the traditional teaching of the Church that capital punishment is legitimate in principle and allow that there might be at least "rare" instances in which it is justifiable in practice. Obviously both documents also call for severely restricting its use, but that is not the same thing as a condemnation. For another thing, Cardinal Ratzinger's statement that even faithful Catholics may be "at odds with the Holy Father" on capital punishment and that "there may be a legitimate diversity of opinion even among Catholics about ... applying the death penalty" entails that it is not necessarily the case that "all Christians and men of good will are called today to fight ... for the abolition of the death penalty ... in all its forms."

Then there are the questions raised by Pope Francis' comparison of a life sentence to a death sentence and the apparent condemnation of the former as well as of the latter. Is the pope saying that all prisoners currently serving life sentences should be released at some point— including serial killers, terrorists, the criminally insane, and the like? Presumably not. But then it is not clear exactly what the practical implications of his remarks are supposed to be. Nor is it clear how those remarks square with Pope John Paul II's teaching, since the late pope's claim that there are in modern circumstances adequate means of protecting society against the most dangerous criminals without executing them was presumably grounded in the supposition that

---

[166] Pope Francis, "Address to the Delegates of the International Association of Penal Law", October 23, 2014, https://w2.vatican.va/content/francesco/en/speeches/2014/october /documents/papa-francesco_20141023_associazione-internazionale-diritto-penale.html.

these criminals could be imprisoned for life instead. (In the 2005 document *A Culture of Life and the Penalty of Death*, the United States Conference of Catholic Bishops explicitly recommended "life without the possibility of parole" as an alternative way of dealing with those who pose a danger to society. If that option is ruled out, what is left?)

There are also other problematic passages in the pope's address. For example, he says that:

> *Regarding the application of criminal sanctions on children* .... [C]hildren ... have not fully developed to maturity and for this reason cannot be held responsible. They must instead benefit from all the privileges that the State is capable of offering, regarding policies of inclusion as much as practices directed at developing in them respect for life and for the rights of others."[167]

By "children" does the pope mean all those who are not yet legally adults (age eighteen in most American states)? Teenagers under eighteen sometimes commit horrific crimes (such as rape murders and school shootings of the kind that have become notorious in recent years). How exactly would the pope have us apply to these cases the principle that children "cannot be held responsible" and the recommendation that they "must instead benefit from all the privileges that the State is capable of offering, regarding policies of inclusion"?

Some passages in Pope Francis' address are highly obscure. In a section dealing with the problem of corruption, the pope says:

> A corrupt person passes through life with shortcuts of opportunism, with an air of one who says: "It wasn't me", managing to internalize his "honest man" mask. It is a process of internalization. . . . .
>
> The corrupt one does not perceive his corruption. It is somewhat like what happens with bad breath: the person who has it is seldom aware of it; it is the others who notice it and have to tell him about it. For this reason it is unlikely that the corrupt person will be able to recognize his state and change through inner remorse.
>
> Corruption is a greater ill than sin. More than forgiveness, this ill must be treated. Corruption has become natural, to the point of becoming a personal and social statement tied to customs, common

---

[167] Ibid, emphasis in the original.

practice in commercial and financial transactions, in public contract-
ing, in every negotiation that involves agents of the State. It is the
victory of appearances over reality and of brazenness over honour-
able discretion.[168]

What exactly does all this mean, and what concrete practical im-
plications does the pope think it has for dealing with corruption?
How could corruption or anything else be "a greater ill than sin"?
And isn't corruption itself a *kind* of sin?

As these passages illustrate, the pope is clearly speaking very loosely
and informally in this address rather than putting forward any carefully formulated doctrinal statements. Indeed, at the beginning of the
address he says that he will be speaking "in summary form" about
"certain issues which ... [are] in part debatable". Given these considerations, together with the fact that the context is not in the first
place an official magisterial statement, such as an encyclical, it seems
clear that the address does not add anything of a doctrinal nature
to the Church's teaching about punishment but constitutes a set
of prudential judgments. Given the obscurity and lack of precision
in some of Pope Francis' remarks, we respectfully submit that the
address also illustrates *Donum Veritatis*'s point about the "deficiencies" that can exist in magisterial statements. This is especially true,
in our view, of recent statements of a prudential nature concerning
capital punishment.

These judgments apply perhaps even more obviously to further
remarks Pope Francis made in a letter of March 20, 2015, to the
International Commission against the Death Penalty, from which we
quote at length:

> The Magisterium of the Church, beginning from Sacred Scripture
> and from the experience of the People of God for millennia, defends
> life from conception to natural death, and supports full human dignity
> as in the image of God (cf. Gen 1:26)....
>
> States can kill by their action when they apply the death penalty,
> when they lead their people to war or when they perform extraju-
> dicial or summary executions. They can also kill by omission, when
> they do not guarantee their people access to the basic necessities of
> life....

[168] Ibid.

Life, human life above all, belongs to God alone. Not even a murderer loses his personal dignity, and God himself pledges to guarantee this. As St Ambrose taught, God did not want to punish Cain with homicide, for He wants the sinner to repent more than to die (cf. *Evangelium Vitae*, n. 9).

In certain circumstances, when hostilities are underway, a measured reaction is necessary in order to prevent the aggressor from causing harm, and the need to neutralize the aggressor may result in his elimination; it is a case of legitimate defence (cf. *Evangelium Vitae*, n. 55). Nevertheless, the prerequisites of legitimate personal defence are not applicable in the social sphere without the risk of distortion. In fact, when the death penalty is applied, people are killed not for current acts of aggression, but for offences committed in the past. Moreover, it is applied to people whose capacity to cause harm is not current, but has already been neutralized, and who are deprived of their freedom.

Today capital punishment is unacceptable, however serious the condemned's crime may have been. It is an offence to the inviolability of life and to the dignity of the human person which contradicts God's plan for man and for society and his merciful justice, and it fails to conform to any just purpose of punishment. It does not render justice to the victims, but rather foments revenge.

For a constitutional state the death penalty represents a failure, because it obliges the State to kill in the name of justice. Dostoyevsky wrote: "To kill a murderer is a punishment incomparably worse than the crime itself. Murder by legal sentence is immeasurably more terrible than murder by a criminal". Justice is never reached by killing a human being.

The death penalty loses all legitimacy due to the defective selectivity of the criminal justice system and in the face of the possibility of judicial error.... With the application of capital punishment, the person sentenced is denied the possibility to make amends or to repent of the harm done; the possibility of confession, with which man expresses his inner conversion; and of contrition, the means of repentance and atonement, in order to reach the encounter with the merciful and healing love of God....

The death penalty is contrary to the meaning of *humanitas* and to divine mercy, which must be models for human justice. It entails cruel, inhumane and degrading treatment, as is the anguish before the moment of execution and the terrible suspense between the issuing of the sentence and the execution of the penalty, a form of "torture" which, in the name of correct procedure, tends to last many years, and which oftentimes leads to illness and insanity on death row.

In some spheres there is debate over the method of execution, as if it were about finding "the best" way. In the course of history, various lethal mechanisms have been defended because they reduced the suffering and agony of the condemned. But there is no humane form of killing another person.

Today, not only are there means of effectively addressing the crime without definitively depriving criminals of the chance to reform (cf. *Evangelium Vitae*, n. 27), but there is also a heightened moral sensitivity regarding the value of human life, arousing public opinion in support of the various provisions aimed at its abolition or at suspending its application and a growing aversion to the death penalty (cf. *Compendium of the Social Doctrine of the Church*, n. 405).

On the other hand, life imprisonment, as well as those sentences which, due to their duration, render it impossible for the condemned to plan a future in freedom, may be considered hidden death sentences, because with them the guilty party is not only deprived of his/her freedom, but insidiously deprived of hope. But, even though the criminal justice system may appropriate the guilty parties' time, it must never take away their hope.

At first glance the pope might seem to be condemning *all* killing as always and in principle wrong. He says that "justice is *never* reached by killing a human being", and that "there is *no humane form* of killing another person." He lumps both the death penalty and war in with "extrajudicial or summary executions". He says that capital punishment "is an offence to the inviolability of life and to the dignity of the human person", that it "does not render justice to the victims", and that it "entails cruel, inhumane and degrading treatment".

However, on closer inspection it is clear that he is not in fact condemning all killing or even capital punishment as always and in principle immoral. For one thing, he allows that the "elimination" of an aggressor is sometimes "necessary", but judges that "*today* capital punishment is unacceptable". Thus Pope Francis both explicitly says that killing can in some cases be justifiable and implies that in previous generations capital punishment, specifically, *was* admissible. For another thing, in support of his remarks, the pope cites the book of Genesis, the *Compendium of the Social Doctrine of the Church*,[169] and

---

[169] The *Compendium of the Social Doctrine of the Church* is a volume on Catholic social teaching published in 2004 by the Vatican's Pontifical Council for Justice and Peace.

Pope John Paul II's *Evangelium Vitae*, and all three not only do not condemn capital punishment as inherently immoral, but explicitly *affirm* that it is in principle justifiable. While Genesis 1:26 does indeed teach that man is made in God's image, we have also seen that Genesis 9:6 sanctions capital punishment, and sanctions it *precisely because* man is made in God's image. Section 405 of the *Compendium of the Social Doctrine of the Church* does indeed take a negative attitude toward capital punishment, but it also affirms that "the traditional teaching of the Church does not exclude the death penalty 'when this is the only practicable way to defend the lives of human beings effectively against the aggressor.'" And we have already examined *Evangelium Vitae* in detail and seen both that what it condemns as inherently immoral is only the taking of *innocent* human life and that it essentially reaffirms all the key elements of traditional Catholic teaching on punishment, including the legitimacy in principle of capital punishment.

In fact, so great is Pope Francis' reliance here on *Evangelium Vitae* and its emphasis on considerations about what is needed for the protection of society against aggressors, that it is clear that the pope is for the most part merely reiterating John Paul II's prudential judgment that capital punishment is no longer necessary under modern circumstances—a prudential judgment with which, as then-Cardinal Ratzinger acknowledged, Catholics are not obliged to agree. Nor, in our judgment, do the considerations raised by Pope Francis add plausibility to this prudential judgment. The pope asserts that capital punishment "foments revenge", that it "definitively depriv[es]" from the criminal "the chance of reform", and that "judicial error" may lead innocent people to be executed. We have already shown what is wrong with such arguments, and we will say more in response to them in chapters 3 and 4. We will also address in chapter 4 the claim that capital punishment is applied arbitrarily (a claim the pope seems to endorse when he refers to "the defective selectivity of the criminal justice system"). The pope also asserts that the "anguish" of those awaiting capital punishment "oftentimes leads to illness and insanity"—an empirical claim for which he offers no support and which, at least in the American context, in fact seems clearly false.

There are additional grave problems facing any suggestion that Pope Francis' remarks here might be read as a reversal or development of doctrine. First, it is hardly plausible that such a major doctrinal shift would be made in a document of such low magisterial authority as a letter to a political organization. Second, read as a statement of doctrinal principle rather than a mere prudential judgment, the pope's remarks would conflict with those of previous popes. For example, we have seen that Pope Pius XII taught that punishment is not to be thought of as a defensive or protective reaction either to an act in progress or to an act that might potentially be committed in the future, but is rather properly inflicted on the offender after the act is committed and whether or not he is likely to commit a further offense, precisely because he is in a state of guilt either way. We have also seen that this is part of an account of the nature of punishment that Pius worked out in some detail over the course of several years and in several documents, and which is grounded in the Thomistic natural law tradition. Now, Pope Francis objects to the death penalty in part on the grounds that it is applied "not for current acts of aggression, but for offences committed in the past" and "is applied to people whose capacity to cause harm is not current, but has already been neutralized". He does not tell us whether there is something wrong with this in *principle*, and if there is, *why* it would be wrong in principle. So, if Pope Francis intended his remarks here to be doctrinal rather than merely prudential, it appears that he would both be contradicting Pius XII and doing so on the basis of groundless assertion rather than on a systematic theological basis of the sort Pius provided. And as Cardinal Dulles has noted, in the case of such a doctrinal conflict between popes, "the faithful would be confronted with the dilemma of having to dissent either from past or from present magisterial teaching", which would raise the question whether "some Catholics [might] be justified in adhering to the earlier teaching on the ground that it has more solid warrants than the new."[170]

A third and even more serious problem is that, as we have argued, one cannot deny either that capital punishment is justifiable in principle, or even that it is in principle justifiable for purposes other than protection of others against the immediate threat of aggression, consistent with the teaching of Scripture, the Fathers of the Church, and previous popes, and thus consistent with Catholic orthodoxy. Hence

---

[170] Dulles, "Catholic Teaching on the Death Penalty", p. 26.

to read Pope Francis as proposing such a doctrinal change would be to attribute to him a heterodox position.

A fourth and final problem is that some of what Pope Francis says here would, if read as having doctrinal significance, be very seriously problematic even apart from the considerations already raised. The pope approvingly cites a remark he attributes to Dostoyevsky, to the effect that "to kill a murderer is a punishment *incomparably worse than the crime itself*. Murder by legal sentence is immeasurably *more terrible than murder by a criminal*" (emphasis added). Now, consider a serial killer such as Ted Bundy, who murdered at least fourteen women. Bundy routinely raped and tortured his victims and also mutilated and even engaged in necrophilia with some of their bodies. He was executed in the electric chair, a method of killing that takes only a few moments. Should we interpret the pope as seriously suggesting that Bundy's execution was "incomparably worse" and an "immeasurably more terrible" crime than what Bundy himself did? Not only would such a judgment lack any grounding whatsoever in Scripture, the Fathers and Doctors of the Church, and the teaching of previous popes; not only would it in fact clearly *contradict* what these sources of Catholic doctrine teach; such a judgment would be manifestly absurd, and indeed, frankly obscene. Surely the pope does *not* intend to teach such a thing, but is rather merely indulging in a rhetorical flourish. In that case, though, his other somewhat peremptory and sweeping remarks about capital punishment in this letter are also plausibly read as having rhetorical rather than doctrinal import.

Then there is the pope's reiteration here of the suggestion that "life imprisonment" amounts to a "hidden" death sentence. If the pope were condemning capital punishment as in principle immoral, then, it would appear to follow that he would also be condemning life imprisonment as in principle immoral. Now, such a teaching has no foundation whatsoever in Scripture, Tradition, or previous papal teaching. It would be a sheer novelty of the pope's own devising. Yet, as we have seen, the First Vatican Council taught that "the Holy Spirit was promised to the successors of Peter *not* so that they might, by his revelation, make known some new doctrine"[171] but rather

---

[171] Tanner, "First Vatican Council", *Decrees*, sess. 4, chap. 4, par. 6, https://www.ewtn.com/library.COUNCILS/VI.HTM, emphasis added.

only that they would guard the doctrines they have inherited. Yet surely the pope does not intend to invent any new doctrine.

Similarly problematic are some remarks about capital punishment that Pope Francis made in his weekly Angelus address of February 21, 2016:

> Tomorrow in Rome begins an international conference entitled "For a World Without the Death Penalty"....
>
> I hope that this conference might give new strength to efforts to abolish the death penalty. A spreading opposition to the death penalty, even as an instrument of legitimate social defence, has developed in public opinion, and this is a sign of hope. In fact, modern societies have the ability to effectively control crime without definitively taking away a criminal's chance to redeem himself. The issue lies in the context of a perspective on a criminal justice system that is ever more conformed to the dignity of man and God's design for man and for society. And also a criminal justice system open to the hope of reintegration in society. The commandment "thou shall not kill" has absolute value and pertains to the innocent as well as the guilty.
>
> The Extraordinary Jubilee of Mercy is a propitious occasion to promote in the world a growing maturity for ways to respect life and the dignity of each person. Because even a criminal has the inviolable right to life, a gift of God. I appeal to the consciences of leaders, that they come to an international consensus aimed at abolishing the death penalty. And to those among them who are Catholic, may they carry out an act of courage, giving an example that the death penalty not be applied in this Holy Year of Mercy.[172]

Note first that we have, once again, a statement lacking the level of magisterial authority that an encyclical or a catechism enjoys. It is merely a set of informal remarks prompted by a forthcoming political conference. We also have, once again, a statement that at least at first glance seems to conflict with official and unbroken Catholic teaching. For the pope says that "the commandment 'thou shalt not kill' ... pertains to the innocent as well as the *guilty*", and that "even a criminal has the *inviolable* right to life." Taken in isolation, such remarks might give the impression that capital punishment is *always*

---

[172] Pope Francis, Angelus, February 21, 2016, https://w2.vatican.va/content/franceso/en/angelus/2016/documents/papa-francesco_angelus_20160221.html.

and intrinsically immoral. As we have seen, such a position would contradict, not only the *Catechism* and the most recent encyclical that addresses this subject (Pope John Paul II's *Evangelium Vitae*), but also the irreformable teaching of Scripture, the Fathers and Doctors of the Church, and all previous popes.

On the other hand, there are aspects of Pope Francis' remarks here that point away from such an interpretation. For one thing, in general, the pope's language in this address fairly closely corresponds to the language of paragraphs 56 and 57 of *Evangelium Vitae*, and paragraph 2267 of the 1997 edition of the *Catechism*. It is clear that his intention is simply to reiterate the teaching of those documents. Yet as we have seen, those documents not only do not condemn capital punishment as intrinsically immoral; they explicitly teach that it is *not* intrinsically immoral. For another thing, Pope Francis calls upon Catholic public officials, "as a gesture of courage" and "an example", to refrain from applying the death penalty during "this Holy Year of Mercy"—namely, the Jubilee Year under way at the time of his address. Now, calling on the faithful to refrain from an act of some kind for a particular, specific period (in this case, for the Jubilee Year) would be very odd if the act were something *intrinsically and gravely* immoral. Rather, one would expect, in the case of some act that is intrinsically and gravely immoral, that the faithful would be commanded to forsake it *absolutely and finally*. It would not be odd, however, to make such a request if one were asking for a display of *supererogatory* virtue—that is, something that goes beyond what is strictly required as a matter of justice but is fitting in some other way (for example, in this case, in light of considerations of mercy).

Then there is the fact that the pope praises increasing opposition to the death penalty "*even* as an instrument of *legitimate* social defence" on the grounds that "*modern societies* have the ability to effectively control crime without definitively taking away a criminal's chance to redeem himself." This seems a clear nod to Pope Saint John Paul II's view that capital punishment is indeed legitimate *in principle* but generally unnecessary under modern circumstances. It seems plausible that if Pope Francis had intended to make the novel claim that capital punishment is *always and intrinsically* wrong, he would not have used the adjective "legitimate" or made reference to the circumstances of "modern societies".

Hence it is doubtful that Pope Francis intended in the first place to say anything in this address that is at odds with the traditional teaching of the Church. At any rate, as we have seen, that teaching cannot be changed.

It is worth adding that Pope Francis has become well known for making remarks that are very striking and even startling but not always doctrinally precise. The pope often seems to have merely pastoral ends in mind when he speaks, rather than the issuing of binding theological formulas. Commenting on the controversy that the pope's remarks on various subjects have sometimes generated, Cardinal Gerhard Müller, prefect of the Congregation for the Doctrine of the Faith under Pope Francis, has noted that "Pope Francis is not a 'professional theologian', but has been largely formed by his experiences in the field of the pastoral care."[173] Asked if he has sometimes had to correct the pope's remarks from a doctrinal point of view, the cardinal replied: "That is what he [Pope Francis] has said already three or four times himself, publicly." Cardinal Müller also emphasized that the pope himself "refers to the teaching of the Church as the framework of interpretation" for his various remarks. In another interview in which he was asked about Pope Francis' sometimes doctrinally imprecise statements, Cardinal Müller acknowledged that churchmen sometimes "express themselves in a somewhat inappropriate, misleading or vague way" and that not all papal pronouncements have the same binding nature.[174] Indeed, Pope Francis himself has acknowledged that some of his public remarks are open to legitimate criticism.[175]

It is also worth noting that New Natural Law theorists have been among those who have criticized Pope Francis' remarks on various subjects for their lack of doctrinal precision, or even for their appearance of contradicting past teaching. For example, Christopher

---

[173] Cardinal Müller's remarks were made in the course of a March 1, 2016, interview with the German newspaper *Kölner Stadt-Anzeiger*. The English translation of the remarks is quoted from Maike Hickson, "Vatican's Doctrine Chief: Pope Is Not a 'Professional Theologian'", *LifeSiteNews.com*, March 14, 2016.

[174] These remarks were made in the course of an interview with the German magazine *Die Zeit*, December 30, 2015.

[175] Cf. John L. Allen Jr., "Under Francis, There's a New Dogma: Papal Fallibility", *Cruxnow .com*, July 13, 2015.

Tollefsen and E. Christian Brugger have argued that some remarks made by Pope Francis on the use of contraception as a means of dealing with the Zika virus cannot be reconciled with binding Catholic teaching on the grave immorality of contraception.[176] Commenting on Pope Francis' famous September 30, 2013, interview with Fr. Antonio Spadaro (wherein the pope stated that the Church "cannot be obsessed with the transmission of a disjointed multitude of doctrines to be imposed insistently"), Germain Grisez complained that Francis' remarks were "bound to confuse and mislead" and that the pope "has failed to consider carefully enough the likely consequences of letting loose with his thoughts".[177]

Given that both Pope Francis himself and his chief doctrinal officer, Cardinal Müller, have acknowledged that the pope's public remarks are not always doctrinally precise, it would be highly implausible to regard the pope's more striking statements on capital punishment as even *intended* to be read as doctrinal statements of any sort, much less as reversals or developments of Catholic doctrine. They are far more plausibly seen as merely pastoral in intention. Moreover, given their own public criticisms of some of Pope Francis' remarks on doctrinal matters, new natural law theorists such as Brugger, Tollefsen, and Grisez could hardly appeal in good faith to Pope Francis' remarks on capital punishment in support of their own call for reversing past Church teaching on the subject. Indeed, as far as we know, these new natural lawyers have not claimed that Pope Francis' remarks support their position or mark any doctrinal development vis-à-vis capital punishment.

We conclude, then, that Pope Francis' various remarks on this subject cannot plausibly be read as having in any way altered Catholic doctrine on the death penalty. They represent, rather, what we have called category-5 magisterial statements (or type-b prudential judgments)—that is, statements of a prudential sort on matters about which there may be a legitimate diversity of opinion among

---

[176] Christopher Tollefsen, "Pope Francis, the Zika Virus, and Contraception", *Public Discourse*, February 23, 2016, http://www.thepublicdiscourse.com/2016/02/16517/; and E. Christian Brugger, "Pope Francis and Contraception: A Troubling Scenario", *National Catholic Register*, February 24, 2016.

[177] Grisez's remarks were made in a letter to Robert Moynihan, which was published on the blog *The Moynihan Letters* on September 29, 2013. The English translation of the pope's interview with Spadaro was published in the September 30, 2013, issue of *America*.

Catholics. Catholics must respectfully consider such statements by the Holy Father, but they need not agree with them.

Two conflicting prudential judgments

Our survey of the evidence from Scripture, the Fathers and Doctors of the Church, and the teaching of the popes has, we think, established the following. First, it is the consensus teaching of Scripture, of the Fathers and Doctors of the Church, and of the popes—and thus the irreformable teaching of the Church—that capital punishment is not intrinsically immoral and can in principle be justifiably inflicted by the state on criminals guilty of the gravest offenses. Second, it is the clear teaching, not only of many saints, Doctors of the Church, and popes, but also of Scripture and the Fathers—and thus is also the irreformable teaching of the Church—that capital punishment can in principle be justifiable for purposes other than directly securing the physical safety of the community against an aggressor, such as for the sake of retributive justice (the upholding of which, we have argued, itself indirectly promotes the safety of the community). Third, given the emphasis on retributive justice present in Scripture, the Fathers and Doctors of the Church, and the popes, as well as the Church's official commitment to natural law as understood by thinkers such as Aquinas, the Church's teaching on capital punishment is best understood in light of the traditional natural law account we expounded and defended in chapter 1. Fourth, given the strong preference of some of the Fathers and popes for mercy over resort to the death penalty, the Church rejects not only the extreme new natural law position according to which capital punishment is always wrong, but also the opposite, Kantian extreme position, according to which capital punishment must always be inflicted when deserved. Fifth, whether and to what extent resort to capital punishment is called for in any particular time and place is *essentially* a matter of prudential judgment and not a matter of doctrinal principle. Hence, in the words of Cardinal Ratzinger, "there may be a legitimate diversity of opinion even among Catholics about ... applying the death penalty"—now and always, in the very nature of the case.

We have also seen that there are two broad prudential judgments that have been defended in the history of the Church. The first, reflected in much of Scripture, in Doctors of the Church such as Aquinas and Bellarmine, and in the *Roman Catechism* and the teaching of popes such as Pius XII, holds that capital punishment is bound to be called for with some frequency. The second, reflected in the Fathers, in Doctors such as Ambrose and Augustine, and in the new *Catechism* and the teaching of popes such as John Paul II, holds that though capital punishment is legitimate in principle, in practice it ought very rarely if ever to be resorted to.

Clearly, the second attitude is the dominant one in the Church in recent decades. But with all due respect to Pope Saint John Paul II and other contemporary churchmen, we believe this is a mistake, and a serious one. We believe that there are very good arguments, not only for keeping the death penalty on the books, but for applying it with some frequency. We also believe that there are no good arguments for abolishing or severely restricting its use, and that some of the arguments for abolition are not only bad but highly damaging both to society and to the credibility of the Church. Let us consider each of these points in turn:

1. The arguments in favor of capital punishment are powerful.

In chapter 1 we spelled out in detail the traditional natural law justification of capital punishment. We will not repeat those arguments, but a brief summary is in order. We have shown how, according to the traditional natural law theory favored by the Church, both punishment and our inclination to inflict it are natural and good and that punishment is fundamentally retributive and ought to be proportional to the gravity of the offense. We have shown how, given these premises, it follows unavoidably that some offenders merit a penalty of death. There is therefore a presumption in favor of execution for certain grave offenses, and though this presumption can be overridden if there is greater good to be obtained by showing mercy, it should not be overridden if there are significant goods to be achieved by execution over and above retribution—in particular, if execution would further the other ends of punishment.

We also noted how capital punishment does indeed significantly further the other ends of punishment. Obviously it protects society insofar as those who are executed can no longer harm others. It also cannot reasonably be doubted that it has at least *some* deterrent effect, even if the precise amount is a matter of controversy. For one thing, what Louis Pojman calls "commonsense and anecdotal evidence" and Steven Goldberg calls "informal evidence" shows that in general, the more severe a penalty, the less likely people are to engage in the behavior penalized. It is simply unreasonable, then, to doubt that capital punishment will deter at least many people in a way lesser punishments would not. Only a vulgar scientism (which no Catholic can accept) could motivate someone to dismiss this commonsense evidence and suppose that formal social-scientific evidence alone could justify the judgment that capital punishment deters.

For another thing, we have argued that it is a crude mistake to think that deterrence is exclusively or even primarily a matter of affecting the calculations that a potential offender will carry out in the moment in which he is considering committing a crime. It is, more fundamentally, a matter of instilling in the citizenry a revulsion against crime so deep that most citizens would not even consider committing it in the first place. As James Fitzjames Stephen wrote:

> Some men, probably, abstain from murder because they fear that if they committed murder they would be hanged. Hundreds of thousands abstain from it because they regard it with horror. One great reason why they regard it with horror is that murderers are hanged with the hearty approbation of all reasonable men. Men are so constituted that the energy of their moral sentiments is greatly increased by the fact that they are embodied in a concrete form.[178]

Now, it simply cannot reasonably be denied that capital punishment reinforces a horror of crimes such as murder. Opponents of capital punishment themselves inadvertently testify to this fact when they express the worry that capital punishment is an expression of hatred for the offender. As we have argued, this need not, in fact, be the case; whereas some who favor capital punishment might be motivated by hatred, others are simply motivated by a desire to see justice done. But there would not even be a danger of hatred unless the offenders who are executed are regarded as having done something

---

[178] James Fitzjames Stephen, *A General View of the Criminal Law in England* (London: Macmillan, 1863), pp. 99–100.

hateful, something unusually wicked and contemptible, something beyond the pale. Capital punishment does indeed reinforce the sense within society that certain crimes are unusually hateful, wicked, contemptible, beyond the pale—and having that sense is a good and healthy thing, for it makes it less likely that people will even consider committing such crimes.

Now, Christopher Kaczor, who favors restricting or abolishing capital punishment, allows that it is at least arguable that capital punishment deters, but judges that "at best the jury is out, and in cases of doubt, one should err on the side of not taking human life."[179] But as we have argued, following Ernest van den Haag, this is precisely the wrong conclusion to draw. If we are going to err, we should rather err on the side of protecting *innocent* life, and that means resorting to capital punishment even if we are not certain that it deters. For if capital punishment does deter and we fail to make use of it, then this failure will result in the deaths of innocent people, whose murderers we would have deterred had we made use of capital punishment. Whereas if we make use of capital punishment and it does not deter, then those who are executed will still have deserved death anyway. Since it is not wrong to execute those deserving of death but it is wrong to fail to prevent the murder of the innocent when we can do so, we should act on the assumption that the death penalty deters.

As we have argued, capital punishment also affords the benefit of providing for a lawful outlet for society's natural (and therefore per se good) desire to see criminals get their just deserts. If even the most cruel and sadistic offenders are permitted to live, a significant portion of society is bound to regard this as a travesty of justice, will doubt the moral legitimacy of any government or society that permits such travesties, and will be tempted to take the law into its own hands. Far from being a remedy for vengeance and hatred, abolitionism is a recipe for encouraging vigilantism.

Finally, capital punishment serves even the rehabilitative end of punishment insofar as it can motivate an offender both to acknowledge the gravity of his crime and to repent and seek his peace with God while he still has time remaining to him. As Samuel Johnson famously put it, "Depend upon it, sir, when a man knows he is to be

---

[179] Kaczor, "Capital Punishment", p. 293.

hanged in a fortnight, it concentrates his mind wonderfully." And as Aquinas argues, if offenders "are so stubborn that even at the point of death their heart does not draw back from evil, it is possible to make a highly probable judgment that they would never come away from evil to the right use of their powers".[180] Indeed, some offenders are only *hardened* in evil by an extended time in prison or will delay repentance as long as they suppose the time remaining to them is indefinitely long. As even Brugger admits:

> Catholic pastors—usually priests—as a rule have ministered to condemned criminals and as a result have been privy to a long train of gallows-side conversions. These conversions can be attributed largely to the pressing influence of the future punishment on the criminal's mind and conscience (as Sister Helen Prejean's celebrated testimony graphically illustrates).[181]

As we have seen, in *Evangelium Vitae*, Pope Saint John Paul II wrote of the need, in inflicting punishment, to fulfill its *purposes* and not merely its retributive end. We maintain that the best arguments show that it is precisely a criminal justice system in which the death penalty plays a significant part that best realizes *all* of the purposes of punishment.

2. There are no good arguments against capital punishment.

In chapter 1 we considered in detail many of the standard objections to capital punishment: that it violates the right to life, is contrary to human dignity, erodes respect for human life, is motivated by vengeance, has no deterrent value, removes the possibility of reform, is something the state has no authority to carry out, and is bound to be inflicted on innocent people. We have shown that these objections reflect a failure to make careful distinctions, involve circular reasoning or non sequiturs, rest on dubious empirical claims, or are otherwise without force. We have also shown that objections to capital punishment often presuppose ethical theories—such as consequentialism, proportionalism, contractarian political philosophy, and new

---

[180] *Summa Contra Gentiles* III, 146.
[181] Brugger, *Capital Punishment*, p. 34.

natural law theory—that are philosophically dubious or irreconcilable with the teaching of the Church, or both.

There are other common objections to capital punishment that are of a less abstract or philosophical sort but appeal to research in social science or other empirical claims. For example, it is often alleged that the death penalty is inflicted arbitrarily rather than in a uniform or principled way, or in a manner that is racially discriminatory or biased against the poor and uneducated. Even if these claims were true, they would argue not for abolishing capital punishment but for applying it more equitably. But in fact, as we argue in later chapters, these claims are not supported by evidence. It is also sometimes claimed that there is positive social-scientific evidence against the deterrence value of capital punishment and that a significant number of innocent people have been executed. We will see in later chapters that those claims do not stand up to the evidence either.

Then there are the theological objections raised by churchmen and others against capital punishment. As we have seen, it is sometimes claimed that abolition of capital punishment will contribute to "building a culture of life" in which the lives of the innocent, such as the victims of abortion and euthanasia, are more likely to be respected. As far as we can see, there is no evidence whatsoever for this claim, and compelling evidence against it. Abortion and euthanasia were much *rarer* in Western societies when capital punishment was more common, and they have become more common in Western society precisely as support for capital punishment has diminished. Indeed, as we noted above, those who are most strongly opposed to abortion and euthanasia seem most likely to support capital punishment, whereas those who most strongly oppose capital punishment also most strongly support abortion and euthanasia (not always, of course, but in general). In fact, there appears to be a *negative* correlation between opposition to capital punishment and respect for innocent life, exactly contrary to what the "culture of life" rhetoric would suggest.

This should not be in any way surprising. Those in contemporary Western society who are most likely to oppose abortion and euthanasia are, of course, those who are also most likely to sympathize with traditional natural law reasoning or the teaching of Scripture, or both. But precisely because they sympathize with traditional natural law reasoning or the teaching of Scripture—both of which strongly support capital punishment—these opponents of abortion and euthanasia are bound (not always, but in general) to support capital punishment. Meanwhile, those who are most strongly opposed to capital punishment tend also to be strongly opposed to traditional morality and traditional religious belief. Precisely because of this opposition, though, opponents of capital punishment will also tend (again, not always, but in general) to support abortion and euthanasia. So, the suggestion that opposition to capital punishment is a natural part of "building a culture of life" appears to be neither true to the sociological facts, nor at all plausible in light of the radically incompatible philosophical, moral, and religious premises that underlie most opposition to abortion and euthanasia, on the one hand, and most opposition to capital punishment on the other.

As we have also noted, it is sometimes suggested that modern secular societies lack the moral premises necessary for a proper understanding of the ethics of capital punishment, insofar as they deny that political authority comes from God or that morality is grounded in natural law. But there are three problems with this objection. First, it would prove too much. Modern secular societies also lack the moral premises necessary for a proper understanding of taxation, national defense, imprisonment, and the other functions of government. But no one would suggest that we should therefore abolish taxation, the military, the criminal justice system, and so forth. Second, the objection is simply a non sequitur. If modern secular society lacks the moral premises necessary for a proper understanding of the ethics of capital punishment, this argues not for abolishing capital punishment but for promoting a more compelling articulation and defense of the moral premises in question. Third, the objection overstates the magnitude of the problem. There is, especially in the United States, very strong resistance to secularism and sympathy for traditional morality and religion in large segments of society, and particularly among those most inclined to support capital punishment. Opposition to capital punishment will only weaken this attachment to traditional morality and religion, not strengthen it, and will demoralize rather than embolden those committed to sound moral and religious premises. Furthermore, and as we noted earlier, ancient pagan cultures in some ways exhibited an even lower regard for innocent human life than ours insofar as they tolerated infanticide, blood sports, and slavery.

Yet this did not prevent Christians such as Saint Paul from upholding capital punishment in the context of such societies, nor did it prevent such societies from moving toward a more Christian (and thus more just) application of the death penalty. So, there simply is no reason to think that our society is somehow so uniquely beyond the pale that it cannot be trusted properly to apply capital punishment.

Nor do appeals to Christian forgiveness and mercy have force. If this were a serious objection to capital punishment, it would constitute a serious objection to *all* punishment, but no one thinks that Christian forgiveness and mercy should lead us to do away with prisons, fines, and punishment in general. With the death penalty, as with other punishments, Christian forgiveness and mercy might moderate, but cannot entirely override, the demands of criminal justice and the public good. As Cardinal Dulles has written:

> It is indeed praiseworthy for victims of crime to forgive their debtors, but such personal pardon does not absolve offenders from their obligations in justice. John Paul II points out that "reparation for evil and scandal, compensation for injury, and satisfaction for insult are conditions for forgiveness."
>
> The relationship of the State to the criminal is not the same as that of a victim to an assailant. Governors and judges are responsible for maintaining a just public order. Their primary obligation is toward justice, but under certain conditions they may exercise clemency. In a careful discussion of this matter Pius XII concluded that the State ought not to issue pardons except when it is morally certain that the ends of punishment have been achieved. Under these conditions, requirements of public policy may warrant a partial or full remission of punishment. If clemency were granted to all convicts, the nation's prisons would be instantly emptied, but society would not be well served.
>
> In practice, then, a delicate balance between justice and mercy must be maintained. The State's primary responsibility is for justice, although it may at times temper justice with mercy.[182]

3. Abolishing capital punishment would do grave harm to society.

There are several respects in which the abolition of capital punishment would seriously harm society. First, as we have argued, it cannot

---

[182] Dulles, "Catholicism and Capital Punishment", p. 34.

reasonably be denied that the death penalty has some significant deterrence value—to some extent insofar as it influences the calculations of those who are considering committing serious crimes, but more importantly insofar as it reinforces the horror of those crimes that keeps most of us from even considering committing them in the first place. Abolishing capital punishment would therefore mean the sacrifice of the lives of those innocent victims who would have been saved had their murderers been deterred.

Second, the abolition of capital punishment would seriously undermine a sound understanding of justice in general. As we argued in chapter 1, punishment in general and capital punishment in particular stand or fall together. To affirm the legitimacy of punishment is to affirm the legitimacy of retributive justice and the principle of proportionality, and therefore implicitly to affirm that a penalty of death can in some cases be legitimate. To deny that such a penalty can be legitimate is thus implicitly to deny the legitimacy of retribution and proportionality and therefore implicitly to deny the legitimacy of punishment itself. Now, if capital punishment were abolished on the grounds that it is inherently immoral—and surely most abolitionists oppose it precisely because they think it *is* inherently immoral—then this could not fail to weaken within society the general sense of the justice of retribution, and thus of the justice of punishment itself. And if a sense of the legitimacy of retributive punishment is weakened, this can in turn lead only to the weakening of the very idea of punishment or to a reconceptualization of punishment in essentially consequentialist terms, with all the dangers that (as C. S. Lewis argued, as we saw in chapter 1) follow upon such a conception. The result would be either a trend toward excessive leniency (if the very idea of punishment were abandoned or weakened) or a trend toward excessive harshness (if a consequentialist attitude were to dominate, so that considerations about "what works" supplanted considerations about what an offender deserves).

The same outcome is bound to follow, regardless of the views and motives of most opponents of capital punishment. In an age when most offenses, whatever their character, are punished with jail time or fines, the death penalty is by far the clearest instance—perhaps the only one—of a punishment that clearly "fits the crime". It teaches the reality and nature of retributive justice and proportionality as no other punishment does or can. It therefore provides an indispensable moral and conceptual "anchor" for the sense of justice in a society. When that anchor is removed, the general sense of justice cannot fail to go with it. That punishment is fundamentally a matter of proportional retribution will no longer be palpable to society as a whole, and either the idea of punishment as such will come to seem suspect, or proportionality will be replaced by a consequentialist conception of justice. The law is a moral teacher, and, especially in modern times, it can teach proportional retribution via capital punishment with an effectiveness that no other means affords. Hence, even supposing that a movement toward abolitionism were led by people who acknowledged that capital punishment is legitimate in principle but merely opposed it on prudential grounds (a supposition we think is sociologically highly implausible), it is unlikely that a sound conception of criminal justice could survive abolition.

Then there is the fact that abolition would leave society without a lawful outlet for its natural desire to see justice done, and, as James Fitzjames Stephen, Joseph Rickaby, and Louis Pojman argue (as we saw in chapter 1), this is damaging to the health of society, as it would be damaging to society if marriage were forbidden and no lawful outlet were provided for the fulfillment of our natural sexual impulses. Forbidding such an outlet in the latter case would inevitably lead to sexual frustration followed by sexual excess, with all of its bad social consequences. Something similar is true of the denial of a lawful outlet for people's natural desire to see criminals get their just deserts. It is simply part of human nature to feel a deep and abiding sense of injustice when men as wicked and unrepentant as Saddam Hussein and Osama bin Laden, John Wayne Gacy and Richard Allen Davis are permitted to live. Smugly to be told that letting such monsters live is what human dignity requires, and that the average person's natural outrage and desire to see justice done is somehow indecent, is to have insult added to this injured sense of justice. Some citizens may be inclined when the next murderer comes around to preempt the justice system with acts of vigilantism, convinced that the lynch mob alone can secure the justice that the state refuses to pursue. Like the tendency to regard sex as per se shameful, abolitionism reflects an otherworldly puritanism, not the sober realism that is the hallmark of Catholic thinking at its best.

In other ways too, abolitionism tends both to reflect and to foster attitudes that are deeply antithetical to a Catholic understanding of moral and social order. Brugger admits that modern abolitionism had its origins precisely in philosophical ideas and social movements hostile to Catholicism, such as the thought of Voltaire, Diderot, Hume, and Bentham, in social contract theory and utilitarianism, in the loss of belief in the afterlife and a consequent emphasis on prolonging this life, and in Enlightenment and secularist thinking in general.[183] Cardinal Dulles nicely summarizes the long-standing historical relationship between abolitionism, on the one hand, and heretical and secularist anti-Catholic thinking on the other:

> The abolitionist position ... has been held by sectarian Christians at least since the Middle Ages. Many pacifist groups, such as the Waldensians, the Quakers, the Hutterites, and the Mennonites, have shared this point of view. But, like pacifism itself, this absolutist interpretation of the right to life found no echo at the time among Catholic theologians, who accepted the death penalty as consonant with Scripture, tradition, and the natural law.
>
> The mounting opposition to the death penalty in Europe since the Enlightenment has gone hand in hand with a decline of faith in eternal life. In the nineteenth century the most consistent supporters of capital punishment were the Christian churches, and its most consistent opponents were groups hostile to the churches. When death came to be understood as the ultimate evil rather than as a stage on the way to eternal life, utilitarian philosophers such as Jeremy Bentham found it easy to dismiss capital punishment as "useless annihilation."
>
> Many governments in Europe and elsewhere have eliminated the death penalty in the twentieth century, often against the protests of religious believers. While this change may be viewed as moral progress, it is probably due, in part, to the evaporation of the sense of sin, guilt, and retributive justice, all of which are essential to biblical religion and Catholic faith. The abolition of the death penalty in formerly Christian countries may owe more to secular humanism than to deeper penetration into the gospel.
>
> Arguments from the progress of ethical consciousness have been used to promote a number of alleged human rights that the Catholic Church consistently rejects in the name of Scripture and tradition.

[183] Brugger, *Capital Punishment*, pp. 130–31.

The magisterium appeals to these authorities as grounds for repudiating divorce, abortion, homosexual relations, and the ordination of women to the priesthood. If the Church feels herself bound by Scripture and tradition in these other areas, it seems inconsistent for Catholics to proclaim a "moral revolution" [in the direction of abolitionism] on the issue of capital punishment.[184]

We believe that the arguments we have marshaled in the previous chapter and in this one amply demonstrate that this historical relationship is no accident. It is also no accident that within the contemporary Western world, support for capital punishment is much stronger in the (still largely religious) United States than it is in (now largely secularized) Europe. As we noted above, since classical natural law reasoning and Catholic Tradition firmly support the legitimacy of capital punishment, there is bound to be a strong correlation between hostility to capital punishment and hostility to classical natural law reasoning and Catholic orthodoxy. The correlation is not without exceptions, of course, but it is undeniably very strong. Hence it is inevitable that a tendency toward abolitionism within a society will tend to reflect, and to reinforce, a trajectory away from theological orthodoxy and traditional morality. Abolitionism thus inadvertently provides powerful "aid and comfort" to ideas and movements that any Catholic must regard as morally and socially destructive.

4. The contemporary Catholic trend toward abolitionism damages the credibility of the Church.

As we have argued, Pope Saint John Paul II's teaching on capital punishment in *Evangelium Vitae* and the *Catechism* is consistent with Catholic Tradition and represents a prudential judgment rather than a reversal or development of doctrine. We have also suggested, however, that in certain respects it could have been formulated with greater clarity and precision. And we have noted that some of the pope's less formal and less authoritative statements (such as his remark that capital punishment is "cruel and unnecessary") have been even less precise.

Other churchmen routinely condemn capital punishment in terms that are more imprecise still, and harder to reconcile with Scripture

[184] Dulles, "Catholicism and Capital Punishment", p. 32.

and Tradition. For example, in 2011 the Catholic bishops of Colorado issued a statement opposing capital punishment, in part on the grounds that "all people have a natural right to life, because every human being is made in the image and likeness of God." Yet Genesis 9:6 teaches that man's being made in the image of God is precisely a reason to *support* capital punishment rather than a reason to oppose it. How would the bishops reconcile their position with Scripture? And if our having a right to life is a reason to oppose capital punishment, is our having a right to property and a right to personal liberty a reason to oppose fining and imprisoning offenders? The bishops do not answer such obvious objections and do not even seem to be aware that their arguments are in any way problematic.

Examples could easily be multiplied. Catholic churchmen now ritualistically denounce capital punishment, typically by appealing to stock arguments that, as we have shown, are of extremely poor quality and sometimes irreconcilable with the teaching of Scripture and Catholic Tradition. Often they offer no arguments at all but resort to mere platitudes. The content of the remarks often seems to have less to do with scriptural teaching or natural law reasoning than with conventional wisdom about crime and punishment prevailing within liberal and secularist circles. Sometimes, as with Pope Francis' condemnation of life imprisonment, the remarks on the subject of crime and punishment might even seem, if not significantly qualified, to defy common sense.

Occasionally there are exceptions. Cardinal Avery Dulles, though he agreed with Pope Saint John Paul II's prudential judgment about the death penalty, repeatedly cautioned that contemporary teaching on the subject of capital punishment must maintain continuity with Scripture and Tradition.[185] Fr. George Rutler is a prominent churchman who not only supports capital punishment but has also been critical of the inclusion within the 1997 *Catechism* of what amounts to a prudential judgment.[186] Fr. Richard John Neuhaus emphasized that "Catholics ... may in good faith disagree over whether the death penalty is necessary for the defense of society" and that "many ...

---

[185] Dulles, "Catholicism and Capital Punishment" and "Catholic Teaching on the Death Penalty".

[186] Rutler, "Scalia's Right" and "Hanging Concentrates the Mind".

people ... depend upon the constancy of the Church's teaching."[187] In 1977, Francis Furey, the archbishop of San Antonio, stated:

> To those who say "Capital punishment is not a deterrent to crime" I say this is a lot of hogwash. Without capital punishment and swift justice life would have been unlivable in the pioneer days of our West. It would be unlivable today in vast areas of the wastelands of the world. ...
>
> What about the position, if any, of the Catholic Church with regard to the death penalty? The truth of the matter is that there is no such position. It is a divisive issue in the church in this country. Perhaps that is as it should be. There are arguments on both sides. ...
>
> The church has always supported the right of the state to impose the death penalty in order to protect itself and its citizens. The question is when and in what manner this right should be used. In the humble opinion of this writer, the when is now and the manner depends on circumstances. I am thoroughly convinced that people who commit heinous crimes, such as brutal murder, and other crimes against society, should be made to pay with their most precious possession, their life. Only in this way can the punishment be made to fit crime.[188]

The overwhelming tendency of Catholic churchmen today, however, is not only toward opposition to capital punishment, but opposition that presents Catholic teaching in a manner that is simplistic, one-sided, incomplete, unrigorous, and indeed often reckless. We speculate that part of the reason for this is the enormous pressure Catholic churchmen face from the surrounding secular and liberal culture. The firm and unalterable opposition of the Church to abortion, euthanasia, homosexual behavior and "same-sex marriage", divorce and remarriage, fornication, and other practices common in contemporary society puts Catholic bishops in the position of facing relentless and harsh criticism from opinion makers, political activists, academics, and dissidents within the Church. The temptation to find *some* common ground, *some* way to seem to the wider culture to be progressive rather than reactionary, can be overwhelming. Vigorous opposition to the death penalty appears to them to fit the bill.

---

[187] Richard John Neuhaus, "The Public Square", *First Things* 56 (October 1995): 83–84.

[188] "Statement on the Death Penalty", USCCB website, http://www.usccb.org/issues-and-action/human-life-and-dignity/death-penalty-capital-punishment/statement-by-bishop-furey-on-the-death-penalty-1977.cfm.

No doubt churchmen think they are doing the Church some good, but we would argue that they are in fact doing great harm, in several ways. First, as we have shown, the standard arguments against the death penalty, which churchmen who oppose capital punishment have tended to adopt uncritically, are simply no good. As Aquinas famously said, we should always avoid presenting bad arguments for theological claims, lest we "furnish infidels with an occasion for scoffing".[189] When churchmen put these arguments forward with such vigor and give the false impression that every Catholic must agree with them, many people of goodwill who might otherwise be attracted to the Church are bound to be put off. They will, wrongly but understandably, conclude that to be a Catholic one must accept a teaching that seems to them clearly to be false and poorly argued for. Then there are those who are *not* otherwise attracted to the Church. Atheist critics of the Church allege that her claim to indefectibility and unbroken continuity in doctrine is a myth. Protestant critics falsely accuse the Church of contradicting Scripture and the popes of manufacturing doctrine by fiat. When churchmen say things about capital punishment that seem to contradict Scripture and past teaching, they lend credibility to these accusations.

Meanwhile, many faithful Catholics are bound to be left confused and troubled, Some, falsely supposing that the Church has contradicted Scripture and Tradition and thereby falsified her claim to indefectibility, or that to be a Catholic one must accept a teaching they believe is clearly false, might lose their faith. By contrast, dissident Catholics are emboldened by the sharp turn against capital punishment and suppose that it opens the door to changes in Church doctrine regarding homosexuality, ordination of women, divorce and remarriage, and so on.

We do not expect all Catholics to agree with our judgment that capital punishment is called for with some regularity even under contemporary circumstances. Like Pope Benedict XVI, we believe there can be legitimate disagreement among Catholics on this subject. We do maintain, though, that the pendulum has gone too far in the abolitionist direction and that those aspects of Catholic tradition favorable to capital punishment have in recent decades not received sufficient

---

[189] *ST* I, 46, 2.

attention. Balance needs to be restored. Catholics, and especially Catholic churchmen, who make the prudential judgment that capital punishment should in contemporary circumstances be "very rare, if not practically non-existent" should be careful not to present this position as if it were anything *more* than a prudential judgment, and should be careful always to respect the "hermeneutic of continuity".

3

Serving Justice in This World and
Salvation in the Next

On April 11, 2012, the seven Catholic bishops of the state of Florida called on Governor Rick Scott to stop the execution of convicted murderer David Alan Gore. They asked Scott "to resist the natural instinct to punish [Gore's] evil deeds ... with the ultimate penalty— death by lethal injection".[1] The bishops acknowledged that they too felt "anger, revulsion" at "Gore's heinous crimes", "but responding to murder by killing the criminal sanctions violence". "The claim for justice", they held, "needs to be balanced by mercy." Here the bishops seemed to concede that Gore did indeed deserve to die for his crimes but that mercy trumped justice. Yet they pointed to nothing about the circumstances of the crimes or anything in Gore's life history to justify punishing him less than justice demanded. Indeed, in their very next sentence they maintained that "society can be protected and justice served by keeping Mr. Gore in prison until his natural death." Yet, as we shall see momentarily, Gore's crimes were so horrific that, in our view, no reasonable person could claim that life in prison would have been a proportional, and thus a just, punishment for Gore's acts.

In the second paragraph of their brief 220-word statement, the bishops seemed to reduce justice to mere revenge: "Revenge does not bring peace, only forgiveness as proclaimed by our Lord on the cross when he said, 'Forgive them, Father! They don't know what they are doing.' (Luke 23:34)." As we have seen in the previous chapter, Catholic teaching at least since the time of Paul's Letter to the Romans has consistently distinguished the personal desire of victims to inflict pain

[1] Press release, "Florida Bishops Appeal to Governor Scott to Stop Execution of David Alan Gore", April 11, 2012, http://www.flaccb.org/documents/2015/8/120411GoreExecution .pdf.

on their offenders from the duty of the state to protect public order by exacting retribution for serious crimes. Yet here the Florida bishops made no such distinction and seemed to imply that retribution is no more than vengeance, which must be replaced by forgiveness. But if all are forgiven, why is anyone punished at all? What principle, if any, justifies punishing even violent offenders? And what principle, one may well ask, would justify confining Gore in prison for his natural life?

In their third and final paragraph the bishops affirmed that "all human life has dignity and is sacred, created in God's image, even those who have done great harm. Violence begets violence and coarsens the culture so that life is no longer valued as a gift from God." Apparently, executing even the vilest of murderers is an affront to the sacredness of human life and makes for a more violent society. This position, as we have seen, is contradicted by God's command to Noah and his sons in Genesis 9:6—where the sacredness of the *victim's* life ("a gift from God", as the bishops rightly say) *demands* the death penalty for murderers—and is radically inconsistent with two thousand years of Catholic teaching. As the bishops concluded their statement, "Today, we are able to protect society and also give criminals a chance to reform and repent. Governor, we ask you to stay the execution of David Alan Gore." In their concern for the reformation and repentance of murderers, the bishops were, of course, echoing an essential element of long-standing Catholic teaching. A key question, as we noted in an earlier chapter, is whether the death penalty, compared with life in prison, makes repentance (and thus the offender's salvation) less likely or more likely: less likely by shortening the time the offender has to get right with his Maker, or more likely by spurring the kind of soul-searching that the prospect of imminent death may occasion.

In the next chapter, we examine in some detail the campaign against the death penalty by American Catholic bishops, especially through the United States Conference of Catholic Bishops (USCCB). There we assess the range of theological and prudential arguments that the bishops advance to justify abolition. In this chapter, we focus on two key issues raised by the opposition of the Florida bishops to Gore's execution, issues that are central to the Catholic debate on capital punishment: (1) whether the death penalty is the only punishment that can reasonably be considered just and proportionate for the specific kinds of murders that result in execution in the United States and (2) whether the death penalty positively promotes the salvation of offenders. We argue that, at least in many cases, the answer to both questions is clearly in the affirmative.

We begin with the issue of just punishment, taking as case studies the details of Gore's crimes and those of other offenders of the sort typically condemned to death today in the United States. We warn the reader in advance that these details are in some cases highly disturbing. But consideration of such details is simply unavoidable if we are responsibly to address the question of what would be a just and proportionate punishment for these crimes. It is also absolutely essential to addressing the question (also explored in the next chapter) of whether capital punishment, not merely in principle but also as it is applied concretely in the United States today, is just. For to have a well-informed opinion about whether it is just, we need to know exactly what sorts of offenders are being executed today.

Proportionate Punishment: The 43 Murderers Executed in 2012

Key case studies

1. David Alan Gore

In the 1970s David Alan Gore and his cousin Fred Waterfield began abducting and raping women in and around Vero Beach, Florida. Waterfield paid Gore $1,000 to find pretty victims.[2] In February 1981, Gore flashed a badge he had from his job as an auxiliary sheriff's

---

[2] The details of Gore's crimes presented here are from the court records in his case as included in materials on executions in the United States compiled by the prosecuting attorney of Clark County, Indiana. For information on all executions between 1977 and 2014, visit www.clarkprosecutor.org/html/death/usexecute.htm. For information on David Alan Gore, visit www.clarkprosecutor.org/html/death/US/gore1290.htm. For additional information on Gore's crimes, including details disclosed in letters he wrote from prison, and their effects on the victims' loved ones and on the young girl who survived his last crime, see Pete Earley, *The Serial Killer Whisperer* (New York: Simon and Schuster, 2012), pp. 3, 118–37, 150–54, 226–69, 309–10, 319–23.

deputy and tricked a seventeen-year-old girl into getting into his car. After driving her to her home, Gore pretended to arrest her forty-eight-year-old mother and handcuffed her to her daughter. He drove the women to a citrus orchard, where he and his cousin raped and murdered them, killing the mother by tying her up in such a way that she slowly choked herself to death while struggling to break free. Five months later, responding to Waterfield's request to find a blonde, Gore offered to help a thirty-five-year-old woman whose vehicle, parked at an isolated beach, he had disabled. She accepted a ride to get help, but once she was inside the pickup truck, Gore pulled a gun on her and handcuffed her. He called Waterfield to arrange to meet at the orchard. There Gore and Waterfield raped and murdered her and "fed her to the alligators" by throwing her body into a swamp. Pleased with Gore's choice, Waterfield paid him $1,500. Within a few weeks of this crime police arrested Gore for armed trespass when they found him crouched in the backseat of a woman's car with a pistol, handcuffs, and a police scanner. He was sentenced to prison and paroled less than two years later. In May 1983, two months after his release, Gore and Waterfield picked up two fourteen-year-old female hitchhikers and raped and murdered them. They dismembered one body, burying it in a shallow grave, and dumped the other in a nearby canal.

On July 26, 1983, Gore and his cousin picked up two teenage girls, fourteen and seventeen, who were hitchhiking to the beach. They took the girls at gunpoint to Gore's parents' house. Once there, Gore bound each of the girls and placed them in separate bedrooms. Gore sexually assaulted the girls multiple times. At one point the seventeen-year-old escaped and ran from the house naked, with her hands still tied behind her back. A fifteen-year-old neighbor riding by on his bicycle saw Gore chase down the girl, drag her back toward the house, and shoot her twice in the head. The boy's mother called the police, who were able to rescue the fourteen-year-old and apprehend Gore (Waterfield had already left). After his arrest Gore admitted to the five previous murders and led the police to what remained of his victims. In January 1984 Gore was convicted and sentenced to death for the most recent crimes and received four life sentences for the previous murders. After state courts upheld the conviction and the sentence, a federal court in

August 1989 overturned the sentence (though it upheld the conviction). In December 1992 Gore was resentenced to death. The state of Florida executed Gore by lethal injection on April 12, 2012: nineteen years and four months after his resentence and more than twenty-eight years after his conviction for the capital crime.

Few outside Florida have likely heard of David Alan Gore. Even the state's governor, Rick Scott, who signed Gore's death warrant in 2012, had not previously heard of him.[3] Gore's crimes in the early 1980s did not attract the national attention engendered by such infamous cases as those of Ted Bundy, executed in Florida in 1989 after murdering and raping dozens of women across the United States; John Wayne Gacy, executed in Illinois in 1994 for sexually assaulting and murdering thirty-three teenage boys and young men; or Timothy McVeigh, executed by the federal government in 2001 for killing 168 in the bombing of the federal building in Oklahoma City in 1995. Such cases are (thankfully) fairly rare; but every year American states execute vile murderers, like Gore, for whom no lesser punishment could reasonably be considered proportionate to the crimes they committed. In 2012 (the most recent year with complete data when we began work on this book), Gore was one of forty-three murderers executed in the country. Here we describe in some detail the capital crimes committed by sixteen additional offenders, with at least one executed each month throughout the year.[4]

2. Gary Roland Welch

On August 25, 1994, Gary Roland Welch and an accomplice, apparently motivated by a dispute over drugs, confronted and assaulted an acquaintance at his apartment, chased him down outside when he fled, cornered him in a roadside ditch, and beat and stabbed him with a knife. Welch then retrieved and smashed a beer bottle and used it to stab and slash his victim, who died from blood loss caused by at least ten stab wounds, three of which penetrated his lungs. Welch had been convicted in 1981 of aggravated assault and battery on a police

---

[3] Earley, *The Serial Killer Whisperer*, p. 321.

[4] For the detailed information on each offender, visit www.clarkprosecutor.org/html /death/usexecute.htm, scroll down to "U.S. Executions in 2012", and click on the name of the offender.

officer and in 1982 of assault and battery with a dangerous weapon. At his sentencing hearing in the capital case, the state presented evidence of four additional serious assaults on his ex-girlfriend: (1) breaking down a door and then hitting and throwing the woman against a Christmas tree; (2) demanding sex, beating the woman in front of her two children, tearing off her clothes, and putting her head through a cabinet and a wall; (3) hitting the woman in the head with a shotgun that she had just fired at him, fearing for her life; and (4) sticking her head inside a washing machine, throwing her down on a coffee table, and holding a knife to her throat. In addition, one hour before the capital crime, Welch had pulled a knife on another man demanding drugs. The state of Oklahoma executed Welch on January 5, 2012: fifteen years and seven months after he was sentenced to death.

3. Edwin Hart Turner

On December 12, 1995, Edwin Hart Turner and an accomplice entered a convenience store at two o'clock in the morning. Turner ordered the clerk to get down on the floor, but before the clerk could comply, Turner shot him in the chest with a rifle. When the offenders could not open the cash register and with the wounded clerk on the ground pleading for his life, Turner placed the barrel of his rifle to the face of the clerk and shot and killed him. The two men then went to a gas station and store a few miles away. With his accomplice inside robbing the store, Turner confronted a man pumping gas and ordered him to the ground. After taking cash from the man's wallet and with the victim on the ground pleading for his life, Turner shot him in the head, killing him. The state of Mississippi executed Turner on February 8, 2012: fifteen years after sentencing.

4. Robert Brian Waterhouse

At one o'clock in the morning on January 2, 1980, Robert Brian Waterhouse left a bar with a twenty-nine-year-old woman. Sometime later, he beat her with a hard instrument, causing thirty lacerations and thirty-six bruises, including severe lacerations on the head and bruises around the throat. He raped the woman, assaulted her in the rectum with a large object, and stuffed her bloody tampon down her throat. She was alive throughout this assault. He then dragged his victim into the water, where she drowned. She was discovered completely naked, and her injuries were so severe that she was unrecognizable. Fourteen years before, Waterhouse had broken into a home and killed a seventy-seven-year-old woman, for which he pleaded guilty to second-degree murder and served eight years before being paroled. At the sentencing hearing in the capital case, the state presented additional evidence that after his arrest for the 1980 rape and murder, Waterhouse committed or attempted to commit sexual battery on a cellmate. The state of Florida executed Waterhouse on February 15, 2012: thirty-one years and five months after his original sentence; twenty-one years and ten months after resentencing following a successful appeal.

5. Timothy Shaun Stemple

In 1996, Timothy Shaun Stemple concocted a plan to kill his wife to collect her life insurance. He recruited two assistants, including the sixteen-year-old cousin of the woman with whom he was having an extramarital affair. On October 24, 1996, after leaving his truck on the side of the road as if it had broken down, Stemple and his wife arrived at the truck in another vehicle. While Stemple pretended to work on the truck, his accomplice hit Stemple's wife twice on the head with a baseball bat. When this did not render her unconscious, Stemple took the bat and hit her in the head twenty to thirty times. Stemple and his accomplice then laid the victim in front of the pickup and attempted unsuccessfully to run over her head. When the victim tried to get up, Stemple grabbed the bat and hit her several more times. The pair then placed her body under the truck and drove over her chest. They returned in the pickup to make sure their victim was dead but found that she had crawled into the grass beside the road. Stemple then sped up and, traveling at about sixty miles per hour, ran over her as she lay in the grass, killing her. According to an appellate court, the victim "suffered great physical pain before she died".[5] At the sentencing hearing, the state presented evidence that while he was awaiting trial, Stemple tried to get other inmates to arrange the death of several

---

[5] The quotation is from *Stemple v. State*, 994 P.2d 61 (Okla. Crim. App. 2000), http://www.clarkprosecutor.org/html/death/US/stemple1286.htm.

witnesses in his case. The state of Oklahoma executed Stemple on March 15, 2012: thirteen years after sentencing.

6. William Gerald Mitchell

On the evening of November 21, 1996, William Gerald Mitchell abducted a thirty-eight-year-old woman from a mall parking lot and drove her to an area under a bridge, where he beat her with hard blows to the head, sexually assaulted her vaginally and anally (causing severe damage to her vagina and anus), and strangled her. The sexual injuries occurred while she was still alive. Mitchell then ran over his victim several times with his car, crushing her skull. At the time of the murder, Mitchell had been on parole for eleven months, following his release from prison for the 1974 stabbing murder of a woman.[6] The state of Mississippi executed Mitchell on March 22, 2012: thirteen years and eight months after sentencing.

7. Buenka Adams

During the late evening on September 2, 2002, Buenka Adams and an accomplice robbed a convenience store. They abducted two women who were working at the store and a nineteen-year-old customer, a mentally challenged man. The offenders drove the three to a secluded spot outside town. Pointing a shotgun, the accomplice ordered the man and one of the women into the trunk of the car. Adams took the other woman to a more secluded spot and sexually assaulted her. He then led her back to the car and let the other two out of the trunk. He tied the women's arms behind their backs and made them kneel on the ground. After starting to flee, the offenders returned, ordered the man (who had been left untied) to kneel on the ground, and shot and killed him. They then shot one of the women, who fell forward. The other woman also fell forward, pretending to be hit. Adams approached the second woman and asked her if she was

---

[6] The jury knew that Mitchell had been paroled from a life sentence but apparently did not know what crime had led to this sentence until his sister, testifying on his behalf during the penalty phase, said, "A person who has committed two murders reads the Bible and that's what he does every day." During this earlier murder, Mitchell had also stabbed the victim's daughter, but this was also unknown to the jury, as were two beatings of women for which Mitchell was charged in 1973.

bleeding. When she did not respond, he threatened to shoot her in the face if she did not answer. When she answered that she was not bleeding, Adams shot her in the face, hitting her lip. Adams and his accomplice then went to the first woman and asked the same question. When she didn't answer, they picked her up by her hair and held a lighter to her face to see if she was still alive. Convinced that she was dead, the two men escaped. The second woman was able to secure help. The first woman also survived but suffered broken ribs, a broken shoulder blade, a collapsed lung, and the loss of skin and tissue over her left shoulder blade. Adams was in charge throughout the ordeal, initiating the kidnapping, giving the orders, sexually assaulting one of the women, ordering the shooting of the man (and threatening to kill his accomplice if he did not do so), and personally shooting the women. At the sentencing hearing the state presented evidence that in the days prior to the capital crime, Adams and his accomplice had committed two armed robberies. The state of Texas executed Adams on April 26, 2012: seven years and eight months after sentencing.

8. Michael Bascum Selsor

At 11:00 P.M. on September 15, 1975, Michael Bascum Selsor and an accomplice entered a convenience store, each armed with a .22-caliber handgun. Brandishing his gun, Selsor approached the fifty-five-year-old man working at the cash register and demanded the contents. Meanwhile the accomplice confronted another employee, who was restocking the walk-in cooler, and ordered her to get down. When she replied, "You've got to be kidding me", the accomplice shot her in the shoulder. When the employee at the cash register handed Selsor a sack filled with money, Selsor shot him several times in the chest, killing him. Upon hearing the shots, the accomplice emptied his weapon through the cooler door, firing at the other employee. She survived the seven gunshot wounds: in her right shoulder, on the back and top of her head, underneath her jaw, in her back, and in her neck. Two bullets were left in her neck. Selsor and his accomplice had agreed before the crime that they would leave no witnesses. In the two weeks before the crime Selsor and his accomplice had (1) robbed a convenience store during which the clerk was shot in the back but survived; (2) robbed another store during which Selsor had stabbed a clerk in the back more than twenty times after she screamed for help; and (3) committed two more robberies (though it is not clear from the record whether all this information was known to the jury prior to sentencing). The state of Oklahoma executed Selsor on May 1, 2012: thirty-six years and eight months after the original sentence; fourteen years after resentencing in 1998.

9. Henry "Curtis" Jackson

On the evening of November 1, 1990, Henry "Curtis" Jackson's mother and four of her older grandchildren left home for church. Her daughter, Regina Jackson, stayed home with her two daughters (ages five and two) and four nieces and nephews (ages eleven, three, two, and one). Once Regina, Henry Jackson's younger sister, was alone with the children, Henry cut the telephone line to the house and then knocked on the door and came inside. A short while later, he grabbed his sister from behind and demanded twenty dollars. When she said she did not have the money, he stabbed her in the chin and stomach. Regina yelled for her eleven-year-old niece, Sarah, who came running and jumped on Jackson's back. The three struggled, and Regina pleaded for Jackson not to kill them. He said he had come to get the contents of his mother's safe and that he had to kill them. He stabbed Sarah in the neck. Regina picked up some iron rods and started hitting Jackson with them. When Jackson used the one-year-old as a shield, Regina relinquished the rods and let Jackson tie her up with a belt. He then stabbed Regina in the neck and, while she watched, fatally stabbed her two-year-old daughter. Jackson then dragged the safe down the hall, which awakened Regina's five-year-old daughter. He fatally stabbed her and threw her on the floor. He stabbed Regina again in the neck, and she pretended that she was dead. At one point, Sarah told the three-year-old boy to run for help, but Jackson called him back. Jackson grabbed Sarah and stabbed her again in the neck. When the knife broke, he retrieved another one from the kitchen, stabbed her yet again, and threw her on a bed. Sarah, too, pretended she was dead. Jackson then stabbed to death the two- and three-year-old boys. He murdered a total of four young children. Regina and Sarah survived their injuries, and the one-year-old suffered a stab wound to her neck that left her unable to walk and with no fine-motor control in her arms. Jackson had previously been convicted of burglary with the intent to commit kidnapping. The state of Mississippi executed him on June 5, 2012: twenty years and nine months after sentencing.

10. Samuel Villegas Lopez

During the night of October 28, 1986, or the early morning of October 29, Samuel Villegas Lopez broke into a fifty-nine-year-old woman's apartment, where, according to court records, "a terrible and prolonged struggle" took place.[7] Lopez gagged his victim by stuffing a scarf into her mouth and blindfolded her with her pajama pants. He raped and sodomized her; stabbed her more than twenty times in the head and face, breast and upper chest, and lower abdomen; and slit her throat. The state of Arizona executed Lopez on June 27, 2012: twenty-five years from the original sentence; twenty-one years and ten months after resentencing following a successful appeal.

11. Yokamon Laneal Hearn

On March 25, 1998, Yokamon Laneal Hearn and three accomplices (armed with two shotguns, a .22.-caliber pistol, and a TEC-9 semiautomatic rifle) confronted a twenty-three-year-old man at a coin-operated car wash, forced him into his car at gunpoint, and drove him to a secluded industrial area. They forced him out of his car, and with the man's hands raised (and apparently pleading for his life), Hearn shot him in the face with the rifle and continued shooting after the victim fell to the ground. An accomplice also shot the victim several times. The offenders stole the victim's car and his license and drove off. Although Hearn had no prior felony convictions on his record, the state presented evidence at the sentencing hearing that he had been involved in numerous prior offenses, including the burglaries of four homes, arson, an aggravated robbery, an aggravated assault, a sexual assault, and a terroristic threat combined with unlawful carrying of a weapon. The state of Texas executed Hearn on July 18, 2012: thirteen years and seven months after sentencing.

---

[7] The quotation is from *State v. Lopez*, 175 Ariz. 407, 857 P.2d 1261 (Ariz. 1993), http://www.clarkprosecutor.org/html/death/US/lopez1300.htm.

12. Daniel Wayne Cook

In July 1987, Daniel Wayne Cook and his accomplice lived in an apartment with a twenty-six-year-old Guatemalan national, with whom they worked at a local restaurant and from whom Cook devised a plan to steal money. On July 19 at their apartment, the accomplice distracted the man while Cook stole ninety dollars from his money pouch. When the man questioned the two about the money, the offenders lured him into an upstairs bedroom, pushed him down on the bed, gagged him, and tied him to a chair. Over the next six or seven hours, they cut him with a knife; beat him with their fists, a metal pipe, and a wooden stick; burned him with cigarettes on the stomach and the genitals; sodomized him; and drove a staple through his foreskin. Later, the accomplice tried unsuccessfully to strangle the victim with a sheet. He then put him on the floor and pushed down on his throat with a metal pipe. When that failed to kill the man, Cook pressed down on one end of the pipe while the accomplice pressed on the other. Finally, the accomplice stood on the pipe as it lay across the man's throat and killed him. They then put the body in a bedroom closet. A few hours later, a dishwasher at the restaurant, who was a sixteen-year-old runaway, stopped by the apartment. Cook and the accomplice told him that they had a dead body upstairs, and Cook took him upstairs to show it to him. The boy was crying when he and Cook returned downstairs. Cook told him to undress, and he complied. Cook and his accomplice then gagged him and tied him to a chair in the kitchen. Cook sodomized the boy and placed him on the couch, bound and gagged. After the two men tried unsuccessfully to strangle the boy with a sheet, Cook placed him on the floor and strangled him to death. Cook then put the body in the closet with the other victim. Two days later, the accomplice turned himself in to the police and gave a full confession. The state of Arizona executed Cook on August 8, 2012: twenty-four years after sentencing.

13. Robert Wayne Harris

Robert Wayne Harris worked at a car wash for ten months before he was fired for exposing himself to a customer. Five days later, on March 20, 2000, Harris returned to the car wash at 7:15 A.M., before it opened for business. He forced the manager and two other employees into the office. He ordered the manager to open the safe, and the manager complied and gave Harris the cash. Harris then forced all three to the floor and shot each of them in the back of the head at close range. He also slit the manager's throat. Before Harris could leave, three other employees arrived for work, unaware of the danger. He forced them to kneel on the lobby floor and shot each of them in the back of the head at close range. One of the victims survived with permanent disabilities. When a seventh employee arrived shortly thereafter, Harris claimed to have discovered the crime scene. The two then crossed the street to a donut shop, and the employee called the police. Harris fled the scene and was later apprehended. When he was interviewed by police about the capital offense, he volunteered that in November 1999 he had abducted and murdered a woman. He led police to her remains in a field. At the sentencing hearing prosecutors presented additional evidence that around the time he was arrested Harris had planned to drive to Florida to kill an old girlfriend. They also presented evidence of an extensive record of violent behavior as a juvenile and of convictions at age eighteen for three burglaries and resisting arrest. These adult convictions had resulted in eight years in a state prison, from which Harris was paroled in May 1999. The state of Texas executed Harris on September 20, 2012: twelve years after sentencing.

14. Eric Donald Robert

On April 12, 2011, while serving an eighty-year sentence in a state prison for kidnapping, Eric Donald Robert and an accomplice secured a metal pipe from another inmate and used it to strike a sixty-three-year-old prison guard in the head repeatedly, fracturing his skull in three places. They then wrapped the guard's head in plastic wrap to prevent him from crying out and to suffocate him. Robert dressed himself in the guard's uniform, and his accomplice got into a box on a four-wheel cart. A short while later, when a suspicious guard confronted Robert about his identity, the accomplice jumped out of the box and the two offenders beat the guard with the radio taken from the murder victim. When other officers responded, Robert attempted to grab one of their guns. When he failed, the offenders surrendered. Robert had been serving his sentence for kidnapping an eighteen-year-old female driver by impersonating a police officer. He had stuffed the woman into the trunk of her car, where she used her cell phone to summon help. Prosecutors subsequently argued that the discovery of a bed, an ax, a rope, and pornography in the back of Robert's truck showed that he had planned to rape his victim. At the sentencing hearing in the capital case, the state also presented testimony from a woman with whom Robert had had a long-term relationship that he had physically assaulted her, including punching, tackling, and pointing a gun to her head, and that once he had beaten her until she acquiesced to sex. The state of South Dakota executed Robert on October 15, 2012: one year after his sentencing.

15. Donald Eugene Moeller

On the evening of May 8, 1990, Donald Eugene Moeller abducted a nine-year-old girl after she left her parents' home to buy candy at a nearby store. He drove the girl to the woods, where he raped her vaginally (when she was alive) and anally (when she was dead), and caused knife wounds to her neck, shoulder, chest, back, hip, and hands. She died from a cut to her jugular vein. At the sentencing hearing in his first trial, prosecutors presented evidence of three prior completed or attempted sexual assaults. The state of South Dakota executed Moeller on October 30, 2012: twenty years after the original sentence; fifteen years after resentencing following a new trial that had resulted from a successful appeal.

16. Ramon Torres Hernandez

While driving with his girlfriend and a male accomplice on October 21, 2002, Ramon Torres Hernandez saw a thirty-seven-year-old woman at a bus stop. When the accomplice tried to grab her purse and she resisted, he pulled her into the car and covered her head as Hernandez drove away. After getting tape at Hernandez's house, they bound and gagged the woman. They took her to a motel, where Hernandez stood guard while his accomplice raped her. Hernandez then told his girlfriend to buy a shovel. While she was out, one of the men (the testimony is conflicting) killed the woman by asphyxiation. She was also beaten about her face and neck. The men wrapped her body in a blanket and placed it in their car. They drove to a remote location and used the shovel to bury their victim. During the crime, they took money and an ATM card from the victim's purse (having previously forced the woman to disclose her PIN). Hernandez had previously been convicted of unlawfully carrying a weapon and of three burglaries. At the sentencing hearing prosecutors presented evidence that a DNA test conducted in 2001 showed that Hernandez's semen had been in the body of a twelve-year-old girl found dead in an isolated area in December 1994. Next to her was the lifeless body of her thirteen-year-old cousin. Both had been severely beaten about the head and face, violently sexually assaulted, and strangled to death. The state of Texas executed Hernandez on November 14, 2012: ten years and one month after his sentencing.

17. Richard Dale Stokley

On the evening of July 7, 1991, Richard Dale Stokley and a twenty-year-old accomplice showed up at a campsite where two thirteen-year-old girls were staying. The accomplice, who knew the older sister of one of the girls, had a discussion with them. Sometime after 1:00 A.M. the two men abducted the girls and drove them to a remote area. They raped them and then discussed the need to kill them. Each offender strangled one girl. Stokley then stabbed both in the eye, and each man stomped on the neck of one girl, causing internal and external injuries. They then threw the naked bodies down an abandoned mineshaft. At the sentencing hearing, prosecutors presented evidence of a history of misdemeanor arrests and offenses, including assaults on two former wives. At the hearing the wives testified that Stokley had physically abused them, threatened them with death, and threatened to throw their bodies down a mineshaft. The state of Arizona executed Stokley on December 5, 2012: twenty years and five months after his sentencing.

An individualized determination

Under U.S. Supreme Court rulings, the decision to sentence a murderer to death in the United States (which is usually by a jury but occasionally by a judge alone) must result from "an individualized determination on the basis of the character of the individual and the circumstances of the crime".[8] So when juries and judges decide whether the death penalty is the just punishment in a particular case, they consider not just the details of the crime but also the character, or blameworthiness, of the murderer. Of course, the facts themselves shed light on the character of the offender (as the above examples surely demonstrate), as does his criminal history. Moreover, juries and judges must consider any mitigating evidence that the defense offers. Thus, when deciding whether death is the appropriate punishment, they have available to them the whole picture, including the gruesome details not often reported in the media (though a few states limit the jury's access to the murderer's criminal history during the sentencing phase of the trial). Even just from the summaries given above, it is not hard to understand why juries (nearly always by unanimous votes) or judges decided that these murderers deserved to die for these crimes and that life in prison would not have been sufficiently severe.

Because space does not permit a detailed summary of the crimes committed by the other twenty-six murderers executed in 2012, here we list simply the essential facts of their crimes and their criminal histories:

- The rape and strangulation murder of a snack-food vendor by an offender with numerous prior convictions, including felony assault. Six years after his conviction in the capital case, he was linked by DNA to the beating, rape, and murder of a seventy-seven-year-old woman.
- The beating death of the offender's seventy-seven-year-old adoptive mother while the offender was on a three-day furlough from a prison sentence for kidnapping a nine-year-old girl.
- The murder of a police officer by a prison escapee who had been serving seventeen life sentences for kidnapping and robbery.
- The murder of the offender's estranged wife and new boyfriend in front of their six-year-old son. The offender had a long history of violence against women.
- The strangulation murder of the offender's sixty-nine-year-old former employer during a robbery at his house.

[8] *Zant v. Stephens*, 462 U.S. 862 (1983), 879.

- The rape and beating death of the wife of the offender's former employer, who had recently fired him.
- The beating death with a flashlight of a ten-month-old boy and nonfatal assault of a four-year-old girl. The offender had once beaten his ex-wife with a baseball bat and burned his girlfriend's child with cigarettes.
- The fatal shooting of the new boyfriend of the offender's ex-girlfriend and the attempted murder of the ex-girlfriend. Previously, the offender had raped an eighteen-year-old who was seven to eight months pregnant. While awaiting trial in the capital case, the offender had solicited fellow inmates to kill his ex-girlfriend.
- The abduction, robbery, and murder of a twenty-five-year-old man.
- The murder and likely sexual assault of a thirty-one-year-old woman in her bed after breaking into her home.
- The murder of the offender's ex-wife, her mother and father, and her three-year-old daughter.
- The murder of a twenty-one-year-old man and the kidnapping and rape of his girlfriend.
- The abduction, beating, and shooting death of a twenty-one-year-old man. The offender had been convicted of three prior robberies, during one of which he pointed a shotgun at a convenience-store clerk.
- The murder of the offender's ex-girlfriend and her five-year-old daughter and three-year-old son. The offender had a history of violence against women.
- The murder and robbery of two strangers in consecutive incidents after a minor traffic accident.
- The abduction, sexual assault, and shooting death of a twenty-eight-year-old woman. The offender had been convicted of armed robbery, had a history of violence against his ex-wife, and was linked by ballistics evidence to the murder of another woman.
- The abduction, rape, and strangulation of a twelve-year-old girl. The offender had a history of violence against women and fellow jail inmates.

- The stabbing and strangulation death of a twenty-six-year-old woman in her apartment. The offender had been convicted of two burglaries as an adult and had a lengthy record of violence as a juvenile.
- The shooting murder and robbery of the offender's forty-four-year-old girlfriend. The offender confessed to having murdered a man a decade earlier, and he had a history of armed robbery and assault.
- The shooting death of the offender's girlfriend and attempted murder of the police officer who responded to the scene. The offender had twice before been convicted of crimes in which he held people at gunpoint.
- The bludgeoning, stabbing, and strangulation death of a forty-four-year-old woman when she returned home during a burglary. The offender had a long history of violence against women.
- The stabbing and strangulation death of a forty-six-year-old woman in her home.
- The murder (and possible rape) of a fifteen-year-old girl and the girl's three-year-old cousin. The offender had a record of sexual assault and aggravated assault against teenage girls.
- The shooting murder of a husband and wife while they slept after the offender forcibly entered the home.
- The murder of nine people (six men and three women) in five separate incidents over a four-month period.

Key Characteristics

Altogether, the forty-three offenders executed in 2012 killed a total of seventy individuals and injured another twelve during the capital offenses that resulted in their death sentences. The nonfatal injuries included sexual assault (three victims), a beating with a flashlight, a beating with a radio, gunshot wounds (five victims), and knifings (three victims). At least two victims were left with permanent disabilities. Twelve of the forty-three offenders (28%) killed more than one, and five (12%) killed more than two: specifically, seven killed two persons, one killed three, two killed four, one killed five, and one killed nine. By contrast, fewer than 5% of all homicide incidents in the United States involve multiple murder victims, and fewer than 1% involve three or more murder victims.[9] These figures for those executed in 2012, however, count only the murders for which the offenders were sentenced to death. We know that eight of the forty-three (19%) had killed at least one person prior to the capital crime that resulted in their execution, totaling thirteen prior homicide victims. (In two of these cases the prior homicides were discovered after the conviction in the capital case.) Thus, in their criminal careers the forty-three executed in 2012 had killed at least eighty-three men, women, and children.

The offenders had also committed serious crimes other than homicide in the past: ten (23%) had committed a sexual assault; ten (23%) had committed a robbery; eighteen (42%) had committed a felony assault (also called aggravated assault); and two (5%) had committed a kidnapping. Altogether, twenty-nine (67%) had previously committed a homicide, sexual assault, robbery, felony assault, or kidnapping. (And these figures likely undercount prior criminal acts because of offenses not known to authorities.) At least two-thirds, then, had committed a serious violent crime in the past.

The above descriptions also show the prevalence of rape homicides in capital cases. Nearly every state with the death penalty (currently thirty-one states, but thirty-eight during most of the period when the above crimes were committed) specifically lists rape homicide as a type of murder than can qualify the offender for the death penalty. For the crimes that led to the executions in 2012, 35% to 40% (two were cases of possible sexual assault) involved the rape of the murder victim or another person by the executed offender or his accomplice. Yet, among all homicides in the United States in recent decades, only about 1% involved a sexual assault.[10]

[9] Erica L. Smith and Alexia Cooper, *Homicide in the U.S. Known to Law Enforcement, 2011* (Washington, D.C.: Bureau of Justice Statistics, 2013), p. 14, table 5 and figure 22, http://www.bjs.gov/content/pub/pdf/hus11.pdf; Alexia Cooper and Erica L. Smith, *Homicide Trends in the United States, 1980–2008* (Washington, D.C.: Bureau of Justice Statistics, 2011), pp. 24–25, http://www.bjs.gov/content/pub/pdf/htus8008.pdf.

[10] The figures on rape murders, robbery murders, and age of murder victims for all homicides in the United States are based on calculations from data published in the annual FBI publication *Crime in the United States*, covering the years 1978–2011. Publications going back to 1995 are online at http://www.fbi.gov/about-us/cjis/ucr/ucr-publications#Crime. Printed copies of these and earlier volumes are published by the U.S. Government Printing Office.

Robbery murders also stand out among those executed in 2012. Eighteen of the forty-three offenders (42%) committed their murder during a robbery. Robbery murder is another type of homicide that most death-penalty states list as qualifying the offender for the death penalty. Excluding the four robbery murders that also involved rape (to make the data comparable with national FBI data), 33% of the forty-three committed a robbery murder. (The FBI uses the most serious crime when classifying homicides accompanied by other felonies; thus, a homicide in which a rape and robbery both occurred is classified simply as a rape homicide.) The 33% rate for robbery murders among those executed in 2012 is about three times the rate for all homicides in the United States.

Finally, of the seventy murder victims for which the forty-three offenders were executed in 2012, sixteen (23%) were under eighteen years old, and nine (13%) were under nine years old. The first figure is about two and a half times higher than for all murder victims in the United States, and the second figure is three times higher.

The selection of some killers for the ultimate penalty is the result of three sets of decisions: legislative determinations that certain kinds of murder qualify the offender for the death penalty, prosecutors' judgments that death is the appropriate penalty to seek in a particular murder case, and the decisions of juries (and sometimes judges), familiar with all the details of the crime, to sentence a convicted offender to death. The data (qualitative and quantitative) from the forty-three executions in 2012 vividly illustrate the kinds of murders and murderers that legislators, prosecutors, and juries in the United States believe merit death as the just punishment. As the details from the crimes behind the forty-three executions in 2012 demonstrate, the death penalty, as it is applied in the United States, falls particularly on those who kill multiple victims, who have killed or committed a serious violent crime in the past, who sexually assault or rob their murder victims, and who kill the very young.

"Justice to Us Is No Less Than the Death Penalty"

We have devoted considerable space to describing the crimes that led to the execution of forty-three murderers in 2012. Many of the details are highly disturbing and, like the better-known cases of such serial killers as Jeffrey Dahmer, Ted Bundy, and John Wayne Gacy, exhibit a degree of cruelty and depravity that is almost unimaginable. And although some of the other murders and murderers seem relatively tame by comparison, taken together these cases show that offenders *ordinarily* condemned to death in the United States are typically guilty of crimes that go far beyond simple murder, or they have a history of violent, and even murderous, behavior.

Critics will say that in describing such details we are playing on the reader's emotions rather than appealing to reason. That is the reverse of the truth. What is required for a dispassionate and rational determination of what would be a proportionate penalty for these offenses is *precisely* attention to the details. In fact, it is, we would suggest, the opponents of capital punishment who in their neglect of these details are too often guilty of letting themselves be swayed by emotion rather than reason. The danger of ignoring the grisly details of such offenses is that we can be led thereby into a sentimentalized conception of the offenders. We can end up modeling our notion of what a murderer is like on paradigms drawn from pop culture, such as the wise old Morgan Freeman character in the film *The Shawshank Redemption*—rather than on real-life killers such as David Alan Gore, Robert Brian Waterhouse, and Timothy Shaun Stemple, grubby and sadistic individuals who are impossible to romanticize.

Given what we have argued in previous chapters, and given that the crimes of such individuals go well beyond simple murder (or that the offenders have very serious violent histories), it is clear that nothing less than death would be a proportionate punishment for these crimes and offenders. Thus, unless there are compelling prudential reasons not to employ the death penalty at all, it follows that such offenders ought to be executed, particularly if executing them would also further some of the other ends of punishment, such as deterrence and the protection of society against the offenders. This assumes, of course, that the civil authority fully respects the rights of the accused, that it ascertains guilt through a proper deliberative process, and that it punishes not out of hatred but, as the *Catechism of the Catholic Church* affirms, to defend the common good. The *Catechism* calls for "inflict[ing] punishment *proportionate to the gravity of the offense*", thereby "redressing the disorder introduced by the offense" (*CCC* 2266, emphasis added). There is a *presumption* in favor of proportionate punishment, even if this presumption can be overridden.

We consider below the question of whether considerations about rehabilitation override this presumption in the case of capital punishment, and in the next chapter we consider whether there are yet other prudential considerations that override the presumption. But first we want to note a benefit of capital punishment that is paid insufficient attention—namely, the assurance it provides citizens that theirs is a *just* society, one that does indeed "redress ... the disorder introduced by the offense[s]" that are committed within it.

Evidence from those executed in 2012 shows just how important respect for the principle of just and proportionate punishment is to the parties involved in death-penalty cases, including the authorities who bring the offender "to justice", the loved ones of the murder victims, and, at times, even the offenders themselves. Here are illustrations from the official records and media accounts of the forty-three executions in 2012.[11]

Public authorities

Public officials of all types have a responsibility to serve justice, but none more so than those who work in criminal justice. The very phrase "criminal justice" signifies the centrality of the principle of justice in combatting crime and punishing criminals. By contrast, we do not normally speak about transportation justice or housing justice or educational justice, though all these are subjects of public policy in the modern era. This is not to say that issues of justice are absent in these policy areas but only that they are less central to the task of formulating and carrying out the policies.

It is no surprise, then, that police and prosecutors often view the execution of a heinous murderer as serving the cause of justice. For example, after the state of Arizona executed the prison inmate who murdered his seventy-four-year-old adoptive mother while he was on furlough, state Attorney General Tom Horne commented that "justice was carried out against convicted murderer Robert

---

[11] Unless otherwise noted, all quotations are from the materials collected by the prosecuting attorney of Clark County, Indiana, available at www.clarkprosecutor.org/html/death/usexecute.htm. For the detailed information on each offender, scroll down to "U.S. Executions in 2012", and click on the name of the offender. For the following quotations we identify the offender at issue, the state, and the date of execution.

Moorman today, approximately 28 years after he brutally murdered and dismembered his adoptive mother, following a sentence of 9 years to life for kidnapping an eight year old girl."[12] Similarly, when Arizona executed Samuel Lopez for his horrific sexual assault and murder of a fifty-nine-year-old woman after breaking into her apartment, Horne said, "Almost 26 years later, justice has been served for the family of [the victim]."[13] When the state of Idaho executed Richard Leavitt for a similar sexual assault and murder, Tom Moss, the former county attorney who prosecuted the case, said simply, "Justice has been served."[14] When the state of Texas executed the escaped convict serving multiple life sentences who murdered a police officer, Assistant District Attorney Toby Shook, who had prosecuted the case, said that "today is about justice for Aubrey Hawkins and Aubrey's fellow police officers."[15] Finally, after the state of Mississippi executed Jan Brawner for murdering a family of four, the sheriff commented that "what we saw, or what I saw tonight was justice for the citizens of Tate County, for the State of Mississippi, and most importantly, for the victims and ... [their] family."[16]

What did these public officials mean when they described the executions as serving justice? Although the statements were short, lacking elaboration, what comes through in each case is an understanding of justice as paying the offender back for his horrendous acts, giving him what he deserved, pure and simple. In only one case did a public official connect the punishment to the more utilitarian benefit of eliminating the continuing threat posed by the offender. This was Shannon Johnson, who murdered his ex-girlfriend's new boyfriend, tried to murder his ex-girlfriend, had previously raped an eighteen-year-old woman who was seven to eight months pregnant, and while awaiting trial in the capital case solicited fellow inmates to kill his ex-girlfriend. After the state of Delaware executed Johnson, Attorney General Joseph R. Biden III commented that "Shannon Johnson is

[12] The offender was Robert Henry Moorman, executed by the state of Arizona on February 29, 2012.

[13] Lopez was executed by the state of Arizona on June 27, 2012.

[14] Leavitt was executed by the state of Idaho on June 12, 2012.

[15] The offender was George Rivas, executed by the state of Texas on February 29, 2012.

[16] Brawner was executed by the state of Mississippi on June 12, 2012.

a threat to society. His conviction and today's sentence ensures that justice will be served."[17]

In two of the Arizona executions the attorney general expressed his hope that the just punishment of the offender would bring some peace to the loved ones of the victim (though this may have been implicit in the other cases as well). Commenting on the Lopez execution, Attorney General Horne noted that "the judge who sentenced Lopez to death found that the crime was especially heinous, cruel and depraved, and among the worst he had ever seen.... Now that Samuel Villegas Lopez has paid the penalty for his terrible crime, it is my hope that his victims and their families will find some peace that justice has been carried out."[18] And when Arizona executed Thomas Kemp for abducting a man at an ATM machine, robbing him, taking him to a secluded spot, and shooting him twice in the head, Horne said, "Now that Thomas Kemp has paid the penalty for his terrible crimes, it is my hope that his victims and their families will find some measure of peace that justice has been carried out."[19]

In one case from Oklahoma the appellate court took the prosecutor to task for appealing to justice during the sentencing phase of the trial. In reviewing the prosecutor's behavior regarding the sentencing of George Ochoa for breaking into a home and shooting to death a husband and wife while they slept, the court held that "the prosecutor improperly pleaded with the jury to do justice 'and the only way you can do that is bring back a sentence of death.' He also told the jury 'If this isn't a death penalty case, what is?' " In Oklahoma, however, "it is error for the prosecutor to state his personal opinion as to the appropriateness of the death penalty."[20] Though the court could have reversed the sentence, it ruled that the error was "harmless" and had not likely changed the outcome in the case.

The victims' loved ones

It is, of course, the loved ones of a murder victim who feel the loss most acutely and most painfully. To many, it is an affront to justice

---

[17] Johnson was executed by the state of Delaware on April 20, 2012.

[18] Lopez was executed by the state of Arizona on June 27, 2012.

[19] Kemp was executed by the state of Arizona on April 25, 2012.

[20] Ochoa was executed by the state of Oklahoma on December 4, 2012.

that the one who took the life of their mother, father, brother, sister, son, or daughter, often in a particularly calculated or brutal way, should continue to live, even in the confines of a maximum-security prison. For these family members, the disorder created by the offense and the demands of justice to balance the crime with a proportionate punishment are not abstract philosophical principles but palpable realities. As the father of the young man chased across a parking lot and stabbed to death with a knife and broken beer bottle told the sentencing jury, "I don't believe it's justice that my son lies in a cold grave and that Gary Welch should live." The victim's brother pleaded for the death penalty: "Gary Welch deserves the death penalty. Give it to him, please." For the victim's mother, no penalty short of execution would be just: "I would beg this court and this jury to see that justice is done. And justice to us is no less than the death penalty."[21] The daughter of the convenience-store clerk who was shot in the chest multiple times after complying with his robber's demands called for the murderer to suffer the same fate he visited upon her dad: "My dad did not have a choice. He's gone. Michael Selsor should pay the same price."[22] One of the sisters of the fifty-nine-year-old woman who was sexually assaulted and brutally murdered after Samuel Lopez broke into her apartment late one night addressed the offender during a hearing before the clemency board: "Let me ask you, Mr. Lopez, did our sister plead for her life as you stabbed her two dozen times? Did she beg you not to rape her? Did she plead with you to spare her life as you almost decapitated her? Did she? ... Nothing will bring her back, but you should pay for it."[23]

In an interview she granted for a book on serial murderers, the survivor of David Alan Gore's last series of rape murders highlighted the injustice of allowing Gore to live (which he did for twenty-eight years after his original sentence):

He was eating three meals a day, had a television, and didn't have to work or worry about rent. He had gotten married in prison and was having people write to him.... He was costing the state $26,500 per year just in food and lodging.... I was a victim, yet no one was

[21] Welch was executed by the state of Oklahoma on January 5, 2012.
[22] Selsor was executed by the state of Oklahoma on May 1, 2012.
[23] Lopez was executed by the state of Arizona on June 27, 2012.

paying my rent or making sure I got three meals a day. People were feeling sorry for him. But what about Lynn [the survivor's fourteen-year-old friend and Gore's last murder victim] and the others whom he victimized? Everyone was so worried about his rights. What about our rights? This wasn't a case of him being innocent. Everyone knew what he had done. Yet he was sitting on death row with his every need being cared for.[24]

Of course, not every loved one of every murder victim demands the death penalty for the offender. Yet the comments by the family members in the proceedings surrounding the sentencing and punishment of those executed in 2012 are eloquent testimony to the strength of the principle of just deserts. Other illustrations include the following:

- In the end I hope and pray justice will be served.[25]
- I just hope justice can be done as soon as possible.[26]
- I'm glad this is finally over and justice is served for my late husband.[27]
- [The murderer] not only took my father's life, he broke my family apart. [My father] missed my softball games, graduation and wedding. He never got to see his three grandchildren. My father deserves justice.[28]
- We are sorry for watching Mr. Cleve Foster die, but the justice is done.[29]
- Finally, justice for Becky after 22 years and five months and 23 days.[30]
- For over 25 years we have waited for justice to be served and for this sentence to be carried out.[31]

[24] Earley, *The Serial Killer Whisperer*, p. 254.

[25] The offender was Gary Welch.

[26] The offender was Yokamon Laneal Hearn, executed by the state of Texas on July 18, 2012.

[27] The offender was Donald L. Palmer Jr., executed by the state of Ohio on September 20, 2012.

[28] The offender was Donald L. Palmer Jr.

[29] The offender was Cleve Foster, executed by the state of Texas on September 25, 2012.

[30] The offender was Donald Eugene Moeller, executed by the state of South Dakota on October 30, 2012.

[31] The offender was Garry Thomas Allen, executed by the state of Oklahoma on November 6, 2012.

Several family members noted that the death of the offender would bring closure, at least of a certain kind, and foster healing. The daughter of one victim said simply, "I'm here for closure."[32] The sister of the woman killed by her husband with a baseball bat and a truck so that he could collect her life insurance said after the execution that the day was "about justice, finality and closure for my gorgeous sister, Trisha, and my family.... Today we put a period at the end of the chapter that held us captive for far too long.... Today we breathe again. Today we move forward and move on."[33] Others expressed a similar view: "Today, we got that justice.... We're glad that it's finally over. Be at peace. The race is finally over."[34]

But the mother of a woman who was sexually assaulted and beaten to death distinguished two kinds of closure: "Nothing will ever fill that void.... It will always be in our lives, the void that Matt [Larry Matthew Puckett] caused. There will be closure to this on the side of justice, but there will never be closure for us for our daughter as part of our lives."[35] Others also pointed out that even though the execution of the offender would not bring back their loved one, justice demanded it: "It's not going to change what happened ... but justice will be served."[36]

And justice could promote healing. According to the father of one of the victims of an offender who had been convicted of one rape murder and later connected by DNA evidence to another, "Now we have an opportunity—both families—to heal. Justice was served— Mary's, my daughter's death—made right." He added, "In this particular case, when justice is carried out, it will be a vindication of my daughter's life."[37] By "vindication" he seemed to mean that by imposing the ultimate punishment on the murderer, public authority was making a statement about the worth of his daughter's life. To

[32] The offender was Michael Selsor.

[33] The offender was Timothy Shaun Stemple, executed by the state of Oklahoma on March 15, 2012.

[34] The offender was Michael Selsor.

[35] The offender was Larry Matthew Puckett, executed by the state of Mississippi on March 20, 2012.

[36] The offender was Michael Edward Hooper, executed by the state of Oklahoma on August 14, 2012.

[37] The offender was Cleve Foster.

allow the offender to live out his days in prison would be to undervalue the life he took in such a brutal way. (This echoes the justification for the death penalty in God's command to Noah and his sons in Genesis 9:6: murderers must suffer death *because their victims were made in God's image*.)

Despite the failure of many contemporary religious leaders to distinguish just punishment from revenge or vengeance, several family members expressly cited the difference. In the words of the mother of a rape-murder victim who had traveled more than five hundred miles to witness the killer's execution in April 2011, only to learn that the U.S. Supreme Court had issued a stay a few hours before the execution, "I just want it to be over. This is astounding to me. The irony is that my daughter didn't get such consideration. I have been so upset. Sickened.... It's not about revenge. To us, it is about justice."[38]

As we have seen, many of those executed in 2012 had committed extraordinarily brutal crimes. There is no need to repeat the details. Yet by being put to death by lethal injection, the murderers did not suffer nearly as much as many of the victims had. One might say that they got better than they deserved. This fact was not lost on many of the family members. One said that "justice was served" but "only slightly".[39] The daughter of one victim commented after the execution that "This was much kinder, what we did to him today, than what he did to my dad.... This was justice, but it was a much kinder justice."[40] The father, quoted above, of one of the two women raped and murdered by Cleve Foster said of Foster's execution that "it wasn't the violent death that both Mary and my daughter experienced. I feel it was way too easy, but it is what it is."[41] Finally, the nephew of one of Manuel Pardo's nine murder victims described Pardo's execution as "mild justice".[42]

The views of these loved ones are echoed in the hundreds of statements we have from the family members who commented (either before or after) on many of the nearly seven hundred executions

[38] The offender was Cleve Foster.
[39] The offender was William Gerald Mitchell, executed by the state of Mississippi on March 22, 2012.
[40] The offender was Michael Selsor.
[41] The offender was Cleve Foster.
[42] Manuel Pardo was executed by the state of Florida on December 11, 2012.

that occurred between 2000 and 2011.[43] What follows are illustrative examples.

Over and over again family members affirmed that the offender received his just punishment; and no expressions were more common than "justice has been served", "justice was served", or "justice was done." Many of those who did not use the actual word "justice" stated emphatically that the offender got what he deserved. Examples include the following:

- I have always believed in "an eye for an eye." ... I have waited 15 years for the final chapter.[44]
- Well, I do think that he deserves to die.[45]
- I think Jack Walker should pay for what he did to my mother. I think he should die for taking my mom away from me.... We believe if you live by the sword, you should die by the sword. An eye for an eye, a tooth for a tooth.[46]
- You do something of this magnitude, torturing somebody, you're going to have to pay the price for it.[47]
- It was horrible [watching the execution] ... but if anyone deserved to die, it was him.[48]
- He got what he had coming to him.[49]
- We think he got what he deserved.[50]
- The man had to pay the price. He committed the crime.[51]

[43] The following quotations are from the materials collected by the prosecuting attorney of Clark County, Indiana. Citations are to the name, state, and date of the executed offender.

[44] The offender was Mark Andrew Fowler, executed by the state of Oklahoma on January 23, 2001.

[45] The offender was Ronald Dunaway Fluke, executed by the state of Oklahoma on March 27, 2001.

[46] The offender was Jack Dale Walker, executed by the state of Oklahoma on August 28, 2001.

[47] The offender was Lois Nadean Smith, executed by the state of Oklahoma on December 4, 2001.

[48] The offender was Michael Eugene Thompson, executed by the state of Alabama on March 13, 2003.

[49] The offender was Kenneth Eugene Bruce, executed by the state of Texas on January 14, 2004.

[50] The offender was David Jay Brown, executed by the state of Oklahoma on March 9, 2004.

[51] The offender was Eddie Albert Crawford, executed by the state of Georgia on July 19, 2004.

- He got what he deserved.... That's what I wanted to hear—death. He didn't deserve to live.[52]
- It was a horrific crime. It deserved the punishment that was given.[53]
- He got what he deserved [for murdering a family of five].... My only regret is that he has but one life to give.[54]
- It's just the right thing to have happen.[55]
- Elijah Page had the ultimate penalty for the ultimate crime.[56]
- He took a life, and now his was taken.[57]
- All I know is my mother is still in the grave and that's the bottom line. We all have to pay for what we do in life and he paid today.[58]

Even the brother of one offender implicitly recognized the justice of the punishment: "I don't want my brother to die.... But nevertheless, he committed a wrong. He has to face judgment for this."[59]

In emphasizing this principle of desert, some family members described the punishment as the natural consequence of freely choosing to commit such an evil act:

- Jerald Harjo made his choice and this is the price he must pay.[60]
- It was his decision. He decided that night to murder Uncle Ralph, knowing the consequences that may follow. Giving up his rights and facing the death penalty was a risk he was apparently willing to take.[61]

[52] The offender was Hastings Arthur Wise, executed by the state of South Carolina on November 4, 2005.

[53] The offender was John Albert Boltz, executed by the state of Oklahoma on June 1, 2006.

[54] The offender was Jeffrey Don Lundgren, executed by the state of Ohio on October 24, 2006.

[55] The offender was Charles Edward Smith, executed by the state of Texas on May 16, 2007.

[56] The offender was Elijah Page, executed by South Dakota on July 11, 2007.

[57] The offender was Terry Lyn Short, executed by the state of Oklahoma on June 17, 2008.

[58] The offender was Jason Getsy, executed by the state of Ohio on August 18, 2009.

[59] The offender was Jeffrey Henry Caldwell, executed by the state of Texas on August 30, 2000.

[60] The offender was Jerald Wayne Harjo, executed by the state of Oklahoma on July 17, 2001.

[61] The offender was Robert Wayne Frye, executed by the state of North Carolina on August 31, 2001.

- Robert Coulson committed a horrible crime; he received a fair trial and was found guilty by a jury of his peers. He must now accept responsibility for his actions.[62]
- We as individuals make decisions. He made the decision to take their lives. Today the state of Arkansas made the decision to take his life, and I'm glad for that decision.[63]
- God has given us free will—we are each responsible for our actions.[64]
- I feel bad that [the offender is] dead because of his [five] kids, but he chose to do this. I can't feel bad for him.[65]

With time from sentence to execution ranging from an average of eleven years and five months for those executed in 2000 to seventeen years and six months for those executed in 2011 (and with many individuals serving considerably longer), many family members complained about the delay but expressed deep satisfaction that justice was finally done.[66] The execution was a "final act of justice", said the parents of one victim.[67] "[This] is the night justice was finally served, plain and simple, [but] it's way past time", said the mother of a slain police officer.[68] "I feel that justice has finally been served", said the father of one victim.[69] "Today we feel that our family finally has justice", said a murder victim's son.[70] "I am here to see final justice", commented a family member whose brother and sister-in-law

---

[62] The offender was Robert Otis Coulson, executed by the state of Texas on June 25, 2002.

[63] The offender was Riley Dobi Noel, executed by the state of Arkansas on July 9, 2003.

[64] The offender was Jerry Bridwell McWee, executed by the state of South Carolina on April 16, 2004.

[65] The offender was Edward Nathaniel Bell, executed by the state of Virginia on February 19, 2009.

[66] The data on time from sentence to execution is from Tracy L. Snell, *Capital Punishment, 2013—Statistical Tables* (Washington, D.C.: Bureau of Justice Statistics, 2014), p. 14, table 10, http://www.bjs.gov/content/pub/pdf/cp13st.pdf.

[67] The offender was Kelly Lamont Rogers, executed by the state of Oklahoma on March 23, 2000.

[68] The offender was Craig Neil Ogan Jr., executed by the state of Texas on November 19, 2002.

[69] The offender was Daniel Juan Revilla, executed by the state of Oklahoma on January 16, 2003.

[70] The offender was Lawrence Colwell Jr., executed by the state of Nevada on March 26, 2004.

were murdered.[71] "We finally, finally got some justice for Elizabeth and Jennifer", said a man whose daughter was murdered.[72] "Justice was finally served", said the widow of a slain police officer, "[but] twenty-four years is extremely too long for justice to be served."[73]

Some noted just how much pain the delay caused the family. One expressed the hope that the execution would "finally put an end to this 16½ years of pain, grief and sadness".[74] An aunt of a victim said that the family had been "unjustly sentenced to 22 years of hell", and another family member called it "22 years of legalized torture".[75] "He did a horrendous crime to these two girls", said the father of one of the victims, "and he deserved to die. And 17 years later he died— not soon enough. Seventeen years is a long time to have something eating on you like that."[76] Several were quite precise about how long it took for the sentence to be carried out. "We have waited 18 years [and] 29 days for this to happen. It has finally come and we thank God", said the mother of one victim.[77] And one family issued a statement noting that "the execution came 16 years, two months, three weeks and one day after [the victim] was murdered in her home."[78]

These complaints about delay between sentence and execution were quite common, and many specifically noted the injustice of the offender living out all those days that he had denied his victim(s).

- My wife, she missed out on those nine and a half years.... There ain't a holiday that goes by—there ain't a day that goes by—that it doesn't affect me.[79]

[71] The offender was Jesus Ledesma Aguilar, executed by the state of Texas on May 24, 2006.

[72] The offender was Sedley Alley, executed by the state of Texas on June 28, 2006.

[73] The offender was Clarence Edward Gill, executed by the state of Florida on September 20, 2006.

[74] The offender was Gary Alan Walker, executed by the state of Oklahoma on January 13, 2000.

[75] The offender was Darrell Keith Rich, executed by the state of California on March 15, 2000.

[76] The offender was Peter Anthony Cantu, executed by the state of Texas on August 17, 2010.

[77] The offender was Daniel E. Wilson, executed by the state of Ohio on June 3, 2009.

[78] The offender was Eddie Duvall Powell III, executed by the state of Alabama on June 16, 2011.

[79] The offender was Glen Charles McGinnis, executed by the state of Texas on January 25, 2000.

- [The two killers] lived almost 12 years since Jim was murdered; that is 12 years longer than my brother lived.[80]
- He ended up with a whole lot more chances than she did. He was given several appeals. My mother didn't get appeals.[81]
- I think he deserves everything he got.... At least he had eight more years. They didn't.[82]
- We're feeding and clothing him all these years and his family has had all these extra years with him.... They had a chance to say goodbye. We've never had that chance. Something is askew.[83]
- Mr. Allen abused the justice system with endless appeals until he lived longer in prison than the short 17 years of Josephine's life [the victim in one of four murders that the offender ordered from prison while serving a life sentence for another first-degree murder].[84]
- We have been waiting 11 years.... He has been alive and well all this time and I have been without a dad.[85]
- It has been 11 years since his conviction.... He has been housed, clothed, given blankets, pillows, at some point TV, mail, sunlight, clean clothes, food and drink, appeal lawyers all paid by our tax dollars.... The victim, Felecia, our daughter and mother, has been in a sealed concrete vault and casket 6 feet under dirt for the past 17 years, since the crime was committed. Paid for by her family.[86]
- Nobody should have the right to outlive their victims by so many years.[87]

[80] The offender was William Clifford Bryson, executed by the state of Oklahoma on June 15, 2000.

[81] The offender was Paul Selso Nuncio, executed by the state of Texas on June 15, 2000.

[82] The offender was Newton Burton Anderson, executed by the state of Texas on February 22, 2007.

[83] The offender was Joseph Bennard Nichols, executed by the state of Texas on March 7, 2007.

[84] The offender was Clarence Ray Allen, executed by the state of Texas on January 17, 2006.

[85] The offender was Reginald Winthrop Blanton, executed by the state of Texas on October 27, 2009.

[86] The offender was Karl Eugene Chamberlain, executed by the state of Texas on June 11, 2008.

[87] The offender was Dorsie Leslie Jones Jr., executed by the state of Oklahoma on February 1, 2001.

In sometimes searing language, several loved ones explained how deeply important it was that they lived to see the execution. The father of one of the two young girls who had been sexually assaulted and stabbed to death said, "I would go to the end of the earth to see this end."[88] The son of a woman murdered for a $1,000 payment thanked "God for the opportunity to have lived long enough to witness this day.... She was made to know fear and horror as her last conscious thoughts before a bullet permanently destroyed her brain tissue at the command of her assassin."[89] The daughter of a deli worker who had been murdered in an armed robbery was eager to tell her ninety-year-old mother, the victim's widow who could not travel, about the execution: "She is going to be very happy.... She's been waiting since 1982 [25 years]."[90] The son of a victim issued a statement on behalf of the family saying, "I thank God for keeping myself, my four brothers and my sister alive and in good health so that we were able to see justice finally done."[91] At a news conference after the execution, the sister of the victim said, "We waited a long time to see him put to death. I'm very glad to have seen him take his last breath."[92]

Although some described the execution as final justice for the family, many others viewed it as something specifically owed to the victim. Accordingly, family members sometimes spoke of their duty to the victim to see the process through and to witness the execution. Some even suggested that only after the execution of the offender would the soul of the victim be able to rest in peace. The mother of a five-year-old girl who was kidnapped from her home, sexually assaulted, and murdered told the press that as she witnessed the execution she told her daughter, "You're free. You can go.... And then I thanked God for the strength to stand there."[93] Others said:

[88] The offender was Rex Warren Mays, executed by the state of Texas on September 24, 2002.

[89] The offender was John B. Nixon, executed by the state of Mississippi on December 14, 2005.

[90] The offender was Joseph Nichols.

[91] The offender was Willie McNair, executed by the state of Alabama on May 14, 2009.

[92] The offender was Paul Everette Woodward, executed by the state of Mississippi on May 19, 2010.

[93] The offender was Jackie Barron Wilson, executed by the state of Texas on May 4, 2006.

- I promised Richard, as I stood over his coffin that I would live to see this day.... I had to keep my promise to Richard and now I can go to the cemetery and I'll tell him.[94]
- It was a promise I made to my husband 22 years ago when he was lying in his coffin that I was going to see this through to the end. This is the end.[95]
- I feel that justice has finally been served—not for me but for my son Mark.[96]
- She was one of those people you just wanted to be like.... If it is over tomorrow, we will just feel like she can rest in peace.[97]
- Today I followed through with this to fulfill something that I needed to fulfill for Julia.[98]
- Susan and Lisa [a 29-year-old mother and 3-year-old daughter] ... have finally been put to rest after 15 years of legal battles with the court system. They both can rest in peace now knowing that this nightmare has finally come to an end.[99]
- It was like I was the last voice for my sister.[100]
- Rest in peace, Suzanne. The jury's sentence has been carried out.[101]
- I feel, now, that my brother and his wife and his son can rest in peace.[102]

Like the family members of the victims of those executed in 2012, many in the earlier group believed that although justice was done, the offender got off too easily compared with the pain and suffering he caused his victim. Here are a few characteristic examples:[103]

[94] The offender was Ronald Keith Boyd, executed by the state of Oklahoma on April 27, 2000.

[95] The offender was Miguel Richardson, executed by the state of Texas on June 6, 2001.

[96] The offender was Daniel Juan Revilla, executed by the state of Oklahoma on January 16, 2003.

[97] The offender was Amos Lee King Jr., executed by the state of Florida on February 26, 2003.

[98] The offender was Jason Scott Byram, executed by the state of South Carolina on April 23, 2004.

[99] The offender was Stephen Allen Vrabel, executed by the state of Ohio on July 14, 2004.

[100] The offender was Marvin Bieghler, executed by the state of Indiana on January 27, 2006.

[101] The offender was Sedley Alley.

[102] The offender was Jason Oric Williams, executed by the state of Alabama on May 19, 2011.

[103] As we saw in chapter 1, Catholic doctrine distinguishes the legitimate desire to see justice done (a virtue) from a hateful desire to see an offender suffer (a vice). In listing these

- He got off easy. It was like he just went to sleep.[104]
- He lived too long and died too easy.[105]
- I think he had an easy death. He went to sleep. That's not comparable to what he did to my mother.[106]
- I think this crime deserves much more than the legal punishment. I just feel like he is taking the coward's way out by going to sleep.[107]
- It will make me feel better when he dies. It is too bad they cut out hanging. Lethal injection is too easy.[108]
- She got off really easy. These men [the offender's seven victims] suffered. These men's families suffered tremendously all these years. I mean it was cold-blooded murder.
- I wish it would have been a little bit more, a little harder on her. It was very, very easy. Very easy ... even the years in prison that she did. It was a piece of cake. It was a cake walk.[109]
- The death that Lyons had tonight was a painless one. I think of my husband's death and it certainly was not painless.[110]
- William Zuern, Jr. went too easy today. I believe that he should have died the way Phil died.[111]
- It started at 9:18. The burden's been lifted. Oken is dead.... The only problem is that Steven Oken died in peace. My daughter didn't have the luxury to die in peace the way he died tonight.[112]

---

examples, we are not maintaining that each of these family members stayed on the virtuous side of the line separating the two.

[104] The offender was James Henry Hampton, executed by the state of Missouri on March 22, 2000.

[105] The offender was James Edward Clayton, executed by the state of Texas on May 25, 2000.

[106] The offender was James Glenn Robedeaux, executed by the state of Oklahoma on June 1, 2000.

[107] The offender was Ronald Dunaway Fluke.

[108] The offender was Richard William Kutzner, executed by the state of Texas on August 7, 2002.

[109] The offender was Aileen Carol Wuornos, executed by the state of Florida on October 9, 2002.

[110] The offender was Robbie James Lyons, executed by the state of North Carolina on December 5, 2003.

[111] The offender was William G. Zuern Jr., executed by the state of Ohio on June 8, 2004.

[112] The offender was Steven Howard Oken, executed by the state of Maryland on June 17, 2004.

The daughter of an eighty-nine-year-old woman who was brutally knifed to death (and nearly decapitated) when she walked in on a burglary of her apartment contrasted her mother's death with the execution of the offender: "It was very white. It was very sterile. It was just as sweet as you would want to die. No pain, no nothing."[113]

Like the loved ones who witnessed or commented on the executions in 2012, many involved in the earlier cases distinguished justice from revenge, or vengeance:

- I've been asked several times whether I feel that watching the execution would be revenge for me. My answer is after 11 years, there is no revenge; that is justice.[114]
- We did not seek revenge with the death of Robert Clayton. We sought justice and justice was served.[115]
- As Christians, we are not here for revenge but to see justice served for Ruth.[116]
- This is not a vendetta or a social event. We all hurt and hope the [offender's family] ... can understand our grief for the past 13 years waiting for justice to be done.[117]
- We do feel closure. Not vengeance.... But that justice was served.[118]
- I'm there for the family and to see justice carried out as what was sentenced in the lower courts.... I don't want people to think I'm in it for revenge.[119]
- The night she was murdered she had no fanfare, no witnesses, no chaplain, no last meal. Today is not about revenge. Today

---

[113] The offender was Larry Eugene Hutcherson, executed by the state of Alabama on October 26, 2006.

[114] The offender was Gregg Francis Braun, executed by the state of Oklahoma on July 20, 2000.

[115] The offender was Robert William Clayton, executed by the state of Oklahoma on March 1, 2001.

[116] The offender was Jerald Wayne Harjo.

[117] The offender was Jessie Joe Patrick, executed by the state of Texas on September 17, 2002.

[118] The offender was William Robert Jones Jr., executed by the state of Missouri on November 20, 2002.

[119] The offender was Jerry Paul Henderson, executed by the state of Alabama on June 2, 2005.

is not about closure. Today is not about anyone else other than my sister.[120]

As might be expected, with nearly seven hundred executions between 2000 and 2011, not every family member supported the death penalty. Yet, such cases were rare:

- The children of a murdered Virginia state trooper opposed the offender's execution, while his widow supported it.[121]
- The grandmothers of a murdered seven-year-old girl split sharply on the punishment: one ended up heading a statewide anti-capital punishment group, and the other, strongly in favor of the death penalty, founded a support group for the family members of murder victims.[122]
- In two cases, the children of women murdered by their husbands called for the state not to execute their father.[123]
- The mother of a twenty-year-old convenience-store clerk who was stabbed to death during a robbery wrote to the state parole board asking that the offender's sentence be commuted to life.[124]
- The former mother-in-law of a twenty-five-year-old woman who had been sexually assaulted, mutilated, and murdered told the press that she did not believe in the death penalty, though she did think that the execution would "bring closure to the children" (then sixteen-year-old twin boys and a fourteen-year-old daughter).[125]
- The relatives of three adults who were murdered by the estranged husband of one of them split on the appropriateness of the death penalty, with the mother of the murdered wife

[120] The offender was William Josef Berkley, executed by the state of Texas on April 22, 2010.

[121] The offender was Lonnie Weeks Jr., executed by the state of Virginia on March 16, 2000.

[122] The offender was Floyd Allen Medlock, executed by the state of Oklahoma on January 16, 2001.

[123] The offenders were Fred Marion Gilreat Jr., executed by the state of Georgia on November 15, 2001, and Leroy White, executed by the state of Alabama on January 13, 2011.

[124] The offender was Johnny Joe Martinez, executed by the state of Texas on May 22, 2002.

[125] The offender was Dexter Lee Vinson, executed by the state of Virginia on April 27, 2006.

strongly supporting the execution and the mother and niece of the other victims calling for clemency.[126]

- The relatives of a South Korean immigrant, shot in the head during a robbery at the store he owned, opposed the death penalty.[127]

Although the reality of the murders did not shake these individuals from their opposition to the death penalty, in a few other cases it did have such an effect. A professional counselor who had worked with the victim on a substance-abuse problem said, "I believe he deserves it, and I've never been real for or against the death penalty. But when it hits you personally and you see the devastation it causes for the entire family and the entire community ... I wouldn't feel safe with him being turned back out into the community. It is, I think, what prisons are made for and the death penalty is made for."[128] "I didn't believe in the death penalty until all this happened", said the victim's sister with whom he had been living. "[But] he killed my brother and it was a brutal murder."[129]

Finally, some loved ones commented that the world would simply be a better place once the offender was gone:

- I just want him off this Earth.... I just want him away from here so he can go to God and let God deal with it.[130]
- He was nothing but a child predator. He needed to be removed.[131]
- This guy has fouled Oklahoma with every breath since he murdered my aunt.[132]

---

[126] The offender was Matthew Eric Wrinkles, executed by the state of Indiana on December 11, 2009.

[127] The offender was Johnnie Roy Baston, executed by the state of Ohio on March 10, 2011.

[128] The offender was Richard Eugene Dinkins, executed by the state of Texas on January 29, 2003.

[129] The offender was Thomas Wayne Akers, executed by the state of Virginia on March 1, 2001.

[130] The offender was Christopher Cornelius Goins, executed by the state of Virginia on December 6, 2000.

[131] The offender was Rex Warren Mays.

[132] The offender was Loyd Winford Lafevers, executed by the state of Oklahoma on January 30, 2001.

- The memories of his victims and the welfare of society and demands of justice all dictate this final act of cleansing.[133]
- We're glad you're going to be off this Earth.... We think the world will be a better and safer place with you gone.[134]

We have quoted such comments at length to illustrate just how very deep and pervasive—among ordinary people and not merely traditional natural law theorists—is the sense that capital punishment is, for the most heinous crimes, simply what justice demands. As Aquinas argues, the desire to see offenders get their just deserts is not only natural to us but in itself is positively virtuous. Thus, when churchmen and other opponents of capital punishment casually dismiss the natural and decent desire among the families of victims to see justice done as a mere quest for revenge, they harm those who have already suffered tremendously. They harm them, first, by insulting them, however inadvertently, and also by contributing to the perception that our society is no longer just—no longer a society that holds evil men responsible for their acts, comforts their victims, or adheres to basic Christian morality. If *even churchmen* will no longer uphold the natural law, the clear teaching of Scripture, and the traditional doctrine of the Church, who will?

Offenders

Strikingly, three of the offenders themselves who were executed in 2012 acknowledged the justice of their punishment. Facing imminent execution for murdering and robbing two strangers in consecutive incidents after a minor traffic accident, Donald Palmer of Ohio turned down the opportunity to request a recommendation of clemency from the Ohio Parole Board because he believed that he did not deserve mercy. In an interview a week before his September 2012 execution he said, "I killed two people. I've always accepted responsibility for the taking of their lives.... I believe in justice and I believe that the victims, their hatred, their anger, they need to have justice." (Yet, Palmer's ultimate acceptance of

---

[133] The offender was Jeffrey Don Lundgren.

[134] The offender was Robert Brice Morrow, executed by the state of Texas on November 4, 2004.

his punishment did not prevent him from authorizing appeals that lasted twenty-two years.)

Unlike Palmer, Eric Robert of South Dakota, who, while serving an eighty-year sentence for kidnapping a young woman, murdered a sixty-three-year-old prison guard during an escape attempt, pleaded guilty and waived all appeals, resulting in his execution just one year after sentencing. In a letter he wrote a week before his execution, he commended the prosecutor and affirmed the justice of his punishment: "I do not want or desire to die, instead I deserve to die; this I have always stated." In concluding he wrote, "It's not about me or any future killers, it is about ensuring that in contested cases that the victims and their families get their intended and needed swift justice."[135]

Finally, after fighting his conviction and sentence for two decades, Donald Moeller of South Dakota, who had abducted a nine-year-old girl, driven her to the woods, and then raped and stabbed her to death, announced at a hearing in federal court a few weeks before his scheduled execution that "I killed the little girl. It's just that the punishment be concluded. I believe it's a good thing, that the death penalty does inhibit further criminal acts." He added, "I killed. I deserve to be killed."

Punishment and forgiveness

Many today—including many in positions of authority in the Catholic Church—mistakenly believe that the Christian message of mercy and forgiveness trumps the legitimate role of the state in meting out punishments proportional to crimes. They believe this despite the unambiguous teaching of the Catholic Church for two millennia, as restated in the modern *Catechism*, that public authorities have not only the "right" but also the "duty" "to inflict punishment proportionate to the gravity of the offense" (*CCC* 2266). As chapters 12 and 13 of Paul's Letter to the Romans make abundantly clear, the Christian prohibition of private vengeance in no way undermines the authority of public officials to punish the guilty. Indeed, when they do so, they act as "the servant of God to execute his wrath on the wrongdoer"

[135] The offender was Eric Robert, executed by the state of South Dakota on October 15, 2012.

(Rom 13:4). Thus, when the victims of crime (or a murder victim's loved ones) personally forgive a criminal, this in no way absolves the offender of deserved and proportionate punishment. This is a simple point, but one that needs repeating in light of the dangerous notion, at least as applied to criminal justice, that the Christian message inexorably exalts mercy over justice. Hence the wisdom of the young woman who was raped, shot, and severely injured after a robbery and abduction, during which her assailant and an accomplice murdered a nineteen-year-old mentally challenged man and injured another woman: "He asked for forgiveness and I forgive him, but he had to pay the consequences."[136]

Forgiveness was a frequent topic for the hundreds of loved ones who commented on the executions that took place between 2000 and 2011. Some simply stated that they could not forgive the offender for the terrible crime he had committed: "I don't forgive him"; "I cannot forgive this man"; "I believed him that he's sorry but that doesn't mean I can forgive him for what he did"; "I cannot forgive." A larger number, however, stated that they did forgive the offender, often in response to a plea from the inmate himself. Examples include the following:

- I do forgive him. I hope he's gone to heaven.[137]
- We forgive him.... We have no animosity for him.[138]
- I think we already have [forgiven the offender].... We are strong Christians. I believe for my own salvation that I need to forgive him.[139]
- He took something very precious from us, but if my mother can forgive him, I have to.[140]
- God has given me peace with this. I have forgiven him.[141]

[136] The offender was Buenka Adams, executed by the state of Texas on April 26, 2012.

[137] The offender was Prenell Ford, executed by the state of Alabama on June 2, 2002.

[138] The offender was Robert Dewey Glock II, executed by the state of Florida on January 1, 2001.

[139] The offender was Ron Scott Shamburger, executed by the state of Texas on September 18, 2002.

[140] The offender was Larry Kenneth Jackson, executed by the state of Oklahoma on April 17, 2003.

[141] The offender was James Barney Hubbard, executed by the state of Alabama on August 5, 2004.

- I've learned how to forgive the man for doing what he did to our family.... I don't understand it and I'll never understand it, but I forgave him for it already.[142]
- If you don't forgive, it will consume you. It will eat you alive.... He has God to answer to.[143]

As this last quotation suggests, for many of the family members, what really mattered was not whether *they* forgave the offender, but whether *God* did. As the sister of one murder victim said, "It's not up to anybody to forgive him. If God forgives him then he's forgiven. It's not up to me or anybody else."[144] "The good Lord might forgive him", said the father of a victim, "but He's got more heart than I've got."[145] "I really hope that God forgave him", said the mother of a victim, adding, "I really hope someday that I will have the strength to do that."[146] When the man who kidnapped and murdered her twelve-year-old son asked for forgiveness in the moments before his execution, the boy's mother insisted that forgiveness "is God's job".[147] Hours before the man who killed her brother and three others was executed, the victim's sister said before a group gathered at church, "Let us pray that he'll find the forgiveness that only God offers."[148] Confronting the fact that the killer of her brother had shown no remorse, the sister said, "I'm gonna be on my knees praying that at the last minute he asks God for forgiveness."[149] Finally, the family of a seventy-year-old woman who had been raped, sodomized, and shot to death in her home said in a statement, "It is our prayer that Mr.

---

[142] The offender was Sammy Crystal Perkins, executed by the state of North Carolina on October 8, 2004.

[143] The offender was Franklin DeWayne Alix, executed by the state of Texas on March 20, 2010.

[144] The offender was Michael David Clagett, executed by the state of Virginia on July 7, 2000.

[145] The offender was Clay King Smith, executed by the state of Arkansas on May 8, 2001.

[146] The offender was Jose Martinez High, executed by the state of Georgia on November 6, 2001.

[147] The offender was Hilton Lewis Crawford, executed by the state of Texas on July 2, 2003.

[148] The offender was Donald Ray Wallace Jr., executed by the state of Indiana on March 10, 2005.

[149] The offender was Kevin Aaron Conner, executed by the state of Indiana on July 27, 2005.

Powell has found forgiveness from our Lord Jesus and that he will spend eternity in Heaven."[150]

Nearly every family member who brought up forgiveness saw no conflict between forgiving the offender and executing him:[151]

- I feel I have already forgiven him, but I want to see justice done.[152]
- He needed to die for that crime, but, I did appreciate the statement and the fact that in his mind, he has been forgiven as best as I understood it and I hope that's the case. The Lord will judge in the end, and whether or not he truly repented [and] was forgiven, in my mind, he paid the price he needed to pay.[153]
- They say that he has turned his life around and found God, which is wonderful, but he has to pay a price here on Earth.[154]
- I think we forgave him a long time ago. But the consequences still had to be carried out. It was just.[155]
- I can forgive Willie McNair for what he did because he paid the price with his life.[156]
- Justice for Brian ... has been served. We have no anger towards Mr. Bradford and forgive him of his crime against our family.[157]

It is worth remarking that in distinguishing the question of forgiveness from that of whether to inflict a proportionate punishment, these ordinary people show greater moral understanding and subtlety of thought than many educated critics of capital punishment, including some churchmen. So too, if we may say so, do those offenders who *have themselves* affirmed that for them to be executed is simply a matter of justice.

[150] The offender was Eddie Duvall Powell III, executed by the state of Alabama on June 16, 2011.

[151] The exception was in the case of Lonnie Weeks Jr.

[152] The offender was Juan Salvez Soria, executed by the state of Texas on July 26, 2000.

[153] The offender was David Earl Gibbs, executed by the state of Texas on August 23, 2000.

[154] The offender was Norman Richard Cleary, executed by the state of Oklahoma on February 17, 2004.

[155] The offender was Kenneth Wayne Morris, executed by the state of Texas on March 4, 2009.

[156] The offender was Willie McNair.

[157] The offender was Gayland Charles Bradford, executed by the state of Texas on June 1, 2011.

Repentance and the death penalty

The notion that the death penalty forestalls the possibility of repentance is often treated by Catholic opponents of capital punishment as if it obviously and decisively overrides any presumption in favor of inflicting such punishment. But as we saw in chapter 1, no less than Saint Thomas Aquinas regarded this objection as "frivolous", and there are, in fact, serious problems with it. Like Aquinas, we noted that knowledge that their execution is imminent can actually *encourage* repentance among some offenders who might otherwise *not* repent. We now consider some examples of offenders who found repentance before being executed.

On February 3, 1998, the state of Texas executed Karla Faye Tucker for a 1983 murder in which she delivered more than twenty blows with a pickax to a man and woman in their bed, leaving the murder weapon buried in the chest of the woman. In the weeks before the execution, the upcoming event drew widespread national (and even international) attention both because Tucker would be only the second woman executed for murder in the United States since 1976 (and the first in Texas since 1863) and because Tucker had apparently become a truly repentant born-again Christian while behind bars. In an interview with Larry King on CNN just a month before her execution, Tucker described her sudden conversion after just three months in jail (and seven months before her murder conviction):

> TUCKER: A ministry came to [the county] jail [in Houston] to do a service, a puppet show, one night and everybody in my tank was going out to the puppet show and I didn't want to stay alone in my tank, so I decided to go with them and socialize in church. Well, actually, when I walked through the door I never said a word, so I never did any socializing, but when I went back to my tank that night, something got down in there and I had grabbed a Bible. I stole this Bible not realizing Bibles were given out free in jail, 'cause I'd never been there. So ...
>
> KING: Never were a churchgoer or anything?
>
> TUCKER: I was never—no. And had never been in jail. I didn't know that they gave out Bibles out [*sic*] free in here to those who needed them. So I took this Bible into my cell, and I

hid way back in the corner so nobody could see me, because I was like really proud. I didn't want anybody to think I was being weak and reading this Bible. I realize now, you have to be stronger to walk with the Lord in here than you do to not walk with him. It's a whole lot harder, let me tell you. But anyway, that night I started reading the Bible. I didn't know what I was reading and before I knew it, I was just—I was in the middle of my floor on my knees and I was just asking God to forgive me.

Later in the interview, King asked Tucker how she could be so upbeat facing death:

KING: You have to explain that to me a little more. It can't just be God.

TUCKER: Yes, it can. It's called the joy of the Lord. I don't—when you have done something that I have done, like what I have done, and you have been forgiven for it, and you're loved, that has a way of so changing you. I mean, I have experienced real love. I know what real love is. I know what forgiveness is, even when I did something so horrible. I know that because God forgave me and I accepted what Jesus did on the cross. When I leave here, I am going to go be with him.[158]

Although Tucker did not contest her guilt once convicted, she did fight hard to avoid execution. She became something of a celebrity in Christian circles and was featured on televangelist Pat Robertson's program, *The 700 Club*. Robertson urged the Texas Board of Pardons and Paroles and Governor George W. Bush to spare her life. He was joined by such prominent figures as the speaker of the U.S. House of Representatives, the United Nations commissioner on summary and arbitrary executions, the prime minister of Italy, and Pope John Paul II. Their appeals proved unpersuasive. Tucker's fate was sealed when Governor Bush turned down her request to stay the execution so that she could file one more appeal. Bush read the following statement at a press conference:

I have sought guidance through prayer. I have concluded judgments about the heart and soul of an individual on death row are best left

---

[158] "Karla Faye Tucker: Born Again on Death Row", CNN.com, March 26, 2007, www.cnn.com/2007/US/03/21/larry.king.tucker/.

to a higher authority. Karla Faye Tucker has acknowledged she is guilty of a horrible crime. The courts, including the United States Supreme Court have reviewed the legal issues in this case and therefore I will not grant a 30-day stay. May God bless Karla Faye Tucker and God bless her victims and their families.[159]

In her final words just moments before her execution, Tucker apologized to her victims' families and thanked her friends and supporters. She also reaffirmed her belief in her salvation: "I am going to be face to face with Jesus now.... I love all of you very much. I will see you all when you get there. I will wait for you."[160]

The controversy over Tucker's execution turned not on whether her professed repentance and conversion were genuine—few seemed to doubt this—but on the relevance of such a profound personal transformation to the imposition of the death penalty. Her most ardent defenders insisted that she was no longer the same person who had brutally murdered two people. In the words of Pat Robertson, "When we sent a reporter down to talk to her [in 1992], we didn't find some wild-eyed hippie, we found the most beautiful Christian woman we had ever encountered ... sublime, if I can use that term, a lovely spirit. The person who had committed those crimes really wasn't there anymore. She was like a different person."[161] One consequence of this transformation, it was argued, was that Tucker was no longer the danger to society that Texas law required for the death penalty to be imposed.

As noted, Tucker very much wanted to live. She made an eloquent case for clemency in the letter she wrote to Governor Bush just two weeks before her execution.[162] She took "full responsibility for what happened". Though she had pleaded not guilty at her trial on the advice of her attorneys, "they knew I murdered Jerry and Deborah. I did not lie to them about it.... I am, in fact, guilty. Very

[159] "Execution of Karla Faye Tucker", YouTube video, 1:54, from a PBS interview with Clay Johnson and Doug Wead, posted by Doug Wead, February 4, 2009, http://youtube /ZaoUloApZdo.

[160] "Karla Faye Tucker", website of the prosecuting attorney of Clark County, Indiana, www.clarkprosecutor.org/html/death/US/tucker437.htm.

[161] Quoted in Mary Sigler, "Mercy, Clemency, and the Case of Karla Faye Tucker", *Ohio State Journal of Criminal Law* 4 (2007): 460.

[162] Extensive excerpts from the letter were published in the *Houston Chronicle*, January 20, 1998, and are available at http://murderpedia.org/female.T/t/tucker-karla.htm.

guilty." "I no longer try to lay the blame on my mother", she said of the woman who introduced her to prostitution at age fourteen, "or on society." Nor did she "blame drugs either. When I share that I was out of it on drugs the night I brutally murdered two people, I fully realize that I made the choice to do those drugs. Had I chosen not to do drugs, there would be two people still alive today. But I did choose to do drugs, and I did lose it, and two people are dead because of me." She promised Bush that if he commuted her sentence to life, she would "continue for the rest of my life on this earth to reach out to others to make a positive difference in their lives". In particular, she could help young girls in prison who were "still acting out in violence and hurting others with no concern for another life or for their own life. I can reach out to these girls and try and help them change before they walk out of this place and hurt someone else." Yet despite this plea for mercy, Tucker accepted the justice of her punishment: "I also know that justice and law demand my life for the two innocent lives I brutally murdered that night. If my execution is the only thing, the final act that can fulfill the demand for restitution and justice, then I accept that.... I will pay the price for what I did in any way our law demands it."

Perhaps the other best-known examples of repentance by a death row inmate are those recounted by Sister Helen Prejean in her best-selling 1993 book, *Dead Man Walking*, a story that was portrayed on the screen in the 1995 movie of the same name that starred Susan Sarandon as Sister Prejean (a performance that won her an Academy Award) and Sean Penn as death row inmate Matthew Poncelet.[163] Poncelet was actually an amalgam of two Louisiana death row inmates for whom Sister Prejean became the spiritual adviser: Elmo Patrick Sonnier, who was executed on April 5, 1984, for the rape and murder of an eighteen-year-old woman and the murder of her seventeen-year-old boyfriend, and Robert Lee Willie, who was executed on December 28, 1984, for the kidnap, rape, and murder of an eighteen-year-old woman. We begin with the more ambiguous of the two cases.

Sister Prejean met Robert Lee Willie four years after his capital conviction and two months before his execution. Willie and his

---

[163] Sister Helen Prejean, C.S.J., *Dead Man Walking* (New York: Random House, 2013).

friend Joe Vaccaro had kidnapped their eighteen-year-old victim, took her to a secluded spot, raped her, and murdered her by stabbing her seventeen times. Later, each offender blamed the other for the actual killing, but even in Willie's account he held the woman's hands down so that Vaccaro could stab her. A few days after the murder, the two men abducted a teenage couple from a lover's lane, took turns raping the woman, and knifed and shot the young man while he was tied to a tree. The two survived, but the man was paralyzed from the waist down. During the previous two years, Willie and another man had drowned a drug dealer (for which Willie pleaded guilty after his conviction in the capital case), and Willie was involved in the murder of a police officer, though he was not the shooter.

When Prejean first met Willie, "he didn't mention his crimes; he didn't show any remorse."[164] Later he told Sister Prejean that he was "real, real sorry that girl got killed", but he insisted that he was not responsible for the death.[165] He added that he had been reading the Bible and said "he believes that Jesus died for him on the cross and will 'take care' of him when he appears before the judgment seat of God."[166] (Here Prejean tells the reader, but did not tell Willie, that although she once believed this "theology of 'atonement'"—that "Jesus, by suffering and dying on the cross, 'appeased' an angry God's demand for 'justice'"—she "shed it" when she "discovered that its driving force was fear that made love impossible. What kind of God demands 'payment' in human suffering?"[167]) In the written presentation he prepared for delivery to the pardon board, Willie attacked the political motivation of the district attorney, blamed his sentence on ineffective counsel, and concluded by saying, "I truly regret everything that has happened. But my death is not going to bring Miss Hathaway back to this earth."[168] In response, the prosecutor gave, in Sister Prejean's words, a "very effective" and "in part, very true" presentation: "that Robert lacks remorse and tends to blame everybody but himself".[169] A week or two before his execution, Willie told

---

[164] Ibid., 128.
[165] Ibid., 145.
[166] Ibid., 150.
[167] Ibid.
[168] Ibid., 160–61.
[169] Ibid., 167.

Sister Prejean that he was no longer afraid to die: "I've had a pretty fulfilled life—women, drugs, travel, rock and roll, school, football—about everything there is."[170] He then gave numerous media interviews during which he expressed his admiration for Adolf Hitler and Fidel Castro. As he summarized his life for one reporter, "I'm an outlaw. I've been an outlaw most of my life. If I had it to do all over again, I'd be an outlaw."[171]

Sister Prejean had encouraged Willie to reflect on Jesus' words in John's Gospel: "You will know the truth, and the truth will make you free" (Jn 8:32). Two days before the execution, when Sister Prejean asked if he had been able to sleep, Willie responded, "Yeah, I slept. Funny, but I've told the truth about what happened and, like the Book said, the truth sets you free. I used to always think that the truth could hurt you, but I feel free now, kind of innocent even, knowing it, knowing the truth."[172] He then asked Prejean to arrange a polygraph test so that his mother could know "that I didn't kill Faith Hathaway".[173] In his final hours, Willie told Sister Prejean that when he first heard that she was a nun, "I thought you'd be doin' nothin' but preachin' repentance at me, but after our first visit, I saw I could just talk to you like a friend, and I told my mother that I met this real nice lady."[174] Sister Prejean relates that thirty minutes before the execution, "he thanks me for teaching him about God. 'I know God knows the truth about what happened,' he says. 'I know I'm gonna be okay.'"[175] Sister Prejean then records his final words from the execution chamber: "I would like to say, Mr. and Mrs. Harvey, that I hope you get some relief from my death. Killing people is wrong. That's why you've put me to death. It makes no difference whether it's citizens, countries, or governments. Killing is wrong."[176]

It is hard to know what to make of this case. Facing death, Willie started reading the Bible, professed a belief in Jesus' saving message,

---

[170] Ibid., 182.

[171] Ibid., 182–83.

[172] Ibid., 186.

[173] Ibid.

[174] Ibid., 209.

[175] Ibid., 210.

[176] Ibid., 210–11. Mr. Harvey became stepfather of Faith Hathaway when she was four: hence the different names.

and was apparently convinced that he would be saved. Yet, in Sister Prejean's account there is no real evidence of genuine remorse or of any effort by Willie to seek forgiveness from God for his many past sins. After all, even if he did not actually wield the knife that killed Faith Hathaway, he had abducted and brutalized several young men and women and contributed directly to one death, and by his own hands had murdered at least one person and possibly several others. Rather than confronting the truth of his sinfulness and the evil of his past deeds, Willie felt, even two days before his execution, "kind of innocent even, knowing it, knowing the truth".

In the case of Elmo Patrick Sonnier, the evidence of genuine repentance is much more compelling. Sister Prejean started corresponding with Sonnier about five years after he entered death row and two years before his execution. A few months later, she began visiting him in prison. The prison had a Catholic chaplain, "an elderly man" whose "face is kind" and who "is strictly an old-school, pre–Vatican [II] Catholic". He told Prejean that if she became Sonnier's spiritual adviser, "Your job is to help this fellow save his soul by receiving the sacraments of the church before he dies."[177] Later, as the execution approached, Sister Prejean asked Sonnier whether he believed God had forgiven him. He responded, "At first no. I felt that even God hated me, but I know now that God forgives me. I went to confession to the old priest." He then discussed the murders for the first time and related that "nobody was supposed to get killed" and that his younger brother had done the actual killings. He added, "I will go to my grave feeling bad about those kids. Every night when they dim the lights on the tier I kneel by my bunk and pray for those kids and their parents."[178] At this point, Sister Prejean was "not sure how to measure his sincerity. Even if he didn't do the shooting, he participated in the kidnappings—not just this couple. There had been others [referring to other abductions and rapes attributed to the Sonnier brothers for which, apparently, they had not been charged or convicted]."[179]

In his final days he told Sister Prejean, "I appreciate all the efforts to save me, but me and God have squared things away. I'm ready to

[177] Ibid., 25.
[178] Ibid., 38.
[179] Ibid., 39.

go if it comes down."[180] (By "save" Sonnier apparently meant save from execution, which Prejean and an attorney tried to do during Sonnier's final months.) Prejean then arranged a prayer and Communion service, which the chaplain attended. In the hours before the execution the chaplain asked Sister Prejean to tell Sonnier that he was "available for the last sacraments", but Sonnier turned down the offer.[181] (Later several Catholic chaplains resisted Sister Prejean's efforts to become Willie's spiritual adviser because of their concern that she had not done enough—or perhaps anything at all—to persuade Sonnier to receive "the last rites of the Church", a refusal that, they believed, may have jeopardized his salvation. She responded that "he said that he had already confessed his sins and received communion, and he didn't see the point of 'doing it all over again.' "[182])

Strapped to the electric chair, Sonnier offered his last words. According to Sister Prejean: "Mr. LeBlanc [the father of one of Sonnier's victims], I don't want to leave this world with any hatred in my heart. I want to ask your forgiveness for what me and Eddie done, but Eddie done it." A few moments later, his eyes found Sister Prejean among the witnesses and said to her, "I love you."[183] In its coverage of the execution the *Times-Picayune* of New Orleans recorded a somewhat different version of Sonnier's final words: "Mr. LeBlanc, I can understand the way you feel. I have no hatred in my heart, and as I leave this world, I ask God to forgive what ... I have done." The reporter added, "He then asked LeBlanc's forgiveness."[184] The version published in the 2010 collection *Last Words of the Executed* is nearly identical to what the *Times-Picayune* reported: "Mr. LeBlanc, I can understand the way you feel. I have no hatred in my heart, and as I leave this world, I ask God to forgive what ... I have done. I ask you to have forgiveness."[185] Although it is impossible to know which of the two versions is accurate, it is interesting that the second

---

[180] Ibid., 76.
[181] Ibid., 91.
[182] Ibid., 121.
[183] Ibid., 93.
[184] James Hodge, "Sonnier Executed for Double Murder", *Times-Picayune*, April 5, 1984, http://www.pbs.org/wgbh/pages/frontline/angel/articles/timespicayune45.html.
[185] Robert K. Elder, *Last Words of the Executed* (Chicago: University of Chicago Press, 2010), p. 160. This book does not cite a specific source for Sonnier's words.

version makes an even stronger case for Sonnier's repentance than does Prejean's. In Sister Prejean's version, Sonnier neither asks for God's forgiveness nor accepts full responsibility for his acts (though he had apparently done both earlier).

As we have argued, some religious leaders oppose the death penalty because in their view it denies the offender the opportunity to repent for his sins and thus to save his soul. For example, in January 1998 Bishop William S. Skylstad, speaking as chairman of the Domestic Policy Committee of the United States Conference of Catholic Bishops, called on Governor Bush of Texas to grant clemency to Karla Faye Tucker: "Our opposition to the use of the death penalty reflects our commitment to human life and human dignity. Executions end a life, deny that dignity and remove any chance for repentance and forgiveness."[186] (Perhaps it goes without saying that this was an odd objection to raise in that context, given that Tucker already *had* in fact expressed repentance.) A year later the California Catholic Conference of Bishops issued a report on the death penalty that said in part, "By abolishing the death penalty, we would make a powerful statement in favor of life and reaffirm our belief that God grants all people the opportunity for conversion, reconciliation and reparation for evil done."[187] What these and other religious leaders fail to recognize is that the death penalty may promote repentance, not foreclose it, in the two ways we discussed earlier: first, by forcing the sinner to confront his mortality and God's judgment for his acts and, second, by conveying to the offender the gravity of his offense. Of course, philosophers, theologians, social scientists, and policymakers can never know with *certainty* whether a murderer has repented and saved his soul; only God can know that. Nonetheless, we can, and should, assess the evidence of the offender's own behavior.

In the case of Karla Faye Tucker, the evidence is about as strong as it could be that her repentance was genuine. Coming so early in her confinement (after just three months of incarceration), it did

---

[186] The statement, issued by the United States Conference of Catholic Bishops on January 29, 1998, was formerly at www.usccb.org/comm/archives/1998/98-021a.shtml, but apparently is no longer available.

[187] California Catholic Conference, "The Gospel of Life and Capital Punishment", July 1999, http://www.cacatholic.org/news/california-bishops-statements/gospel-life-and-capital -punishment.

not result from confronting the consequences of imminent death. Yet, Tucker committed her crime in Texas, one of only seven states that at that time had executed a murderer since the Supreme Court had upheld new state death-penalty statutes in 1976.[188] Just seven months before Tucker's crime, Texas had executed Charlie Brooks Jr. for kidnapping, binding, and murdering a twenty-six-year-old auto mechanic. The execution had been widely publicized: Brooks was the first person executed in Texas in nineteen years; he was the first person executed in the United States by lethal injection; and he was the first black American executed in the United States since executions had resumed in 1977. Moreover, during the four decades prior to the Supreme Court's 1972 decision that had overturned all existing capital punishment statutes, Texas had executed 297 persons, the third most of any state in the nation.[189] In the thirty years after Tucker committed her crime, Texas would go on to execute 507 murderers, more than a third of the nation's total. In any ranking of states in which use of the death penalty might have the effect of reinforcing the gravity of the crime of murder, Texas would be at the top. If Tucker had instead committed her brutal crimes in Michigan, which abolished the death penalty more than a century and a half ago, would she have repented so suddenly and so forthrightly?

There is, of course, no way to know. As we saw in the previous chapter, the *Roman Catechism* (1566), the first universal catechism of the Catholic Church, had taught that "the most efficacious [of the remedies against murder] is to form a just conception of the wickedness of murder.... The murderer is the worst enemy of his species, and consequently of nature."[190] (Even the current *Catechism of the Catholic Church*, which is less enthusiastic about using the death penalty, calls murder "a sin that cries out to heaven for vengeance" [*CCC* 2268].) Not only is the death penalty justified by the wickedness of murder; it also reinforces belief in the wickedness of murder. It is this message that capital punishment sends concerning murder's

---

[188] The cases that first upheld new death penalty statutes were *Gregg v. Georgia*, 428 U.S. 153 (1976), *Proffitt v. Florida*, 428 U.S. 242 (1976), and *Jurek v. Texas*, 428 U.S. 262 (1976).

[189] The case was *Furman v. Georgia*, 408 U.S. 238 (1972). The data on executions in Texas are derived from table 14 in Snell, *Capital Punishment, 2013—Statistical Tables* (December 2014), p. 17, www.bjs.gov/content/pub/pdf/cp13st.pdf.

[190] Available at www.cin.org/users/james/ebooks/master/trent/tcommo5.htm.

wickedness, and not merely the prospect of imminent execution, that may encourage murderers to repent and save their souls. Indeed, the willingness of some offenders to accept the death penalty as society's giving them their just deserts is surely a sign that they have come to grasp the enormity of what they have done and are truly sorry for it.

Evidence that Elmo Patrick Sonnier sincerely repented for his crimes seems equally persuasive. Yet here repentance came much more slowly than it did for Tucker. By Sister Helen Prejean's account, Sonnier was on death row for at least five years before he confessed his sins to the prison's Catholic chaplain. And there is every reason to believe that Sister Prejean's intervention in the final two years of Sonnier's life assisted his spiritual development. Although Sonnier turned down the last rites, it was apparently because he believed he had already accomplished what was necessary with confession and Communion, not because he had backtracked.[191] As he said to Sister Prejean in his final days, "me and God have squared things away."[192] In the moments before he died, he said (according to the Times-Picayune), "I ask God to forgive what ... I have done."[193] What causes such a radical transformation of the soul of a multiple murderer-rapist? Surely, much must remain a mystery to human observers. Yet there is every reason to believe that the prospect of imminent death concentrated Sonnier's mind and, with the help of the Catholic prison chaplain and Sister Prejean, promoted his repentance and salvation.

Although the evidence that Robert Lee Willie genuinely repented is not as strong, it is certainly possible, even here, that the imminence of his demise got Willie reading the Bible and reflecting on salvation. Despite the absence of contrition in the interviews he did in the final weeks—"If I had to do it all over again, I'd be an outlaw"— just thirty minutes before his execution, he thanked Sister Prejean for teaching him about God. However halting Willie's steps toward

[191] Because Prejean makes no mention of any effort by her to convey to Sonnier the special graces that the sacrament of anointing of the sick conveys, we can assume that Sonnier's refusal to receive the sacrament was not a rejection of the Church's mediation but rather a mistaken sense that the sacrament merely duplicated his previous confession and Communion.

[192] Prejean, Dead Man Walking, p. 76.

[193] Hodge, "Sonnier Executed".

genuine repentance were, they may not have been taken at all had he been killing time year after year on a life sentence.

How often do those who commit horrific crimes manifesting a corrupt and evil soul turn toward God to seek salvation? Are cases like those of Karla Faye Tucker and Elmo Patrick Sonnier rare exceptions, or is this kind of transformation a more common occurrence for those on death row? Evidence from the public record of those executed in 2012 supports the conclusion that this is a surprisingly common phenomenon (though only God can know for certain). Here is evidence from eighteen of the forty-three cases, beginning with the offender's last words where relevant.[194] In some cases there is evidence of little more than contrition for terrible deeds, but in others the evidence reveals the offender turning toward God for forgiveness and salvation.

- *Robert Henry Moorman*, who had murdered his seventy-four-year-old adoptive mother while he was on furlough from a prison sentence for kidnapping a eight-year-old girl, said little just before his execution but did ask for forgiveness: "I'm sorry for the pain I caused. I hope this brings closure and [the families] can start healing now. I just hope that they can forgive me in time." For the previous ten years of Moorman's twenty-six years on death row, a deacon from a Catholic parish in Tuscon, Arizona, had served as his spiritual adviser. After the execution the deacon said, "At the end, Robert was at a peaceful place and for some time had come to terms with what he had done and his fate. You could hear it in his last words, his thoughts and concerns were for others, not himself." He added that Moorman had received last rites from the bishop of Tuscon eight days before and final Communion on the day of the execution: "He received his communion and was very grateful for our years of working together as he found his relationship with

---

[194] Details presented here are from the court records on executions in the United States compiled by the prosecuting attorney of Clark County, Indiana, available at www.clark prosecutor.org/html/death/usexecute.htm. For the detailed information on each offender, visit www.clarkprosecutor.org/html/death/usexecute.htm, scroll down to year of the execution and click on the name of the offender.

the Lord.... He moved from shame to guilt, to asking for mercy and reconciliation.... His soul is now in God's hands." In prison Moorman had written an essay about God and his role in human affairs: "God gave each person 'free will' to choose the path they want to follow.... God lets us make our own decisions.... We are all children of God. He created us and sent His own Son to teach us and guide us. He died on the cross so that we can all go to Heaven.... Trust in Our Creator's forgiveness and forgive those who have done you wrong.... You are God's work every moment of every day.... We see his wonders but still many cannot believe. He is helping them too. He loves us but will not force us to believe in Him. We must want to. That is free will. Satan wants to enslave all God's children to hate, lust, revenge, distrusting etc. God is in each of us and will always love us if we just ask and believe He will forgive us our sinful past. Each of you has to live his own life. With God's love or by following Satan. I choose to follow God (Jesus)!!'"

- *George Rivas*, who had murdered a police officer after escaping with six others from a maximum-security prison, apologized to the victim's family moments before his execution: "I do apologize for everything that happened. Not because I'm here, but for closure in your hearts. I really do believe you deserve that." He addressed his very final words to his wife: "Take care of yourself. I will be waiting for you. I love you. God bless. I am ready to go." A reporter who had interviewed Rivas from his prison cell related that "Rivas said that prison was a constant reminder of the wrong decisions he made in life. He said he thought of [the police officer] frequently, especially every Christmas. He said he regretted that 'I didn't find Christ sooner.'"

- *Robert Charles Towery*, who had murdered his sixty-nine-year-old former employer during a robbery at his home, apologized emotionally to the victim's family and his own. He then added, "So many times in my life I went left when I should have gone right and I went right when I should have gone left. It was mistake after mistake." He began crying and said, "I love my family." Earlier in the day he had put his final entry in his prison diary, which read in part: "I just finished my visit with Deacon Ed and receiving communion. Now I'm just waiting for y'all, at which point I'm going to give you my legal work and my Bible. Please give my Bible to [name blacked out]. As this is my last entry, I just want to say thank you. Thank you all for the kindness. Please give everyone my best and know that I will carry y'all on my lips to God."

- *Jesse Joe Hernandez*, who beat to death a ten-month-old boy with a flashlight and severely injured a four-year-old girl, said at the end, "Tell my son I love him very much. God bless everybody. Continue to walk with God."

- *David Alan Gore*, who had kidnapped, raped, and murdered young girls, expressed his contrition just before execution: "I want to say to the ... family I am sorry for the death of your daughter. I am not the same man I was back then 28 years ago. I hope they can find it in their hearts to forgive me." At his sentencing hearing years before, "a minister testified that [Gore] was a 'born again' Christian since his arrest for murder." One newspaper account reported that in his last statement "Gore called himself a Christian." On his final day, he was visited by his "spiritual adviser, a Baptist minister".

- *Mark Wayne Wiles*, who had stabbed to death a teenage boy during a home burglary, told the witnesses to the execution: "I pray that my dying brings some solace and closure to the ... family and their loved ones.... May God bless us all that fall short." According to new reports, "during his original trial, Wiles did not want to be defended. His attorneys, in seeking clemency for him, said Wiles was very remorseful and could never forgive himself for killing [the boy]." (That remorse, however, did not prevent Wiles from appealing his conviction and sentence for twenty-six years.) One newspaper reported that on Wiles' final day, he "said the rosary with his spiritual adviser, a Roman Catholic priest who works at Ohio's death row in Chillicothe". Another newspaper reported, "He said the rosary and took communion with his spiritual adviser."

- *Buenka Adams*, who had abducted three young people, murdered the mentally challenged man, raped one woman, and shot and injured both women, said in his last statement: "To the victims, I'm very sorry for everything that happened. Everything that happened that night was wrong. If I could take it back, I would.... I messed up and can't take that back.... I am not the malicious person that you think I am. I was real stupid back then. I made a great many mistakes."

- *Michael Bascum Selsor*, who murdered a clerk at a convenience store during a robbery, expressed his belief in the afterlife in his final words: "My son, my sister, I love you. Till I see you again next time, be good. Eric, keep up the struggle. I'll be waiting at the gates of heaven for you. I hope the rest of you will make it there as well. I'm ready." Two weeks earlier he had told the Oklahoma Pardon and Parole Board, "Is it too late to say I'm sorry? I am truly sorry for the suffering and damage I have caused."

- *Jan Michael Brawner*, who had murdered his ex-wife, their three-year-old daughter, and his ex-wife's parents, used his brief final words to apologize to the family of his victims: "I can't bring anything back. I can't change what I've done. Maybe this will bring you a little peace." According to the corrections commissioner, who spent much of Brawner's last day with him, "he said he deserved to be executed for what he did." At his sentencing hearing a decade earlier, Brawner had told the jury, "I don't feel that I deserve life to live."

- *Samuel Villegas Lopez*, who had brutally raped, sodomized, and murdered a fifty-nine-year-old woman in her apartment, gave no final words but had earlier written to the clemency board that "what happened to [his victim] was so horrible and so wrong. I've been always been sorry for what she went through that night and for what her family has gone through ever since."

- *Marvin Lee Wilson*, who had abducted, beaten, and shot to death an acquaintance, said at the end, "Give mom a hug for me and tell her that I love her. Take me home, Jesus. Take me home, Lord. I ain't left yet, must be a miracle. I am a miracle. Y'all do understand that I came here a sinner and [am] leaving a saint?"

- *Daniel Wayne Cook*, who had raped, tortured, and murdered two men, apologized for his crime in his final words: "I'd like to say sorry to the victim's family. I know that's not enough."

- *Michael Edward Hooper*, who had murdered his ex-girlfriend and her five-year-old daughter and three-year-old son, invoked Jesus in his final words: "I ask that my spirit be released directly into the hands of Jesus. I'm ready to go. I love you all." According to a newspaper account, "a clergy member, sitting next to Hoop-er's mother, turned to her and said, 'He's at peace. When you have the assurance that Michael had, he was ready to go.'" The statement strongly implies that the clergy member had counseled Hooper through a process of repentance and, as Hooper's last words suggest, led him to believe in his salvation, but this cannot be known for sure. Although Hooper was on death row for sev-enteen years, after his original sentence was overturned (about ten years after his conviction) Hooper had waived his right to a jury trial in his resentencing and "had explicitly directed counsel not to contact experts, family, friends, or anyone else for the purpose of presenting mitigating evidence".

- *Donald L. Palmer Jr.*, who had murdered and robbed two strang-ers after a minor traffic accident, told the six women relatives of the two men he killed, "I want you to know I have carried you in my heart for years and years. I'm sorry for what I took from you.... I wish I could bring it back to you, but I can't. I hope the pain and hurt die with me here today. May God bless you and give you good lives. I'm sorry." Earlier, Palmer had decided not to request clemency from the Ohio Parole Board. His attorney said that "he has always accepted responsibility for this and wants the families of his victims to have justice." The attorney added that Palmer had told the parole board that he was "filled with shame and remorse and regrets the harm he caused". In an interview Palmer told a reporter that he was "searching for God and I found him in 2007 [after eighteen years on death row]". According to the reporter, "he said he has been forgiven for his sins." Two clergy members witnessed the execution.

- *Cleve Foster*, who had abducted, sexually assaulted, and mur-dered a twenty-eight-year-old woman, said in his final words, "I love you all. I'm looking to leave this place on wings of a homesick angel. Ready to go home to meet my maker. What a friend we have in Jesus, oh my God I lay in awe cause I love you God.... When I close my eyes, I'll be with the father. God is everything. He's my life. Tonight I'll be with him."

- *Gary Thomas Allen*, who had murdered his girlfriend (who was the mother of their two young children) and then tried to murder the arresting officer, at first "rambled unintelligibly" in his final words but then spoke about Jesus: "I hope that more realize Jesus is the son of God—the only son of God. Jesus is the one and only savior." When Allen testified at his sentencing hearing twenty-four years before (according to court records), "he spoke extensively about his faith. He detailed his religious upbringing. He said he now devoted about three hours a day to Bible study and prayer and, if the judge spared his life, he would devote himself to the Lord."

- *Ramon Torres Hernandez*, who had abducted a thirty-seven-year-old woman and murdered her after his accomplice raped her, briefly expressed contrition to his victim's relatives in his final words: "I am very sorry for all the pain."
- *Richard Dale Stokley*, who with an accomplice had abducted, raped, and murdered two thirteen-year-old girls, said moments before his execution twenty years later, "What I am guilty of is being an irresponsible person for most of my life, running from responsibility, living in a fantasy world, and it was my irresponsibility on the night that this incident occurred that involved me in the incident.... There is no words that can express the grief and the sorrow and the torment I have experienced over this, but I am just going to leave everything in the hands of God because that's where it is anyway."

Of these eighteen offenders (fully two-fifths of those executed in 2012), eleven expressed sorrow or contrition for what they had done, and two who did not conveyed the hope that their death would bring solace or closure to the victims' families. Eleven of the eighteen also mentioned God, several at considerable length (and another mentioned heaven, though not God); six specifically invoked Jesus Christ. Based on information from the public record, at least a third of the eighteen had a spiritual adviser (though the number could have been much higher). Finally, at least three of the offenders received Catholic sacraments at some point before execution: Moorman received last rites eight days before execution and Communion on his final day; Towery received Communion on his final day; and Wiles said the Rosary and received Communion on his final day. Presumably, all three made a sacramental Confession prior to receiving Communion, and it is likely that Towery and Wiles also received last rites.

As noted earlier in the chapter, there is no reason to think that those executed in 2012 were dissimilar from those executed in previous (or subsequent) years. Although space does not allow a complete account, here are a few of the more powerful examples of repentance from those executed in 2010 and 2011.

- *Kevin Scott Varga* was executed by the state of Texas in May 2010 for robbing and beating to death two men in separate incidents. In his final words, he said, "I know I took someone very precious to you. I wish what was torn from you was not." According to news reports, "he asked for forgiveness and said that God had forgiven him." He told his mother that he would "go to sleep and wake up with Jesus. This is the only way God could save me, Mom." As the lethal drugs took effect, he finished with "Thank you, Jesus. I'm going, Mom."

- *Michael Francis Beuke,* was executed by the state of Ohio in May 2010 for shooting to death one man and shooting two others (leaving one paralyzed for life) in three separate hitchhiking incidents. According to news reports, "before the chemicals flowed into his bloodstream, he spent 17 minutes reciting the Rosary. He also recited an early Christian creed and the Lord's Prayer as tears rolled down his left cheek." In his clemency request to the governor, Beuke had accepted responsibility for his crimes and expressed the hope that "that God will ease the pain I have caused my victims". The Associated Press reported that "Beuke's attorneys and a retired Orthodox priest who visits Beuke say he is a 'changed man' involved in religious and community service programs and has had a positive impact on other inmates." A clergy member said, "He is probably the most reformed prisoner I have met and certainly the most remorseful."

- *Teresa Wilson Bean Lewis* was executed by the state of Virginia in September 2012 for paying two men, one her lover, to kill her husband and stepson with multiple shotgun blasts as they slept, while she stood by in the kitchen. In her brief final words she told the daughter and sister of the two murdered men, "I love you and I'm very sorry." A month earlier, she wrote a message to her fellow inmates: "Man wants me to die, but I'm not worrying over this, I'm trusting Jesus.... Please my precious friends in Christ if you don't know our awesome Savior, and father, please let Him in your heart; He will forgive you of all your sins and He will bring you into His loving arms and He will bless you and guide you and show you so much, He loves you more than you'll ever know! Trust Him! Believe in Him!"

- *Michael Wayne Hall* was executed by the state of Texas in February 2011 for abducting and brutally murdering a nineteen-year-old female friend for sport. In his final words he apologized to his victim's family: "I would like to give my sincere apology to Amy's family. We caused a lot of heartache, grief, pain, and suffering, and I am sorry. I know it won't bring her back." He then spoke about his faith in Jesus Christ: "Even though I have to die for my mistake, he paid for mine by wages I could never pay." According to one account, he said that "he was changed by Christ and was not the same person anymore." At some point before his execution, "Hall asked to watch the 2004 movie 'The Passion of the Christ,' but prison officials were unable to locate a rental copy."

- *Johnnie Roy Baston* was executed by the state of Ohio in March 2011 for robbing and murdering a storekeeper. In his five-minute final statement, Baston said that he wanted his children to know that "even through my time in prison I wanted to better myself, encourage others." He thanked "all the members of my church, my friends who petitioned, letters, faxed, Twittered, hopefully, to the governor, to show mercy". He ended: "Dear heavenly father, I have sinned, and I repent of my sins, I pray for forgiveness. As I close my eyes on the light of this world, I hope to open my eyes to the light in heaven."

- *Clarence Carter* was executed by the state of Ohio in April 2011 for beating to death a fellow prison inmate. In a brief final statement he said, "I'd like to say I'm sorry for what I did, especially to his mother. I ask God for forgiveness and them for forgiveness."

- *Benny Joe Stevens* was executed by the state of Mississippi in May 2011 for using a shot gun to kill his ex-wife, her new husband, and two children. Just before his execution he said, "I am sorry.... Lord knows I am sorry. What I've taken from God and you, I can't replace. I'm sorry." He then asked the witnesses to read their Bibles. "Don't let me be a stumbling block to your salvation. I'm not worth it. That's it."

- *Milton Wuzael Mathis* was executed by the state of Texas in June 2011 for shooting to death two people at a crack house, shooting and paralyzing a fifteen-year-old girl, and trying to shoot two more. At his execution he apologized to his paralyzed victim but did not ask for her forgiveness: "All I have to worry about is God forgiving me. I hope you get better." He added, "Lord, have mercy on my soul. Lord, have mercy on these people's soul. Life is not supposed to end this way. I ask God that when I knock at the pearly gates, that you open up and let me in." One account reported that "Mathis did not apologize for his actions but repeatedly asked for divine assistance."

- *Mark Anthony Stroman* was executed by the state of Texas in July 2011 for murdering a convenience-store cashier during a robbery. Stroman also admitted to shooting two other men of Middle Eastern descent, killing one, in the weeks after the terrorist attacks of September 11, 2001. Among his last words: "The Lord Jesus Christ be with me. I am at peace. Hate is going on in this world, and it has to stop. One second of hate will cause a lifetime of pain. Even though I lay on this gurney, seconds away from my death, I am at total peace."

- *Frank Martinez Garcia* was executed by the state of Texas in October 2011 for murdering his wife and the police officer who responded to the domestic disturbance. As he was being prepared for execution he said, "Thank you for this. My God is a God of salvation. Only through you, Jesus Christ, people will see that you're still on the throne. For this reason I was born and raised. Thank you for this miracle you are performing in my life. My God is holy, holy, holy. Hallelujah!" Then he repeatedly shouted, "Thank you, Yahweh", until he lost consciousness.

Although we cannot be certain of the sincerity of all these statements and actions, it seems more likely that these examples undercount, rather than exaggerate, the number of cases in which inmates facing execution repent and turn toward God for salvation. After all, an inmate may have repented without leaving evidence of having done so in the public record.

We cannot overstate just how dramatic some of these transformations are. Men and women guilty of the most despicable acts that a person can commit against another (even here we have not reported all the gruesome details), exhibiting at times a depravity of soul that seems almost beyond comprehension, become profoundly remorseful for what they have done and put their souls in the hands of a merciful and loving God, particularly in the care of his Son, Jesus Christ. What can account for such a radical transformation if not the murderer's consciousness that he has done great wrong—which, we have argued, the death penalty itself reinforces—and the awful reality that death and judgment await at some time certain, however long after the crime itself? And although we cannot say that these examples *prove* that the death penalty promotes the reform of the offender's soul, we can say that this is *precisely the kind of evidence we would expect* if Aquinas and others are correct that the death penalty encourages, and may even be necessary for, rehabilitation. As double murderer Kevin Varga told his mother moments before his execution in 2010, "This is the only way God could save me, Mom." Those whose life's work it is to care for men's souls ought not to ignore the evidence that the death penalty promotes not only justice in this world but also salvation in the next.

4

The American Bishops' Campaign
against the Death Penalty

A profound change in attitudes

In late October 2012, just two weeks before the citizens of California were to vote on whether to retain the state's death penalty for aggravated murders, parishioners at the local church of one of the authors of this volume heard both a homily against capital punishment and a request by the celebrant to consult the parish bulletin for "A Prayer to End the Use of the Death Penalty". Here is part of that prayer:

> Merciful Father, we ask your blessing on all we do to build a culture of life....
>
> We pray for all people, that their lives and dignity as children of a loving God may be respected and protected in all stages and circumstances....
>
> We pray for those on death row, that their lives may be spared, that the innocent may be freed and that the guilty may come to acknowledge their faults and seek reconciliation with you....
>
> We pray for civic leaders, that they may commit themselves to respecting every human life and ending the use of the death penalty in our land.
>
> Compassionate Father, give us wisdom and hearts filled with your love. Guide us as we work to end the use of the death penalty and to build a society that truly chooses life in all situations....
>
> Amen.[1]

---

[1] Saint Anthony Catholic Church, Upland, California, weekly bulletin, October 21, 2012. During the writing of this chapter, the other author was asked at a different church, in the Prayer of the Faithful, to pray for the end of the death penalty. Full prayer text is available at http://www.usccb.org/prayer-and-worship/prayers-and-devotions/prayers/prayer-to-end -the-use-of-the-death-penalty.cfm.

This same author, who learned the essentials of the faith from his parents and weekly Sunday school in a Boston suburb in the 1950s and 1960s, learned the following about the Church's position on the death penalty from the *Baltimore Catechism*, the standard text used throughout Catholic parishes in the United States for more than half a century:

> Q. 1276. Under what circumstances may human life be lawfully taken?
>
> A. Human life may be lawfully taken: 1. In self-defense, when we are unjustly attacked and have no other means of saving our own lives; 2. In a just war, when the safety or rights of the nation require it; 3. By the lawful execution of a criminal, fairly tried and found guilty of a crime punishable by death when the preservation of law and order and the good of the community require such execution.[2]

For most of the twentieth century, American boys and girls learning the faith were taught that the death penalty was a legitimate punishment if imposed after a fair trial and if it was necessary to preserve "law and order and the good of the community". This is hardly surprising given the mass of evidence we presented in chapter 2 that this has been the standard teaching of the Catholic Church for two millennia. Nor is it surprising that during the 1950s and 1960s Catholics were not asked to pray that "those on death row ... be spared", that "civic leaders ... commit themselves to ... ending the use of the death penalty in our land", or that God "guide us as we work to end the use of the death penalty".

The death penalty, self-defense, and just war, then, do not violate the Fifth Commandment's rule "Thou shall not kill" (which many modern editions of the Bible translate as "Thou shall not murder").[3] These three types of lawful killing depend on contingent

---

[2] The *Baltimore Catechism* is available online. The death penalty is addressed in the third volume of the catechism, which is for older students. See www.baltimore-catechism.com /lesson33.htm.

[3] Translations with "murder" include the International Standard Version, the English Standard Version, the New International Version, the New Revised Standard Version, the English Revised Version, the New American Standard Bible, Holman's Christian Study Bible, and Young's Literal Translation. For a convenient comparison of translations, go to https://www .biblegateway.com or http://biblehub.com/.

circumstances. According to the *Baltimore Catechism*, killing in self-defense was legitimate if there were "no other means" to save lives. War was licit only if "the safety or rights of the nation require[d] it." And, as noted, the death penalty was lawful if necessary to preserve "law and order and the good of the community". In each of these cases, standard Catholic teaching presumed that in particular circumstances the conditions justifying killing might well be met. It might indeed be necessary to kill an aggressor to protect life; it might be necessary to prosecute war to defend a nation; and it might be necessary to execute criminals to preserve law and order and the good of the community. The *Baltimore Catechism* sharply distinguished these kinds of killings, which might be licit in particular contingent circumstances, from those that are always wrong:

> Q. 1275. Is it ever lawful for any cause to deliberately and intentionally take away the life of an innocent person?
>
> A. It is never lawful for any cause to deliberately and intentionally take away the life of an innocent person. Such deeds are always murder, and can never be excused for any reason, however important or necessary.

Thus, there are no contingent circumstances, no prudential judgments, that can ever make licit the intentional killing of an innocent person (a position that, as we noted in chapter 2, Pope John Paul II strongly affirmed in *Evangelium Vitae*).

Because it is never licit to take the life of an innocent person intentionally, it is never permissible for private individuals or public authorities to authorize such killings or to establish rules or criteria permitting them in particular circumstances. Thus, abortion and euthanasia are categorically ruled out by Catholic doctrine. By contrast, prudential judgments are at the core of decisions regarding self-defense, just war, and capital punishment. It is public officials who must decide what laws should govern the use of force in self-defense, whether to take the nation to war, and whether to make death a punishment for certain grave crimes and according to what procedures. The current *Catechism of the Catholic Church* makes this quite explicit regarding decisions to go to war. After summarizing four conditions that must be present to justify the use of military force—which it calls "the traditional elements ... [of] the 'just war' doctrine"—it adds: "The evaluation of these conditions for moral legitimacy belongs to the prudential judgment of those who have responsibility for the common good" (*CCC* 2309). As Cardinal Joseph Ratzinger affirmed in 2004 (as we noted earlier and will say more about below), both just war and capital punishment are prudential matters and thus radically distinct from abortion and euthanasia, which are intrinsic evils and always wrong. The faithful Catholic may kill in a just war or support the death penalty but may not be a party to abortion or euthanasia.

To put it simply, half a century ago the Church in the United States consistently taught that capital punishment could be lawfully applied against those fairly convicted of serious crimes if public officials concluded that it was necessary to preserve law and order and the good of the community. Much has changed since then. American Catholic bishops have become leading figures and a major political force in the movement to abolish capital punishment in the United States. In 1980, the nation's Catholic bishops—organized initially as the National Conference of Catholic Bishops (NCCB) but since 2001 the United States Conference of Catholic Bishops (USCCB)—issued a major statement calling for the abolition of the death penalty. Numerous other statements followed. In 2005, the USCCB invited Catholics to join a "Catholic Campaign to End the Use of the Death Penalty".[4] Although the bishops' 1980 statement had acknowledged that the pro–capital punishment position was not "incompatible with the Catholic tradition", by 2007 the bishops were arguing that the teaching that "human life is sacred .... *compels us as Catholics* to oppose genocide, torture, unjust war, and the use of the death penalty".[5]

---

[4] "Catholic Bishops Launch Major Catholic Campaign to End the Use of the Death Penalty", USCCB website, March 21, 2005, http://www.usccb.org/issues-and-action/human -life-and-dignity/death-penalty-capital-punishment/catholic-bishops-launch-major -catholic-campaign-to-end-the-use-of-the-death-penalty.cfm and *Catholic Campaign to End the Use of the Death Penalty* (Washington, D.C.: USCCB Publishing, n.d.), http://www .usccb.org/issues-and-action/human-life-and-dignity/death-penalty-capital-punishment /upload/5-723DEATHBI.pdf.

[5] Emphasis added. The quotation is from a summary of "Forming Consciences for Faithful Citizenship", United States Conference of Catholic Bishops, 2007. A revised edition of the full document was published in 2011, available at http://www.usccb.org/issues-and-action /faithful-citizenship/index.cfm. The major statements by the USCCB on the death penalty, or by bishops acting officially on behalf of the USCCB, include the following: "Bishops'

The bishops have been active in the political sphere, especially in efforts to abolish the death penalty at the state level. In recent years legislatures in Connecticut (2012), Illinois (2011), Maryland (2013), Nebraska (2015), New Jersey (2007), and New Mexico (2009) have all voted to abolish the death penalty (although in a few of these states the abolition was not applied retroactively to those already under sentence of death). In all these states Catholic bishops urged abolition and applauded the change. Later we will examine in some detail the arguments that American bishops have advanced in opposition to the death penalty. Here we note briefly the key points raised by the three Nebraska bishops in the most recent successful repeal effort (2015): "The Roman Catholic Church has long called for a culture of life"; although "Catholic teaching allows the use of the death penalty under certain clear and specific conditions", these conditions do not "exist in Nebraska at this time"; "we do not believe that violence is best fought with violence"; "too often, the death penalty serves our cultural desire for vengeance", but we should temper "our natural outrage against violent crime with a recognition of the dignity of all people, even the guilty"; too many sentenced to death were "wrongly convicted"; "racial minorities and the poor are disproportionately sentenced to death"; and the death penalty does not serve any of the key purposes of the criminal justice system: it does not rehabilitate, there is "no clear evidence" that it deters crime, it is not necessary for public safety, and justice does not require it. The bishops concluded their appeal by asking those who disagree to "reflect prayerfully on the words of Jesus Christ himself: 'love your enemies, and

Statement on Capital Punishment, 1980"; "A Good Friday Appeal to End the Death Penalty, 1999"; "A Witness to Life: The Catholic Church and the Death Penalty", an address by Cardinal Roger Mahony to the National Club, Washington, D.C., May 25, 2000; *Responsibility, Rehabilitation, and Restoration: A Catholic Perspective on Crime and Criminal Justice*, November 15, 2000; *A Culture of Life and the Penalty of Death*, December 2005; and *Forming Consciences for Faithful Citizenship: A Call to Political Responsibility from the Catholic Bishops of the United States*, 2007 (rev. ed., 2011). For additional materials on the death penalty made available through the USCCB website, including many statements by individual bishops or bishops conferences in particular states, see http://www.usccb.org/issues-and-action /human-life-and-dignity/death-penalty-capital-punishment/ and http://www.usccb.org/issues -and-action/human-life-and-dignity/death-penalty-capital-punishment/archived -documents-for-criminal-justice-death-penalty.cfm.

pray for those who persecute you, that you may be children of your heavenly Father.' "[6]

Although the objections advanced by the Nebraska bishops are now quite common among Catholic churchmen in the United States, not so long ago significant numbers of American bishops refused to call publicly for the abolition of the death penalty. The American bishops first addressed the subject in a general meeting in 1974.[7] Philosopher-theologian Germain Grisez (the founder of new natural law theory and a prominent Catholic opponent of the death penalty) was commissioned to write a background study. He submitted a fifty-one-page document, from which a committee produced a seven-page brief against the death penalty, including scriptural, theological, and practical arguments for its abolition. The statement proved to be highly controversial. Some bishops objected that it "implied rejection of the teaching of the church regarding the limited right of the state to take life". Others objected to the interpretation of scriptural passages. A cardinal questioned "whether the reference to capital punishment being discriminatory was sufficiently compelling" and "whether there was sufficient evidence to say that capital punishment was not being applied in an even-handed application". The next day, after the document was revised, the same cardinal "noted that the reference to deterrence in the statement ignored the legitimate vindictive aspect of punishment". After it was announced "that the statement, because of its length, would fall under the rule of a two-thirds vote", passage failed: 119 in favor, 103 against, and 3 abstentions. The next day the bishops voted on a short substitute motion: "The United States Catholic Conference goes on record as opposed to capital punishment." It passed: 108 in favor, 63 opposed. (Later some bishops maintained that the two-thirds rule—63% had voted in favor—should have been applied for the short resolution as well, which would have resulted in its defeat.) Although the minutes of the meeting did not record whether there were any

---

[6] The full statement is available at http://www.wowt.com/home/headlines/Nebraska-Bishops--Repeal-the-Death-Penalty-296634531.html.

[7] The events at the bishops' meetings in 1974 and 1980 are recounted in James J. Megivern, *The Death Penalty: An Historical and Theological Survey* (New York: Paulist Press, 1997), pp. 345–69. We also draw on the minutes of the 1974 meeting, provided to authors by the USCCB, April 8, 2015. All quotations are from the minutes.

abstentions on the second vote, if all 225 who voted the day before were present for the final vote, then 54 abstained. The vote for the motion (108) was actually 11 fewer than the vote for the document (119), while the vote against the motion (63) was 40 fewer than the vote against the document. There is no way to know whether the 54 fewer votes on the second motion represent bishops not in attendance or those present who abstained. The best we can say is that somewhere between 37% (63 of the 171 voters on the short statement) and 46% (103 of the 225 voters on the lengthy document) of the bishops opposed the organization's adopting an anti–capital punishment position.

The sharp division on this issue among the bishops in 1974, as well as the forcefulness with which many bishops then opposed the new policy (as is evident from the meeting's minutes), has been obscured by later accounts by abolitionist bishops. Just three years after the 1974 meeting, Archbishop Joseph Bernardin, president of the National Conference of Catholic Bishops, wrote in a statement on the death penalty: "In 1974, the United States Catholic Conference declared its opposition to the reinstitution of capital punishment."[8] In a 1981 appeal, the Montana bishops wrote the same.[9] In 1984 the Oregon bishops reported: "In 1974, out of a commitment to the value and dignity of human life, the Bishops of the United States declared their opposition to capital punishment."[10] (Oddly, the Oregon statement purports to give the *reason* the bishops opposed capital punishment—"a commitment to the value and dignity of human life"—even though what passed was in fact a mere resolution of opposition.) In 1989, Cardinal Bernardin, testifying before the U.S. Senate on behalf of the USCCB, said that "the United States Catholic Bishops first declared their opposition to the use of the

[8] The official link for this document through the USCCB is no longer active, but the text can be found here: http://www.baylorfans.com/forums/showthread.php?t=74346.

[9] Montana Catholic Conference on Capital Punishment, "Statement on the Death Penalty", USCCB website, November 1981, http://www.usccb.org/issues-and-action/human -life-and-dignity/death-penalty-capital-punishment/statement-by-montana-catholic-bishops -on-the-death-penalty-1981-11.cfm.

[10] Oregon Catholic Bishops, "Statement on the Death Penalty", USCCB website, October 1984, http://www.usccb.org/issues-and-action/human-life-and-dignity/death-penalty -capital-punishment/statement-by-oregon-catholic-bishops-on-the-death-penalty-1984-10 .cfm.

death penalty in 1974."[11] Then, in 1999, the Administrative Board of the USCCB issued "A Good Friday Appeal to End the Death Penalty", which began: "For more than 25 years, the Catholic bishops of the United States have called for an end to the death penalty in our land."[12] From these and similar statements one might think that beginning in 1974 the bishops were as one in their opposition to capital punishment. Yet there was a real debate at the 1974 meeting, with serious arguments advanced both for and against abolition. At the end of that debate one-third to one-half of the bishops refused to call for an end to the death penalty. As Archbishop Francis Furey of San Antonio, Texas, an outspoken proponent of the death penalty, wrote in 1977: "It is a divisive issue in the Church in this country. Perhaps that is as it should be. There are arguments on both sides. However, to say that the U.S. hierarchy, as such, is opposed to capital punishment, is just a plain lie."[13]

In 1980, the bishops returned to the death penalty and debated and passed a 3,000-word document, "Bishops' Statement on Capital Punishment", calling for the abolition of the death penalty. Although several bishops argued against adopting the document, in the six years since 1974 the majority for abolition had grown: 145 in favor, 31 opposed, and 41 abstaining. Thus, of the 217 present, 67% supported abolition, meaning that up to a third of the bishops did not concur. The bishops' statement served as the foundational document for what would become an increasingly aggressive campaign against the death penalty. It made three kinds of arguments, all of which would be repeated many times in the years ahead: that capital punishment failed to serve the legitimate purposes of punishment; that it was inconsistent with the values of the gospel and the example of Jesus; and that it was fraught with errors and discrimination in its application. In the following pages we address these arguments in some detail.

[11] The official link for this document through the USCCB is no longer active. Cardinal Bernardin's testimony before the Judiciary Committee of the United States Senate was delivered on September 28, 1989.

[12] Administrative Board of the United States Conference of Catholic Bishops, "A Good Friday Appeal to End the Death Penalty", April 2, 1999, http://www.usccb.org/issues-and -action/human-life-and-dignity/death-penalty-capital-punishment/good-friday-appeal.cfm.

[13] "Statement on the Death Penalty", USCCB website, http://www.usccb.org/issues-and -action/human-life-and-dignity/death-penalty-capital-punishment/statement-by-bishop -furey-on-the-death-penalty-1977.cfm.

As we demonstrated in chapter 2, the Catholic Church has always taught that the death penalty is, in principle, a legitimate punishment for grievous crimes. Indeed, we have also shown that Scripture, the Fathers, and several popes have taught that resort to capital punishment can in principle be legitimate even for purposes other than the defense of society against the immediate threat posed by the offender. And we have argued that this teaching cannot possibly be reversed by the Church, consistent with the authority that the Church attributes to Scripture, the Fathers, and the popes. Hence, whether capital punishment *should* in fact be used, and *how extensively*, is in the nature of the case a prudential judgment about which faithful Catholics, including those in the highest positions in the Church, can disagree and have often disagreed. Catholic laymen are not well served when national or state organizations of bishops fail to acknowledge the existence and legitimacy of disagreement on this prudential matter among faithful Catholics, including among Catholic churchmen. Yet from 1974 to 2007, the nation's bishops moved from, by one measure, nearly an equal division on the abolition of the death penalty to the position that Catholic teaching "compels us ... to oppose ... the use of the death penalty". As we have shown, this is simply not true, as we know from the testimony of Saint Paul, the Fathers and Doctors of the Church, the Church's greatest theologians, the universal catechisms of the Church, and the popes themselves. Indeed, as we saw earlier, just three years before the USCCB told the laity that they were compelled to oppose the death penalty, Cardinal Ratzinger, then prefect of the Congregation for the Doctrine of the Faith (and soon to become Pope Benedict XVI), wrote to the American bishops that "there may be a legitimate diversity of opinion even among Catholics about waging war and applying the death penalty, but not however with regard to abortion and euthanasia." Of course, this *must mean* that Catholics are *not* compelled to oppose the death penalty.

Strikingly, just a month before Ratzinger sent his memorandum, Archbishop William Levada, chairman of the USCCB Committee on Doctrine, issued on behalf of the USCCB "Theological Reflections on Catholics in Political Life and the Reception of Holy Communion". In language that was obviously worked out with the Vatican's doctrinal authorities, Levada wrote that "there may be a legitimate diversity of opinion even among Catholics about waging war and applying the death penalty, but not with regard to abortion and euthanasia."[14] Thus, when it asserted in 2007 that Catholics were compelled to oppose the death penalty, the USCCB not only contradicted two thousand years of Catholic teaching and the contemporaneous views of the person who is (next to the pope) the Vatican's highest doctrinal official but also *contradicted itself.*

In the following pages we show both that the bishops' case against the death penalty rests on seriously problematic scriptural, philosophical, and moral arguments and that the bishops' allegation that the administration of the death penalty in the United States today is "deeply flawed" is simply mistaken. We make these statements with all due respect for the office of the bishops, and we emphasize that we are here simply exercising the right of the faithful that the U.S. bishops themselves recognized in their 1968 pastoral letter, which we cited in chapter 2. As we there noted, the U.S. bishops taught in that letter that "there exist in the Church a lawful freedom of inquiry and of thought and also general norms of licit dissent", indeed of "responsible dissent," where "non-infallible" matters are concerned (though, as we have also noted, the word "dissent" has, in the decades since 1968, come to have unwelcome connotations—we prefer the term "disagreement"). And again, Archbishop Levada stated on behalf of the U.S. bishops that *capital punishment, specifically,* is a matter about which Catholics may legitimately disagree. Hence in respectfully taking issue with the U.S. bishops' arguments vis-à-vis capital punishment, we are simply adopting a position that the *bishops' own statements* show can be a legitimate one for loyal Catholics to take. As the bishops themselves carefully noted in their 1986 pastoral letter *Economic Justice for All,* when they address prudential matters they speak with less authority than when they address doctrine: "As bishops, we do not claim to make these prudential judgments with the same kind of authority that marks our declarations of principle."[15]

---

[14] Archbishop William J. Levada, Chairman of the USCCB Committee on Doctrine, "Theological Reflections on Catholics in Political Life and the Reception of Holy Communion", June 13, 2004, USCCB website, http://www.usccb.org/issues-and-action/faithful -citizenship/church-teaching/theological-reflections-tf-bishops-politicians-2004-06-13.cfm.

[15] United States Catholic Bishops, *Economic Justice for All: Pastoral Letter on Catholic Social Teaching and the U.S. Economy* (Washington, D.C.: United States Conference of Catholic Bishops, 1986), http://www.usccb.org/upload/economic_justice_for_all.pdf.

Scriptural interpretations

Because the Catholic Church has consistently maintained that Scripture is divinely inspired and inerrant in what it teaches about faith and morals, it is not possible to make a Catholic argument for or against the death penalty without addressing what Scripture has to say on the subject. So it is not surprising that American Catholic bishops have done so; though, at least quantitatively, this is not a large part of their case against capital punishment. In reviewing and assessing the bishops' interpretations, we will refer back to the more extensive discussion of Scripture at the beginning of chapter 2, as there is no need to repeat here what we argued there. In what follows we focus on statements issued by the USCCB or by bishops acting in an official capacity on behalf of the USCCB, though we occasionally cite the interpretations of state conferences of Catholic bishops and of individual American bishops.[16] We focus on USCCB statements because the views expressed therein are (presumably) widely shared among members of the Catholic hierarchy in the United States and also because the USCCB has worked so aggressively to try to move American Catholic opinion (about a quarter of the electorate) in the direction of abolition of the death penalty.

Note that we are not saying that statements issued by the USCCB, even if endorsed by a large majority of the membership, carry greater teaching authority than those issued by individual bishops. In fact, they do *not* carry greater authority. This is an important point that is too little understood by lay Catholics and, frankly, not often noted or emphasized by national conferences of bishops. As Cardinal Joseph Ratzinger, then prefect of the Congregation for the Doctrine of the Faith, affirmed in 1984:

> We must not forget that the episcopal conferences have no theological basis, they do not belong to the structure of the Church, as willed by

---

[16] We have not tracked down every statement by an American bishop on the death penalty; rather, we have relied primarily on the documents in the "Criminal Justice/Death Penalty Archive" on the USCCB website, http://www.usccb.org/issues-and-action/human-life-and -dignity/death-penalty-capital-punishment/archived-documents-for-criminal-justice-death -penalty.cfm. Thus we are relying—reasonably, it seems to us—on the USCCB itself for identifying the most important statements by individual bishops and by state conferences of bishops. Of all the statements linked, only one—by Archbishop Francis Furey in 1977—endorsed the death penalty.

Christ, that cannot be eliminated; they have only a practical, concrete function....

No episcopal conference, as such, has a teaching mission; its documents have no weight of their own save that of the consent given to them by the individual bishops....

It happens ... that with some bishops there is a certain lack of a sense of individual responsibility, and the delegation of his inalienable powers as shepherd and teacher to the structures of the local conference leads to letting what should remain very personal lapse into anonymity....

In many episcopal conferences, the group spirit and perhaps even the wish for a quiet, peaceful life or conformism lead the majority to accept the positions of active minorities bent on pursuing clear goals.... I know bishops who privately confess that they would have decided differently than they did at a conference if they had had to decide by themselves. Accepting the group spirit, they shied away from the odium of being viewed as a "spoilsport," as "backward," as "not open."[17]

The Old Testament

Rarely do USCCB documents on the death penalty address the bearing of the Old Testament on the issue and, as best we can tell, not a single such document even mentions Genesis 9:6: "Whoever sheds the blood of man, by man shall his blood be shed; for God made man in his own image." This is a striking omission both because this was part of God's covenant with Noah and his family, who constituted the entire human race after the Flood—and thus cannot be dismissed as merely a temporarily binding part of the later Mosaic Law— and because it appears not merely to allow the death penalty but positively to require it, and to do so precisely because the victim was made in the image of God. Nor have we found a statement on the death penalty by an individual American bishop or by a state conference of bishops that addresses Genesis 9:6. Because, as we will see, some bishops' statements do address other Old Testament passages, the omission is all the more glaring.

Among official USCCB documents, the most common reference to the Old Testament is its teaching that man is, as the bishops'

---

[17] Joseph Cardinal Ratzinger with Vittorio Messori, *The Ratzinger Report* (San Francisco: Ignatius Press, 1985), pp. 59–62, emphasis added.

foundational 1980 statement said, "a creature made in the image and likeness of God".[18] The reference, of course, is to the creation of man in Genesis 1:26–27. In a lengthy statement on criminal justice released in 2000 (which included, but was not limited to, discussion of the death penalty) the USCCB elaborated:

> The fundamental starting point for all of Catholic social teaching is the defense of human life and dignity: every human person is created in the image and likeness of God and has an inviolable dignity, value, and worth, regardless of race, gender, class, or other human characteristics. Therefore, both the most wounded victim and the most callous criminal retain their humanity. All are created in the image of God and possess a dignity, value, and worth that must be recognized, promoted, safeguarded, and defended.[19]

Later the same document says: "Capital punishment ... fails to live up to our deep conviction that all human life is sacred."[20] In the same year, Cardinal Roger Mahony, speaking for the USCCB at the National Press Club, explained how "these principles that uphold human life and dignity apply to the complex matter of capital punishment":

> In reflecting on Catholic teaching, we must conclude that "even the most hardened criminal remains a human person, created in God's image, and possessing a dignity, value, and worth which must be recognized, promoted, safeguarded and defended" [quoting a 1999 presentation by Father Bryan Massingale]. Simply put, we believe that every person is sacred, every life is precious—even the life of one who has violated the rights of others by taking a life. Human dignity is not qualified by what we do. It cannot be earned or forfeited. Human dignity is an irrevocable character of each and every person.

The following year, Cardinal Mahony joined Cardinal William Keeler in issuing a statement on behalf of the USCCB decrying the

---

[18] "Bishops' Statement on Capital Punishment, 1980" USCCB website, http://www.usccb.org/issues-and-action/human-life-and-dignity/death-penalty-capital-punishment/statement-on-capital-punishment.cfm.

[19] *Responsibility, Rehabilitation, and Restoration: A Catholic Perspective on Crime and Criminal Justice* (Washington, D.C.: USCCB, 2000), http://www.usccb.org/issues-and-action/human-life-and-dignity/criminal-justice-restorative-justice/crime-and-criminal-justice.cfm.

[20] Ibid.

upcoming execution of Timothy McVeigh. They connected opposition to capital punishment with man's nature as created in God's image and Pope John Paul II's promotion of a "culture of life":

> With Timothy McVeigh's execution we add to our culture of death. The Holy Father has urged all people of good will to replace this culture with a culture of life. But a culture of life rests on the foundational principle that all are created in God's image. We are called to uphold the life and dignity of every human being at all times including the lives of those justly convicted of horrible crimes.[21]

The American bishops returned to this point in their important 2005 document *A Culture of Life and the Penalty of Death*, their most extensive discussion of capital punishment: "The opening chapters of the Book of Genesis teach that every life is a precious gift from God (see Gn 2:7, 21–23). This gift must be respected and protected. We are created in God's image and redeemed by Jesus Christ, who himself was crucified."[22]

Note that while these passages seem to imply that capital punishment is wrong because it entails the intentional killing of a being made in God's image, they do not formally assert this (although the claim that it "fails to live up to our deep conviction that all human life is sacred" comes quite close).[23] To do so would be directly to contradict (1) the teaching of the Old Testament—which holds both that man is made in God's image *and* that the death penalty is the appropriate punishment for murder (in the covenant with Noah, the

---

[21] Cardinal Roger Mahony and Cardinal William Keeler, "Statement on the Approaching Execution of Timothy McVeigh", USCCB website, May 2, 1001, http://www.usccb.org/issues-and-action/human-life-and-dignity/death-penalty-capital-punishment/statement-by-cardinals-mahony-and-keeler-on-the-execution-of-timothy-mcveigh-2001-05-02.cfm.

[22] *A Culture of Life and the Penalty of Death* (Washington, D.C.: USCCB, 2005), http://www.usccb.org/issues-and-action/human-life-and-dignity/death-penalty-capital-punishment/culture-of-life-penalty-of-death.cfm.

[23] Note also that after the execution of Timothy McVeigh in June 2001, Bishop Joseph A. Fiorenza, president of the USCCB, issued a statement on behalf of the bishops that read in part: "We believe it is important to emphasize that human life is a gift from God, and no one or any government should presume to kill God's gift." Although not quite a formal assertion that the death penalty in itself violates man's nature as a creature of God, it would seem rhetorically to amount to as much, and surely many faithful Catholics reading such a statement would so interpret it. Bishop Fiorenza's statement is available at http://www.usccb.org/issues-and-action/human-life-and-dignity/death-penalty-capital-punishment/statement-by-bishop-fiorenza-on-the-execution-of-mcveigh-2001-06-11.cfm, accessed June 22, 2015.

repeated principle of "a life for a life", and the specific Mosaic Law on homicide)—and (2) the universal unchanging Catholic teaching that intentionally taking the life of a murderer, though created in God's image and possessing inviolable human dignity, is not intrinsically wrong. Indeed, as we have argued, the teaching of Genesis 9:6 is that because the *victim* of a murder is made in God's image, the death of the offender is *the required, or at least presumptive, punishment*. Genesis 9:6 teaches that the death penalty affirms the dignity of both the *victim*, because he is made in God's image, and the *offender*, by holding him morally responsible for intentionally destroying a precious part of God's creation. Were the USCCB statements quoted so far formally to have asserted that capital punishment is contrary to man's dignity as made in the image of God, they would flatly have been in conflict with the teaching of Scripture.

At least two state conferences of Catholic bishops, however, have gone beyond the USCCB and asserted the incompatibility of the death penalty with man's nature as a being created by God in His image. In 2007, the Catholic bishops of Texas issued a statement on the death penalty that read in part:

> Since the reinstatement of the death penalty in the United States in 1976, the Catholic Bishops of the United States have repeatedly condemned its use as a violation of the sanctity of human life. Capital punishment, along with abortion and euthanasia, is inconsistent with the belief of millions of Texans that all life is sacred.... As religious leaders, we are deeply concerned that the State of Texas is usurping the sovereign dominion of God over human life by employing capital punishment for heinous crimes.[24]

Two years later, in a lengthy statement on the death penalty, the California bishops wrote, "It is our Catholic belief that every human person is a precious and unrepeatable gift of God and this fact cannot be reconciled with capital punishment."[25]

---

[24] General Assembly of Texas Conference of Churches, "Resolution Opposing the Death Penalty", February 24, 1998, http://www.usccb.org/issues-and-action/human-life-and-dignity/death-penalty-capital-punishment/statement-by-texas-catholic-conference-on-death-peanlty-1998-02-24.cfm.

[25] California Catholic Conference of Bishops, "The Gospel of Life and Capital Punishment", California Catholic Conference website, July 1999, http://www.cacatholic.org/news/california-bishops-statements/gospel-life-and-capital-punishment.

We can see no way to square these statements with either the Old Testament or two millennia of Catholic moral teaching. The Catholic Church has never taught—nor does she *now* teach—that the death penalty, in itself, violates the sanctity of human life. She has never taught—nor does she *now* teach—that man usurps God's dominion over human life by executing murderers (just as man does not usurp God's dominion when he kills in self-defense or in a just war). She has never taught—nor does she *now* teach—that capital punishment cannot be reconciled with the "Catholic belief that every human person is a precious and unrepeatable gift of God". We are, of course, reluctant to correct Catholic bishops on, as it were, their own turf. Yet the conclusion that the Texas and California bishops misrepresented Catholic doctrine is inescapable.

Perhaps these bishops can be partly excused by the ambiguity of the many statements of the USCCB that connect man's special creation and dignity with the death penalty. Although the Texas bishops misrepresented the teachings of the USCCB when they claimed that "the Catholic Bishops of the United States have repeatedly condemned [the death penalty's] use as a violation of the sanctity of human life", the USCCB itself seems to share in the blame. When official USCCB documents and spokesmen repeatedly introduce into discussions of the death penalty the principle, universally shared among faithful Christians, that even a murderer is "a human person, created in God's image" who possesses "dignity, value, and worth", one wonders what the point is if not to get the reader or listener to reject the death penalty *precisely* as a violation of this principle. The implicit thesis seems to be that the death penalty *in itself* denies human dignity and thus contradicts the very nature of man as created in God's image. That such documents and spokesmen do not *flatly* assert the (in fact nonbiblical and non-Catholic) doctrine that man's sacred nature renders the death penalty illicit does not excuse the USCCB for making arguments and statements that seem designed to imply just such a connection. Otherwise, what is the point? Man's sacred nature and his character as a being created in God's image is not exactly a disputed matter among Christians. Surely, not a single Church Father, Doctor, theologian, or pope who acknowledged the legitimacy in principle of the death penalty would have disagreed that man is made in God's image. Neither the popes of the nineteenth century who authorized more than five hundred executions in the Papal States nor the Church authorities of the early twentieth century who inserted the death penalty into the Lateran Treaty of 1929, which established Vatican City, had somehow forgotten how Genesis describes God's creation of man: "Then God said, 'Let us make man in our image, after our likeness.'" ... So God created man in his own image, in the image of God he created him" (Gn 1:26–27).

The most extensive discussion by the USCCB of the relevance of the Old Testament teaching to the death penalty came in 2005 in *A Culture of Life and the Penalty of Death*:

> The opening chapters of the Book of Genesis teach that every life is a precious gift from God (see Gn 2:7, 21–23). This gift must be respected and protected.... Some argue that biblical statements about "life for life, eye for eye, tooth for tooth" (see Ex 21:23–25, Lv 24:17, Dt 19:21) require that the death penalty be used for certain crimes. A correct interpretation of these passages indicates, however, that the principal intent of such laws was to limit the retribution that could be exacted for an offense, not to require a minimum punishment. Furthermore, it is important to read individual passages in the context of Sacred Scripture as a whole. While the Old Testament includes some passages about taking the life of one who kills, the Old Testament and the teaching of Christ in the New Testament call us to protect life, practice mercy, and reject vengeance. When Cain killed Abel, God did not end Cain's life. Instead, he sent Cain into exile, not only sparing his life but protecting it by putting "a mark on Cain, lest anyone should kill him at sight" (Gn 4:15). Jesus refused to stone the woman accused of adultery (Jn 8:1–11), reminding us to be cautious in judging others and to have hope in the possibility of reform and redemption.[26]

Here the authors, while again ignoring Genesis 9:6, address the lex talionis of strict proportional punishment—"life for life, eye for eye, tooth for tooth"—and the story of the first murder: Cain's slaying of his brother Abel. Although the authors are right to affirm that the lex talionis limited punishment to *no more than* the injury sustained

---

[26] USCCB, *A Culture of Life*, p. 11.

by the victim, thus restraining escalating cycles of violence, they are wrong to deny that it also requires punishment *as severe as* the harm caused by the offender. In *every case* the text actually mandates, rather than merely allows, a penalty equivalent to the harm: if fighting men harm a pregnant woman, "then you shall give life for life, eye for eye, tooth for tooth, hand for hand, foot for foot, burn for burn, wound for wound, stripe for stripe" (Ex 21:23–25); if a man "causes a disfigurement in his neighbor, as he has done it shall be done to him, fracture for fracture, eye for eye, tooth for tooth; as he has disfigured a man, he shall be disfigured" (Lev 24:19–20); if one man testifies falsely against his brother, "then you shall do to him as he had meant to do to his brother; so you shall purge the evil from the midst of you. And the rest shall hear, and fear, and shall never again commit any such evil among you. Your eye shall not pity; it shall be life for life, eye for eye, tooth for tooth, hand for hand, foot for foot" (Deut 19:19–21). The language demanding punishments *as severe as*—not merely *no more severe than*—the offense could hardly be more emphatic.

Although the lex talionis expressly included the death penalty for murder—"life for life"—Mosaic Law had a rather sophisticated treatment of homicide that distinguished grades of the offense depending on the intention of the offender and the degree of culpability. In general, purely accidental killings did not result in a death sentence but rather in a period of exile in a city of refuge. No such mitigated punishment was available for intentional killers: "if a man willfully attacks another to kill him treacherously, you shall take him from my altar, that he may die" (Ex 21:14). If such an offender, in violation of the law, fled to a city of refuge, "then the elders of his city shall send and fetch him from there, and hand him over to the avenger of blood, so that he may die. Your eye shall not pity him, but you shall purge the guilt of innocent blood from Israel, so that it may be well with you" (Deut 19:12–13). Natural human sentiments of pity, compassion, or sympathy for the offender must not trump the demands of the law for punishment that causes as much harm to the offender as he caused to his victim. Any other interpretation simply misreads the plain—and often repeated—language on punishing murder in the first five books of the Old Testament.

The bishops also note that "when Cain killed Abel, God did not end Cain's life. Instead, he sent Cain into exile, not only sparing his life but protecting it by putting 'a mark on Cain, lest anyone should kill him at sight' (Gn 4:15)."[27] Genesis does not tell us why God spared Cain's life. The Fathers of the Church offered different explanations. For Cyril of Jerusalem the episode showed God's "loving kindness" and his "forbearance". According to the Septuagint, the Greek translation of the Old Testament in common use at the time, God had sentenced Cain to "groaning and trembling ... upon the earth". Cyril added, "Though the sin was great, the sentence was light."[28] Yet John Chrysostom emphasized the severity of the sentence and its beneficial effect on others and on Cain himself:

> The punishment of which God spoke seems to be excessively harsh, but rightly understood it gives us a glimpse of his great solicitude. God wanted men of later times to exercise self-control. Therefore, he designed the kind of punishment that was capable of setting Cain free from his sin. If God had immediately destroyed him, Cain would have disappeared, his sin would have stayed concealed, and he would have remained unknown to men of later times. But as it is, God let him live a long time with that bodily tremor of his. The sight of Cain's palsied limbs was a lesson for all he met. It served to teach all men and exhort them never to dare to do what he had done, so that they might not suffer the same punishment. And Cain himself became a better man again. His trembling, his fear, the mental torment that never left him, his physical paralysis kept him, as it were, shackled. They kept him from leaping again to any other like deed of bold folly. They constantly reminded him of his former crime. Through them he achieved greater self-control in his soul.[29]

Neither Cyril nor Chrysostom denied that God could have justly destroyed Cain for the enormity of his crime. In his exegesis of the text, Pope John Paul II explained that "God cannot leave the crime

[27] Pope John Paul II also mentions this episode from Genesis in *Evangelium Vitae* (The Gospel of Life) (March 25, 1995), nos. 7–10.

[28] Cyril of Jerusalem, *Catechetical Lectures*, quoted in *Ancient Christian Commentary on Scripture: Old Testament*, ed. Andrew Louth (Downers Grove, Ill.: InterVarsity Press, 2001), 1:108.

[29] John Chrysostom, *Against Judaizing Christians*, quoted in *Ancient Christian Commentary on Scripture: Old Testament*, 1:108.

unpunished; from the ground on which it has been spilt, the blood of the one murdered demands that God should render justice. From this text the Church has taken the expression 'sins which cry to God for justice', and, first among them, she has included wilful murder."[30] Where Cyril emphasized God's mercy, Chrysostom seemed to see the punishment as *worse than* death and one that, in addition to serving justice, also incapacitated Cain from repeating his crime, deterred others from like crimes, and contributed to Cain's rehabilitation.

As we acknowledged in earlier chapters, neither natural law nor Catholic teaching demands that every murder be punished with death. We are not calling for a wholesale return to Old Testament methods of punishment but are merely criticizing arguments that misrepresent what the Old Testament teaches vis-à-vis punishment in general and capital punishment in particular. While we cannot know with certainty why God spared Cain, we *can* know that this story was not meant to be a teaching against capital punishment. We know this because, as we have seen, the first five books of the Old Testament unambiguously endorse the death penalty for murder, an endorsement that begins in Genesis itself, just a few chapters away from the story of Cain's murder of Abel, when God instructs Noah and his family: "Whoever sheds the blood of man, by man shall his blood be shed; for God made man in his own image."

The New Testament

It is not surprising that when addressing the death penalty the bishops devote more attention to the New Testament than to the Old, and it is true that the New Testament does not expressly *command* the death penalty for murder (though, as we saw in chapter 2, it certainly *allows* it). Of course, the New Testament, unlike the Old, has rather little to say about government and criminal law at all. Yet the bishops argue, or at least strongly imply, that the "values of the Gospel" are contrary to the use of the death penalty.[31] Other than a few references to Saint Paul, nearly the entire New Testament case against the death penalty promulgated by the bishops (including the USCCB, state conferences of bishops, and individual bishops) draws from the following:

---

[30] John Paul II, *Evangelium Vitae*, no. 9, internal citations omitted.
[31] "Bishops' Statement on Capital Punishment, 1980".

1. Chapter 5 of Matthew's Gospel, in which Christ rejects "an eye for an eye and a tooth for a tooth" and teaches that we should love our enemies and forgive those who harm us
2. Luke's account of Christ's forgiving his executioners and the good thief during the Crucifixion
3. John's account of Jesus' refusal to stone the adulteress

Here are several illustrations of how American bishops, either collectively or individually, have interpreted and applied these Gospel teachings and episodes:

- We must not remain unmindful of the example of Jesus who urges upon us a teaching of forbearance in the face of evil (Matthew 5:38–42) and forgiveness of injuries (Matthew 18:21–35).... We urge our brothers and sisters in Christ to remember the teaching of Jesus who called us to be reconciled with those who have injured us (Matthew 5:43–45) and to pray for forgiveness for our sins "as we forgive those who have sinned against us" (Matthew 6:12). We call on you to contemplate the crucified Christ who set us the supreme example of forgiveness and of the triumph of compassionate love.[32]
- [Jesus] rejected punishment for its own sake, noting that we are all sinners (Jn 8).[33]
- Jesus, our Redeemer, who taught peace and forgiveness by word and example, was Himself the Victim of capital punishment, the innocent Victim of the death penalty, who would pray for His executioners, "Father, forgive them, for they know not what they do" (Luke 23:34). As our Savior gave his life on the cross, He forgave the thief who repented, promising him, "This day you will be with me in Paradise" (Luke 23:43). He forgave many others who repented and saved the woman taken in adultery for the death penalty with the words, "Let the one who is without sin cast the first stone" (John 8:7).[34]
- It would not be out of place to speculate on how Jesus would deal with capital crime. In the case of the woman accused of

---

[32] Ibid.
[33] USCCB, *Responsibility, Rehabilitation, and Restoration.*
[34] Oregon Catholic Bishops, "Statement on the Death Penalty".

adultery (John, 8), a capital crime at the time, he invited those without sin to cast the first stone. And when the death penalty was applied to him, Jesus responded by praying: "Father forgive them ..." (Luke 23:34).[35]

In chapter 2 we explained in some detail why these passages from the Gospels cannot possibly be read as promulgating an anti–capital punishment teaching, and we also showed that they were *not* so read by Saint Paul, Saint Augustine, and the Fathers of the early Church. We need not repeat the details of those arguments here. To see principles or values in Christ's teaching that render the death penalty illicit, a view that increasing numbers of American bishops have adopted, is to accept what is largely an invention of the mid- to late twentieth century, one at odds with nearly two millennia of Catholic teaching. Indeed, it is doubtful that one could find a single American bishop today who would publicly endorse the following:

- Saint Paul's teaching that rulers "bear the sword ... [as] the servant of God to execute his wrath on the wrongdoer" (Rom 13:4)
- Saint Augustine's praise for the "great and holy men [who] ... punished some sins with death .... [in the] spirit of concern for the good of humanity"[36]
- Pope Innocent III's insistence that a breakaway group seeking reconciliation with Rome formally renounce its view that the death penalty is morally wrong
- the *Roman Catechism*'s affirmation in the sixteenth century that "the just use of [capital punishment] ... is an act of paramount obedience to this Commandment which prohibits murder"[37]
- the authorization of more than five hundred executions in the Papal States by popes of the nineteenth century
- the inclusion of the death penalty in the treaty of 1929 that established Vatican City

[35] Testimony by Bishop John F. Kinney of Saint Cloud, Minnesota (apparently before the Minnesota state legislature), December 7, 1995, http://www.usccb.org/issues-and-action/human-life-and-dignity/death-penalty-capital-punishment/testimony-by-bishop-kinney-before-judicial-committee-1995-12-07.cfm.

[36] Augustine, *On the Sermon on the Mount* I, 20, 64.

[37] *Catechism of the Council of Trent*, trans. John A. McHugh and Charles J. Callan (Rockford, Ill.: TAN Books, 1982), p. 421.

The key to the conclusion of so many American bishops that the death penalty is inconsistent with the "values of the Gospel" is a fundamental misunderstanding of the application of Christ's call for forgiveness to matters of criminal justice. As we noted in chapter 2, if Christ's demand that we forgive those who harm us means that murderers should not be executed, then why would it not also mean that murderers should not be punished at all? Why would forgiveness eliminate the death penalty as an appropriate punishment but not eliminate life in prison, or indeed, *any* time in prison? And what of rapists, robbers, and those who commit serious assaults? If they are all to be forgiven, then none will be punished. But no serious person argues that when Christ taught the crowds to pray, "Forgive us our trespasses as we forgive those who trespass against us" (cited many times by the bishops), he was calling for an end to the criminal justice system. Over and over again, as the excerpts above illustrate, American bishops tell us that Christ's call for forgiveness is inconsistent with the use of the death penalty. Yet as recently as 2015, the USCCB endorsed life sentences for at least some murderers: "Life in prison without parole provides a non-lethal alternative to the death penalty."[38] It must then follow that we can forgive our trespassers and still punish them, even punish them severely. Indeed, as we will discuss below, the USCCB itself acknowledges the legitimacy of retributive punishment. As we saw in chapter 3, the loved ones of murder victims well understand that forgiveness does not cancel punishment. In the words of the young woman who was raped, shot, and severely injured after a robbery and abduction during which her assailant and an accomplice murdered a nineteen-year-old man and also injured another woman: "He asked for forgiveness and I forgive him, but he had to pay the consequences."

Remarkably, we can find no explanation in any document from the USCCB, state conferences of bishops, or individual bishops that explains why forgiveness prohibits the death penalty but not life in prison. There are, of course, other arguments that distinguish the two penalties, such as that the irrevocable nature of capital

---

[38] "The Church and the Death Penalty: Questions and Answers", USCCB website, http://www.usccb.org/issues-and-action/human-life-and-dignity/death-penalty-capital -punishment/q-and-a.cfm.

punishment makes it impossible to rectify mistakes that are discovered too late. Although we do not agree that this argument undermines the case for the death penalty (time in prison is also irrevocable), at least it is a real argument. By contrast, the argument from forgiveness provides no principle for distinguishing capital punishment from life in prison. It simply cannot stand as an argument against the death penalty unless we are willing to throw out punishment altogether. And, of course, this was not Christ's intention. As we argued in chapter 2, Christ was not calling for an end to the death penalty when he urged forgiveness, because he was addressing the personal attitude of victims and not the legitimate authority of the state to punish malefactors.

Vengeance or justice?

As noted above, the USCCB's first substantial written treatment of the death penalty (1980) acknowledged the legitimacy of retributive punishment: "the restoration of the order of justice which has been violated by the action of the criminal". This was, of course, long-standing Catholic teaching. The 1997 *Catechism of the Catholic Church* reaffirmed this teaching with admirable clarity:

> The efforts of the state to curb the spread of behavior harmful to people's rights and to the basic rules of civil society correspond to the requirement of safeguarding the common good. Legitimate public authority has the right and the duty to inflict punishment proportionate to the gravity of the offense. *Punishment has the primary aim of redressing the disorder introduced by the offense.* (*CCC* 2266, emphasis added)

Unfortunately, many American bishops' statements on the death penalty reduce the natural (and wholesome) human desire for retribution to mere vengeance and hatred, and some seem at least implicitly to deny the legitimacy of retributive punishment altogether. Here are characteristic examples from USCCB documents or spokesmen:

- We seek a society of justice, not vengeance and violence.[39]
- Our passions cry out for vengeance. However, our God calls for justice and mercy, to love our enemies and pray for those who persecute us. We are called to seek justice without vengeance.[40]
- Our faith calls us to seek justice, not vengeance.[41]
- We believe in justice without vengeance.[42]
- We see the death penalty as perpetuating a cycle of violence and promoting a sense of vengeance in our culture.[43]
- What is needed is a moral revolution .... [that] calls on our leaders and the media to seek the common good and not appeal to our worst instincts. This is a time for a new ethic—justice without vengeance.... Let us also remember that we can not restore life by taking life, that vengeance cannot heal....[44]
- The crimes for which Mr. [Juan Raul] Garza and others on death row have been convicted are horrible and deserve punishment. As pastors, we understand the human emotion of anger and the desire for revenge.[45]

[39] Testimony by Cardinal Joseph Bernardin on behalf of the USCCB before the Judiciary Committee of the United States Senate, September 28, 1989. The official link for this document through the USCCB is no longer active.

[40] Statement by Bishop William S. Skylstad on behalf of the USCCB on the conviction of Timothy McVeigh for the bombing of the federal building in Oklahoma City, June 1997. The official link for this document through the USCCB is no longer active.

[41] Statement by Cardinal Bernard Law on behalf of the USCCB on the federal jury's decision to sentence Timothy McVeigh to death, June 13, 1997. The official link for this document through the USCCB is no longer active.

[42] Statement by Bishop William S. Skylstad on behalf of the USCCB appealing to Texas governor George W. Bush to grant clemency to Karla Faye Tucker, January 29, 1998. The official link for this document through the USCCB is no longer active.

[43] Administrative Board of the USCCB, "A Good Friday Appeal".

[44] Cardinal Roger Mahony, "A Witness to Life: The Catholic Church and the Death Penalty," address to the National Press Club, Washington, D.C., May 25, 2000, http://www.usccb.org/issues-and-action/human-life-and-dignity/death-penalty-capital-punishment/address-by-cardinal-mahony-to-national-press-club-on-death-penalty-2000-05-25.cfm.

[45] Most Rev. Joseph A. Fiorenza, "Letter to President Clinton Calling for a Moratorium on the Death Penalty", July 10, 2000, http://www.usccb.org/issues-and-action/human-life-and-dignity/death-penalty-capital-punishment/letter-to-president-clinton-from-bishop-fiorenza-calling-for-moratorium-on-death-penalty-2000-07-10.cfm. Garza had been convicted in federal court of ordering or carrying out three murders to further his drug-trafficking operation. At his sentencing hearing prosecutors presented evidence that Garza was responsible for five other murders as well.

- We seek justice, not vengeance. We believe punishment must
  have clear purposes: protecting society and rehabilitating those
  who violate the law.... [Jesus] rejected punishment for its own
  sake, noting that we are all sinners (Jn 8). Jesus also rejected
  revenge and retaliation and was ever hopeful that offenders
  would transform their lives and turn to be embraced by God's
  love.... Punishment for its own sake is not a Christian response
  to crime. Punishment must have a purpose. It must be coupled
  with treatment and, when possible, restitution.... We ask all
  Catholics—pastors, catechists, educators, and parishioners—to
  join us in rethinking this difficult issue and committing ourselves
  to pursuing justice without vengeance.[46]
- Public policies that treat some lives as unworthy of protection,
  or that are perceived as vengeful, fracture the moral conviction
  that human life is sacred.... We support policies that ensure
  accountability and safety for society without the illusion of vengeance or the search for simple answers.[47]

Individual bishops and state conferences have been equally insistent
that popular support for the death penalty stems from an unhealthy
desire for vengeance and that this is un-Christian and must be resisted:

- "The attachment of the death penalty to a law", wrote a Florida
  bishop in 1976, "would seem to stem usually from one or both
  of two motives: vengeance and deterrence."[48]
- "Vengeance is morally inadmissible on Christian grounds",
  wrote the Catholic bishops of Georgia in 1980. "Our scriptures
  are explicit in declaring vengeance to be God's prerogative, not
  humanity's."[49]

---

[46] USCCB, *Responsibility, Rehabilitation, and Restoration.*

[47] USCCB, *A Culture of Life.*

[48] Bishop Rene H. Gracida of Pensacola-Tallahassee, "A Florida Bishop Speaks against
the Death Penalty", June 1976, available at http://www.usccb.org/issues-and-action/human
-life-and-dignity/death-penalty-capital-punishment/statement-on-the-death-penalty-by
-bishop-gracida-1976-06.cfm.

[49] Catholic bishops of Georgia and the Episcopal bishop of Atlanta, "Ecumenical Statement
by Georgia Churches on the Death Penalty 1980", June 2, 1980, http://www.usccb.org
/issues-and-action/human-life-and-dignity/death-penalty-capital-punishment/ecumenical
-statement-by-georgia-churches-on-the-death-penalty-1990.cfm.

- "Revenge is the only word that reflects adequately why 80 percent of Virginians favor the death penalty", according to the bishop of Richmond in 1992. "Vengeance or revenge, the only 'valid' reason for putting another to death, is contrary to the gospel message."[50]
- "Experience has shown", wrote the bishop of Saint Cloud, Minnesota, in 1995, that the relatives and friends of murder victims "who wait for years for the death of the perpetrator find themselves trapped in a commitment to wrathful vengeance that compounds and extends the horror of the initial violent act, leaving them empty and unhealed."[51]
- "Capital punishment", argued the Texas bishops in 1997, "does nothing for the families of the victims of violent crime other than prolonging their suffering through many wasted years of criminal proceedings. Rather than fueling their cry for vengeance, the state could better serve them by helping them come to terms with their grief."[52]
- "We must resist at all cost", wrote the California bishops in 1999, "the humanly understandable motive of revenge against the perpetrator of evil."[53]

It is hard to see how statements such as these, and the attitudes about punishment that they reflect, comport with long-standing Catholic teaching defending retributive punishment. "Legitimate public authority", says the *Catechism*, "has the right and the duty to inflict punishment proportionate to the gravity of the offense." Such punishment "has the primary aim of *redressing the disorder introduced by the offense*" (2266, emphasis added). And, as noted, the bishops themselves maintained in 1980 that punishment should promote "the restoration of the order of justice which has been violated by the action of the criminal". Human beings have a natural desire to see justice done. It is not at all surprising that citizens, legislators, prosecutors,

[50] Bishop Walter F. Sullivan, "Statement on the Death Penalty", July 1992, http://www .usccb.org/issues-and-action/human-life-and-dignity/death-penalty-capital-punishment /statement-by-bishop-sullivan-on-the-death-penalty-1992-07.cfm.
[51] Testimony by Bishop Kinney.
[52] Texas Conference of Churches, "Resolution Opposing the Death Penalty".
[53] California Catholic Conference of Bishops, *The Gospel of Life and Capital Punishment*.

and juries believe that some murders are so heinous (see chapter 3) that nothing less than death would be "proportionate to the gravity of the offense" or would restore "the order of justice". As we have seen in the words of the loved ones of murder victims, this desire for justice runs very deep indeed. And even some murderers themselves acknowledge the justice of their execution. As we saw in chapter 2, Augustine, though generally opposed in practice to the execution of criminals, defended the "just revenge due to the injured person from his assailant".[54] According to Aquinas, "man resists harm by defending himself against wrongs, lest they be inflicted on him, or he avenges those which have already been inflicted on him, with the intention, not of harming, but of removing the harm done."[55] The desire for just punishment reflects not "our worst instincts" but some of our best. It orients human behavior to the natural moral law and in so doing provides the foundation for retributive punishment, which, as we have argued throughout this book, is essential for promoting the common good.

Like their argument for forgiveness, the bishops' case against revenge, or vengeance, makes no distinction between the death penalty and lesser punishments. If desiring the death of a vicious murderer is to indulge our base passion for revenge, then what of desiring that such murderers serve, at the very least, life in prison without parole, a punishment endorsed by the bishops themselves? What of the desire that an offender be punished with some lesser punishment? Why would even that not count as vengeance of the sort the bishops object to?

Think again of the case we used to open the previous chapter. David Alan Gore had made a sport of abducting young women and then brutally raping and murdering them. He was convicted of five such murders and likely committed others. Surely the desire of men and women to punish evil men like Gore severely is not only a natural and understandable human reaction but also a positive good. We would think something was seriously wrong with a loved one of a murder victim, a juror in a murder case, or a member of a murder victim's community if that desire was entirely lacking, whether or not that individual supported the death penalty as the appropriate

---

[54] Augustine, *Contra Faustum* 19, 25.
[55] *ST* II-II, 108, 2.

punishment. Men *should* be angry at injustice and should desire, as the bishops say, to restore "the order of justice".

In his extended treatment of the passion of anger, Aquinas is quite clear on this. He approvingly quotes John Chrysostom: "Without anger, teaching will be useless, judgments unstable, crimes unchecked"; and "He who is not angry, whereas he has cause to be, sins. For unreasonable patience is the hotbed of many vices, it fosters negligence, and incites not only the wicked but even the good to do wrong."[56] Even the Florida bishops who urged their governor to commute Gore's sentence recognized "the natural instinct to punish the evil deeds of David Alan Gore with the ultimate penalty—death by lethal injection", acknowledging that "we, too, feel the anger, revulsion."[57] As political scientist Walter Berns explained in one of the few books by a modern academic to defend the death penalty:

> [Anger] is an expression of that element of the soul that is connected with the view that there is responsibility in the world; and in holding particular men responsible, it pays them that respect which is due them as men. Anger recognizes that only men have the capacity to be moral beings and, in so doing, acknowledges the dignity of human beings. Anger is somehow connected with justice, and it is this that modern penology has not understood.[58]

Anger, then, or what we sometimes call "righteous anger" or "moral indignation", moves men to want to punish wrongdoers. Over and over the bishops denounce "vengeance", but they never, in any document or statement we have seen, distinguish between the vice of vengeance (for the bishops it is never a virtue) and the legitimate desire of men and women, whether the victims of crime or not, to see criminals justly punished. Here the bishops seem to ignore the rich Catholic tradition in which this distinction is carefully

---

[56] *ST* II-II, 158, 1 and 8. Aquinas is citing the work *Opus Imperfectum* or *Incomplete Commentary on Matthew*, which, according to the translator of the modern edition, "was wrongly ascribed for centuries to John Chrysostom". The true author is unknown. See Thomas C. Oden, ed., *Incomplete Commentary on Matthew*, trans. James A. Kellerman (Downers Grove, Ill.: IVP Academic, 2010), 1:xvii.

[57] "Florida Bishops Appeal to Governor Scott to Stop Execution of David Alan Gore", Florida Conference of Catholic Bishops website, April 11, 2012, http://www.flaccb.org /documents/2015/8/120411GoreExecution.pdf.

[58] Walter Berns, *For Capital Punishment: Crime and the Morality of the Death Penalty* (1979; Lanham, Md.: University Press of America, 1991), p. 154.

drawn. In chapter 1, we showed how Aquinas identified two kinds of vengeance, one a vice and the other a virtue. (We note again how unfortunate it is that the English word "vengeance" today carries almost entirely negative connotations, which was not true of the Latin word "vindicatio", which Aquinas used and from which the English "vindication" derives.) If the desire to punish stems from hatred of the offender and pleasure in seeing him suffer, then it is a vice and should be resisted. If, however, "the avenger's intention be directed chiefly to some good, to be obtained by means of the punishment of the person who has sinned (for instance that the sinner may amend, or at least that he may be restrained and others be not disturbed, that justice may be upheld, and God honored), then vengeance may be lawful, provided other due circumstances be observed."[59] This kind of vengeance—or what we often call "retribution"—is a virtue, not only for Aquinas but (as we saw in previous chapters) for later Catholic moral theologians well into the twentieth century. As we noted in chapter 2, in the mid-twentieth century Pope Pius XII defended the retributive purpose of punishment as nothing less than essential to human well-being.

Also largely absent from the bishops' denunciations of vengeance and of the death penalty is the essential distinction between the acts of private citizens and those of public officials. It is standard Catholic doctrine that only public officials, those who bear the responsibility of caring for the common good, may mete out punishment for criminal acts. Private citizens may indeed defend themselves if attacked without waiting for the police to arrive, but once the immediate danger has passed, only public officials may punish wrongdoers. As we noted in chapter 1, Aquinas explained that because some men are not restrained from wrongdoing by fear of God's punishment, "it has been ordered accordingly by divine providence that there be men in various countries whose duty it is to compel these people, by means of sensible and present punishments, to respect justice"; thus, "men who are in authority over others do no wrong when they reward the good and punish the evil."[60] Hence, though private citizens, even if well intended, may not punish malefactors, public officials may and ought to do so.

[59] ST II–II, 108, 1.
[60] Summa Contra Gentiles III, 146, 1 and 2.

Strikingly, though, American bishops sometimes speak in a way that implies that retribution is reserved exclusively to God Himself. As the Catholic bishops of Georgia wrote in 1980, "Vengeance is morally inadmissible on Christian grounds. Our scriptures are explicit in declaring vengeance to be God's prerogative, not humanity's."[61] Four years earlier, religious leaders in Rhode Island (apparently including Catholic bishops) made a similar point: "There are many scriptural references that make the point that the murderer must be punished. Nevertheless, biblical tradition is also replete with reminders that vengeance belongs to the Lord and that he enjoins the qualities of compassion and forgiveness on those believers in the biblical revelation of God."[62] This second statement, unfortunately, strongly implies (though its authors surely could not have meant) that the punishment of murderers must be left to God. And while the Rhode Island religious leaders referenced chapter 12 of Saint Paul's Letter to the Romans, neither they nor the Georgia bishops mentioned or cited chapter 13 of the same letter. In chapter 12 Paul does indeed instruct the Christians in Rome, "Never avenge yourselves, but leave it to the wrath of God" (v. 19). Yet, immediately thereafter, in chapter 13, he teaches that the governing authority "is the servant of God to execute his wrath on the wrongdoer" (v. 4). Hence, the prohibition of private vengeance in no way undermines the right of public authorities to punish criminals.

Paul's treatment of the authority of the state to punish criminals is the *locus classicus* of Christian doctrine on the subject; yet, in all the documents from American bishops that we have examined, we can find only one reference to it, and that reference clearly misreads it. This is from the lengthy treatment of the death penalty, *The Gospel of Life and Capital Punishment*, issued by the California bishops in 1999: "St. Paul recognizes the legitimacy of civil authority to represent divine authority in Romans 13:1–7. The passage acknowledges the validity and propriety, even the necessity, of the punitive function of the state (the state bears 'the power of the sword'), but the text does

---

[61] "Ecumenical Statement by Georgia Churches".

[62] Rhode Island religious leaders, "Ecumenical Statement by Rhode Island Churches on the Death Penalty 1976", February 19, 1976, http://www.usccb.org/issues-and-action/human -life-and-dignity/death-penalty-capital-punishment/ecumenical-statement-by-rhode-island -churches-on-the-death-penalty-1976.cfm.

not suggest that, in practice, the state should engage in bloodshed."
For bishops to maintain that when Saint Paul wrote, "But if you
do wrong, be afraid, for [the ruler] does not bear the sword in vain;
he is the servant of God to execute his wrath on the wrongdoer"
(Rom 13:4), he wasn't even suggesting that the state might legitimately shed blood is to offer a remarkably strained and tendentious
interpretation. It is one thing for modern scholars opposed to the
death penalty to come up with creative interpretations to explain
away scriptural endorsement of capital punishment, but it is quite
another for Catholic bishops themselves to endorse such novel readings. As the First Vatican Council taught (see chapter 2), "it is not
permissible for anyone to interpret Holy Scripture in a sense contrary
to" the meaning "which Holy mother Church held and holds" or
which is "against the unanimous consent of the fathers".

In condemning as merely vengeful the desire to deny life to those
who deny life to others, the bishops' statements strike at the very
principle of proportionate punishment. While they formally (at
least occasionally) acknowledge the legitimacy of retributive punishment, their rhetoric denouncing the death penalty seems to cut
the ground out from under the case for retribution as legitimate
social policy. Note that this would not be the case if they opposed
capital punishment only for reasons unrelated to whether murderers
deserve death. For example, they could argue that even if murderers deserve execution, in practice the system is so imperfect that it
should be abandoned. Or they could argue that abolishing capital punishment, though deserved, would enhance the likelihood of
moving public opinion decisively against abortion, euthanasia, and
destructive stem cell research—a trade-off that many supporters of
capital punishment might well accept. For reasons already stated and
those to come, we find these arguments unpersuasive; but at least
they do not attack the core of the case for retributive punishment.

Consider these passages, quoted above, from the USCCB's *Responsibility, Rehabilitation, and Restoration: A Catholic Perspective on Crime
and Criminal Justice* (2000), the bishops' most extensive treatment of
criminal justice in the United States:

> We seek justice, not vengeance. We believe punishment must have
> clear purposes: protecting society and rehabilitating those who violate

the law.... [Jesus] rejected punishment for its own sake, noting that we are all sinners (Jn 8). Jesus also rejected revenge and retaliation and was ever hopeful that offenders would transform their lives and turn to be embraced by God's love.... Punishment for its own sake is not a Christian response to crime. Punishment must have a purpose. It must be coupled with treatment and, when possible, restitution.... We ask all Catholics—pastors, catechists, educators, and parishioners—to join us in rethinking this difficult issue and committing ourselves to pursuing justice without vengeance.

Apart from the unjustified inference that Christ's refusal to countenance the stoning of the adulteress (Jn 8:1–11) was a biblical teaching about punishment (see our earlier discussion), what does it mean to say that Christ rejected "punishment *for its own sake*" or that "punishment *for its own sake* is not a Christian response to crime" because "punishment must have a purpose"? What kind of punishment, exactly, was Christ supposedly rejecting in the bishops' view? Apparently, he was, in their view, rejecting purposeless punishment, which Christians should always reject. When the bishops formally address the matter (most fully in their first systematic treatment of the death penalty in 1980), they identify three key justifications for punishment: "retribution, deterrence, and reform".[63] These are the purposes that punishment is meant to serve, all of which the bishops accept as legitimate. What, then, counts as punishment *without a purpose*, and who has ever urged that criminals be punished for no purpose? Who *today* calls for punishing criminals—whether with the death penalty, prison, or fines—for no reason at all? Surely, those in ancient Israel who wished to stone adulterers had a very specific purpose in mind: to discourage adultery. Perhaps the key to understanding the force of the bishops' point is the sentence that follows "Punishment must have a purpose" in the document we cite: "It must be coupled with treatment and, when possible, restitution." Retribution has seemingly disappeared from view, even though, as we have seen, the bishops themselves elsewhere acknowledge retribution as one of the legitimate purposes of punishment, and, as we showed in earlier chapters, it is in the Catholic tradition the *chief* purpose. The current

[63] "Bishops' Statement on Capital Punishment, 1980".

Catechism of the Catholic Church reaffirms this traditional view: those responsible for "safeguarding the common good" have "the right and the duty to inflict punishment proportionate to the gravity of the offense. Punishment has the primary aim of redressing the disorder introduced by the offense" (*CCC* 2266). We should not be surprised if most readers interpret the bishops' phrase "punishment for its own sake" as code for retributive punishment. Unfortunately, then, the bishops' statements strongly imply that Christ was simply opposed to retributive punishment, a position quite contrary to traditional Catholic teaching.

We hasten to emphasize that we do not believe that the bishops *intend* in statements like this to contradict the Church's traditional teaching. Rather, we think that, in their zeal to rally others to the abolitionist cause, they have too frequently resorted to making statements that have rhetorical and emotional force, but that are theologically highly imprecise and misleading.

Deterrence

In its 1980 statement on capital punishment, the USCCB affirmed that "the protection of society and its members from violence ... is a value of central and abiding importance; and we urge the need for prudent firmness in ensuring the safety of innocent citizens." Similarly, the *Catechism of the Catholic Church* teaches that "legitimate defense can be not only a right but a grave duty for one who is responsible for the lives of others" (*CCC* 2265). It would seem to follow that if public officials had good reason to believe that capital punishment saves innocent lives by deterring murder, they would have a duty to employ it, assuming, first, that it "is carried out not in hatred but with good judgment, not inconsiderately but after mature deliberation" (Pope Innocent III),[64] and, second, that its negative effects, if any, do not outweigh the benefits. Although the Church has traditionally left such prudential judgments to public officials, Catholic authorities and theologians have often acknowledged that the death

---

[64] Quoted in E. Christian Brugger, *Capital Punishment and Roman Catholic Moral Tradition* (Notre Dame, Ind.: University of Notre Dame Press, 2003), p. 104.

penalty does, in fact, deter crime. Here are three key examples cited earlier in this book:

- In defending Moses' order at the foot of Mount Sinai to execute the worshippers of the golden calf, Augustine writes, "he impressed their minds at the time with a wholesome fear, and gave them a warning for the future, by using the sword in the punishment of a few."[65]
- Aquinas held that "when a thief is hanged, this is not for his own amendment, but for the sake of others, that at least they may be deterred from crime through fear of the punishment."[66]
- The *Roman Catechism* of the sixteenth century taught that "the just use of [capital punishment] ... is an act of paramount obedience to this Commandment which prohibits murder" (presumably because it saves lives).[67]

It follows, then, that Catholics who oppose the death penalty must confront the deterrence issue. And, indeed, the American bishops have, but, as we will show, not very effectively.

The USCCB first addressed the subject in its 1980 statement:

The deterrence of actual or potential criminals from future deeds of violence by the threat of death is also advanced as a justifying objective of punishment. While it is certain that capital punishment prevents the individual from committing further crimes, it is far from certain that it actually prevents others from doing so. Empirical studies in this area have not given conclusive evidence that would justify the imposition of the death penalty on a few individuals as a means of preventing others from committing crimes. There are strong reasons to doubt that many crimes of violence are undertaken in a spirit of rational calculation which would be influenced by a remote threat of death. The small number of death sentences in relation to the number of murders also makes it seem highly unlikely that the threat will be carried out and so undercuts the effectiveness of the deterrent.

[65] Augustine, *Reply to Faustus the Manichaean* XXII, 79.
[66] *ST* I–II, 87, 3.
[67] *Catechism of the Council of Trent*, p. 421.

Here we see three common related criticisms of the deterrence argument for capital punishment: (1) there is no conclusive evidence that the death penalty deters; (2) violent criminals do not act from rational calculation; and (3) there are too few death sentences to make a difference. In their 1999 appeal "To End the Death Penalty", a committee of the bishops' conference, joined by the National Council of Synagogues, reiterated two of those criticisms:

> Some would argue that the death penalty is needed as a deterrent to crime. Yet the studies that lie behind our statements over the years have yet to reveal any objective evidence to justify this conclusion. Criminals tend to believe they will escape any consequences for their behavior; or simply do not think of consequences at all, so an escalation of consequences is usually irrelevant to their state of mind at the time of the crime.[68]

And in *A Culture of Life and the Penalty of Death* (2005), the USCCB briefly restated its judgment about the empirical studies and added a point about comparing states with and without the death penalty:

> The question of the death penalty's deterrence value remains unproven. States with more executions do not generally have lower murder or crime rates. There is no clear evidence that the death penalty prevents or deters crime.

None of these statements denies outright that capital punishment may deter murder. Rather, they say that it is "far from certain" that it does; that there is "no conclusive evidence"; that there are "strong reasons to doubt"; that studies have "yet to reveal any objective evidence"; and that the matter "remains unproven". Of course, one would hardly expect religious leaders, Catholics or not, to have any particular insight into the controversial and highly contested question of whether the death penalty deters. Here the bishops are opining on

[68] "To End the Death Penalty", a report of the National Jewish/Catholic Consultation, cosponsored by the National Council of Synagogues and the Bishops' Committee for Ecumenical and Interreligious Affairs of the National Conference of Catholic Bishops, 1999, http://www.usccb.org/issues-and-action/human-life-and-dignity/death-penalty-capital-punishment/statement-to-end-the-death-penalty-1999-12-03.cfm.

a subject that is far removed from their religious training and pastoral experience. When they assert, for example, that studies "have yet to reveal any objective evidence" that "the death penalty is needed as a deterrent to crime", they are obviously relying on what others have told them. It is unlikely that the bishops have read the relevant studies or that they could understand and evaluate the highly complex mathematical models and techniques that modern deterrence studies regularly employ. Of course, it is no criticism of the bishops that they are not quantitatively trained social scientists (who, as we will see, themselves disagree about deterrence); but it does raise the question of just how much credence Catholics should give to bishops' claims about purely practical or empirical matters regarding the administration of the death penalty in the United States.

This, however, has not stopped some individual bishops or state conferences of bishops from flatly asserting that the death penalty does not deter. "The death penalty is no deterrent to the types of violent crimes committed by the types of persons who presently occupy death row in our prisons", a Florida bishop told his flock in 1976.[69] "The death penalty is not a deterrent to serious crimes", wrote the Oregon bishops in 1984.[70] "All studies show that capital punishment does not deter crime", claimed a Virginia bishop in 1992.[71]

One would not know from such confident assertions or from the more ambiguous statements of the USCCB that social scientists (mainly economists) have published many quantitative studies in peer-reviewed journals in recent years that, according to their authors, provide evidence that the death penalty *does* deter murder. Here are the leading examples just since the year 2000:

- A 2001 study of executions and murder rates in Texas published in *Applied Economics* found evidence "that is consistent with the deterrent hypothesis". Acknowledging that no single study can prove deterrence, the authors add, "This study is but another on a growing list of empirical work that finds evidence consistent with the deterrence hypothesis. These studies as a whole provide

---

[69] Bishop Gracida, "A Florida Bishop Speaks".
[70] Oregon Catholic Bishops, "Statement on the Death Penalty".
[71] Sullivan, "Statement on the Death Penalty".

robust evidence ... obtained from a variety of different models, data sets and methodologies that yield the same conclusion."[72]

- Using county-level data, a 2003 study published in *American Law and Economics Review* found that the death penalty had "a strong deterrent effect". More specifically, "our most conservative estimate is that the execution of each offender seems to save, on average, the lives of eighteen potential victims."[73]

- A 2003 study published in the *Journal of Law and Economics* found that "each additional execution decreases homicides by about five, and each additional commutation [reducing the sentence to life in prison or some lesser sentence] increases homicides by the same amount, while one additional removal from death row generates one additional homicide."[74]

- A 2004 study in the *Journal of Applied Economics* that examined state-level data for 1978–1997 concluded: "It is estimated that each state execution deters somewhere between 4 and 25 murders per year" (14 being the average).[75]

- A study of state-level data for 1977–1999 published in the *Journal of Legal Studies* in 2004 concluded that "capital punishment indeed deters murders", including "crime of passion murders". In 1999, the author reported, "Each execution resulted in approximately three fewer murders." Also, "each death sentence resulted in approximately 4.5 fewer murders in 1999. Thus, the threat of execution, in addition to the execution itself, deters murders."[76]

- A study published in *Applied Economics* in 2006 estimated that the moratorium on executions instituted by the Illinois'

[72] Dale O. Cloninger and Roberto Marchesini, "Execution and Deterrence: A Quasi-Controlled Group Experiment", *Applied Economics* 33 (2001): 576.

[73] Hashem Dezhbakhsh, Paul H. Rubin, and Joanna M. Shepherd, "Does Capital Punishment Have a Deterrent Effect? New Evidence from Postmoratorium Panel Data", *American Law and Economics Review* 5, no. 2 (2003): 344, 373.

[74] H. Naci Mocan and R. Kaj Gittings, "Getting Off Death Row: Commuted Sentences and the Deterrent Effect of Capital Punishment", *Journal of Law and Economics* 46 (October 2003): 474.

[75] Paul R. Zimmerman, "State Executions, Deterrence, and the Incidence of Murder", *Journal of Applied Economics* 7, no. 1 (May 2004): 190.

[76] Joanna Shepherd, "Murders of Passion, Execution Delays, and the Deterrence of Capital Punishment", *Journal of Legal Studies* 33 (June 2004): 315–16, 308.

governor in January 2000 resulted in 150 additional homicides in the four years after the moratorium was announced.[77] (In January 2003 the governor emptied Illinois' death row by commuting the sentences of 167 murderers to life in prison and pardoning four. In 2011 the state legislature abolished the death penalty.)

- A study that compared murder rates in the fifty states before and after changes in their death-penalty laws between 1960 and 2000, published in *Economic Inquiry* in 2006, found strong evidence of deterrence: "The results are boldly clear: Executions deter murders, and murder rates increase substantially during moratoriums. The results are consistent across before-and-after comparisons and regressions regardless of the data's aggregation level, the time period, or the specific variable used to measure executions." The authors call this "convincing evidence for the deterrent effect".[78]

- A study published in the *American Law and Economics Review* in 2009 found that in the sixteen states that added the murder of a child as an eligibility factor for the death penalty between 1985 and 2001, that change was "associated with an approximately 20% reduction in the homicide rate of youth victims, corresponding to close to four fewer child homicides annually in a state of average size".[79]

- A study of the use of the death penalty in Texas between January 1994 and December 2005, published in *Criminology* in 2009, estimated that each execution led to between 0.5 and 2.5 fewer homicides. As the authors conclude about even the more conservative estimate: "Nonetheless, with a total number of executions in Texas of 10 to 20 in some years, even the estimated .5 deterrent per execution yields an estimated reduction in the

[77] Dale O. Cloninger and Roberto Marchesini, "Execution Moratoriums, Commutations and Deterrence: The Case of Illinois", *Applied Economics* 38 (2006): 971.

[78] Hashem Dezhbakhsh and Joanna M. Shepherd, "The Deterrent Effect of Capital Punishment: Evidence from a 'Judicial Experiment'", *Economic Inquiry* 44, no. 3 (July 2006): 532–33.

[79] Michael Frakes and Matthew Harding, "The Deterrent Effect of Death Penalty Eligibility: Evidence from the Adoption of Child Murder Eligibility Factors", *American Law and Economics Review* 11, no. 2 (2009): 494–95.

expected numbers of monthly homicides of 5 to 10 during the subsequent 12 months."[80]

Of course, there are social scientists who disagree with these findings. Some studies since 2000 have failed to find a deterrent effect, and academic critics have challenged the persuasiveness of the evidence and conclusions of the studies cited above. And some critics argue that any deterrent effect is offset in whole or in part by a "brutalization effect" of increased murders after a state execution.[81] In turn, the authors of the key pro-deterrence studies have defended their findings against the critics and pointed to what they claim are serious deficiencies in the critics' quantitative methods and analyses.[82] Because of the importance of the deterrence issue to the public policy debate on the death penalty, the National Research Council (the "principal operating agency" of the National Academy of Sciences and the National Academy of Engineering) empaneled a committee of eight (six of whom were quantitatively trained social scientists) to assess the evidence. In 2012, it concluded that "research to date on the effect of capital punishment on homicide is not informative about whether capital punishment decreases, increases, or has no effect on homicide rates." It cautioned policymakers not to rely on claims that social-science research "demonstrates that capital punishment

---

[80] Kenneth C. Land, Raymond H. C. Teske Jr., and Hui Zheng, "The Short-Term Effects of Executions on Homicides: Deterrence, Displacement, or Both?" *Criminology* 47, no. 4 (October 2009), 1038. Note that the phrase "monthly homicides" in the quotation does not mean homicides per month, which would imply an annual reduction twelve times as high. The authors make clear that they are estimating the reduction in the number of homicides over the twelve months following an execution.

[81] For a recent list of studies cited by the academic critics of the deterrence hypothesis, see "Brief of Amicus Curiae Empirical Scholars" in the California death penalty case *Jones v. Davis*, before the United States Court of Appeals, Ninth Circuit, esp. pp. 16-18, available at http://www.hcrc.ca.gov/news/Brief%20of%20Amici%20Curiae%20Empirical%20Scholars%20Concerning%20Deterrence%20and%20the%20Death%20Penalty%20in%20Support%20of%20Petitioner_Appellee.pdf.

[82] See, for example, Paul R. Zimmerman, "Statistical Variability and the Deterrent Effect of the Death Penalty", *American Law and Economics Review* 11, no. 2 (2009): 370–98; Dale O. Cloninger and Roberto Marchesini, "Reflections on a Critique", *Applied Economics Letters* 16, no. 17 (November 2009): 1709–11; and Hashem Dezhbakhsh and Paul H. Rubin, "From the 'Econometrics of Capital Punishment' to the 'Capital Punishment' of Econometrics: On the Use and Abuse of Sensitivity Analysis", *Applied Economics* 43, no. 25 (2011): 3655–70.

decreases or increases the homicide rate by a specified amount or has no effect on the homicide rate".[83] In the judgment of the eight committee members, the evidence did not prove deterrence. Yet they were careful to add that "lack of evidence is not evidence for or against the hypothesis." That is, the committee was by no means claiming that the death penalty did not deter, only that "the scholarly evidence on the deterrent effect of capital punishment is too weak to guide decisions."[84] In its final paragraph, the committee recalled a similar study in 1978 that had concluded that "research on this topic is not likely to produce findings that will or should have much influence on policymakers." It added, "Today, more than 30 years later, perhaps the primary lesson learned from the latest round of empirical research on the deterrent effect of the death penalty is that researchers and policy makers must cope with ambiguity."[85]

It remains the case that there are highly trained quantitative social scientists who are convinced that the death penalty deters homicide—though estimates of the size of the effect vary widely—and highly trained quantitative social scientists who are convinced that it does not. Among the former is such a prominent figure as Nobel Prize–winning economist Gary S. Becker, who pioneered research on the economic analysis of crime. In 2006, he wrote:

> I believe [capital punishment] deters murders.... The available data are quite limited, however, so one should not base any conclusions solely on the econometric evidence. Still, I believe the preponderance of evidence does indicate that capital punishment deters.... Of course, public policy on punishments cannot wait until the evidence is perfect. Even with the limited quantitative evidence available, there are good reasons to believe that capital punishment deters murders. Most people, and murderers in particular, fear death, especially when it follows swiftly and with considerable certainty following the commission of a murder.... As [federal judge and scholar Richard] Posner indicates, the deterrent effect of capital punishment would be greater if the delays on its implementation were much shortened, and if this

---

[83] National Research Council, *Deterrence and the Death Penalty*, ed. Daniel S. Nagin and John V. Pepper (Washington, D.C.: National Academies Press, 2012), p. 2.

[84] Ibid., p. 3.

[85] Ibid., p. 121.

punishment was more certain to be used in the appropriate cases. But I agree with Posner that capital punishment has an important deterrent effect even with the way the present system actually operates.[86]

As this brief review demonstrates, from the perspective of quantitative social science, the deterrent effect of the death penalty is very much an open question. Thus, for a bishop to assert that "all studies show that capital punishment does not deter crime", as one did in 1992 (seventeen years after University of Chicago economist Isaac Ehrlich had published a highly influential paper that argued that each execution in the United States between 1933 and 1967 saved an average of eight lives through deterrence), is grossly to mischaracterize the state of the empirical research.[87] And for other bishops flatly to assert that the death penalty does not deter murder is to convey to their flocks the false impression that empirical support for deterrence is simply lacking in the professional literature.

Moreover, bishops do not serve their flocks well when they cite the fact that states without the death penalty tend to have lower murder rates than states with the death penalty as proof that the death penalty does not deter, as the USCCB did in 2005 and the Oregon bishops did in 1984: "The six states with the lowest murder rates have all abolished capital punishment."[88] While it is true that the original empirical deterrence studies more than half a century ago (mainly by sociologists and criminologists) relied on just such a comparison, social scientists quickly recognized that these comparisons do not prove the absence of deterrence. The reason is simple: low murder rates in some states may have made them more likely to drop the death penalty. For example, when North Dakota abolished the death penalty for all murders in 1973, its murder rate was less than one-tenth of the national average. Thus, we cannot conclude that the death penalty does not deter simply because states without the death penalty may have lower average murder rates than states with the death penalty. For example, states with very high violent-crime rates tend to have much higher

[86] Gary S. Becker, "On the Economics of Capital Punishment," *Economists' Voice* 3, no. 3 (March 2006): 1–2.

[87] Isaac Ehrlich, "The Deterrent Effect of Capital Punishment: A Question of Life and Death", *American Economic Review* 65, no. 3 (June 1975): 397–417.

[88] Oregon Catholic Bishops, "Statement on the Death Penalty".

incarceration rates (number of prisoners divided by the state's population) than do states with low violent-crime rates. Obviously, one should not conclude from this that prisons do not reduce crime. On the contrary, if states with very high crime rates suddenly reduced their incarceration rates to that of states with very low crime rates, we would expect to see an increase in crime in those states as they put thousands, or even tens of thousands, of repeat (and often violent) offenders on the street.

There is a good reason why it is so hard to demonstrate quantitatively whether the death penalty deters murder in the United States: the relatively small number of executions compared with the total number of homicides each year. Since the U.S. Supreme Court reinstated the death penalty in 1976, annual executions exceeded 74 only twice (98 in 1999 and 85 in 2000). Executions reached a low of 20 in 2016, though admittedly recent numbers have been suppressed by the failure of California to execute anyone since January 2006 (despite a death row population of at least 646 during this entire period). Between 2000 and 2015, executions averaged just over 51 per year (with a downward trend). If each execution saves 5 to 10 lives (a midrange for the various estimates discussed above), then 51 executions would have saved 255 to 510 lives each year (or roughly 4,000 to 8,000 for the 16-year period). Yet during this same period, homicides averaged about 15,600 per year. So, the total lives saved would have amounted to between 1.6% and 3.3% of all homicides. Although these percentages would be somewhat higher if we examined only the 31 to 38 states with the death penalty during these years, the fact is that even a fairly robust deterrent effect, saving perhaps several hundred lives every year, would necessarily be hard to discover among the vastly larger number of homicides not deterred. This is one reason some social scientists despair that quantitative methods will ever provide conclusive evidence that capital punishment deters murder even if it actually saves several hundred lives each year. Of course, the problem of detecting deterrence would be even greater if, say, an execution on average saved only a single life. Yet, such a statistically low—and almost certainly undetectable—deterrent effect would mean that at least 1,400 lives would have been saved by the equivalent number of executions in the United States since 1976. And if the death penalty does deter (at whatever level) and were used more frequently—since the reform of capital punishment laws in the 1970s, executions dropped from a peak of 98 in 1999 to 20 in 2016—then many more lives would be saved and there would be a greater likelihood that quantitative social science could detect the effect.

Though statistical studies are inconclusive on the deterrence question, the scholarly literature documents several clear examples of innocent lives saved by an offender's fear of death. One case was recounted by California senator Diane Feinstein on the floor of the U.S. Senate in 1995:

> I strongly believe that the death penalty can act as a deterrent to the most violent of crimes and is an appropriate punishment for those who knowingly take another life. There has been a lot of discussion as to whether the death penalty is or is not a deterrent. But I remember well in the 1960's when I was sentencing a woman convicted of robbery in the first degree [referring to Feinstein's service on the California parole board] and I remember looking at her commitment sheet and I saw that she carried a weapon that was unloaded into a grocery store robbery. I asked her the question: "Why was your gun unloaded?" She said to me: "So I would not panic, kill somebody, and get the death penalty." That was firsthand testimony directly to me that the death penalty in place in California in the sixties was in fact a deterrent.[89]

Another appeared in the journal *Criminology* in 2009:

> During a seminar presentation of the results from the present research by one of the authors, a colleague recalled the following incident. Some years ago his mother was in her late 70s and living alone in an apartment in Westchester County, New York. She had several collectibles. One afternoon the door rang, and two men, who must have known about her collectibles, forced their way in. They bound her to a chair while they went around the living room where most of her valuables were displayed. After they had taken what they wanted and were about to exit, one said to the other: "She has seen us and can identify us, should we kill her?" "No," answered the other, "we don't

[89] The speech was given on June 5, 1995, and is recounted in Paul G. Cassell, "In Defense of the Death Penalty" in *Debating the Death Penalty*, ed. Hugo Adam Bedau and Paul G. Cassell (Oxford: Oxford University Press, 2004), p. 190.

want to risk the death penalty." And so, to the great relief of my colleague's mother, they left her alone. This incident illustrates the kind of "second thought" process that may occur during instrumental crimes but is less likely to occur during highly emotional interactions.[90]

A third was recounted by law professor Robert Blecker, who spent twelve years interviewing inmates of the Washington, D.C., prison in Lorton, Virginia:

> Yes, I've spent thousands of hours among convicted killers and they've opened up to me and I've heard stories—I won't regale you with them—but one particular one was a guy who broke into a house to rob drug dealers and discovered more drugs than he expected. He had [a man] duct taped and tied up and he was about to kill him and he didn't, and I asked him why not and what went through his mind. And he said he remembered looking at the electric chair as a child through the window of the DC jail. And he also remembered the time he spent on [sic] Richmond penitentiary when he used to sweep the halls and look at the ... electric chair. And he said he couldn't tolerate that happening to him, so he let him live.... That was a half perfect datum. So I asked him whether he had a similar situation in Washington, DC, which has no death penalty. He in fact had. He had a drug dealer again tied up, and I asked him what did he do, and he said, "I killed him." And I asked him why, and he said, "Because I can tolerate what they got waiting for me here. I just couldn't tolerate what they had waiting for me in Virginia."[91]

These examples put the lie to the notion that criminals never think about the death penalty when engaged in criminal activity.

Yet, contemplating the risks of a death sentence during criminal activity is not the only way that the death penalty may deter murder. Another is through the leverage that the death penalty gives prosecutors to negotiate guilty pleas that result in longer sentences than would be the case if the jurisdiction did not authorize the death

---

[90] Land, Teske, and Zheng, "The Short-Term Effects", 1016–17.

[91] Robert Blecker, presentation at a "mock trial event" held in London in March 2010. The defendant is the American system of capital punishment. A video of the trial is available through the website of the Criminal Justice Legal Foundation at http://www.cjlf.org /media/dpontrial/London.htm. The one-minute clip that is transcribed in the quotation is at http://www.crimeandconsequences.com/crimblog/files/videos/Blecker.mpg.

penalty. These longer sentences themselves may have a deterrent effect on potential murderers, which would mean that the death penalty might deter even when it is not actually used. Law professor and Independent Institute research fellow Charles Keckler calls this "a secondary deterrent effect of capital punishment".[92]

Keckler reports that studies of those who are convicted of, or plead guilty to, a murder eligible for the death penalty "reinforce the essential point that life is preferred to death" and that consequently "the option of the death penalty gives prosecutors an important amount of leverage in plea negotiations."[93] Defendants charged with capital murder, with plenty of time to think through their options and counseled by their attorneys, often choose to avoid the risk of a death sentence by pleading guilty in exchange for a sentence to life without parole or to a very long fixed sentence.[94] For most offenders, life without parole (or a sentence, for example, of 30 years or more) would

---

[92] Charles N. W. Keckler, "Life v. Death: Who Should Capital Punishment Marginally Deter?" *Journal of Law, Economics and Policy* 2, no. 1 (2006): 51.

[93] Ibid., p. 93.

[94] For example: "I find the death penalty leads defendants to accept plea bargaining with harsher terms." Ilyana Kuziemko, "Does the Threat of the Death Penalty Affect Plea Bargaining in Murder Cases? Evidence from New York's 1995 Reinstatement of Capital Punishment", *American Law and Economics Review* 8, no. 1 (2006): 116. "Thus, generally, prosecutors and defense attorneys agree that without the threat of death, a case is unlikely to be resolved by a plea of life without parole.... The state benefits by securing a plea to a higher sentence than might otherwise be obtained." Susan Ehrhard, "Plea Bargaining and the Death Penalty: An Exploratory Study", *Justice System Journal* 29, no. 3 (2008): 320, 323. "Significantly more defendants plea bargain to a life or long sentence in states where the death penalty is available." Kent S. Scheidegger, "The Death Penalty and Plea Bargaining to Life Sentences" (working paper 09-01, Criminal Justice Legal Foundation, 2009), p. 1, http://www.cjlf.org/publications/papers /wpaper09-01.pdf. "The results provide strong evidence that the threat of the death penalty has a robust causal effect on the likelihood of a plea agreement." Sherod Thaxton, "Leveraging Death", *Journal of Criminal Law and Criminology* 103, no. 2 (2013): 475. Two studies that partially dissent from these findings are Susan Ehrhard-Dietzel, "The Use of Life and Death as Tools in Plea Bargaining", *Criminal Justice Review* 37, no. 1 (2012): 89–109 and John C. Douglass, "Death as a Bargaining Chip: Plea Bargaining and the Future of Virginia's Death Penalty", *University of Richmond Law Review* 49, no. 3 (2015): 873–94. Though Ehrhard-Dietzel, who surveyed thirty-five prosecutors and defense attorneys in Michigan (no death penalty) and thirty-two in Ohio (death penalty), largely discounts the importance of the death penalty as leverage in plea negotiations in murder cases, her own data (table 6, p. 95) show that murder defendants were much more likely to plead guilty in the death-penalty state. Douglass, though skeptical about the size of the effect that the death penalty has on sentence length in plea bargains, acknowledges that "it does seem likely that, on the whole, prosecutors who charge capital murder will obtain higher bargained-for sentences than prosecutors who negotiate pleas from the starting point of an indictment for first-degree murder" (pp. 892–93).

result in many more years behind bars than would a typical sentence for murder. With the average age of murderers in the range of 28 to 31 years old, a true life sentence would likely mean 30 to 50 years behind bars.[95] This compares to an average time served in prison of just over 14 years for the 2,600 murderers released from state prisons in 2009 (the most recent year with published data).[96] Of course, those released for murder in 2009 were sentenced mainly in the mid-1990s. What of those sentenced more recently? How long can we expect that they will serve for murder? Here, though the data are imperfect, the best estimate is perhaps a year or two longer than the 14 years for those released in 2009.[97] Because so many convicted murderers

[95] Sean Rosenmerkel, Matthew Durose, and Donald Ferole Jr., *Felony Sentences in State Courts, 2006: Statistical Tables* (Washington, D.C.: Bureau of Justice Statistics, 2009), table 3.1, p. 16, http://www.bjs.gov/content/pub/pdf/fssco6st.pdf.

[96] Thomas P. Bonczar, et al., *National Corrections Reporting Program, Time Served in State Prison, By Offense, Release Type, Sex, and Race* (Washington, D.C.: Bureau of Justice Statistics, 2009), table 9, available at http://www.bjs.gov/index.cfm?ty=pbdetail&iid=2045 (download data for 2009 and select file ncrp0909.csv). The mean for all those released for murder was 14 years and 3 months; the median—or middle value—was 13 years and 7 months. Note that while published data often include murder and nonnegligent manslaughter in a single category, this report separates them; thus, the time-served data here exclude all manslaughter convictions.

[97] We can derive this estimate in the following way: The most recent published national data for felony sentencing by state courts are from a Bureau of Justice Statistics (BJS) report published in 2009, which covers felony convictions and sentences in 2006. In that year state courts convicted an estimated 6,240 persons of murder and another 2,420 of nonnegligent manslaughter (often called voluntary manslaughter). Note that these numbers exclude negligent manslaughter (also called involuntary manslaughter), such as accidental killings in which someone is criminally culpable (Rosenmerkel, Durose, and Ferole, *Felony Sentences in State Courts*, table 1.1, p. 3). From here on, the BJS report presents detailed data on the single category "Murder/Nonnegligent manslaughter". Of the estimated 8,670 persons convicted of murder or nonnegligent manslaughter in 2006, 2% were sentenced to death, 23% to life in prison (whether or not eligible for parole), 68% to prison for a term of years, 2% to local jail for up to a year, and 5% to probation or other nonincarceration sentence (table 4.4, p. 28; table 1.2, p. 4). The figure of 68% for sentences to prison for a term of years is derived by subtracting 25% (the total of sentences to death and to life in prison) from the 93% who received a prison sentence (which in table 1.2 includes both sentences to life in prison and to death). The 68% received an average sentence of 20 years and 10 months (table 1.3, p. 6). Because murderers eligible for release typically serve about 61% of their sentence (see Bureau of Justice Statistics, *State Court Sentencing of Convicted Felons, 2004—Statistical Tables*, table 1.5, available at http://www.bjs.gov/content/pub/html/scscf04/tables/scso4105tab.cfm), we can expect that this group of murderers will serve on average just under 13 years before release. However, because roughly one-quarter of these offenders were convicted of nonnegligent manslaughter, for which prison sentences average about half as long as for murder (see Bonczar, *National Corrections Reporting Program*, table 9), the actual figure for murder, if it could be known, would be, perhaps, a few years higher than the 13-year estimate.

serve much less than life behind bars, sentences to life without parole are considerably more severe than a typical murder sentence. They may, therefore, more effectively deter murder than prison sentences that allow eventual release.

Despite the views of some critics of capital punishment that life in prison is a punishment as severe as (or even worse than) death, the vast majority of murderers who end up on death row show that they disagree; they reveal their preference for life in prison over death by appealing their sentences until all hope is lost. Though some forgo appeals—so-called volunteers—Keckler estimates that these constitute no more than 4 to 5% of those sentenced to death: "in excess of 95% of death row inmates would prefer to stay alive."[98] Moreover, as we saw in chapter 3, some who eventually stop appealing do not do so until many years after their original sentence; and others stop appealing because they recognize the justice of the punishment, not because death will free them of more painful years in prison.

Thus, there is ample evidence that the vast majority of murderers prefer life in prison to death, given a choice. Both after arrest—if offered a plea bargain—and after sentence—when deciding whether and how often to appeal—they give every evidence of acting quite rationally and preferring life to death. One effect of this rational behavior, as we have seen, is longer plea-bargained sentences in death-penalty jurisdictions and therefore a possible secondary deterrent effect even when the death penalty is not used (though, for the threat of death to be credible, it must sometimes be applied).

What about prior to arrest—when potential murderers are on the streets, often engaging in serious criminal activity? We have already seen that the scholarly literature documents several cases of criminals sparing innocent lives for fear of a death sentence. Engaging the broader argument about the deterrent effects of criminal sanctions, Keckler notes that some criminologists argue that criminals are so "peculiarly present-oriented, impulsive and driven by emotion" that they cannot be deterred by criminal sanctions.[99] (Many American bishops seem to think that all murderers and potential murderers are of this type, despite the incontrovertible fact that hit men, terrorists,

[98] Keckler, "Life v. Death", p. 82.
[99] Ibid., p. 76.

gang members, and many others plan their murders and do not act out of sudden impulse.) Other criminologists, however, make "a completely contrary claim", holding "that the threat of punishment would be most salient for, and thus have the greatest impact on, individuals most prone to crime".[100] Keckler concludes that "based on limited evidence, it appears to be the case that 'sanction threats inhibit the criminal activity of those most at risk of offending' despite their greater impulsivity."[101]

Here Keckler offers the fascinating, if deeply disturbing, example of Jeffrey Dahmer, convicted of murdering (and, in some cases, raping, dismembering, and cannibalizing) seventeen men and young boys, all but one in Wisconsin, between 1978 and 1991. Though the court found Dahmer sane, and thus subject to criminal process and punishment, few would consider him the kind of rational criminal who might be deterred by criminal penalties (unlike, say, a professional killer). Yet, to satisfy his sadistic desires, Dahmer invested considerable time and effort in concealing his activities. For example, he rejected "potential subjects who had automobiles, as abandonment of these would create problematic inquiries upon the zombification and disappearance of their drivers".[102] ("Zombification" refers to Dahmer's practice of drilling holes in his victims' heads, while they were still alive, and pouring chemicals into the holes in an attempt to render his victims docile.) He also took great pains to dispose of the remains of many victims by "pulverizing bones or dissolving them with acid".[103] As Keckler notes,

> Obviously, the legal regime and its associated threat of incapacitation and punishment [Wisconsin did not have the death penalty] failed to *fully* deter Dahmer.... Yet the law did alter the *rate* of his crimes [seventeen murders over thirteen years] by increasing the labor and time investment necessary to reduce the chance of capture and, thus, the expected cost. The detection-avoidance investments were sufficiently onerous so that only occasionally was it "rational" for him to violate the legal rules against killing and eating people.

[100] Ibid.
[101] Ibid., pp. 76–77.
[102] Ibid., p. 63.
[103] Ibid.

On most days, Dahmer could not, for fear of the authorities, *act as he otherwise would have,* a phenomenon we usually call deterrence. Dahmer, a very bad man, *was* deterred, and in consequence, lives were saved.[104]

Though Dahmer committed his horrific crimes in a state without the death penalty, Keckler's interpretation is entirely consistent with the three anecdotes cited above: even very evil men with no moral qualms about taking innocent lives may modify their behavior in light of the consequences the state imposes for such behavior.

If Keckler and others are right that the death penalty results in longer prison sentences for murder, then it would also reduce some amount of crime, including some murders, through lengthier incapacitation. We know from three large-scale recidivism studies conducted by the Bureau of Justice Statistics (BJS) of the U.S. Department of Justice that about a fifth of those serving time for homicide who are released from prison are arrested for another violent crime during the three-to-five years after their release and between 1% and 6% are rearrested for another homicide. (For 1983–1986, the homicide rearrest rate was 6.6%; for 1994–1997, 1.2%; and for 2005–2010, 2.1%.)[105] With states releasing from prison between five and ten thousand convicted killers each year, it can be estimated that over the past several decades killers released from prison within the previous three-to-five years accounted for at least many dozens and perhaps as many as several hundred new homicides each year. Indeed, as we saw in chapter 3, nearly a fifth (8 of 43) of the murderers executed in 2012 had killed someone else prior to the murder for which they were sentenced to death. Moreover, BJS data show

---

[104] Ibid., emphasis in the original.

[105] See Allen J. Beck and Bernard E. Shipley, *Recidivism of Prisoners Released in 1983* (Washington, D.C.: Bureau of Justice Statistics, 1989, NCJ-116261), table 9, p. 6, available at http://www.bjs.gov/content/pub/pdf/rpr83.pdf; Patrick A. Langan and David J. Levin, *Recidivism of Prisoners Released in 1994* (Washington, D.C.: Bureau of Justice Statistics, 2002), table 10, p. 9, available at http://www.bjs.gov/content/pub/pdf/rpr94.pdf; Matthew R. Durose, Alexia D. Cooper, and Howard N. Snyder, *Recidivism of Prisoners Released in 30 States in 2005: Patterns from 2005 to 2010* (Washington, D.C.: Bureau of Justice Statistics, 2014), table 8, p. 8, available at https://www.bjs.gov/content/pub/pdf/rprts05p0510.pdf; and the Supplemental Tables to the last report released in December 2016 and available at http://www.bjs.gov/content/pub/pdf/rprts05p0510_st.pdf.

that 9% of the three thousand inmates on death rows throughout the nation had previously been convicted of homicide.[106]

Oregon prosecuting attorney Joshua Marquis, writing in 2005, put a human face on the statistical data:

> Let's tally the *additional* victims of [murderers] freed [from prison]: *Nine*, killed by Kenneth McDuff, who had been sentenced to die for child murder in Texas and then was freed on parole after the death penalty laws at the time were overturned. *One*, by Robert Massie of California, also sentenced to die and also paroled. Massie rewarded the man who gave him a job on parole by murdering him less than a year after getting out of prison. *One*, by Richard Marquette, in Oregon, sentenced to "life" (which until 1994 meant about eight years in Oregon) for abducting and then dismembering women. He did so well in a woman-free environment (prison) that he was released— only to abduct, kill and dismember women again. *Two*, by Carl Cletus Bowles, in Idaho, guilty of kidnapping nine people and the murder of a police officer. Bowles escaped during a conjugal visit with a girlfriend, only to abduct and murder an elderly couple.[107]

It follows that if the existence of the death penalty in a state results in longer prison sentences for murderers, it will very likely also result in fewer future homicides, either because (1) more murderers will never be released at all (life without parole); (2) they will be released at older ages, which we know correlates with lower recidivism rates; and (3) citizens will be protected while the murderer is incarcerated. On the aging effect, online analysis of BJS' database for prisoners released in 1994 shows that within three years of release from a homicide sentence: 25.0% of those over forty were rearrested within three years, compared with 41.9% of those thirty-one to thirty-five and 54.1% of those younger than twenty-six.[108] Keeping convicted murderers

[106] Tracy L. Snell, *Capital Punishment, 2013—Statistical Tables* (Washington, D.C.: Bureau of Justice Statistics, December 2014), table 8, p. 12, available at http://www.bjs.gov/content/pub/pdf/cp13st.pdf.

[107] Joshua Marquis, "The Myth of Innocence", *Journal of Criminal Law and Criminology* 95, no. 2 (2005): 518–19.

[108] The BJS Prisoner Recidivism Analysis Tool is available at http://www.bjs.gov/index.cfm?ty=datool&surl=/recidivism/index.cfm. Note also that BJS' most recent published report on recidivism, *Recidivism of Prisoners Released in 30 States in 2005*, reported that 80.4%

in prison longer, which the death penalty helps to achieve, almost certainly saves lives.

There are other related ways in which the death penalty saves lives. First, some convicted murderers cannot be deterred from killing again. Law professor Ronald Allen and law student Amy Shavell relate the case of Edward Montour, "who, while serving time for killing his eleven-week-old daughter, beat a guard to death and claimed that he would murder again: 'The court knows how little I value human life.... It is self-evident that I would kill again if another opportunity was afforded me. I am antisocial, homicidal and without remorse and will remain a potential threat. The state can kill me, I don't care.'"[109] Short of executing such an offender, we are left only with solitary confinement for perhaps decades with no direct human contact. Apart from the significant added expense of enforcing such extreme measures, is it so clear that this is a more humane way to punish the worst murderers than by giving them their just deserts?

Second, the prospect of the death penalty gives violent prison inmates already serving a very long fixed sentence or life without parole (whatever their conviction offense) a powerful incentive not to kill other inmates or prison staff. A "lifer" may believe that he has nothing to lose by killing in prison (except perhaps some privileges or freedoms within the prison). Allen and Shavell note that "there are numerous inmate murders", and they give examples from more than thirty cases between 1999 and 2005 yielded by a Lexis-Nexis search.[110] Also, BJS reports that from 2000 to 2013 there were 302 homicides of inmates of local jails throughout the country (an average of 22 per year) and from 2001 to 2013 there were 762 homicides of inmates of state prisons (an average of 59 per year).[111] So, inmate murders of other inmates are not extraordinarily rare events, averaging about 80

---

of the youngest violent offenders (twenty-four and younger) released from prison were rearrested within five years, compared with 60.7% of the oldest offenders studied (forty and older) (table 14, p. 12). The report does not show the correlation of age with recidivism for murder specifically or homicide more generally.

[109] Ronald J. Allen and Amy Shavell, "Further Reflections on the Guillotine", *Journal of Criminal Law and Criminology* 95, no. 2 (2005): 630–31.

[110] Ibid., p. 630n9.

[111] Margaret Noonan, Harley Rohloff, and Scott Ginder, *Mortality in Local Jails and State Prisons, 2000-2013—Statistical Tables* (Washington, D.C.: Bureau of Justice Statistics, 2015), table 7, p. 12; table 23, p. 23, http://www.bjs.gov/content/pub/pdf/mljsp0013st.pdf. Although it is likely that most of the reported homicides are inmate murders of other inmates, some may

per year. If the death penalty deters some inmates from killing while in prison, then these numbers would be higher without it. And, as Allen and Shavell argue, even if "an execution does not deter any future murders, a decision not to execute an individual may nevertheless result in deaths of other individuals: namely an inmate who would have been executed may kill others in prison."[112]

Third, the existence of the death penalty can give a lifer who escapes a strong reason not to kill while on the run. Though it happens rarely, very violent criminals do sometimes escape from jails and prisons. One of the men executed in 2012 (described in chapter 3) had escaped with six others from a maximum-security prison in Texas, where he had been serving time for seventeen counts of armed robbery in two separate incidents. In June 2015 the nation was transfixed by the news that two convicted murderers had escaped a maximum-security prison in upstate New York. And in January 2016 southern Californians learned that three men had escaped from a maximum-security jail in Orange County, where one had been held pending trial for murder, another for torture and kidnapping, and the third for attempted murder.

To summarize our argument about deterrence to this point in the chapter:

- If we had good reason to believe that capital punishment, which the Church has always taught is a licit punishment for grave crimes, saved innocent lives through deterrence, there would be a strong presumption *based on Catholic moral principles* that it should be used.
- Church officials have traditionally left such prudential judgments to public officials; yet even so, Catholic authorities and

---

be inmate deaths caused by prison guards in the lawful execution of their authority, and others may be the result of injuries received prior to incarceration. Here is the definition used in the BJS reporting system: "Homicides include all types of intentional homicide and involuntary manslaughter as ruled by a medical examiner or pathologist at autopsy. For example, an inmate may die of positional asphyxia (suffocation caused by the position of the inmate's body) while the inmate is being removed from a cell. A legal-intervention homicide committed while the inmate is trying to escape would also be included. In addition, homicides include cases that are ruled a homicide at autopsy when events that led to the death occurred prior to incarceration. For example, an inmate who was shot in the community years prior to incarceration died from complications of the gunshot wound while incarcerated" (p. 31).

[112] Allen and Shavell, "Further Reflections on the Guillotine", p. 630.

theologians have often acknowledged that the death penalty does in fact deter crime.

- Although American Catholic bishops have either strongly implied or expressly argued that the death penalty does not save lives through deterrence, they have neither the training nor experience to make judgments about the deterrent effects of the death penalty—a question that is of its nature an empirical and prudential one, not a matter of theological or moral principle.

- Numerous empirical studies in recent decades have purported to adduce evidence that the death penalty deters murders. Other researchers have challenged these findings, and social scientists remain divided on the issue. Yet given the relatively small number of executions in the United States compared with the large number of homicides, it is quite possible that each execution saves many innocent lives but that empirical studies will never be able to demonstrate this conclusively.

- Especially (but not only) because of the inconclusive nature of the social-science evidence, it is quite appropriate for policymakers and others to draw on anecdotal and commonsense evidence to reach judgments about the deterrent effect of capital punishment. In our view, such evidence is largely supportive of the deterrence argument; for even hardened criminals and sociopaths give evidence of acting rationally to adjust their criminal behavior to account for criminal sanctions.

- There are sound logical and empirical reasons for believing that the death penalty has a "secondary deterrent effect" by increasing prison sentences for murder through the plea-bargaining process. These longer sentences also reduce murders through lengthier incapacitation of those willing to kill.

- The death penalty likely saves lives of prison inmates and staff (1) by eliminating killers who cannot be deterred from killing again and (2) by giving violent prisoners strong incentives not to kill while incarcerated. It also likely saves lives by giving a lifer who escapes a strong reason not to kill while on the run.

Although we believe that in sum the case outlined here for deterrence is quite strong, we still hold that the argument we made near the end of chapter 1 is even stronger: that the fundamental question regarding capital punishment and deterrence is not what will deter those who are willing to consider murder, but rather what will prevent people from being willing to consider murder in the first place. No one has captured this point more succinctly and pithily than James Fitzjames Stephen, who is worth quoting again: "Some men, probably, abstain from murder because they fear that if they committed murder they would be hanged. Hundreds of thousands abstain from it because they regard it with horror. One great reason why they regard it with horror is that murderers are hanged with the hearty approbation of all reasonable men."[113] Surely, most men and women do not murder others because they know that murder is deeply wrong, not because they have calculated the risks involved. Here the law is a teacher, though not, of course, the only teacher. As David Gelernter has noted (also quoted in chapter 1), "we execute murderers in order to make a communal proclamation: that murder is intolerable. A deliberate murderer embodies evil so terrible that it defiles the community.... By executing murderers, the community reaffirms this moral understanding."[114] The murder-reduction effects of such moral teaching through law are not likely to be observable by comparing murder rates month to month or even year to year with executions.

It is not good enough for opponents of the death penalty to dismiss the empirical evidence as inconclusive; for if we do not have certain knowledge one way or the other, then the prudent course would be to maintain capital punishment. Better to take the lives of those who have brutally murdered others if this will possibly save innocent lives, than to allow the guilty to live at the possible cost of the deaths of more innocent people. Thus, to oppose capital punishment inflexibly in the face of inconclusive empirical evidence of deterrence is, in effect, to act as if one is certain that the death penalty *does not* deter. As Keckler argues, "The executive, the legislators and the citizenry are not at liberty to enjoy the subtle pleasures of intellectual ambivalence. To not execute criminals is to make a choice regarding the effect of the death penalty, just as to execute them reflects such a choice, and there seems to be no way around the fact that the state

[113] James Fitzjames Stephen, *A General View of the Criminal Law in England* (London: Macmillan, 1863), pp. 99–100.

[114] David Gelernter, "What Do Murderers Deserve?" *Commentary* (April 1998), https://www.commentarymagazine.com/articles/what-do-murderers-deserve/.

will do one or the other."[115] As he says about those who oppose the death penalty, "to eliminate the *mere possibility* that innocent lives (by wrongful conviction) might be lost", such opponents "must have at a fundamental level assumed that the deterrence argument was not simply *unproven*, but *implausible*, perhaps *impossible*".[116] But the arguments of this chapter and of chapter 1 show, at the very least, that the deterrence argument *cannot* rationally be dismissed as implausible, much less impossible.

When religious leaders, Catholic or otherwise, call for abolishing the death penalty, as nearly all American bishops now do, they have of necessity reached a judgment that the death penalty does not save innocent lives. Again, it is not good enough to say that the evidence is inconclusive. "Inconclusive" means that the death penalty may well deter even if social science cannot so demonstrate. There is no gainsaying the fact that innocent lives will be lost, perhaps quite a few of them, if the death penalty deters but is abolished. In the face of uncertainty about the findings of quantitative social science and in light of other evidence and strong arguments in favor of deterrence, it is simply irresponsible for religious leaders to call for the abolition of capital punishment on this basis.

Strikingly, in their lengthy 2000 statement *Responsibility, Rehabilitation, and Restoration*, the USCCB held that "even if the death penalty were proven to be a deterrent to crime, the Catholic bishops would still oppose its use because there are alternative means to protect society available to us today." With all due respect to the bishops, we find this statement logically untenable and morally indefensible. If we knew that the death penalty deters crime (meaning, of course, that it deters murder, since murder is the only crime for which states may use the death penalty), we would know that, compared with prison sentences, however long, the death penalty saves lives. It makes no sense to claim that there are "alternative means to protect society" that would, presumably, compensate for the extra murders that criminals could commit if the death penalty were abolished.

One of the authors of this book went to graduate school in a very high-crime neighborhood where, to avert murders, law-abiding people avoided walking the streets after dark except in fairly large groups.

---

[115] Keckler, "Life v. Death", pp. 56–57.
[116] Ibid., 60, emphasis added.

(During this time two graduate students who violated this informal rule were murdered in separate incidents a few years apart.) Surely the bishops are not suggesting that even if the death penalty were known to deter, it would still be preferable for law-abiding citizens to be forced to adopt cumbersome behavioral modifications of this and other sorts so as to avoid being murdered, rather than inflicting a just punishment that might deter potential murderers! If there are sound ways to reduce this worst of crimes—a crime that "cries out to heaven for vengeance" (*CCC* 2268)—then we should employ them. But murderers are a permanent feature of the human landscape, and when caught they must be punished. It seems to us callous in the extreme to say that *even if we knew for certain that executing murderers saved innocent lives*, we should reject it. Of course, our point is not that punishment is justified by its deterrent effects alone. That would be pure consequentialism, which we rejected (following natural law principles) in chapter 1. Punishment must be deserved, and it must be proportional to the harm caused by the crime. The thief deserves to be punished, but he does not deserve to have his hand hacked off, despite the powerful deterrent effects of such punishment. Brutal murderers, by contrast, deserve to be executed, and if such executions also save innocent lives, then the case for employing the death penalty with some frequency is all the more compelling, and rejecting it is all the more irresponsible.

Are there any grounds, then, for rejecting a punishment that justice demands and that saves lives? In addition to their scriptural, theological, and philosophical arguments, the bishops maintain that: (1) the death penalty makes repentance impossible, a result deeply incompatible with Christian principles; (2) it is administered so unfairly in the United States that its continued use cannot be justified; and (3) its use promotes disrespect for human life, and this contributes to a culture of death rather than a culture of life. We address the first two points here and return to the third in the conclusion.

The possibility of repentance

When the American bishops first collectively elaborated their case against the death penalty in 1980, they said the following about repentance, reform, and rehabilitation:

Reform or rehabilitation of the criminal cannot serve as a justification for capital punishment, which necessarily deprives the criminal
of the opportunity to develop a new way of life that conforms to
the norms of society and that contributes to the common good. It
may be granted that the imminence of capital punishment may induce
repentance in the criminal, but we should certainly not think that this
threat is somehow necessary for God's grace to touch and to transform
human hearts....

With respect to the difficulties inherent in capital punishment, we
note first that infliction of the death penalty extinguishes possibilities
for reform and rehabilitation for the person executed as well as the
opportunity for the criminal to make some creative compensation for
the evil he or she has done. It also cuts off the possibility for a new
beginning and of moral growth in a human life which has been seriously deformed.[117]

Here the bishops make three related claims. First, they hold that the
death penalty "deprives the criminal of the opportunity to develop a
new way of life that conforms to the norms of society". If this "new
way of life" means responsibly exercising one's freedoms and meeting
one's social obligations in the outside world, then the death penalty
indeed prevents this, but no more so than does life without parole,
which, as we have noted, the bishops specifically endorse as a legitimate punishment for the worst murderers. If the bishops are simply
referring to behaving properly *within* prison because of an interior
reformation, then the death penalty no more prevents this than does
a prison sentence, especially with nearly all executions taking place at
least a decade, and often two decades or more, after sentencing. Of
course, the death penalty, if actually carried out, does reduce the time
available for reformation of heart and soul, but no doubt this is more
than compensated for by the stimulus that impending death creates
for genuine reform.

Second, the bishops concede that capital punishment "may induce
repentance", but they insist that the threat of death is not "necessary
for God's grace to touch and to transform human hearts". We agree
that it is not necessary in the case of *every* offender, but that is not
really the issue. The question is whether the threat of death is *more*

[117] "Bishops' Statement on Capital Punishment, 1980".

effective at fostering repentance and reform (and therefore salvation) than is a very long prison sentence. Furthermore, there are surely *some* offenders who are so stubborn and set upon evil that they are *not* likely to repent unless they know death is imminent. (Do the bishops claim to know otherwise? How *could* they know this?) Saint Thomas Aquinas, as we saw in chapter 1, not only insisted that the death penalty was good for repentance but held that "if [offenders] are so stubborn that even at the point of death their heart does not draw back from evil, it is possible to make a highly probable judgment that they would never come away from evil to the right use of their powers".[118] Samuel Johnson quipped that the prospect of execution "concentrates ... [the] mind wonderfully". The a priori case for the value of capital punishment in fostering repentance is strongly supported by the wealth of empirical evidence we presented in chapter 3 showing how common it is for death row inmates to repent and seek forgiveness from God. Moreover, as we argued in chapter 1, repentance and reformation require that the wrongdoer appreciate and acknowledge the gravity of his crime. He is more likely to do so if knows that what he has done is *worthy of death*, and he is more likely to believe this if the state punishes murder with death. In this way too, capital punishment can actually promote the reform of an offender's soul. Thus, the Christian message of repentance as the road to salvation—the very first words of Christ's public teaching in the traditional ordering of the Gospels is "Repent, for the kingdom of heaven is at hand" (Mt 4:17)—strengthens, not weakens, the case for the death penalty.

Finally, the bishops argue that the death penalty makes it impossible for the murderer "to make some creative compensation for the evil he or she has done". We wonder what "creative compensation" Richard Alan Gore might have made, had he been serving life in prison, for his brutal abductions, rapes, and murders of young girls in Florida in the 1980s; or what "creative compensation" Richard Dale Stokley might have made for abducting, raping, strangling, and beating to death two thirteen-year-old girls and throwing their naked bodies down an abandoned mine shaft? In 2012, the states of Florida and Arizona gave these men the punishment they richly

---

[118] *Summa Contra Gentiles* III, 146.

deserved for their terrible deeds. Other than by manfully accepting their just punishment, what else could these men *possibly* offer the victims' families for tearing their loved ones from their lives and leaving them with searing memories of how brutally they died? We submit that there is nothing else, and that reassuring the families of their victims that there is at least some justice to be had in this life *is itself* the most fitting form of "creative compensation" there could be.

Of course, this is "compensation" only in a figurative sense. There is no true compensation for murder, not in the here and now. Indeed, one of the essential elements of the Mosaic homicide law—which distinguished it from other Middle Eastern societies of the time—was an absolute ban on money compensation for homicide: "Moreover you shall accept no ransom for the life of a murderer, who is guilty of death; but he shall be put to death" (Num 35:31). Of course, the bishops have not proposed money compensation (they say not a word about what an inmate *could* do to compensate for murder), but the broader biblical principle is that *no compensation is appropriate in the case of murder:* rather, the murderer "shall be put to death".

A "deeply flawed" application?

A frequent theme of the bishops' attack on the death penalty is how unfairly it is applied in practice. "Its application is deeply flawed", the bishops wrote in 2005.[119] All of the bishops' major statements make this point. They allege three key faults: (1) the capital punishment system makes too many mistakes; (2) it discriminates against racial minorities; and (3) it discriminates against the poor. Not only are the bishops themselves convinced that the application of the death penalty in the United States suffers from such serious flaws, but they also "seek to educate and persuade our fellow citizens that this penalty is often applied unfairly and in racially biased ways".[120] Here, as with their argument about deterrence, the bishops are weighing in on matters far removed from their religious training and pastoral

[119] USCCB, *A Culture of Life*, p. 7.
[120] Administrative Board of the USCCB, "A Good Friday Appeal".

experience. If they are convinced that the application of the death penalty is deeply flawed, it is because others have told them so. As with deterrence, however, all these matters are disputed by social scientists and legal practitioners. The bishops have embraced one side of an ongoing debate—the side that lines up with their abolitionist position—and they seek to persuade their flocks to embrace it. Of course, we do not begrudge the bishops or any religious leaders the right to form an opinion about such contested issues. Yet, in our view, it is more than a little inappropriate for the national organization of the nation's Catholic bishops to take an official position on highly contested empirical claims far outside the bishops' expertise and then to "seek to educate and persuade" Catholic laymen. They thereby add their religious authority to the scales in an ongoing debate on empirical issues about which Catholics are free to disagree. What is worse is that their empirical claims themselves are unsound, as we will show in addressing each of their points in turn.

Mistakes in the application of capital punishment

Here are the key passages from USCCB documents on the prevalence of errors in the American capital punishment system:

> The imposition of capital punishment involves the possibility of mistake. In this respect, it is not different from other legal processes; and it must be granted our legal system shows considerable care for the rights of defendants in capital cases. But the possibility of mistake cannot be eliminated from the system. Because death terminates the possibilities of conversion and growth and support that we can share with each other, we regard a mistaken infliction of the death penalty with a special horror, even while we retain our trust in God's loving mercy.[121]

> The discovery of people on death row who are innocent is frightening.[122]

> Some people argue that our system of justice, trial by jury, can ensure that ... the innocent will never be convicted. This is the least persuasive argument of all. Statistics, however weighted, indicate that errors

---

[121] "Bishops' Statement on Capital Punishment, 1980".
[122] Administrative Board of the USCCB, "A Good Friday Appeal".

are made in judgement and convictions.... Our legal system is a very good one, but it is a human institution. Even a small percentage of irreversible errors is increasingly seen as intolerable. God alone is the author of life.[123]

The criminal justice system is run by human beings—and we make mistakes. Since 1973, at least 139 people from 26 states have been exonerated from death row after evidence of innocence was found. Rather than showing the system is working, exonerations provide evidence that our system is flawed. DNA testing cannot solve these problems. DNA evidence exists in only 10% of criminal cases.[124]

In recent decades no criticism of capital punishment has gained more traction than this charge that the criminal justice systems in death-penalty states regularly convict and sometimes execute innocent individuals. The bishops are certainly right that although "our legal system shows considerable care for the rights of defendants in capital cases[,] ... the possibility of mistake cannot be eliminated from the system." Indeed, we know of no responsible defender of the death penalty who denies the possibility of mistakes. After all, as the bishops said in 2011, "The criminal justice system is run by human beings—and we make mistakes." On this proponents and opponents agree. What is in question is just how large the problem is and what conclusions we should draw from it.

As their last quotation shows, a few years ago the bishops claimed that "at least 139 people from 26 states have been exonerated from death row after evidence of innocence was found." This figure, which is from the Death Penalty Information Center (DPIC), covers the period 1973 through 2011.[125] (Despite the neutral-sounding name, DPIC is an avowedly abolitionist organization and a leading force in the movement to rid the nation of capital punishment.) During this time, the states and the federal government sentenced

---

[123] National Jewish/Catholic Consultation, "To End the Death Penalty".

[124] Office of Domestic Social Development, USCCB, *Death Penalty*, February 2011, http://www.usccb.org/issues-and-action/human-life-and-dignity/death-penalty-capital -punishment/upload/Death-Penalty-Backgrounder-2011-2.pdf.

[125] Death Penalty Information Center, "The Innocence List", http://www.deathpenalty info.org/innocence-list-those-freed-death-row.

8,295 individuals to death. So, if this figure of 139 is accurate, then the error rate was 1.7% (and therefore the accuracy rate was 98.3%). The bishops neither place the 139 figure in the larger context nor explain the source of the 139 figure and the controversy surrounding it. Indeed, the bishops seem totally unaware that critics of the DPIC list (which included 155 through June 8, 2015) have argued that the DPIC *vastly overstates* the number of innocent people who have been removed from death row.

First, the bishops misstate what the DPIC list purports to show. It is simply not true that everyone on the list was "exonerated from death row after evidence of innocence was found". The DPIC uses the following criteria for inclusion on its "Innocence List":

> Defendants must have been convicted, sentenced to death and subsequently either-
>
> a. Been **acquitted** of all charges related to the crime that placed them on death row, or
> b. Had all charges related to the crime that placed them on death row **dismissed** by the prosecution, or
> c. Been granted a complete **pardon** based on evidence of innocence.[126]

By the DPIC count, 47 of the 155 were acquitted at retrial, 101 had the charges dismissed by the prosecutor, and 7 were pardoned. Note that inclusion on the list *does not require new evidence of innocence.*[127] Outside of the relatively few pardons, each inmate had his original conviction overturned on appeal and then was not reconvicted, usually because the prosecutor dismissed the charges. While it is true that in some cases the charges were dismissed because new evidence exonerated the defendant, in many others, prosecutors simply concluded that conviction

---

[126] Ibid., bold in the original.

[127] Note that the bishops are not alone in mischaracterizing the DPIC list as requiring new evidence of innocence. Even articles in academic journals do so. See, for example, Charles S. Lanier and James R. Acker, "Capital Punishment, the Moratorium Movement, and Empirical Questions", *Psychology, Public Policy, and Law* 10, no. 5 (2004): 577–617, which says this about the DPIC list: "Since 1973, more than 110 individuals have been released from death rows in 25 different states after evidence surfaced that they had not committed the crimes for which they stood condemned" (p. 593).

was unlikely at a new trial.[128] Higher courts may have excluded key evidence as improperly obtained, witnesses may have died, or essential evidence may have been lost many years after the crime. Also, when new trials occurred, evidence problems may have created too great a hurdle to prove guilt "beyond a reasonable doubt"—the highest standard of proof in the American legal system. Individuals acquitted at retrial or who had their charges dismissed may be legally innocent but factually guilty. That is, they may well have committed the crime. This is a crucial distinction that many death-penalty opponents intentionally obscure. For example, the civil jury in the wrongful-death civil suit against O.J. Simpson found that he was responsible for the death of Ronald Goldman, yet a criminal jury had earlier acquitted him of the murder of Goldman and Simpson's former wife, Nicole Brown Simpson. In the eyes of the criminal law, Simpson was legally innocent of murder; nonetheless, the civil jury found that he was the actual killer. Would it make any sense to include Simpson on an "Innocence List" of those accused of murder? Would it make any sense to label a list of all those acquitted of felonies in criminal courts throughout the United States or who had charges dropped by prosecutors an "Innocence List"? How many of those on the DPIC "Innocence List" are like Simpson, *legally* innocent but very likely *factually* guilty of murder? To estimate this number, we can examine three independent evaluations of some or all of the entries on the DPIC list.

First, in July 2002 federal judge Jed Rakoff of the Southern District of New York ruled the federal death penalty unconstitutional because of the purported prevalence of erroneous convictions throughout the United States (all by state courts). In his decision Judge Rakoff maintained that at least 32 of the 51 individuals on the DPIC list who were removed from death row between 1991 and April 2002 were likely "factually innocent" (12 based on DNA evidence and another 20 on other grounds).[129] Thus, in the judge's

---

[128] According to the DPIC, 20 of the 155 cases (as of June 8, 2015) involved DNA evidence. Some of these are unambiguous examples of a "wrong person" conviction, but others, where two or more were involved in the crime (often a rape murder), are not so clear.

[129] Judge Rakoff issued two related opinions in the case. The first (preliminary) opinion was issued on April 25, 2002 (*United States v. Quinones*, 196 F. Supp.2d 416 [S.D.N.Y 2002]). The final opinion was issued on July 1, 2002 (*United States v. Quinones*, 205 F. Supp.2d 256 [S.D.N.Y. 2002]). In the first opinion, Judge Rakoff wrote that since 1993 "DNA testing has established the factual innocence of no fewer than 12 inmates on death row" (p. 417) and that "at least 20 additional defendants [from the DPIC list of 51 for 1993 through April 2002] who

estimation at least 63% of those on the DPIC list for this eleven-year period were factually innocent.

Second, in 2003 the California District Attorneys Association (CDAA) issued a lengthy report on the death penalty that included a review of the then 102 individuals on the DPIC list. It concluded that only 34 of the 102 (or 33%) had a persuasive claim of actual innocence.[130] Of the three cases on the list from California, the prosecutors argued that "no reasonable doubt exists as to the guilt of any of them."[131] The "confusion of 'actual innocence' and 'legal innocence'", they held, is a "major flaw in the DPIC List".[132] They emphasized that "legally insufficient evidence to convict a defendant or an acquittal does not mean the defendant did not commit the crime. It means the prosecutor could not convince the jury beyond a reasonable doubt that the defendant did commit the crime. Defendants are acquitted for many reasons, the least likely being innocence."[133] By collapsing the distinction between legal innocence and actual innocence, the DPIC had produced "a padded list of allegedly innocent Death Row defendants that overstates the frequency of wrongful convictions in capital cases".[134] In the opinion of the California prosecutors, the DPIC list was intentionally designed to undermine

---

had been duly convicted of capital crimes and were facing execution have been exonerated and released" (p. 418). Although the judge did not formally define the word "exonerated", he made clear in a footnote that he meant factual innocence, not just legal innocence: "At least 20 of the 51 death-sentenced defendants who have been released from prison since 1991 were released on grounds indicating factual innocence derived from evidence other than DNA testing" (n. 5). This opinion did not name the 32 inmates (12 DNA cases plus 20 others). In his final opinion, the judge again referred to the 12 DNA-related exonerations and "at least 20 ... defendants released from death row over the past decade for reasons unrelated to DNA testing [who] were factually innocent" (p. 265). Then in a footnote he listed the 32, at the end of which he added this: "Moreover, even under the Court's cautious approach, substantial arguments could be made for adding at least 8 other names to the list, namely ..." (n. 11). Because the judge uses the number 32 in the text of both opinions and because in the footnote he seems to be saying only that another 8 might possibly have been innocent, we use the 32 figure.

[130] California District Attorneys Association, *Prosecutors' Perspective on California's Death Penalty*, March 2003, pp. vi–x and appendix B, http://www.cjlf.org/deathpenalty/DPPaper.pdf. See also the similar critique of the DPIC list by Ward Campbell, "Exoneration Inflation: Justice Scalia's Concurrence in *Kansas v. Marsh*", *IACJ Journal* (Summer 2008): 49–63, available at http://www.cjlf.org/files/CampbellExonerationInflation2008.pdf.

[131] Ibid., p. vi.

[132] Ibid., p. vii.

[133] Ibid.

[134] Ibid., p. 30.

public support for the death penalty: "The DPIC's gimmicky and superficial List falsely inflates the problem of wrongful convictions in order to skew the public's opinion about capital punishment."[135]

Third, in 2011 the Commission on Capital Cases of the Florida Legislature, which included four legislators and two former judges, issued an even more detailed examination of the 23 Florida inmates on the DPIC list. At the time, no state had more removals from death row. In its 144-page report, the commission concluded that "the guilt of only four defendants [17% of the 23] was subsequently doubted by the prosecuting office or the Governor and Cabinet members."[136] Thus, in 19 of the 23 cases (83%), authorities remained convinced that the defendant had committed the crime even though prosecutors eventually dropped the charges or courts acquitted the defendant at retrial. If the Florida study is accurate and if cases from Florida are similar to those from other death-penalty states (which, of course, we cannot know from the Florida study itself), then only 17% of those on the DPIC "Innocence List" were likely factually innocent of the capital crime.

Thus, for these three evaluations we get proportions of 17% (Florida Commission), 33% (California district attorneys), and 63% (Judge Rakoff). (Note that these figures are not in themselves inconsistent with the DPIC data; for the DPIC *does not claim*—despite its misleading title "Innocence List"—that all of those on its list were *factually innocent* of the crime, only that after their original conviction was thrown out they either were not reconvicted of the crime or, in a few cases, they received a pardon). In Table 1 we apply these

---

[135] Ibid., p. 38. Note that the CDAA report specifically addressed Judge Rakoff's count of erroneous convictions from *U.S. v. Quinones*. It looked at all 40 listed by the judge in footnote 11 of the second opinion and concluded that only 17 belonged on the list as likely cases of factual innocence (p. 37). For another lengthy critique of the "Innocence List" that is very much consistent with the CDAA report, see Ward A. Campbell, "Exoneration Inflation". Campbell discusses many of the same cases addressed in the CDAA report but does not estimate what percentage of the entries on the DPIC list should be stricken. Campbell was supervising deputy attorney general in the California Department of Justice and had served on the committee of the California District Attorneys Association that produced the 2003 report.

[136] Commission on Capital Cases, Florida Legislature, *Truly Innocent? A Review of 23 Case Histories of Inmates Released from Florida's Death Row Since 1973*, May 13, 2011, p. 7, http://www.floridacapitalcases.state.fl.us/Documents/Publications/casehistory05-13-11%20Report.pdf.

Table 1. Error rates for death sentences based on factual innocence

| Period | Death sentences | DPIC list | Estimated number factually innocent* | | | Estimated error rate | | | |
			Florida Comm. (17%)	California DAs (33%)	Judge Rakoff (63%)	Florida Comm.	California DAs	Judge Rakoff
1980–2005	6,424	117	20	39	74	0.3%	0.6%	1.2%
1990–2005	3,837	43	7	14	27	0.2%	0.4%	0.7%

* The percentages are the proportion of those listed by DPIC that are judged by each source to have been factually innocent of the capital crime, assuming, as noted in the text, that cases from Florida are comparable to those from other death-penalty states.

proportions to the number reported on the DPIC list for two over-lapping periods:

- 1980 (after the states had brought their capital punishment stat-utes into line with the new Supreme Court standards set forth in the 1970s) through 2005 (allowing for at least a decade of appeals to demonstrate a wrongful conviction)
- 1990 (after DNA evidence came into regular use) through 2005

Thus, for 1980 through 2005, estimated error rates range from 0.3% to 1.2% (or an accuracy rate of 98.8% to 99.7%) and for 1990 through 2005 from 0.2% to 0.7% (or an accuracy rate of 99.3% to 99.8%). Here it is useful to ask what an ideal error rate would be, as disclosed through criminal appeals. Although we might first think it would be zero, that would mean that our state and federal appeals courts never discovered a single mistaken conviction. Would we be comfortable with this result? Would we be confident that the appellate courts were responsibly doing their job? As the bishops rightly note, "The criminal justice system is run by human beings—and we make mistakes." The purpose of the appellate court system is to catch mistakes in the legal process. Every individual sentenced to death for murder in the American states is afforded three rounds of appeals to challenge his conviction and sentence:

1. A *direct appeal* to the state courts (usually to the state supreme court) that focuses on issues that arose during the trial (such as the admissibility of evidence or the judge's instructions to the jury)
2. A *post-conviction appeal* to the state courts (also called *state habeas*) that can raise issues outside of the trial record itself (such as the competence of defense counsel, newly discovered evidence, or the failure of the prosecutor to disclose exculpatory evidence)
3. A *federal habeas corpus suit*, starting with a federal district court that charges a violation of federal constitutional rights as estab-lished, in particular, by the extensive Supreme Court jurispru-dence on the death penalty

A defendant who loses in stage 1 or 2 can request a hearing by the U.S. Supreme Court. A defendant who loses in stage 3 in the federal district court can request a hearing by a federal appellate court and, if he loses there, by the U.S. Supreme Court. Beyond the courts themselves, the governors in most states (and independent bodies in others) retain the authority to pardon a death row inmate or to commute his sentence to a lesser punishment.[137]

Anyone who has read the (often quite voluminous) record in death penalty appeals can testify to how scrupulous and meticulous higher courts are in reviewing capital convictions and sentences. Appellate courts are far from deferential to the decisions of the trial courts. From 1980 to 2005, trials courts throughout the United States issued 6,424 death sentences. Ultimately, in a third of these cases the inmate was permanently removed from death row through the appellate process: 11% because the capital conviction was overturned and the defendant was not both reconvicted of a capital crime and resentenced to death; and 22% because the capital sentence was overturned (but not the underlying conviction) and the offender was not resentenced to death.[138] Most of these defendants ended up with a prison sentence after a new trial, sentencing hearing, or guilty plea. A small fraction left prison as legally innocent because they were acquitted through a new trial or the charges were dropped. (Some fraction of this fraction were "wrong person" convictions.) Moreover, it is not unusual for governors (or other bodies) to exercise their own independent judgment after appeals have been exhausted. This has resulted in the commutation of 392 death sentences between 1973 and 2013 (nearly 5% of all death sentences).[139]

We know, then, that at the trial stage the American capital punishment system is not perfect, and that of the 8,500 convicted murderers sentenced to death since the *Furman* decision of 1972, at least several dozen were actually innocent of the capital crime.[140] What we do *not*

---

[137] For a useful summary of this process, see "Death Penalty Appeals Process", Capital Punishment in Context, http://www.capitalpunishmentincontext.org/resources/dpappeals process.

[138] Snell, *Capital Punishment, 2013—Statistical Tables*, calculations based on data in table 16, p. 19.

[139] Ibid.

[140] It is possible, of course, that some of those currently on death row may be exonerated in the future. Yet we would not expect the number of actually innocent cases to increase much for three reasons: (1) courts in the United States in recent years have sentenced many fewer individuals to death than a decade or two ago (an average of 87 per year from 2010 to 2014,

know is whether any innocent person was in fact *executed* during this period. From 1977 through 2014, thirty-four American states executed 1,386 convicted murderers and the federal government another 3. Were any of these 1,389 actually innocent of the crimes for which they were sentenced to death? Although there is no way to know this with certainty, it seems likely that *at most 1 or 2 innocent persons—and very possibly none at all*—have been executed since the *Furman* decision of 1972 required every capital punishment jurisdiction to revise their death-penalty statutes.

In 1987, a decade after executions had resumed in the United States, Hugo Bedau and Michael Radelet reported the results of a twenty-five-year study that argued that 350 individuals who have been convicted of "capital or potentially capital crimes in this century, and in many cases sentenced to death, have later been found to be innocent".[141] Of these, 139 were sentenced to death and 23 were executed.[142] By "innocent" Bedau and Radelet meant either that no crime had actually occurred (in a few cases the presumed victim later turned up alive) or that "the defendant was legally and physically uninvolved in the crime."[143] In the judgment of the authors, the 23 who were wrongly executed represent "wrong-person mistakes—the conviction and execution of the factually 'innocent'".[144] Someone else had committed the crime for which they were executed.

Yet critics of Bedau and Radelet's compilation insist that they have not demonstrated that *any* of the 23 persons executed in the twentieth century—a list that included such controversial cases as Nicola Sacco and Bartolomeo Vanzetti (executed in Massachusetts in 1927

---

compared with 166 per year from 2000 to 2004 and 280 per year from 1990 to 1994); (2) because convictions of the innocent have received such wide publicity, there is reason to believe that prosecutors and juries are now more likely to reserve the death penalty for cases in which guilt is quite certain; and (3) routine use of DNA in capital cases now eliminates many potential "wrong person" convictions, especially in rape-homicide cases (which constitute 20% to 30% of death sentences). Note, for example, that even under the DPIC count (which is not limited to those actually innocent), only 5 of the 1,572 individuals sentenced to death between 2000 and 2010 (0.3%) have been "exonerated", even though more three-fifths of these have had at least a decade to appeal their convictions.

[141] Hugo Adam Bedau and Michael L. Radelet, "Miscarriages of Justice in Potentially Capital Cases", *Stanford Law Review* 40, no. 1 (November 1987): 23–24.

[142] Ibid., table 2, p. 36.

[143] Ibid., p. 45.

[144] Ibid.

for an armed-robbery murder) and Bruno Hauptmann (executed in New Jersey in 1936 for kidnapping and murdering the twenty-month-old son of Charles Lindbergh)—were factually innocent of the crimes for which they were convicted. They also emphasize that only one of the 23 executions occurred after the reform of death-penalty laws in the 1970s: James Adams, executed by the state of Florida in 1984. (Between 1977, when executions resumed in the United States, through 1986, the year before Bedau and Radelet published their results, the states had executed 68 convicted murderers.) Because only Adams' execution occurred in the post-*Furman* era, critics have focused on the evidence in that case. Here is the entire entry on Adams from Bedau and Radelet's 1987 article:

ADAMS, JAMES (black). 1974 [the year of conviction]. Florida. Adams was convicted of first-degree murder, sentenced to death, and executed in 1984. Witnesses located Adams' car at the time of the crime at the home of the victim, a white rancher. Some of the victim's jewelry was found in the car trunk. Adams maintained his innocence, claiming that he had loaned the car to his girlfriend. A witness identified Adams as driving the car away from the victim's home shortly after the crime. This witness, however, was driving a large truck in the direction opposite to that of Adams' car, and probably could not have had a good look at the driver. It was later discovered that this witness was angry with Adams for allegedly dating his wife. A second witness heard a voice inside the victim's home at the time of the crime and saw someone fleeing. He stated this voice was a woman's; the day after the crime he stated that the fleeing person was positively not Adams. More importantly, a hair sample found clutched in the victim's hand, which in all likelihood had come from the assailant, did not match Adams' hair. Much of this exculpatory information was not discovered until the case was examined by a skilled investigator a month before Adams' execution. Governor Graham, however, refused to grant even a short stay so that these questions could be resolved.[145]

Bedau and Radelet cited one source for this information: "Application for Executive Clemency *in re* James Adams (May 1, 1984)".[146]

According to Stephen Markman, a former assistant attorney general for legal policy in the U.S. Department of Justice and currently a

[145] Ibid., p. 91.
[146] Ibid., p. 91n350.

justice on the Michigan Supreme Court, "this analysis of the Adams trial record ... seriously distorts and misrepresents the evidence. A more thorough analysis of the testimony reveals the following:

1. The witness driving the truck was able to identify Adams as the driver of the car because the car was weaving so badly that the witness had to pull over to the far side of the road and stop. Indeed, the car came very close to hitting him. The witness identified Adams from the line-up the day after the incident.

2. With respect to Adams's dating the witness's wife, such a theory was raised by the defense counsel in his opening argument. However, no evidence to that effect was ever presented at trial. Indeed, Adams never even raised the issue in his post-trial motions, although it would have been relevant to the witness's credibility.

3. In recalling having heard a "woman's" voice in the house, the second witness was referring to the voice not of the killer but of the person being killed. Furthermore, his general description of the person fleeing the house matched Adams. This witness said only that he could not identify Adams with certainty as the fleeing person, not that it was "positively not Adams."

4. The allegedly exculpatory hair sample was made known to Adams's counsel well before trial. He chose not even to offer it either at trial or on appeal. Most likely, the hair had come from sweepings of the floor of the ambulance carrying the victim to the hospital or from one of several people who attempted to treat the victim's wounds at the death scene, not from the killer's head.

5. Adams's alibi defense was that he was not in the area of the crime on the day of the crime. He was contradicted on this by three other witnesses who placed him or his car at the scene shortly before the crime. In addition, Adams's own alibi witness contradicted him on his whereabouts at the time of the crime.

6. Several hours after the murder, Adams took his car to a body shop and asked to have it painted a different color.

7. When arrested by police later that day driving a friend's car, Adams had in his possession a twenty-dollar bill stained with blood of the victim's type. When asked about the blood, Adams said that it had come from a cut on his finger. Adams's blood type did not match that on the bill.

8. When arrested, Adams had in his possession his own bloodied clothing: the blood matched the victim's. He was also found in the possession of jewelry and eyeglasses from the victim's house.

9. In addition, evidence was presented concerning Adams's demeanor following the murder, the circumstance of his having $200 in his possession shortly after having borrowed $35 from two friends, the likelihood that this amount of money in the particular denominations had been in the victim's possession that day, and a series of conflicting statements made by Adams to the police.[147]

In an earlier and even more extensive discussion, Markman and Paul Cassell, a former associate deputy attorney general in the U.S. Department of Justice and later a federal district judge and law professor, provided greater detail from the trial record. Where, for example, Bedau and Radelet had strongly implied that a woman had committed the murder, the witness at trial testified that he heard the voice say, "In the name of God, don't do it" and that the voice sounded "kind of like a woman's voice, kind of like strangling or something" and that, referring to himself, "if he couldn't hardly talk it would sound that way, if he had been beat up like he was". Markman and Cassell added, "It was not seriously disputed at trial that this must have been Mr. Brown's last plea for life, and therefore it is without consequence that the voice sounded in certain respects like a woman's. Moreover, contrary to the authors' implication that the real killer was a woman, the witness made it clear that the person he saw leaving the scene of the crime was a man, even though he was unable to identify the man positively as Adams."[148] They concluded that the description of the Adams case presented by Bedau and Radelet was "seriously misleading. The authors have misrepresented or excluded critical evidence of the defendant's guilt and have exaggerated the significance of supposedly exculpatory evidence."[149] Defending the death penalty in 2008, Cassell wrote that "a dispassionate review of the facts of [the Adams] case demonstrates ... that Adams was unquestionably guilty."[150]

---

[147] Stephen Markman, "Innocents on Death Row?" *National Review*, September 12, 1994, pp. 74–77.

[148] Stephen J. Markman and Paul G. Cassell, "Protecting the Innocent: A Response to the Bedau-Radelet Study", *Stanford Law Review* 41 (1988): 130.

[149] Ibid., p. 129.

[150] Paul Cassell, "In Defense of the Death Penalty," *IACJ Journal* (Summer 2008): 14–18, 25.

The Adams case is a cautionary tale. It shows that even cases where the evidence of guilt presented at trial was quite strong can be made to look weak through a selective presentation of the evidence and a retelling of defense theories designed to sow doubt on the defendant's guilt. Yet, as strong as the evidence appears for Adams' guilt, opponents pointed to this as one case of an innocent man executed during the first two decades or so after executions resumed.

By the 1990s, the national media were focusing on several cases of putatively innocent men about to be executed. None of these garnered more attention than that of Roger Coleman, scheduled to die in Virginia in 1992 for a 1981 rape and murder. In a Supreme Court case from 2006, Justice Antonin Scalia recounted the media fascination with Coleman:

> Coleman was convicted of the gruesome rape and murder of his sister-in-law, but he persuaded many that he was actually innocent and became the poster child for the abolitionist lobby. Around the time of his eventual execution, "his picture was on the cover of *Time* magazine ('This Man Might Be Innocent. This Man Is Due to Die'). He was interviewed from death row on 'Larry King Live,' the 'Today' show, 'Primetime Live,' 'Good Morning America' and 'The Phil Donahue Show.'" ... Even one Justice of this Court, in an opinion filed shortly before the execution, cautioned that "Coleman has now produced substantial evidence that he may be innocent of the crime for which he was sentenced to die." ... Coleman ultimately failed a lie-detector test offered by the Governor of Virginia as a condition of a possible stay; he was executed on May 20, 1992.
>
> In the years since then, Coleman's case became a rallying point for abolitionists, who hoped it would offer what they consider the "Holy Grail: proof from a test tube that an innocent person had been executed." But earlier this year [2006], a DNA test ordered by a later Governor of Virginia proved that Coleman was guilty, even though his defense team had "proved" his innocence and had even identified "the real killer" (with whom they eventually settled a defamation suit).[151]

In an essay from 2012, Oregon prosecutor Joshua Marquis added that "Coleman was represented, like many death row inmates, by a top-flight law firm—Washington, D.C.'s Arnold & Porter" and that his last words were: "An innocent man is going to

---

[151] Justice Antonin Scalia, concurring opinion in *Kansas v. Marsh*, 548 U.S. 163 (2006), 188–89, citations omitted.

be murdered tonight. When my innocence is proven, I hope America will realize the injustice of the death penalty as all other civilized countries have."[152]

Because of the discrediting of cases like those of Adams and Coleman, by the first decade of the twentieth century, defenders of the death penalty were confidently asserting that opponents had not demonstrated a single case of an innocent person executed in the post-*Furman* era, despite a total of 683 executions between 1977 and 2000 and another 321 between 2001 and 2005.

- Paul Cassell in 2000: "[The authors of a critical study of the death penalty] were unable to find a single case in which an innocent person was executed. Thus, the most important error rate—the rate of mistaken executions—is zero."[153] And in 2008: "Abolitionists have been unable to demonstrate that even a single innocent person has been executed in error."[154]
- Joshua Marquis in 2005: "The well-organized and even better-funded abolitionists cannot point to a single case of a demonstrably innocent person executed in the modern era of American capital punishment."[155]
- Justice Antonin Scalia in 2006: "The dissent does not discuss a single case—not one—in which it is clear that a person was executed for a crime he did not commit."[156]

In more recent years, opponents have pointed to two other executed defendants, both from Texas, who, they claim, were innocent of the murders for which they were convicted: Carlos DeLuna, who was executed in 1989 for murdering a gas station attendant, and Cameron Todd Willingham, who was executed in 2004 for murdering his three young children by arson.[157] Post-execution, the *Chicago*

---

[152] Joshua Marquis, "Rightful Convictions", *Cato Unbound*, March 7, 2012, http://www.cato-unbound.org/2012/03/07/joshua-marquis/rightful-convictions.

[153] Paul G. Cassell, "We're Not Executing the Innocent", *Wall Street Journal*, June 16, 2000, http://www.wsj.com/articles/SB961116188606389139.

[154] Cassell, "In Defense of the Death Penalty", p. 26.

[155] Marquis, "Myth of Innocence", p. 518.

[156] Scalia, concurring opinion in *Kansas v. Marsh*, p. 188.

[157] In 2015, Supreme Court justice Stephen Breyer, dissenting from the Court's opinion upholding Oklahoma's three-drug execution protocol in *Glossip v. Gross* (576 U.S. ____), specifically cited these cases as evidence for the unreliability of the death penalty.

Tribune ran investigative articles raising questions about DeLuna's and Willingham's guilt. The DeLuna case also attracted the attention of a team of researchers from Columbia University, who produced a more than 400-page report of the case that argued that "another Carlos"—namely, Carlos Hernandez—had committed the murder.[158] The Willingham case was also investigated by the *New Yorker*. Numerous other media outlets ran stories on the two cases.

Unlike the cases of Adams and Coleman, it is not so obvious where the truth lies regarding DeLuna and Willingham. Critics have raised serious questions, while law-enforcement officials in both cases remain convinced of the guilt of the two individuals. (And one of Willingham's trial attorneys has publicly stated his belief that Willingham was guilty.)[159] We venture no opinion as to whether DeLuna or Willingham were innocent but reaffirm our judgment of what the evidence to date shows: it seems likely that of the more than 1,400 persons who have been executed in the United States since the 1972 *Furman* decision, at most one or two—and very possibly none at all— were innocent of the crimes for which they were put to death.

All human institutions are imperfect, including those that protect us from the violent and the vicious. We give guns to more than half a million police officers knowing that occasionally an officer may misuse his weapon or a criminal may wrest it away and use it to harm the officer or others. We do not, however, allow the almost certain knowledge that occasionally an innocent person will be harmed by a police firearm to paralyze us in the face of the threat that violent offenders pose. Arming police serves a larger social good, and that

---

[158] The report was originally published in the *Columbia Human Rights Law Review* in the summer of 2012 and later as the book *The Wrong Carlos: Anatomy of a Wrongful Execution* (New York: Columbia University Press, 2014).

[159] See the CNN interview of trial attorney David Martin by Anderson Cooper on October 15, 2009, available at https://youtu.be/L5cFKpjRnXE. Willingham's wife, the mother of the three child victims, was also convinced that Willingham was guilty. After his execution, she made the following statement: "I did witness Cameron Todd Willingham's execution. Todd set our house on fire then stood outside and watched it burn. He knew our three daughters were inside this home taking [their] last breath. He watched them die. I felt like the only thing that I could do is watch their murderer die. I wasn't there for closure. My closure was when he told me what he had done. I stood on the behalf of my three daughters." The statement was printed in the Fort Worth *Star-Telegram* and is available at http://www .crimeandconsequences.com/crimblog/2009/10/statement-on-willingham.html.

good cannot be achieved without the risk of an innocent person being harmed or killed. Similarly, the death penalty serves a larger social good that cannot be achieved without the risk of an innocent person being executed. As Paul Cassell and Stephen Markman affirm, "Through a combination of deterrence, incapacitation, and the imposition of just punishment, the death penalty serves to protect a vastly greater number of innocent lives than may be lost through its erroneous application."[160] Fortunately, the risk that a truly innocent person will be executed in the United States is, as we have shown, extremely low. In the words of Justice Scalia, "The American people have determined that the good to be derived from capital punishment— in deterrence, and perhaps most of all in the meting out of condign justice for horrible crimes—outweighs the risk of error."[161]

Racial discrimination

Although the question of whether racial discrimination affects the application of the death penalty in the United States is highly controversial and hotly debated among practitioners and social scientists, the American bishops not only agree with the charge of racism but, as we noted above, seek to persuade others that it is true: "We seek to educate and persuade our fellow citizens that this penalty is often applied unfairly and in racially biased ways."[162] Once again, the bishops have taken sides on a much disputed empirical matter far removed from their own training and expertise and have sought to tip the scales in the public debate. For reasons we will detail, we believe that the charge of racism in the application of the death penalty is not supported by the empirical data.

Here is the lengthiest statement by the bishops on the allegedly racist application of the death penalty (from their seminal 1980 document on capital punishment):

There is a widespread belief that many convicted criminals are sentenced to death in an unfair and discriminatory manner. This belief can be affirmed with certain justifications. There is a certain presumption

---

[160] Markman and Cassell, "Protecting the Innocent", p. 123.
[161] Concurring opinion in *Kansas v. Marsh*, p. 199.
[162] Administrative Board of the USCCB, "A Good Friday Appeal".

that if specific evidence of bias or discrimination in sentencing can be provided for particular cases, then higher courts will not uphold sentences of death in these cases. But we must also reckon with a legal system which, while it does provide counsel for indigent defendants, permits those who are well off to obtain the resources and the talent to present their case in as convincing a light as possible. The legal system and the criminal justice system both work in a society which bears in its psychological, social, and economic patterns the marks of racism. These marks remain long after the demolition of segregation as a legal institution. The end result of all this is a situation in which those condemned to die are nearly always poor and are disproportionately black. Thus 47% of the inmates on Death Row are black, whereas only 11% of the American population is black. Abolition of the death penalty will not eliminate racism and its effects, an evil which we are called on to combat in many different ways. But it is a reasonable judgment that racist attitudes and the social consequences of racism have some influence in determining who is sentenced to die in our society. This we do not regard as acceptable.

Despite the somewhat hedging and tentative language of the first few sentences, the bishops' position seems to be the following:

1 The legal system harms the poor and minorities (overlapping categories) because well-off defendants can hire better attorneys (more on this below).

2. The broader society remains racist in its psychological, social, and economic patterns, and this societal racism necessarily affects the criminal-justice system in general and capital punishment in particular.

3. As a result, nearly all those condemned to death are poor or disproportionately black.

4. Evidence of the latter is that the proportion of death row inmates who are black is more than four times higher than the black proportion of the U.S. population.

5. Thus, it is reasonable to conclude that racist attitudes influence who is sentenced to death.

Later documents reiterate this critique. A 1999 statement coauthored with the National Council of Synagogues referred to "suspiciously high percentages of those on death row [who] are poor or people of color".[163] The bishops' lengthy statement on criminal justice in 2000 concluded that "the racism and discrimination that continue to haunt our nation are reflected in similar ways in the criminal justice system" and that "racism often shapes American attitudes and policies toward crime and criminal justice [and] we see it in ... who is on death row."[164] Finally, in a list of "Facts about the Death Penalty" in a 2011 document, the USCCB reported that "over 80 percent of those executed in the United States were convicted of killing a white person, even though African Americans are the victims in at least half of all homicides.... Blacks constitute 12.9% of the U.S. population, but 42% of death row inmates."[165]

As best we can tell, the only evidence that the bishops present to support the charge of racism is (1) the disproportion between the percentage of blacks in the population and their percentage on death row and (2) the overrepresentation of white victims among the murderers on death row. The bishops' statements and reports do not evaluate the many studies on race and the death penalty that have appeared since the *Furman* decision, and, as we will see, the little evidence they cite does not demonstrate the influence of racism in the capital punishment system.

The first point to understand is that the disproportion between blacks on death row and blacks in the U.S. population no more proves discrimination against blacks than the disproportion between males on death row (98%) and males in the U.S. population (49%) proves discrimination against males. Only those arrested for murder can end up sentenced to death, and we know that males and blacks are much more likely to be arrested for murder than are females and whites. So, simply comparing the percentages of groups on death row with their percentage in the population in no way demonstrates bias in the capital punishment system. The key starting point is to compare death row populations to those arrested for murder. (Note that, in the following discussion, arrests and convictions for murder include nonnegligent manslaughter because this is how the FBI and

---

[163] National Jewish/Catholic Consultation, "To End the Death Penalty".
[164] USCCB, *Responsibility, Rehabilitation, and Restoration*.
[165] Office of Domestic Social Development, USCCB, *Death Penalty*.

Table 2. Murder arrests, death sentences, and
executions, 1990–2013[166]

	Whites	Blacks
Arrests for murder*	45.9%	52.1%
Death sentences	56.0%	41.4%
Executions	64.3%	34.4%
Death sentences per 1,000 arrests	21.1	13.7

*Those 18 and over.

the Bureau of Justice Statistics report the data.) Table 2 summarizes twenty-four years of death-penalty sentencing in the United
States. If, as the bishops (and many other critics of capital punishment) claim, racism influences "who is on death row" in the United
States, we would expect that, once arrested for murder, blacks would
be *more likely* than whites to be sentenced to death. But, as the table
shows, blacks arrested for murder are considerably *less likely* to be
sentenced to death (13.7 per 1,000 arrests) than are whites (21.1 per
1,000 arrests). Put another way, whites arrested for murders in the
United States are 54% more likely to be sentenced to death than are
blacks arrested for murders.

We can also compare death sentences with convictions for murder in state courts between 1990 and 2006 (when the Bureau of
Justice Statistics discontinued this biannual series). Table 3 shows
that what is true of whites *arrested* for murder is also true of whites
convicted of murder: they are more likely than blacks to be sentenced

[166] All data are derived from calculations based on annual figures from the following
sources: arrest data for 1991–2013 are from FBI, *Crime in the United States*, table 43, available
online for 1995–2013 at https://www.fbi.gov/about-us/cjis/ucr/crime-in-the-u.s; arrest data
for 1990 are from BJS, Arrest Data Analysis Tool, available at http://www.bjs.gov/index
.cfm?ty=datool&surl=/arrests/index.cfm#; data on death sentences and executions are from
BJS, annual series, *Capital Punishment*, available at http://www.bjs.gov/index.cfm?ty=pbtp
&tid=18&iid=1. All data accessed August 19, 2015. Note that the categories "Whites" and
"Blacks" include Hispanics of both races. The U.S. Census Bureau, which sets the data-
collection standards for the federal government, defines "Hispanic" or "Latino" as an eth-
nic designation, not a racial one. Nonetheless, some federal data does distinguish Hispanics
from whites and blacks by using the designations "white, non-Hispanic" and "black, non-
Hispanic". Note that arrests include data for non–capital punishment states.

Table 3. Murder convictions and death sentences, 1990–2006

	Whites		Blacks	
	Murder convictions	Death sentences	Murder convictions	Death sentences
1990	42%	60%	56%	39%
1992	41%	56%	58%	43%
1994	37%	53%	62%	45%
1996	44%	58%	54%	40%
1998	42%	51%	57%	46%
2000	43%	57%	54%	40%
2002	45%	52%	51%	46%
2004	44%	60%	53%	40%
2006	46%	63%	51%	37%

Source: see the footnote.[167]

to death. For every year since 1990 with the available data, whites constituted a considerably higher percentage of death sentences than of murder convictions. Conversely, for every year, blacks constituted a considerably lower proportion of death sentences than of murder convictions.

If the races were reversed in these two tables, critics of the death penalty would insist that the numbers prove racism. Yet no one maintains that the disproportions reported here prove that the death penalty in the United States is biased against whites. Why not? Because practitioners and researchers are well aware that there are legitimate criminal justice reasons why whites arrested for murder and convicted of murder seem to be treated more harshly than blacks: in general, white killers are more likely than black killers to commit the kinds of aggravated murders that qualify for a death sentence.

[167]Data on death sentences are from the same sources as in the previous table. Data on convictions for murder (which includes nonnegligent manslaughter) are from the BJS publication *Felony Sentences in State Courts* for each year, available at http://www.bjs.gov/index .cfm?ty=pbaz.

For example, between 1976 and 2002, white offenders were responsible for 47% of all murders but 57% of rape murders and 58% of murders that resulted in the death of two or more persons.[168] As we saw in chapter 3, these two factors—rape murders and multiple murders—correlate very highly with whether a convicted murderer is sentenced to death: 28% of the forty-three murderers executed in 2012 had committed a multiple murder (which are only 5% of all murders), and over a third had participated in a rape murder (which are only 1% or less of all murders). So it is no surprise that between 1990 and 2013, whites constituted 46% of all murder arrests but 56% of death sentences.

Because the data show unmistakably that white murderers are more likely to be sentenced to death than black murderers, critics today rarely charge that there is *race-of-offender* discrimination in the capital punishment system. Instead, the argument has shifted to purported *race-of-victim* discrimination, as reflected in the bishops' 2011 statement that "over 80% of those executed in the United States were convicted of killing a white person, even though African Americans are the victims in at least half of all homicides." The claim is that mostly white prosecutors and juries tend to undervalue the lives of black murder victims and thus punish those who murder blacks less severely than those who murder whites.

Just how large is the disparity between the race of the victims of those executed and the race of all murder victims? Although the bishops claim that "over 80%" of the victims of those executed were white, the Death Penalty Information Center (a harsh critic of capital punishment) reports that 76% of the victims of all those executed since 1976 were white. Our own analysis of the 794 executions between 2000 and 2014 yields a slightly lower figure: 72%. These figures compare to 51% for all murders reported to the FBI between 1976 and 2002.[169] So we are talking about the difference between roughly 51% (white victims in all homicides) and 72% to 76% (white victims in cases resulting in executions). As we saw

---

[168] Online analysis of "Uniform Crime Reports [United States]: Supplementary Homicide Reports, 1976–2002—Part 1: Offender Data", through the National Archive of Criminal Justice Data (NACJD) of the Inter-University Consortium for Political and Social Research (ICPSR) of the University of Michigan, http://www.icpsr.umich.edu/icpsrweb/NACJD/.

[169] Ibid.

with the data on race of offenders, there may be perfectly legitimate criminal-justice reasons why death row inmates do not mirror all murderers. Indeed, just as the most aggravated murders tend to involve white offenders disproportionately, they also involve white victims disproportionately. Between 1976 and 2002, whites were 70% of the victims of rape murders and 62% of the victims of multiple murders (which rises to 65% in homicides in which three or more were killed).[170] These numbers alone suggest that much of the reason why white victims are "overrepresented" among those executed for murder is because they are overrepresented among the kinds of murders marked out by state law as death eligible and for which juries impose the death sentence.

Another likely contributing factor is that, in many states, rural counties (with lower minority populations) are more likely to sentence a murderer to death than are urban counties (with larger minority populations). Researchers note, for example, that "while Maryland retained the death penalty, 'a death-eligible case in Baltimore County [which is almost two-thirds white] [was] twenty-three times more likely ultimately to result in a death sentence than a death-eligible case in Baltimore City [which is less than a third white].'"[171] Similarly, a detailed study of death sentencing in Illinois (prior to its abolition of capital punishment in 2011) found that "the odds of receiving a death sentence for killing a victim(s) in Cook County [which includes Chicago] are on average 83.6% lower than for killing a victim(s) in the rural county region of Illinois controlling for the other twenty-six variables in the analysis."[172] Other studies found the same urban-rural differences in New York and Virginia.[173] If mostly-white counties in capital punishment states are more likely to use the death penalty than are counties with large minority populations, then we would expect more white murderers to enter death row than would be the case if counties behaved identically. Moreover, since white murderers choose white victims

---

[170] Ibid.

[171] James R. Acker, *Questioning Capital Punishment: Law, Policy, and Practice* (New York: Routledge, 2014), p. 217.

[172] Glenn L. Pierce and Michael L. Radelet, "Race, Region, and Death Sentencing in Illinois, 1988–1997", *Oregon Law Review* 81 (2002): 65.

[173] See the discussion in Lanier and Acker, "Capital Punishment", p. 599.

over 90% of the time, any sentencing patterns that result in more white murderers entering death row will increase the percentage of white victims accounted for by death row inmates.[174]

The best-known statistical study that purported to find a race-of-victim effect in capital sentencing was the one directed by University of Iowa College of Law professor David Baldus. Baldus and his colleagues studied capital sentencing in Georgia from 1973 to 1979—that is, the first years after Georgia adopted a new capital punishment statute in the wake of the *Furman* decision (1972). The results of the study were then used by Warren McCleskey, a black man with three prior armed-robbery convictions who murdered a white police officer during an armed robbery at an Atlanta furniture store, to challenge the Georgia capital punishment system as racially biased. McCleskey argued in the federal courts that the Baldus study had demonstrated that murder cases involving black offenders and white victims were more likely to result in a death sentence than other combinations of the race of offender and victim. Even after controlling statistically for hundreds of other factors about the crime, if the victim was white, the risk of a death sentence increased measurably. McCleskey's lawyers maintained that this race-of-victim effect rendered the Georgia capital punishment system unconstitutional.

The case went all the way to the U.S. Supreme Court, where a five-justice majority held that even if "the Baldus study is statistically valid", McCleskey had offered "no evidence specific to his own case that would support an inference that racial considerations played a part in his sentence".[175] Death-penalty opponents sometimes argue that even though McCleskey lost his case, the Supreme Court had accepted the substantive conclusions of the authors of the Baldus study. But this is incorrect, for the Court saw no need to evaluate the study itself since McCleskey had provided no evidence that his particular case was influenced by racial considerations. The legal issue turned not on the validity of the study but on the absence of evidence of racial discrimination in McCleskey's case.

---

[174] Based on online analysis of the Supplementary Homicide Reports of the Uniform Crime Reports for single offender-single victim murders for 1976–2002.

[175] *McCleskey v. Kemp*, 481 U.S. 279 (1987), pp. 291n7, 292–93 (Justice Lewis Powell for the majority).

More egregiously, opponents of the death penalty ignore the findings of the federal district court in Georgia, which held an evidentiary hearing on the Baldus study during which Baldus and two other social scientists defended the study while two experts relied on by the state critiqued it.[176] Although Judge J. Owen Forrester overturned McCleskey's murder conviction on other grounds (he was later reversed on this), he concluded after a lengthy and detailed analysis that the Baldus study had *"failed to make out a prima facie case of discrimination based either on race of the victim or race of the defendant disparity."*[177] He gave many reasons for his conclusions but emphasized three: "the data base is substantially flawed, ... even the largest models are not sufficiently predictive, and ... the analyses do not compare like cases."[178] One can read widely in the literature on race and the death penalty and never learn that a federal judge, after extensive review, had found that the most famous of the studies purporting to demonstrate racism in the post-*Furman* era had not even made a "prima facie case of discrimination".

This last reason given by Judge Forrester points to a very deep limitation of using complex statistical models involving multiple-regression analysis to assess the effects of race in the application of the death penalty. Baldus had quantified hundreds of factors about each case and then generated an index to classify the aggravation level of each murder. Thus, the model assumed that the heinousness of the murder could be reduced to a number and, consequently, that murders with the same measure on the aggravation index were equally heinous. But Judge Forrester disputed this assumption: "The major premise is that he is comparing cases with similar levels of aggravation and mitigation. He is not.... He is merely comparing cases which have similar aggravation indices based on the variables included in the model."[179] As the federal appellate court that upheld Judge Forrester's decision noted:

The Baldus approach ... would take the cases with different results on what are contended to be duplicate facts, where the differences could

[176] *McCleskey v. Zant*, 580 F. Supp. 338 (N.D. Ga. 1984).
[177] Ibid., pp. 364–65, emphasis in the original.
[178] Ibid., p. 365.
[179] Ibid., p. 364.

not be otherwise explained, and conclude that the different result was based on race alone.... This approach ignores the realities. It not only ignores quantitative differences in cases: looks, age, personality, education, profession, job, clothes, demeanor, and remorse, just to name a few, but it is incapable of measuring qualitative differences of such things as aggravating and mitigating factors. There are, in fact, no exact duplicates in capital crimes and capital defendants.[180]

In Judge Forrester's view, the reason white-victim cases were so common among those sentenced to death was because "white-victim cases tend to be more aggravated while black-victim cases tend to be more mitigated.... Each aggravating factor was present in a markedly higher percentage of white-victim cases than in black-victim cases, and conversely, the vast majority of the mitigating circumstances appeared in higher proportions in black-victim cases."[181] Thus, "to the extent that there are unaccounted-for aggravating or mitigating circumstances, white-victim cases become a proxy for aggravated cases, and black-victim cases become a proxy, or composite variable, for mitigating factors."[182] In McCleskey's case, three aggravating factors, all of which individually correlate highly with the likelihood of receiving a death sentence, were more than sufficient to explain why the prosecutor requested and the jury imposed a death sentence: murder during another felony, murder of a police officer, and murder to avoid arrest.

Both Judge Forrester and the federal appellate court emphasized that Baldus' data demonstrated the essentially rational character of the post-*Furman* Georgia sentencing system. By Baldus' account, the higher a case ranked on his aggravation index, the more likely the offender was to receive the death penalty. As Judge Forrester summarized, "When the 500 most aggravated cases in the system were divided into eight categories according to the level of the aggravation index, the death penalty rate rose dramatically from 0 in the first two categories, to about 7% in the next two, to an average of about 22% in the next two, to a 41% rate at level seven, and an 88% rate at level eight. Level eight was composed of 58 cases. The death

---

[180] *McCleskey v. Kemp*, 753 F.2d 877 (11th Cir. 1985), p. 899.
[181] *McCleskey v. Zant*, U.S. District Court, pp. 363–64.
[182] Ibid., p. 364.

sentencing rate in the 40 most aggravated cases was 100%."[183] For Forrester, these data and the testimony of "all of the experts" "*put to rest ... any notion that the imposition of the death penalty in Georgia is a random event unguided by rational thought.*"[184] The appellate court concurred: "The Baldus study revealed an essentially rational system, in which high aggravation cases were more likely to result in the death sentence than low aggravation cases."[185] "The system as a whole", concluded the appellate court, "is operating in a rational manner, and not in a manner that can fairly be labeled arbitrary or capricious."[186]

In evaluating the death worthiness of homicide cases, prosecutors and jurors do not assign points for aggravating and mitigating aspects of the event and of the offender and then tally the results. Instead, they draw on everything they have learned about the crime and the criminal to decide whether death is the appropriate punishment. Statistical studies can identify specific aggravating factors—e.g., the number killed, whether the victim was raped or tortured, or whether the offender had previously murdered someone else—but they cannot capture the complex qualitative reality of each case. Just imagine trying to quantify the heinousness of the murders described in chapter 3 and then deciding on death based on some number or set of numbers. Surely, no one would seriously propose using a statistical formula to determine death worthiness. Obviously, prosecutors and jurors in capital cases have available to them a vastly richer understanding of the heinousness of a particular crime, the character of a particular criminal, and the nature of any mitigating factors than could possibly be captured by numbers. Judge Forrester concluded that white victims were overrepresented among murderers sentenced to death in Georgia in the 1970s because they were overrepresented among the more aggravated, or heinous, homicides and that key aspects of heinousness cannot be captured statistically. No aggravation index can represent the full reality of the crime and

---

[183] Ibid., p. 374.

[184] Ibid., p. 365, emphasis in the original.

[185] *McCleskey v. Kemp*, 753 F.2d 877 (11th Cir. 1985), p. 896.

[186] Ibid., p. 898. Baldus and his coauthors defend their study and discuss the federal court cases in David C. Baldus, George Woodworth, and Charles A. Pulaski, *Equal Justice and the Death Penalty: A Legal and Empirical Analysis* (Boston: Northeastern University Press, 1990).

the offender that a judge and jury learn through weeks or months of a trial.[187]

In the end, the race-of-victim version of the charge that racism affects capital sentencing turns on some very odd logic. We are asked to believe that mostly white prosecutors and jurors, influenced (perhaps subconsciously) by racist attitudes, ignore the race of the offender and instead make their decisions based on the race of the victim. But if racial attitudes are at work, why not punish the offender more harshly if he is black? Why would racist attitudes skip over the offender's race to land on the victim's race? Indeed, in so doing the supposedly racist prosecutor or juror is actually giving a break to the black defendant because in nearly every murder case in which the victim is black the offender is also black. (According to FBI data, 94% of all murders of black victims were by black offenders between 1976 and 2002.)[188] Thus, we must believe that the prosecutors or jurors give a break to the black offender because they devalue the life of the black victim. In the twentieth-first century (through 2014) American states executed 105 offenders who each killed a single black or, in multiple murders, only blacks. Ninety-nine of these offenders were also black. If the critics are right, then, had the lives of all murder victims been equally valued during these fourteen years, the number of black offenders sent to death row would have been higher. It is a strange kind of racism, indeed, that operates to spare black offenders from death row.

---

[187] In 2015, in a concurring opinion in *Glossip v. Gross* (576 U.S. ____), Justice Clarence Thomas critiqued the whole notion of trying to quantify the egregiousness of murders: "The results of these studies are inherently unreliable because they purport to control for egregiousness by quantifying moral depravity in a process that is itself arbitrary, not to mention dehumanizing." He then described one study that assigned "depravity points" for different kinds of homicides: three points for killing a prison guard, three for killing to make a political statement, two for killing a police officer, two for killing a child under twelve, two for killing out of racial hatred, one for killing someone over seventy, and so forth. "We owe victims", Thomas insisted, "more than this sort of pseudoscientific assessment of their lives. It is bad enough to tell a mother that her child's murder is not 'worthy' of society's ultimate expression of moral condemnation. But to do so based on cardboard stereotypes or cold mathematical calculations is beyond my comprehension. In my decades on the Court, I have not seen a capital crime that could not be considered sufficiently 'blameworthy' to merit a death sentence." Slip opinion, pp. 5–6.

[188] The 94% figure is for single offender–single victim murders between 1976 and 2002, based on online analysis of "Uniform Crime Reports".

Other empirical data also strongly cuts against the racism hypothesis. First, blacks on death row are more likely than whites to have a prior felony conviction and, in particular, a prior homicide conviction—refuting the notion that the bar is lower for blacks when courts decide sentences. Second, blacks sentenced to death since 1977 have been less likely than whites to be executed, demonstrating that the appeals system is not biased against them.[189]

Discrimination against the poor

Finally, the bishops charge that the death penalty is applied unfairly against the poor. Here are the more important statements from USCCB documents or by bishops speaking on behalf of the USCCB:

- But we must also reckon with a legal system which, while it does provide counsel for indigent defendants, permits those who are well off to obtain resources and the talent to present their case in as convincing a light as possible.... Those condemned to die are nearly always poor....[190]
- A disproportionate number of those in prison and on death row are poor and non-white and unable to avail themselves of the best legal resources.[191]
- In many states, underfunded and overworked defense attorneys struggle to keep up with large caseloads. It is simply unacceptable that defendants charged with capital crimes should have to rely on counsel that is underfunded, inexperienced, or simply incompetent.[192]
- Policymakers and citizens are facing the unpleasant reality that the poor and marginalized of the society are more likely to be convicted and sentenced to death than the rich and powerful.[193]
- Over 90% of those on death row were too poor to afford their own attorney.[194]

---

[189] Snell, *Capital Punishment, 2013—Statistical Tables*, table 8, p. 12; table 12, p. 15.
[190] "Bishops' Statement on Capital Punishment, 1980".
[191] Testimony by Cardinal Joseph Bernardin.
[192] Mahony, "A Witness to Life".
[193] Fiorenza, "Letter Calling for a Moratorium".
[194] Office of Domestic Social Development, USCCB, *Death Penalty*.

The bishops' critique seems to have three elements:

1. It is fundamentally unfair that poor people are disproportionally sentenced to death.
2. It is unfair that "well off" defendants can afford better legal counsel than can poor defendants.
3. Even apart from the comparison with those better off, poor defendants too often receive inadequate legal representation.

To the bishops' credit, they do not expressly embrace the larger critique of American society, so common in the academy, that economic stratification or income inequality drives the poor to crime and thus absolves them of full responsibility for their deeds. So, one wonders what kind of unfairness is demonstrated by the mere fact that death row inmates, like prisoners generally, are more likely to be poor than is the nation's population. If males disproportionately commit more murders than females, we would expect them to be disproportionately represented on death row. Similarly, if the poor disproportionately commit more murders than the nonpoor, we would expect them also to be disproportionately represented on death row. We should not be surprised that violent criminals, and especially the worst among them, do not have stellar work histories. Many have been in and out of prison for much of their adult lives, have been deeply involved in the drug subculture, have drifted in and out of the job market, or have otherwise lived on the fringe of society. They tend to lack the very character traits that have moved tens of millions of Americans from modest beginnings into a solid middle-class life. Thus, it is not that poverty has driven these offenders to crime; rather, the same bad character traits that have led them to crime have also led them into poverty.

Think again of the forty-three murderers executed in 2012. Would we expect many of them to have worked overtime or two jobs or to have gone to night school to improve their economic prospects? One of these, Robert Wayne Harris, had worked for ten weeks at a car wash in 2000 just before he murdered the manager and four other employees (and left another permanently disabled). But he had lost that job five days before the murder because he had exposed himself to a customer. Harris was twenty-eight at the time of the murder. As a juvenile he had had an extensive record of violent behavior, and when he was eighteen he was convicted of three burglaries. He spent the next eight years in state prison before being paroled in May 1999. Six months later he abducted and murdered a woman (a crime to which he confessed after his arrest for the car-wash murders, leading the police to the remains). Roughly four months after his first murder (for two and a half months of which he was employed at the car wash), he murdered five innocent people. By any statistical test, Harris was "poor" his entire adult life. He was, as the bishops put it, one of "the poor and marginalized of the society"; for "those condemned to die are nearly always poor." Harris was certainly poor, and he was indeed condemned to die (and did die), but we fail to see the slightest bit of injustice in the combination of those two facts.

Secondly, the bishops see unfairness in the fact that those who are "well off" can "obtain resources and the talent to present their case in as convincing a light as possible". In some of the bishops' statements, this critique seems independent of the issue of the adequacy of the poor defendant's defense. That is, they suggest that even if a poor defendant receives a fully adequate defense, it is not likely to be as effective as the defense that a "well off" defendant could secure. One thinks, of course, of multimillionaire O.J. Simpson's "Dream Team" of legal and professional talent that worked to acquit him in his 1995 murder trial. A much older case, but equally famous at the time, was the murder trial in Chicago of Nathan Leopold and Richard Loeb, two wealthy college students (nineteen and eighteen at the time of the crime), for kidnapping and murdering for sport a fourteen-year-old boy from their upscale neighborhood in 1924. Although the two pleaded guilty to the murder charge, their trial to determine the sentence lasted thirty-two days. Famed defense attorney Clarence Darrow, hired by Loeb's wealthy parents, represented the defendants. Darrow's now famous twelve-hour concluding argument convinced the judge to spare the defendants' lives. While it is certainly possible that the employment of less skilled attorneys might have resulted in Simpson's conviction for double murder and the death sentence for Leopold and Loeb, cases of this type are extraordinarily rare and hardly undermine the value and justice of the death penalty. As the late American philosopher Ernest van den Haag famously argued, "Guilt is personal. No one becomes less guilty or less deserving of

punishment because another was punished leniently or not at all."
That some rich people might escape punishment does not reduce the
guilt of the less-than-rich or make them deserving of a lesser punishment.[195] Indeed, currently in the United States more than a third of
homicides go unsolved: no one is even arrested for the crime.[196] Yet
no one argues that because one-third of killers get away with murder,
we should stop arresting, convicting, and punishing the others.

The key is not whether the typical capital defendant can afford
to hire the legal profession's greatest talent but whether the typical
capital defendant receives a competent defense. Critics of the death
penalty cite anecdotes of bad lawyering in capital cases, usually from
relatively poor states or counties without public-defender systems;
but proponents of the death penalty insist that: (1) cases of inadequate representation are relatively few, (2) they are not widespread
throughout the United States, and (3) the criticism is outdated because
current appointment procedures in death-penalty states ensure high-
quality legal representation. Paul Cassell, then a federal judge in Salt
Lake City, Utah, wrote in 2004 that

> Utah has a carefully developed procedure for appointing counsel in
> capital cases. The court must appoint at least two attorneys for the
> accused. At least one of the attorneys must meet stringent require-
> ments for experience in criminal cases generally and capital cases in
> particular. The court is further required to make specific findings
> about the capabilities of the lawyers to handle a capital defense. These
> new procedures have worked well to insure high quality representa-
> tion for capital defendants in Utah.[197]

Prosecuting attorney Joshua K. Marquis wrote the following about
Oregon's capital defense system in 2004:

> Oregon is similar to many states in that a government-funded
> agency, the Indigent Defense Board, contracts with lawyers for all

[195] Ernest van den Haag, "The Death Penalty Once More", in *The Death Penalty in America: Current Controversies*, ed. Hugo Adam Bedau (New York: Oxford University Press, 1997),
p. 449.
[196] Federal Bureau of Investigation, *Crime in the United States, 2013*, table 25, https://www
.fbi.gov/about-us/cjis/ucr/crime-in-the-u.s/2013/crime-in-the-u.s.-2013/tables/.
[197] Cassell, "In Defense of the Death Penalty", pp. 209–10.

court-appointed capital cases.... Oregon taxpayers spent almost seventy-five million dollars in 2001 to fund indigent defense. By comparison, the total budget of all prosecutorial offices was just under fifty million dollars.... A person with no visible means of support or assets who is charged with aggravated (capital) murder in Oregon will receive a defense that would do the "Dream Team" proud.[198]

About Colorado, state district judge Morris B. Hoffman wrote in 2007:

Despite [the abolitionists'] anecdotes about sleeping, drunk, and otherwise incompetent defense lawyers, this picture of rampant defense incompetence couldn't be further from the truth, at least in my experience. I have told friends, and even written, that if they get into serious criminal trouble in Denver, the first thing they should do is to give away their assets in order to qualify for a public defender. Yes, public defenders are overburdened and underpaid, but on the whole they are also the finest single collection of criminal defense lawyers around, and for good reason—experience. I would stack the best of our public defenders against any private defense lawyer I know.[199]

On capital defense in California, the state's district attorneys wrote in 2003:

Only the most experienced criminal-defense attorneys are assigned to death-penalty cases. This alone is an extraordinary reflection of the seriousness placed upon protecting defendants faced with capital punishment. In January 2003, the Judicial Council of California promulgated standards for the appointment of trial counsel in capital cases, with particular emphasis on tenure and related experience. These standards mirror California's long-standing practice of appointing only the very best to handle these most important cases.... California is recognized nationwide for its outstanding training of counsel in death-penalty cases. Each year, the California Public Defenders Association (CPDA) and California Attorneys for Criminal Justice (CACJ) hold death-penalty seminars attended by about 1,000 defense

---

[198] Joshua K. Marquis, "Truth and Consequences: The Penalty of Death", in *Debating the Death Penalty*, ed. Hugo Adam Bedau and Paul G. Cassell (Oxford: Oxford University Press, 2004), pp. 141–42.

[199] Morris B. Hoffman, "The Myth of Factual Innocence", in *Chicago-Kent Law Review* 82, no. 2 (2007): 686.

attorneys from all over the nation. They provide extensive manuals, sample legal pleadings, demonstrations, and excellent instruction on how best to defend capital prosecutions.... Capital-case attorneys are paid much higher fees than attorneys appointed in noncapital cases. Significantly more funding also is available for defense investigators and other experts. Often, thousands of dollars are spent hiring multiple defense experts, including psychiatrists, forensic scientists, criminalists, jury-selection experts, and penalty-phase coordinators, to ensure no stone is left unturned.[200]

In 2015, law professor John Douglass of the University of Richmond School of Law described reforms in Virginia's assignment of defense attorneys in capital cases:

> The most significant change in capital litigation [since 1999] ... has been in capital case defense. In 2002 the Virginia General Assembly authorized the creation of four regional CDOs [Capital Defender Offices] under the supervision of the VIDC [Virginian Indigent Defense Commission]. In all capital cases since 2004, Virginia courts have been required to appoint two defense attorneys, including one from a CDO. State funds were appropriated to staff CDOs with experienced, specialized defense counsel and to provide for investigators and mitigation specialists. At about the same time, Virginia adopted detailed standards for appointment of counsel, increased compensation, and removed fee caps for appointed counsel in capital cases.

The result, according to Douglass, is a "capable and vigorous defense" in capital cases.[201]

Paul Cassell, who served as Associate Deputy Attorney General and an Assistant U.S. Attorney in the U.S. Department of Justice in the 1980s, also notes that in the federal system the law "requires appointment of extremely well-qualified counsel and provides them with seemingly unlimited resources". "The federal government", he adds, "spent in excess of $13.8 million to pay for attorneys and cover other costs of McVeigh's defense until his execution. Yet even with what may have been the most expensive defense in the history of the

---

[200] *Prosecutors' Perspective on California's Death Penalty*, p. 15.

[201] John G. Douglass, "Death as a Bargaining Chip: Plea Bargaining and the Future of Virginia's Death Penalty", *University of Richmond Law Review* 49, no. 3 (2015): 887.

world, McVeigh was sentenced to death and ultimately executed—disproving [the claim] ... that the ultimate penalty falls only on those who have 'the misfortune to be assigned the worst lawyers.' "[202] Hoffman, the Colorado state judge, also disputes the impact of lawyering skills on outcomes in capital cases:

> Contrary to public perception, the best facts win, not the best lawyers. Trials are contests of facts, not contests of lawyers. Some of the best lawyering I have ever seen has resulted in spectacular losses, some of the worst in spectacular wins. It's the evidence that's important to outcome, not the oratorical or sartorial abilities of the messengers.
>
> The view that the best lawyers win and the worst lawyers lose, that public defenders are bad and highly paid private defense lawyers are good, not only does terrible damage to the public's already waning confidence in the system, it has the pernicious effect of reinforcing all the worst stereotypes of the system as being hopelessly racist and classist. Not only do innocent people get wrongly convicted, so this stereotype goes, it is the poor and disenfranchised—those who cannot afford Perry Mason—who are getting disproportionately wrongfully convicted. Conversely, rich white men who are guilty are regularly getting off because of their highly paid lawyers.
>
> People who believe this may watch lots of movies and TV, but they are not spending much time in our courtrooms.[203]

The picture that emerges from these descriptions hardly supports the bishops' belief that bad lawyering is responsible for the number of poor people on death row. Moreover, there is an added "failsafe" in the system that we have not mentioned: ineffective assistance of counsel is a major grounds for the second and third stages of appeals in capital cases (discussed above)—*post-conviction appeal* to the state courts (also called *state habeas*) and *habeas corpus* appeal to the federal courts. As we noted earlier, about a third of all those sentenced to death since 1980 ended up getting off death row because of a successful appeal of their conviction (11% of all cases) or their sentence (22% of all cases). Thus, if someone who has been sentenced to death can persuade state or the federal courts that his counsel at trial

[202] Cassell, "In Defense of the Death Penalty", p. 210.
[203] Hoffman, "The Myth of Factual Innocence", pp. 686–87.

provided an ineffective defense, he will receive either a new trial or a new sentencing hearing. In combination with the kinds of reforms described above, it is hard to imagine what more could be done to ensure that everyone charged with a capital crime receive an effective defense.

* * *

We have shown, then, that every element of the bishops' case against the death penalty fails, including their scriptural interpretations, their moral and philosophical arguments, and their understanding of the practical application and effects of capital punishment. In the conclusion we return to the charge, made by the bishops and many other Catholic critics of the death penalty, that executing murderers undermines the teaching that killing is wrong and therefore capital punishment promotes a culture of death rather than a culture of life.

CONCLUSION

We have now set out a detailed philosophical, theological, and social-scientific defense of capital punishment. Most simply put, the Catholic case for capital punishment rests on two propositions:

1. There is a strong moral presumption in favor of capital punishment for grave crimes such as murder.
2. This presumption can be overridden only when resorting to capital punishment would fail to serve the common good as well as a lesser punishment would.

For Catholics to advocate the use of capital punishment, both propositions must be true. If capital punishment were inherently contrary to Catholic moral teaching, faithful Catholics would be required to reject it, no matter how effective it might be in saving the lives of the innocent or otherwise serving the common good. Also, if it were less effective than lesser punishments at saving lives or otherwise serving the common good, or if it carried social costs that outweighed its benefits, Catholics would be required to reject it, despite its principled legitimacy.

In the previous chapters, we have shown that capital punishment is philosophically justified, consistent with Scripture and long-standing Church teaching, and necessary to achieve the common good. Specifically and to summarize, our arguments have addressed:

Philosophy

- Catholic moral theology embraces the essential elements of natural law philosophy, especially as articulated by Saint Thomas Aquinas. According to this philosophic tradition, when we punish criminals we restore "the equality of justice" by answering the offender's overindulgence of his will with the infliction of something that is contrary to his will. Punishment that serves

375

this purpose is inherently good, and thus the human desire to inflict such punishment on wrongdoers is also inherently good.

- Because the main (or first) purpose of punishment is to restore "the equality of justice", punishments must be proportional to the offense. Though retribution is punishment's fundamental end, punishment may also serve other purposes, such as correcting or rehabilitating the offender, deterring others from similar crimes, incapacitating the offender, and compensating victims.
- The principle of proportionality fully justifies the death penalty for murderers. To deny this is implicitly to deny the principle of desert itself and thus implicitly to deny the very legitimacy of retributive punishment.
- The imposition of the death penalty for murder upholds human dignity by treating the offender as a free and rational agent responsible for his acts and by acknowledging that nothing less than death would reflect the gravity of what has been done to the victim.

Scripture and Church teaching

- The Old Testament unambiguously affirms the appropriateness and necessity of the death penalty through, for example, (1) God's command to Noah that "Whoever sheds the blood of man, by man shall his blood be shed; for God made man in his own image" (Gn 9:6); (2) the incorporation of the lex talionis into the law of ancient Israel: "You shall give life for life, eye for eye, tooth for tooth, hand for hand, foot for foot, burn for burn, wound for wound, stripe for stripe" (Ex 21:23–25); and (3) the Mosaic Law's delineation of homicide into different degrees, with the demand that those who intentionally kill the innocent must die (e.g., Deut 19:11–13).
- Christ's Sermon on the Mount in Matthew's Gospel is not a teaching against punishment in general or capital punishment in particular, but rather an admonition to the victims of violence not personally to seek redress in kind. Nothing in the sermon disputes the right of public authorities to punish crime. Other passages in the New Testament not only do not condemn capital punishment, but clearly take for granted its legitimacy, such as Luke's account of the words of the "good thief" crucified next

to Christ, who acknowledged that he and his fellow thief were condemned "justly" and were "receiving the due reward of our deeds" (Lk 23:41).

- In his Letter to the Romans, Saint Paul emphatically affirmed the right of the state to execute criminals. Moreover, all the Fathers and Doctors of the Church who addressed the death penalty affirmed its moral legitimacy.

- Until recently, popes rarely addressed the death penalty. Of those who did, none condemned it as immoral, and several by word or deed affirmed its legitimacy, including Pope Saint Innocent I, who in 405 upheld the authority of Christian civil officials to impose the penalty of death; Pope Innocent III, who in 1210 demanded that the breakaway Waldensians take an oath recognizing the moral legitimacy of the death penalty; Pope Leo X, who in 1520 condemned the proposition that heretics could not be executed; Pope Saint Pius V, who in 1566 issued the *Roman Catechism*, which explicitly affirmed the legitimacy of the death penalty; the popes who headed the Papal States (for more than a thousand years) and authorized many hundreds (perhaps even thousands) of executions for murder and other violent crimes (with more than five hundred executions in the nineteenth century alone); and Pope Pius XII, who in the mid-twentieth century defended retributive punishment and the death penalty in major public addresses.

- The view of new natural lawyers that it is always wrong intentionally to take the life of another cannot be reconciled with orthodox Catholic teaching and centuries of Church practice.

- The reservations expressed by very recent popes about the death penalty and their stated wish to see it abolished constitute prudential judgments with which faithful Catholics may legitimately disagree.

- The current *Catechism of the Catholic Church* (1997), which incorporates part of Pope John Paul II's teaching, affirms that punishment is fundamentally retributive and must be commensurate with the gravity of the crime. Insofar as it argues that a very limited use of the death penalty will be sufficient to protect society, it is making a prudential judgment, not a doctrinal one. Thus, current Church teaching neither reverses traditional Catholic doctrine on the death penalty nor constitutes a development of doctrine. In 2004, nine years after Pope John Paul II addressed the death penalty in *Evangelium Vitae*, Cardinal Joseph Ratzinger, prefect of the Congregation for the Doctrine of the Faith, acknowledged the prudential character of Pope John Paul II's teaching when he wrote that Catholics may legitimately "be at odds with the Holy Father on the application of capital punishment".

Current application

- The death penalty in the American states is reserved for the most heinous murders—including rape murders, torture murders, multiple murders, and the murders of children—and for the most dangerous murderers—including those with long histories of violent behavior such as other homicides, rapes, and serious assaults. (Federal law also allows the death penalty for the national crimes of treason and espionage.) Given the nature of these crimes and offenders, no punishment less than death would be commensurate with the offense.
- The desire simply to see justice done—rather than hatred or personal score settling—is a powerful force in motivating prosecutors and the victims' loved ones to demand the execution of the offender. Even some offenders themselves come to acknowledge the justness of their execution. In general, loved ones rightly see no conflict between the Christian demand for forgiveness and the justice (and therefore the necessity) of the punishment. As one said, "He asked for forgiveness and I forgive him, but he had to pay the consequences."
- There is substantial evidence that the prospect of execution encourages many condemned murderers to repent for their crimes, often through the assistance of a spiritual adviser. This is consistent with Thomas Aquinas' argument that the death penalty could encourage criminals to repent and thereby save their souls.

The American bishops

- The national association of Catholic bishops in the United States first opposed the death penalty in 1974, though a large minority (between 37% and 46%) refused to endorse this position. By 1980, two-thirds of the bishops voted to oppose capital punishment, issuing their first document calling for abolition. Despite the large numbers of bishops who dissented in 1974 and 1980, by 2007 the bishops were maintaining (incorrectly) that Catholic teaching "compels us ... to oppose ... the use of the death penalty". This new position contradicted both Cardinal Joseph Ratzinger, writing three years before as head of the Congregation for the Doctrine of the Faith, and Cardinal William Levada, writing at the same time as chair of the Committee on Doctrine of the United States Conference of Catholic Bishops, who held that "there may be a legitimate diversity of opinion even among Catholics about ... applying the death penalty."

- Statements issued by the USCCB or made by bishops acting on behalf of the USCCB often assert, or strongly imply, that capital punishment (1) is morally unacceptable because it entails the intentional killing of a being made in God's image, (2) violates the values of the Gospel, (3) is contrary to Christ's call for forgiveness, or (4) stems from an unhealthy desire for vengeance. As we have shown, these positions cannot be squared with two millennia of Catholic moral teaching.

- American Catholic bishops frequently assert that capital punishment does not deter murder, despite their lack of expertise in this area and despite the fact that this question is hotly debated among quantitatively trained social scientists.

- Although social scientists have reached no consensus on the deterrent effect of the death penalty, anecdotal and common-sense evidence strongly support the conclusion that the death penalty deters some potential murderers. It also likely reduces murders by increasing prison sentences for murder through plea bargaining—thereby (1) deterring some by increasing the cost for committing the crime and also (2) incapacitating killers for longer periods—and it gives prisoners serving life sentences (for whatever crime) strong incentives not to kill other inmates or prison staff. Most fundamentally, it reduces murders by reinforcing the community's sense of the appalling nature of the crime, making it less likely that someone would be willing to consider murder in the first place.

- Although the bishops claim that the death penalty "is deeply flawed" in how it is applied, a fair assessment of the evidence demonstrates both (1) that mistaken convictions are rare and mistaken executions perhaps nonexistent since the reform of capital punishment laws in the 1970s and (2) that the capital punishment system in the United States neither discriminates against minorities nor is unfair to the poor.

We believe it is time to recover the traditional Catholic case for the death penalty, both so as to restore clarity and balance to the Church's presentation of her doctrine and to help uphold a punishment that promotes the common good of society. Catholic teaching and traditional Church practice allow no room for rejecting the death penalty as intrinsically wrong. God's covenant with Noah after the Flood (Gn 9:6) did not order that human societies engage in intrinsically immoral acts. The Mosaic Law of ancient Israel did not order intrinsically immoral acts. Saint Paul did not advocate that public officials engage in intrinsically immoral acts. The Fathers and Doctors of the Church, including her greatest theologians, did not defend the legitimacy of intrinsically immoral acts. The popes who defended the legitimacy of the death penalty and who authorized many hundreds (perhaps thousands) of executions in the Papal States were not countenancing or commanding intrinsically immoral acts. By including in its legal code the death penalty for the attempted assassination of the pope from 1929 to 1969, Vatican City was not prescribing an intrinsically immoral punishment.

As with personal self-defense and just wars, the death penalty's appropriateness, morally and practically, depends on the circumstances. As long as (in the words of Pope Innocent III) "the punishment is carried out not in hatred but with good judgment, not inconsiderately but after mature deliberation", the death penalty may be imposed if it genuinely serves the common good. Generally, the Church has left these and similar prudential judgments to public officials. The current *Catechism of the Catholic Church* expressly affirms that when it comes to judging whether a decision to go to war is morally justified, "the evaluation of these conditions for moral legitimacy belongs to the prudential judgment of those who have the responsibility for the common good." The institutional Church respects the authority and responsibility of public officials, guided by sound moral principles, to make these judgments. Similarly, to the best of our knowledge, the Church has fully respected the authority of lawmakers to write statutes on self-defense that detail the conditions under which individuals may use force, including deadly force, to protect themselves and others.

Unfortunately, churchmen have in recent years not been equally respectful of the authority and duty of public officials to exercise their prudential judgment in applying Catholic teaching when it comes to the death penalty. Thus, an influential American bishop such as Charles Chaput both affirms the traditional Church teaching yet simultaneously calls for the immediate abolition of capital punishment. He has said, on the one hand, that "the death penalty is not intrinsically evil. Both Scripture and long Christian tradition acknowledge the legitimacy of capital punishment under certain circumstances. The Church cannot repudiate that without repudiating her own identity." On the other hand, he alleges that capital punishment serves no useful purpose, claiming that "in modern industrialized states, killing convicted murderers adds nothing to anyone's safety. It is an excess.... We need to end the death penalty and we need to do it soon."[1] Now, whether the death penalty contributes to public safety is precisely the point at issue, and churchmen bring to that debate no particular expertise, certainly no expertise derived from their religious training and pastoral experience.

It follows, then, that whether a Catholic should support the death penalty depends on whether, properly administered to those convicted of the most heinous offenses, it makes the world a safer place and otherwise upholds the common good. We believe that it does, and we have elaborated the reasons at some length throughout this book:

- It protects prison guards and other inmates by (1) preventing killers from killing again and (2) giving violent criminals in prison (including those who have not killed before) powerful incentives not to kill while incarcerated.

---

[1] "Archbishop Chaput Clarifies Church's Stance on Death Penalty", *Catholic News Agency*, October 18, 2005, http://www.catholicnewsagency.com/news/archbishop_chaput_clarifies _churchs_stance_on_death_penalty_says_in_industrialized_societies_it_must_end/.

- It protects members of the community by giving lifers who escape strong reasons not to kill while on the run.
- It almost certainly has a deterrent effect on at least some potential murderers by threatening to take from them that which they value most: their lives.
- It may also prevent murders by increasing the average sentence for murder through the plea-bargaining process compared with jurisdictions in which prosecutors cannot threaten to seek the penalty of death. Longer sentences for murder may have both a "secondary deterrent effect" (by increasing the cost of the crime) and an incapacitative effect (by reducing the number of years that a potential recidivist killer spends in society and also by releasing him at an older age).
- It powerfully reinforces society's condemnation of the crime of murder, making it less likely that those growing up in a community with the death penalty would even consider killing someone in the first place.
- It anchors the entire schedule of punishments for serious crimes to the principle of just deserts, ensuring the survival of retributive punishment as a key element in the criminal justice system.
- It reassures the families and other loved ones of the victims of grave crimes that they live in a society that is just and that shows respect for the lives of victims by inflicting on their killers a penalty that is truly proportionate to the gravity of the offense.
- It encourages repentance insofar as it makes offenders aware of the extreme gravity of their offenses and also of the shortness of the time remaining to them to get themselves right with God and to ask forgiveness of the families of their victims.
- Perhaps most importantly, it promotes belief in and respect for the majesty of the moral order and for the system of human law that both derives from and supports that moral order.

In our view, if capital punishment for murder does indeed promote the common good in these ways, then traditional Catholic doctrine virtually demands that it be used. Otherwise, we send the message that the lives of the innocent must be sacrificed to save the lives of those who richly deserve to lose their own and that letting evil men live out their days in relative comfort is of greater value than encouraging their repentance, upholding a sense of justice in society at large, and reassuring the loved ones of victims that the most evil acts will be punished with a truly proportionate penalty. Such a position cannot be squared with two millennia of Catholic moral teaching.

Thus, we now find ourselves in the rather odd situation in which the majority of churchmen appear to be against the death penalty but Catholic teaching itself is not. This is a recipe for massive confusion among the faithful. It cannot help but demoralize or disaffect faithful Catholics who support the death penalty for the very reasons that the Church Fathers and Doctors, her leading theologians, and her popes traditionally have supported it. From a merely prudential point of view, how is it good for the American Catholic Church to take an increasingly strident abolitionist position in a country where support for the death penalty has been between 60% and 80% for the past forty years?[2] Currently, three-fifths of Americans support the death penalty (including a majority of Catholics), and this includes the residents of the nineteen states that have abolished it. Presumably, popular support is even higher in the thirty-one states that retain it. And note that these survey results are in response to a very generic question: "Are you in favor of the death penalty for a person convicted of murder?" Yet, as we have shown, the death penalty in the United States is meted out not to the "typical" murderer but to a handful of the most brutal and heinous killers. Surely, public support for executing the murderers of the especially brutal sort we described in chapter 3 would be even higher than the 61% most recently measured by Gallup. What separates the American bishops from the majority of their flock on the death penalty is not a theological dispute (though some bishops seem to think so) but a prudential one. All else being equal, Catholic clergy have no greater insight into whether the death penalty promotes public safety than do the Catholic laity, and likely much less than do the public officials charged with keeping us safe.

We also worry that the strident opposition to the death penalty among so many churchmen may prove a hindrance to conversions

[2] See http://www.gallup.com/poll/1606/death-penalty.aspx. In March 2015 a Pew Research Center poll reported that 56% of Americans supported the death penalty with 38% opposed. Yet another question from the same survey showed that 63% believed that "the death penalty is morally justified [for murder]", and another 6% said that it "depends". Only 31% said that the "death penalty is morally wrong". Pew measured support among Catholics at 53% (down from 59% in 2011).

among death-penalty proponents who either (1) look askance at the weakly supported prudential judgments of so many churchmen or (2) question the soundness of Catholicism itself if it seems to demand policies that threaten public safety and appear to conflict with Scripture and traditional Christian doctrine.

The results of the elections of November 8, 2016, testified to the wisdom of average citizens when voters in California, Nebraska, and Oklahoma reaffirmed their support for the death penalty. Unless the U.S. Supreme Court removes the issue of capital punishment from popular control (think abortion and same-sex marriage), it will remain for the people and their representatives to decide whether to preserve the ultimate punishment. Catholic churchmen will likely continue their campaign to persuade their flocks to reject this most salutary punishment. We hope that this volume will stand as a reminder to the bishops and the Catholic faithful in general that there is a rich Catholic tradition that affirms the justice of the death penalty and its importance to securing the common good.

If in the end capital punishment is absolutely rejected even for the most heinous offenses, the fundamental principle, reaffirmed repeatedly by the Church, that an offender deserves a punishment proportional to his crime will be fatally undermined. Society will lose sight, first of the idea of proportionality, then of the idea of desert, and finally of the idea of punishment itself. And when the idea of punishment goes, the very idea of justice will go with it, replaced by a therapeutic or technocratic model that treats human beings as cases to be managed and socially engineered than as morally responsible persons. Nothing less is at stake in the death-penalty debate.

The Catholic Church stands as the world's preeminent advocate of human dignity and the culture of life against enormously powerful forces of modern secularism. As we have argued, by saving innocent lives, by affirming the sacredness of the lives of murder victims, and by treating murderers as morally accountable creatures who deserve punishment proportional to their crimes, the death penalty plays a vital role in *upholding* human dignity and in *promoting* a culture of life. The solemn affirmation in Genesis 9:6 of both human dignity and capital punishment alike is as relevant today as it was to earlier generations: "Whoever sheds the blood of man, by man shall his blood be shed; for God made man in his own image."

BIBLIOGRAPHY

Acker, James R. *Questioning Capital Punishment: Law, Policy, and Practice*. New York: Routledge, 2014.

Agius, George. *Tradition and the Church*. Boston: Stratford, 1928.

Allen, John L. "He Executed Justice". *National Catholic Reporter*, September 14, 2001.

Allen, Ronald J., and Amy Shavell. "Further Reflections on the Guillotine". *Journal of Criminal Law and Criminology* 95, no. 2 (2005): 625–36.

Ambrose. *Letters*. Translated by Sister Mary Melchior Beyenka, O.P. Washington, D.C.: Catholic University of America Press, 1954.

Anscombe, G.E.M. "War and Murder". In *Ethics, Religion, and Politics*, 51–61. Oxford: Basil Blackwell, 1981.

"Archbishop Chaput Clarifies Church's Stance on Death Penalty". *Catholic News Agency*, October 18, 2005. http://www.catholicnewsagency .com/news/archbishop_chaput_clarifies_churchs_stance_on_death _penalty_says_in_industrialized_societies_it_must_end/.

Athenagoras. *A Plea for the Christians*. Translated by B.P. Pratten. In *Ante-Nicene Fathers*, vol. 2, edited by Alexander Roberts, James Donaldson, and A. Cleveland Coxe, 123–48. Buffalo, N.Y.: Christian Literature, 1885.

Augustine. *The City of God*. Translated by Marcus Dods. In *Nicene and Post-Nicene Fathers*, 1st ser., vol. 2, edited by Philip Schaff. Buffalo, N.Y.: Christian Literature, 1887.

———. *Contra Faustum*. Translated by Richard Stothert. In *Nicene and Post-Nicene Fathers*, 1st ser., vol. 4, edited by Philip Schaff, 155–345. Buffalo, N.Y.: Christian Literature, 1887.

———. *On the Sermon on the Mount*. Translated by William Findlay. In *Nicene and Post-Nicene Fathers*, 1st ser., vol. 6, edited by Philip Schaff. Buffalo, N.Y.: Christian Literature, 1888.

Baird, Robert M., and Stuart E. Rosenbaum, eds. *Punishment and the Death Penalty: The Current Debate*. Amherst, N.Y.: Prometheus Books, 1995.

Baldus, David C., George Woodworth, and Charles A. Pulaski. *Equal Justice and the Death Penalty: A Legal and Empirical Analysis*. Boston: Northeastern University Press, 1990.

Baltimore Catechism No. 3. Third Plenary Council of Baltimore, 1891, http:// www.baltimorecatechism.com.

Beccaria, Cesare. *On Crimes and Punishments*. Translated by Henry Paolucci. Indianapolis: Bobbs-Merrill, 1963.

Beck, Allen J., and Bernard E. Shipley. *Recidivism of Prisoners Released in 1983*. Washington, D.C.: Bureau of Justice Statistics, 1989. http://www.bjs.gov/content/pub/pdf/rpr83.pdf.

Becker, Gary S. "On the Economics of Capital Punishment". *Economists' Voice* 3, no. 3 (March 2006): 1–4.

Bedau, Hugo Adam, and Michael L. Radelet. "Miscarriages of Justice in Potentially Capital Cases". *Stanford Law Review* 40, no. 1 (November 1987): 21–179.

Bellarmine, Robert. *De Laicis, or The Treatise on Civil Government*. Edited by Kathleen E. Murphy. New York: Fordham University Press, 1928.

Berns, Walter. *For Capital Punishment: Crime and the Morality of the Death Penalty*. New York: Basic Books, 1979. Reprinted Lanham, Md.: University Press of America, 1991.

Biggar, Nigel, and Rufus Black, eds. *The Revival of Natural Law: Philosophical, Theological and Ethical Responses to the Finnis-Grisez School*. Aldershot: Ashgate, 2000.

Bittle, Celestine N. *Man and Morals: Ethics*. Milwaukee: Bruce, 1950.

Bonczar, Thomas P., Timothy A. Hughes, Doris James Wilson, Paula M. Ditton. *National Corrections Reporting Program, Time Served in State Prison, By Offense, Release Type, Sex, and Race*. Washington, D.C.: Bureau of Justice Statistics, 2009.

Boonin, David. *The Problem of Punishment*. Cambridge: Cambridge University Press, 2008.

Bradley, Gerard V. "No Intentional Killing Whatsoever: The Case of Capital Punishment". In *Natural Law and Moral Inquiry: Ethics, Metaphysics, and Politics in the Work of Germain Grisez*, edited by Robert P. George, 155–73. Washington, D.C.: Georgetown University Press, 1998.

Brugger, E. Christian. *Capital Punishment and Roman Catholic Moral Tradition*. Notre Dame, Ind.: University of Notre Dame Press, 2003.

———. *Capital Punishment and Roman Catholic Moral Tradition*. 2nd ed. Notre Dame, Ind.: University of Notre Dame Press, 2014.

Budziszewski, J. "Capital Punishment: The Case for Justice". *First Things* 145 (2004): 39–45.

California Catholic Conference of Bishops. "The Gospel of Life and Capital Punishment", California Catholic Conference website. July 1999. http://www.cacatholic.org/news/california-bishops-statements/gospel-life-and-capital-punishment.

California District Attorneys Association. *Prosecutors' Perspective on California's Death Penalty*. March 2003. http://www.cjlf.org/deathpenalty/DPPaper.pdf.

Campbell, Ward. "Exoneration Inflation: Justice Scalia's Concurrence in *Kansas v. Marsh*". *IACJ Journal* (Summer 2008): 49–63. http://www.cjlf.org/files/CampbellExonerationInflation2008.pdf.

Carlson, John W. *Words of Wisdom: A Philosophical Dictionary for the Perennial Tradition*. Notre Dame, Ind.: University of Notre Dame Press, 2012.

Cassell, Paul G. "In Defense of the Death Penalty". In *Debating the Death Penalty*. Edited by Hugo Adam Bedau and Paul G. Cassell. Oxford: Oxford University Press, 2004.

———. "In Defense of the Death Penalty" *IACJ Journal* 2 (Summer 2008):14–28.

———. "We're Not Executing the Innocent". *Wall Street Journal*, June 16, 2000.

Catechism of the Catholic Church, Second Edition, Latin Typical Edition. 1997. (Libreria Editrice Vaticana)

Catechism of the Council of Trent (Roman Catechism). Translated by John A. McHugh and Charles J. Callan. Rockford, Ill.: TAN Books, 1982.

Chinigo, Michael, ed. *The Pope Speaks: The Teachings of Pope Pius XII*. New York: Pantheon Books, 1957.

Clark, Ramsey. *Crime in America*. New York: Simon and Schuster, 1970.

Clement of Alexandria. *The Stromata*. Translated by William Wilson. In *Ante-Nicene Fathers*, vol. 2, edited by Alexander Roberts, James Donaldson, and A. Cleveland Coxe. Buffalo, NY: Christian Literature, 1885.

Cloninger, Dale O., and Roberto Marchesini. "Execution and Deterrence: A Quasi-Controlled Group Experiment". *Applied Economics* 33 (2001): 569–76.

———. "Execution Moratoriums, Commutations and Deterrence: The Case of Illinois". *Applied Economics* 38 (2006): 967–73.

———. "Reflections on a Critique". *Applied Economics Letters* 16, no. 17 (November 2009): 1709–11.

Commission on Capital Cases, Florida Legislature. 2011. *Truly Innocent? A Review of 23 Case Histories of Inmates Released from Florida's Death Row Since 1973*. May 13, 2011. http://www.floridacapitalcases.state.fl.us/Documents/Publications/casehistory05-13-11%20Report.pdf.

Congregation for the Doctrine of the Faith. 1989. "Profession of Faith" *Origins* 18.

Cooper, Alexia, and Erica L. Smith. *Homicide Trends in the United States, 1980–2008*. Washington, D.C.: Bureau of Justice Statistics, 2011. http://www.bjs.gov/content/pub/pdf/htus8008.pdf.

Cottingham, John. "Punishment and Respect for Persons". In *Law, Morality, and Rights*, edited by M. A. Stewart, 421–29. Dordrecht: Reidel, 1983.

Cronin, Michael. *The Science of Ethics*. Vol. 1, *General Ethics*. Dublin: M.H. Gill and Son, 1939.

Cyril of Jerusalem. *Catechetical Lectures*. In *Ancient Christian Commentary on Scripture: Old Testament*, vol. 1, edited by Andrew Louth. Downers Grove, Ill.: InterVarsity Press, 2001.

Denzinger, Henry. *The Sources of Catholic Dogma*. Translated by Roy J. Deferrari. St. Louis: B. Herder, 1957.

Dewan, Lawrence. "St. Thomas, John Finnis, and the Political Good". *Thomist* 64 (2000): 337–74.

———. "Thomas Aquinas, Gerard Bradley, and the Death Penalty". In *Wisdom, Law, and Virtue: Essays in Thomistic Ethics*, 312–25. New York: Fordham University Press, 2007.

Dezhbakhsh, Hashem, Paul H. Rubin, and Joanna M. Shepherd. "Does Capital Punishment Have a Deterrent Effect? New Evidence from Postmoratorium Panel Data". *American Law and Economics Review* 5, no. 2 (2003): 344–76.

Dezhbakhsh, Hashem, and Paul H. Rubin. "From the 'Econometrics of Capital Punishment' to the 'Capital Punishment' of Econometrics: On the Use and Abuse of Sensitivity Analysis". *Applied Economics* 43, no. 25 (2011): 3655–70.

Dezhbakhsh, Hashem, and Joanna M. Shepherd. "The Deterrent Effect of Capital Punishment: Evidence from a 'Judicial Experiment'". *Economic Inquiry* 44, no. 3 (July 2006): 512–35.

Di Blasi, Fulvio. *God and the Natural Law*. South Bend, Ind.: St. Augustine's Press, 2006.

Douglass, John C. "Death as a Bargaining Chip: Plea Bargaining and the Future of Virginia's Death Penalty". *University of Richmond Law Review* 49, no. 3 (2015): 873–94.

Dulles, Avery. "Catholicism and Capital Punishment". *First Things* 112 (2001): 30–35.

———. "Catholic Teaching on the Death Penalty: Has It Changed?" In *Religion and the Death Penalty: A Call for Reckoning*, edited by Erik C. Owens, John D. Carlson, and Eric P. Elshtain, 23–30. Grand Rapids, Mich.: William B. Eerdmans, 2004.

———. *Magisterium: Teacher and Guardian of the Faith*. Naples, Fla.: Sapientia Press, 2007.

———. "The Magisterium and Theological Dissent". In *The Craft of Theology: From Symbol to System*, expanded ed., 105–18. New York: Crossroad, 1995.

Durose, Matthew R. *State Court Sentencing of Convicted Felons, 2004—Statistical Tables*. Washington, D.C.: Bureau of Justice Statistics, 2007. http://www.bjs.gov/content/pub/pdf/fssc04.pdf.

Durose, Matthew R., Alexia D. Cooper, and Howard N. Snyder. *Recidivism of Prisoners Released in 30 States in 2005: Patterns from 2005 to 2010*. Washington, D.C.: Bureau of Justice Statistics, 2014. https://www.bjs.gov/content/pub/pdf/rprts05p0510.pdf.

Earley, Pete. *The Serial Killer Whisperer*. New York: Simon and Schuster, 2012.

Ehrhard, Susan. "Plea Bargaining and the Death Penalty: An Exploratory Study". *Justice System Journal* 29, no. 3 (2008): 313–25.

Ehrhard-Dietzel, Susan. "The Use of Life and Death as Tools in Plea Bargaining". *Criminal Justice Review* 37, no. 1 (2012): 89–109.

Ehrlich, Isaac. "The Deterrent Effect of Capital Punishment: A Question of Life and Death". *American Economic Review* 65, no. 3 (June 1975): 397–417.

Elder, Robert K. *Last Words of the Executed*. Chicago: University of Chicago Press, 2010.

Fagothey, Austin. *Right and Reason*. 2nd ed. St. Louis: C. V. Mosby, 1959.

Falvey, Joseph L. "Crime and Punishment: A Catholic Perspective". *Catholic Lawyer* 43 (2004): 149–68.

Federal Bureau of Investigation. *Crime in the United States*. Annual volumes, 1978–2011.

Feser, Edward. *Aquinas*. Oxford: Oneworld Publications, 2009.

———. "Being, the Good, and the Guise of the Good". In *Neo-Aristotelian Perspectives in Metaphysics*, edited by Daniel D. Novotny and Lukas Novak, 84–103. London: Routledge, 2014.

———. "In Defense of Capital Punishment". *Public Discourse*, September 29, 2011. http://www.thepublicdiscourse.com/2011/09/4033/.

———. "Punishment, Proportionality, and the Death Penalty: A Reply to Chris Tollefsen". *Public Discourse*, October 13, 2011. http://www.thepublicdiscourse.com/2011/10/4126/.

———. *Scholastic Metaphysics: A Contemporary Introduction*. Heusenstamm: Editiones Scholasticae, 2014.

Figueiredo, Anthony J. *The Magisterium-Theology Relationship: Contemporary Theological Conceptions in the Light of Universal Church Teaching since 1835 and the Pronouncements of the Bishops of the United States*. Rome: Gregorian University Press, 2001.

Finnis, John. *Aquinas*. Oxford: Oxford University Press, 1998.

———. *Fundamentals of Ethics*. Washington, D.C.: Georgetown University Press, 1983.

———. "Is Natural Law Theory Compatible with Limited Government?" In *Natural Law, Liberalism, and Morality*, edited by Robert P. George, 1–26. Oxford: Oxford University Press, 1996.

———. *Natural Law and Natural Rights*. Oxford: Clarendon Press, 1980.

Flannery, Kevin L. "Capital Punishment and the Law". *Ave Maria Law Review* 5 (2007): 399–428.

Foot, Philippa. *Natural Goodness*. Oxford: Clarendon Press, 2001.

Ford, John C., and Gerald Kelly. *Contemporary Moral Theology*. Vol. I, *Questions in Fundamental Moral Theology*. Westminster, Md.: Newman Press, 1958.

Frakes, Michael, and Matthew Harding. "The Deterrent Effect of Death Penalty Eligibility: Evidence from the Adoption of Child Murder Eligibility Factors". *American Law and Economics Review* 11, no. 2 (2009): 451–97.

Gauthier, David. *Morals by Agreement*. Oxford: Oxford University Press, 1986.

Gelernter, David. "What Do Murderers Deserve?" *Commentary* (April 1998): 21–24.

George, Robert P. *In Defense of Natural Law*. Oxford: Oxford University Press, 1999.

Goldberg, Steven. "Does the Death Penalty Deter?" In *When Wish Replaces Thought*, 25–45. Buffalo, N.Y.: Prometheus Books, 1991.

Goyette, John. "On the Transcendence of the Political Common Good: Aquinas versus the New Natural Law Theory". *National Catholic Bioethics Quarterly* 13 (2013): 133–55.

Grisez, Germain. "Toward a Consistent Natural-Law Ethics of Killing". *American Journal of Jurisprudence* 15 (1970): 64–96.

——. *The Way of the Lord Jesus*. Vol. 1, *Christian Moral Principles*. Chicago: Franciscan Herald Press, 1983.

——. *The Way of the Lord Jesus*. Vol. 2, *Living a Christian Life*. Quincy, Ill.: Franciscan Press, 1993.

Haydock, George Leo. *Haydock's Catholic Family Bible and Commentary*. New York: Edward Dunigan and Brother, 1859.

Higgins, Thomas J. *Man as Man: The Science and Art of Ethics*. Rev. ed. Milwaukee: Bruce, 1958.

Hittinger, Russell. *A Critique of the New Natural Law Theory*. South Bend, Ind.: University of Notre Dame Press, 1987.

Hoffman, Morris B. "The Myth of Factual Innocence". *Chicago-Kent Law Review* 82, no. 2 (2007): 663–90.

Incomplete Commentary on Matthew (Opus imperfectum). Ancient Christian Texts. Translated by James A. Kellerman. Edited by Thomas C. Oden. Downers Grove, Ill.: InterVarsity Press, 2010.

John Chrysostom. *Against Judaizing Christians*. In *Ancient Christian Commentary on Scripture: Old Testament*, vol. 1, edited by Andrew Louth. Downers Grove, Ill.: InterVarsity Press, 2001.

————. *Homilies on the Statues*. Translated by W. R. W. Stephens. In *Nicene and Post-Nicene Fathers*, 1st ser., volume 9, edited by Philip Schaff. Buffalo, N.Y.: Christian Literature, 1889.

John Paul II. *Evangelium Vitae* (The Gospel of Life). March 25, 1995.

Kaczor, Christopher. "Capital Punishment and the Catholic Tradition: Contradiction, Circumstantial Application, or Development of Doctrine?" *Nova et Vetera*. English ed. 2 (2004): 279–304.

Kant, Immanuel. *The Metaphysical Elements of Justice*. Translated by John Ladd. New York: Macmillan, 1965.

Kaufmann, Walter. *Without Guilt and Justice*. New York: Peter H. Wyden, 1973.

Keckler, Charles N. W. "Life v. Death: Who Should Capital Punishment Marginally Deter?" *Journal of Law, Economics and Policy* 2, no. 1 (2006): 51–104.

Koritansky, Peter Karl. *Thomas Aquinas and the Philosophy of Punishment*. Washington, D.C.: Catholic University of America Press, 2012.

Kuziemko, Ilyana. "Does the Threat of the Death Penalty Affect Plea Bargaining in Murder Cases? Evidence from New York's 1995 Reinstatement of Capital Punishment". *American Law and Economics Review* 8, no. 1 (2006): 116–42.

Lactantius. *The Divine Institutes*. Translated by William Fletcher. In *Ante-Nicene Fathers*, vol. 7, edited by Alexander Roberts, James Donaldson, and A. Cleveland Coxe. Buffalo, N.Y.: Christian Literature, 1886.

————. *A Treatise on the Anger of God*. Translated by William Fletcher. In *Ante-Nicene Fathers*, vol. 7, edited by Alexander Roberts and James Donaldson. Edinburgh: T&T Clark, 1886.

Lamont, John. "Finnis and Aquinas on the Good of Life". *New Blackfriars* 83 (2002): 365–80.

Land, Kenneth C., Raymond H. C. Teske Jr., and Hui Zheng. "The Short-Term Effects of Executions on Homicides: Deterrence, Displacement, or Both?" *Criminology* 47, no. 4 (October 2009): 1009–43.

Langan, Patrick A., and David J. Levin. *Recidivism of Prisoners Released in 1994*. Washington, D.C.: Bureau of Justice Statistics, 2002. http://www.bjs.gov/content/pub/pdf/rpr94.pdf.

Lanier, Charles S., and James R. Acker. "Capital Punishment, the Moratorium Movement, and Empirical Questions". *Psychology, Public Policy, and Law* 10, no. 5 (2004): 577–617.

Laurence, Patrick M. "He Beareth Not the Sword in Vain: The Church, the Courts, and Capital Punishment", *Ave Maria Law Review* 1 (2003): 215–57.

Levada, Archbishop William J. "Theological Reflections on Catholics in Political Life and the Reception of Holy Communion." 2004.

Lewis, C. S. "The Humanitarian Theory of Punishment". In *God in the Dock*, 287–94. Grand Rapids, Mich.: William B. Eerdmans, 1970.

Liebman, James S., and the Columbia DeLuna Project. *The Wrong Carlos: Anatomy of a Wrongful Execution*. New York: Columbia University Press, 2014.

Lisska, Anthony J. *Aquinas's Theory of Natural Law*. Oxford: Clarendon Press, 1996.

Long, Steven A. "*Evangelium Vitae*, St. Thomas Aquinas, and the Death Penalty". *Thomist* 63 (1999): 511–52.

———. "Fundamental Errors of the New Natural Law Theory". *National Catholic Bioethics Quarterly* 13 (2013): 105–31.

———. "Natural Law or Autonomous Practical Reason: Problems for the New Natural Law Theory". In *St. Thomas Aquinas and the Natural Law Tradition: Contemporary Perspectives*, edited by John Goyette, Mark S. Latkovic, and Richard S. Myers, 165–93. Washington, D.C.: Catholic University of America Press, 2004.

———. *The Teleological Grammar of the Moral Act*. Naples, Fla.: Sapientia Press, 2007.

Markman, Stephen. "Innocents on Death Row?" *National Review*, September 12, 1994.

Markman, Stephen J., and Paul G. Cassell. "Protecting the Innocent: A Response to the Bedau-Radelet Study". *Stanford Law Review* 41 (1988): 121–60.

Marquis, Joshua. "The Myth of Innocence". *Journal of Criminal Law and Criminology* 95, no. 2 (2005): 501–21.

———. "Rightful Convictions". *Cato Unbound*, March 7, 2012. http://www.cato-unbound.org/

———. "Truth and Consequences: The Penalty of Death". In *Debating the Death Penalty*, edited by Hugo Bedau and Paul Cassell, 117–51. Oxford: Oxford University Press, 2004.

Martin, Christopher. "The Fact/Value Distinction". In *Human Values: New Essays on Ethics and Natural Law*, edited by David S. Oderberg and Timothy Chappell, 52–69. New York: Palgrave Macmillan, 2004.

May, William E. *An Introduction to Moral Theology*. Rev. ed. Huntington, Ind.: Our Sunday Visitor, 1994.

McDonald, John F. *Capital Punishment*. London: Catholic Truth Society, 1964.

McHugh, John A., and Charles J. Callan. *Moral Theology*. Vol. 2. Rev. ed. New York: Joseph F. Wagner, 1958.

McInerny, Ralph. *Ethica Thomistica*. Rev. ed. Washington, D.C.: Catholic University of America Press, 1997.

————. "Opposition to the Death Penalty". *Catholic Dossier* 4 (1998): 5–8.

————. "The Principles of Natural Law". *American Journal of Jurisprudence* 25 (1980): 1–15.

Megivern, James J. *The Death Penalty: An Historical and Theological Survey.* New York: Paulist Press, 1997.

Menninger, Karl. *The Crime of Punishment.* New York: Viking Press, 1968.

Miller, J. Michael. *The Shepherd and the Rock: Origins, Development, and Mission of the Papacy.* Huntington, Ind.: Our Sunday Visitor, 1995.

Mocan, H. Naci, and R. Kaj Gittings. "Getting Off Death Row: Commuted Sentences and the Deterrent Effect of Capital Punishment". *Journal of Law and Economics* 46 (2003): 453–78.

Narveson, Jan. *The Libertarian Idea.* Philadelphia: Temple University Press, 1988.

Nathanson, Stephen. *An Eye for an Eye? The Immorality of Punishing by Death.* 2nd ed. New York: Rowman and Littlefield, 2001.

National Research Council. *Deterrence and the Death Penalty.* Edited by Daniel S. Nagin and John V. Pepper. Washington, D.C.: National Academies Press, 2012.

Neuhaus, Richard John. "The Public Square". *First Things* 56 (October 1995): 83–84.

Noonan, Margaret E., Harley Rohloff, and Scott Ginder. *Mortality in Local Jails and State Prisons, 2000–2013—Statistical Tables.* Washington, D.C.: Bureau of Justice Statistics, 2015.

Norko, Michael A. "The Death Penalty in Catholic Teaching and Medicine: Intersections and Places for Dialogue". *Journal of the American Academy of Psychiatry and the Law* 36 (2008): 470–81.

O'Brien, Matthew B., and Robert C. Koons. "Objects of Intention: A Hylomorphic Critique of the New Natural Law Theory". *American Catholic Philosophical Quarterly* 86 (2012): 655–703.

Oderberg, David S. *Applied Ethics: A Non-Consequentialist Approach.* Oxford: Blackwell, 2000.

————. "The Metaphysical Foundations of Natural Law". In *Natural Moral Law in Contemporary Society,* edited by H. Zaborowski, 44–75. Washington, D.C.: Catholic University of America Press, 2010.

————. *Moral Theory: A Non-Consequentialist Approach.* Oxford: Blackwell, 2000.

————. *Real Essentialism.* London: Routlege, 2007.

Optatus. *Against the Donatists.* Translated by Mark Edwards. Liverpool: Liverpool University Press, 1997.

Origen. *Homilies on Leviticus.* Translated by Gary Wayne Barkley. Washington, D.C.: Catholic University of America Press, 1990.

Owens, Erik C., John D. Carlson, and Eric P. Elshtain, eds. *Religion and the Death Penalty: A Call for Reckoning*. Grand Rapids, Mich.: William B. Eerdmans, 2004.

Pierce, Glenn L., and Michael L. Radelet. "Race, Region, and Death Sentencing in Illinois, 1988-1997". *Oregon Law Review* 81 (2002): 39–96.

Pius XII. "Discourse to the Catholic Jurists of Italy". In *Catholic Documents*, vol. 17, 1955. http://www.apropos.org.uk/documents/Punishment-PiusXII-speechtoItalianJurists5thDec1954.pdf.

———. Encyclical *Divino Afflante Spirtu*. September 30, 1943.

———. Encyclical *Humani Generis*. August 12, 1950.

———. "An International Code for the Punishment of War Crimes". *St. John's Law Review* 28 (December 1953): 1–18. http://scholarship.law.stjohns.edu/cgi/viewcontent.cgi?article=4716&context=lawreview

Pojman, Louis P., and Jeffrey Reiman. *The Death Penalty: For and Against*. New York: Rowman and Littlefield, 1998.

Prejean, Sister Helen. *Dead Man Walking*. New York: Random House, 2013.

Prümmer, Dominic M. *Handbook of Moral Theology*. New York: P.J. Kenedy and Sons, 1957.

Putnam, Hilary. *The Collapse of the Fact/Value Dichotomy and Other Essays*. Cambridge, Mass.: Harvard University Press, 2002.

Ratcliff, Roy, with Lindy Adams. *Dark Journey Deep Grace: Jeffrey Dahmer's Story of Faith*. Abilene, Tex.: Leafwood Publishers, 2006.

Ratzinger, Cardinal Joseph. "Worthiness to Receive Holy Communion: General Principles". Memorandum sent to Cardinal Theodore McCarrick of Washington, D.C. 2004.

Ratzinger, Joseph, and Tarcisio Bertone. "Commentary on the Profession of Faith's Concluding Paragraphs". *Origins* 28 (1998): 116–19.

Ratzinger, Cardinal Joseph, with Vittorio Messori. *The Ratzinger Report*. San Francisco: Ignatius Press, 1985.

Rawls, John. "Justice as Fairness: Political Not Metaphysical". *Philosophy and Public Affairs* 14 (1985): 223–51.

Rice, Charles. "Papal Teaching Deserves 'Submission'". *National Catholic Register*, March 24–31, 2002.

Rickaby, Joseph. *Moral Philosophy*. 4th ed. London: Longmans, Green, 1919.

Roberti, Francesco Cardinal, and Pietro Palazzini, eds. *Dictionary of Moral Theology*. London: Burns and Oates, 1962.

Roman Catechism. See *Catechism of the Council of Trent*.

Rosenmerkel, Sean, Matthew Durose, and Donald Ferole Jr. *Felony Sentences in State Courts, 2006: Statistical Tables*. Washington, D.C.: Bureau of Justice Statistics, 2009. http://www.bjs.gov/content/pub/pdf/fssc06st.pdf .

Rutler, George. "Hanging Concentrates the Mind". *Crisis*, February 8, 2013.
————. "Scalia's Right: Catechism's Problematic". *National Catholic Register*, March 24–31, 2002.
Ryan, John A. "Compensation." In *Catholic Encyclopedia*. Vol. 4. New York: Robert Appleton, 1908.
Sarat, Austin. *When the State Kills: Capital Punishment and the American Condition*. Princeton, N.J.: Princeton University Press, 2002.
Scheidegger, Kent S. "The Death Penalty and Plea Bargaining to Life Sentences". Working Paper 09-01, Criminal Justice Legal Foundation, 2009. http://www.cjlf.org/publications/papers/wpaper09-01.pdf.
Second Vatican Council. Dogmatic Constitution on Divine Revelation *Dei Verbum*. November 18, 1965.
Shepherd, Joanna. "Murders of Passion, Execution Delays, and the Deterrence of Capital Punishment". *Journal of Legal Studies* 33 (June 2004): 282–321.
Sigler, Mary. "Mercy, Clemency, and the Case of Karla Faye Tucker". *Ohio State Journal of Criminal Law*, 4 (2007): 455–86.
Slater, Thomas. *A Manual of Moral Theology*. Vol. 1. 5th ed. New York: Benziger Brothers, 1925.
Smith, Erica L., and Alexia Cooper. *Homicide in the U.S. Known to Law Enforcement, 2011*. Washington, D.C.: Bureau of Justice Statistics, 2013. http://www.bjs.gov/content/pub/pdf/hus11.pdf.
Snell, Tracy L. *Capital Punishment, 2012—Statistical Tables*. Washington, D.C.: Bureau of Justice Statistics, 2014; rev. November 3, 2014. http://www.bjs.gov/content/pub/pdf/cp12st.pdf.
————. *Capital Punishment, 2013—Statistical Tables*. Washington, D.C.: Bureau of Justice Statistics, 2014. http://www.bjs.gov/content/pub/pdf/cp13st.pdf.
Spirago, Francis. *The Catechism Explained*. Edited by Rev. Richard F. Clarke. Rockford, Ill.: TAN Books, 1993.
Stephen, James Fitzjames. *A General View of the Criminal Law in England*. London: Macmillan, 1863.
Tanner, Norman, ed. *Decrees of the Ecumenical Councils*. 2 vols. Washington, D.C.: Georgetown University Press, 1990.
Tanquerey, A. *A Manual of Dogmatic Theology*. Vol. 1. Translated by John J. Byrnes. New York: Desclée, 1959.
Taylor, Greg. "Jeffrey Dahmer's Story of Faith". *Christianity Today*, September 2006. http://www.christianitytoday.com/ct/2006/september/34.125.html.
Tertullian. *A Treatise on the Soul*. Translated by Peter Holmes. In *Ante-Nicene Fathers*, vol. 3, edited by Alexander Roberts, James Donaldson, and A. Cleveland Coxe. Buffalo, N.Y.: Christian Literature, 1885.

Thaxton, Sherod. "Leveraging Death". *Journal of Criminal Law and Criminology* 103, no. 2 (2013): 475–552.

Thomas Aquinas. *On Law, Morality, and Politics*. 2nd ed. Translated by Richard J. Regan. Indianapolis: Hackett, 2002.

———. *Summa Contra Gentiles*. 5 vols. Translated by Anton C. Pegis, James F. Anderson, Vernon J. Bourke, and Charles J. O'Neil. South Bend, Ind.: University of Notre Dame Press, 1975.

———. *Summa Theologiae*. Vol. 41. Translated by T. C. O'Brien. Cambridge: Cambridge University Press, 1972.

———. *Summa Theologica*. 5 vols. Translated by the Fathers of the English Dominican Province. New York: Benziger Brothers, 1948.

———. *Truth*. 3 vols. Translated by Robert W. Mulligan, James V. McGlynn, and Robert W. Schmidt. Indianapolis: Hackett, 1994.

———. *Lectures on the Letter to the Romans*. Translated by Fabian Larcher, O.P. Edited by Jeremy Holmes. Ave Maria, Fla.: Aquinas Center for Theological Renewal, n.d.

Thompson, Michael. "The Representation of Life". In *Virtues and Reasons: Philippa Foot and Moral Theory*, edited by Rosalind Hursthouse, Gavin Lawrence, and Warren Quinn, 247–96. Oxford: Clarendon Press, 1995.

Tollefsen, Christopher O. "Capital Punishment, Dignity, and Authority: A Response to Ed Feser". *Public Discourse*, September 30, 2011. http://www.thepublicdiscourse.com/2011/09/4045/.

———. "Capital Punishment, Sanctity of Life, and Human Dignity". *Public Discourse*, September 16, 2011. http://www.thepublicdiscourse.com/2011/09/3985/.

———. "The New Natural Law Theory". *Lyceum* 10 (2008): 1–18.

———. "Punishment: Political, Not Metaphysical". *Public Discourse*, October 14, 2011. http://www.thepublicdiscourse.com/2011/10/4135/.

Van den Haag, Ernest. "On Deterrence and the Death Penalty". In *Punishment and the Death Penalty: The Current Debate*, edited by Robert M. Baird and Stuart E. Rosenbaum, 125–36. Amherst, N.Y.: Prometheus Books, 1995.

———. "The Death Penalty Once More". In *The Death Penalty in America: Current Controversies*, edited by Hugo Adam Bedau, 445–56. New York: Oxford University Press, 1997.

Van Noort, G. *Dogmatic Theology*. Vol. 3, *The Sources of Revelation* and *Divine Faith*. Translated and revised by John J. Castelot and William R. Murphy. Westminster, Md.: Newman Press, 1961.

Veatch, Henry. "Natural Law and the 'Is-Ought' Question: Queries to Finnis and Grisez". In *Swimming against the Current in Contemporary*

Philosophy, 293–311. Washington, D.C.: Catholic University of America Press, 1990.

Westmoreland-White, Michael L., and Glen H. Stassen. "Biblical Perspectives on the Death Penalty". In *Religion and the Death Penalty: A Call for Reckoning*, edited by Erik C. Owens, John D. Carlson, and Eric P. Elshtain, 123–38. Grand Rapids, Mich.: William B. Eerdmans, 2004.

Wilhelm, Joseph. "Roman Catechism". In *Catholic Encyclopedia*. Vol. 13. New York: Robert Appleton Company, 1912.

Wilhelm, Joseph, and Thomas B. Scannell. *A Manual of Catholic Theology Based on Scheeben's "Dogmatik"*. Vol. 1. 4th ed. New York: Benziger Brothers, 1909.

Wuellner, Bernard. *Dictionary of Scholastic Philosophy*. Milwaukee: Bruce, 1956.

Zimmerman, Paul R. "State Executions, Deterrence, and the Incidence of Murder". *Journal of Applied Economics* 7, no. 1 (May 2004): 163–93.

———. "Statistical Variability and the Deterrent Effect of the Death Penalty". *American Law and Economics Review* 11, no. 2 (2009): 370–98.

Statements issued by the United States Conference of Catholic Bishops (USCCB); its predecessor, the National Conference of Catholic Bishops (NCCB); or individual bishops speaking on behalf of the national organization:

"Bishops' Statement on Capital Punishment, 1980". USCCB website, http://www.usccb.org/issues-and-action/human-life-and-dignity/death-penalty-capital-punishment/statement-on-capital-punishment.cfm.

Economic Justice for All: Pastoral Letter on Catholic Social Teaching and the U.S. Economy. 1986. http://www.usccb.org/upload/economic_justice_for_all.pdf

Testimony by Cardinal Joseph Bernardin on behalf of the USCCB before the Judiciary Committee of the United States Senate. September 28, 1989.

Kinney, Bishop John F. "Testimony on the Death Penalty". December 7, 1995. http://www.usccb.org/issues-and-action/human-life-and-dignity/death-penalty-capital-punishment/testimony-by-bishop-kinney-before-judicial-committee-1995-12-07.cfm.

Statement by Bishop William S. Skylstad on behalf of the USCCB on the conviction of Timothy McVeigh for the bombing of the federal building in Oklahoma City. June 1997.

Statement by Cardinal Bernard Law on behalf of the USCCB on the federal jury's decision to sentence Timothy McVeigh to death. June 13, 1997.

Statement by Bishop William S. Skylstad on behalf of the USCCB appealing to Texas governor George W. Bush to grant clemency to Karla Faye Tucker. January 29, 1998.

Administrative Board of the USCCB. *A Good Friday Appeal to End the Death Penalty, 1999.*

"A Witness to Life: The Catholic Church and the Death Penalty". Address by Cardinal Roger Mahony to the National Club, Washington, D.C., May 25, 2000. http://www.usccb.org/issues-and-action/human-life -and-dignity/death-penalty-capital-punishment/address-by-cardinal -mahoney-to-national-press-club-on-death-penalty-2000-05-25.cfm.

Fiorenza, Most Reverend Joseph A. "Letter to President Clinton Calling for a Moratorium on the Death Penalty". July 10, 2000. http:// www.usccb.org/issues-and-action/human-life-and-dignity/death -penalty-capital-punishment/letter-to-president-clinton-from -bishop-fiorenza-calling-for-moratorium-on-death-penalty-2000-07 -10.cfm.

Responsibility, Rehabilitation, and Restoration: A Catholic Perspective on Crime and Criminal Justice. November 15, 2000. http://www.usccb.org/issues -and-action/human-life-and-dignity/criminal-justice-restorative -justice/crime-and-criminal-justice.cfm.

Cardinal Roger Mahony and Cardinal William Keeler. "Statement on the Approaching Execution of Timothy McVeigh". May 2, 2001. http:// www.usccb.org/issues-and-action/human-life-and-dignity/death -penalty-capital-punishment/statement-by-cardinals-mahony-and -keeler-on-the-execution-of-timothy-mcveigh-2001-05-02.cfm.

Fiorenza, Most Rev. Joseph A. "Statement on the Execution of Timothy McVeigh". June 11, 2001. http://www.usccb.org/issues-and -action/human-life-and-dignity/death-penalty-capital-punishment /statement-by-bishop-fiorenza-on-the-execution-of-mcveigh-2001 -06-11.cfm.

A Culture of Life and the Penalty of Death. December 2005. http://www .usccb.org/issues-and-action/human-life-and-dignity/death-penalty -capital-punishment/culture-of-life-penalty-of-death.cfm

Forming Consciences for Faithful Citizenship: A Call to Political Responsibility from the Catholic Bishops of the United States. 2007; rev. ed. 2011. http:// www.usccb.org/issues-and-action/faithful-citizenship/index.cfm.

Death Penalty. February 2011. http://www.usccb.org/issues-and-action /human-life-and-dignity/death-penalty-capital-punishment/upload /Death-Penalty-Backgrounder-2011-2.pdf

Federal court cases

Furman v. Georgia, 408 U.S. 238 (1972)

Gregg v. Georgia, 428 U.S. 153 (1976)

Zant v. Stephens, 462 U.S. 862 (1983)

McCleskey v. Zant, 580 F. Supp. 338 (N.D. Ga. 1984)

McCleskey v. Kemp, 753 F.2d 877 (11th Cir. 1985)

McCleskey v. Kemp, 481 U.S. 279 (1987)

United States v. Quinones, 196 F. Supp.2d 416 (S.D.N.Y 2002)

United States v. Quinones, 205 F. Supp.2d 256 (S.D.N.Y. 2002)

Kansas v. Marsh, 548 U.S. 163 (2006)

Glossip v. Gross, 576 U.S. _____ (2015)

INDEX

Abel, Cain and, 187, 295, 297–98
abolition of death penalty
    damage to credibility of Catholic
        Church, 207–11
    Francis on, 183–84, 192–93
    John Paul II on, 10, 123, 181, 184
    relationship with anti-Catholic
        thinking, 206–7
    social-scientific arguments for, 14
    societal harm resulting from, 73,
        203–7
    USCCB on, 265, 282–84, 285–86, 379
    vigilante justice resulting from, 68,
        199, 205
abortion
    culture of life rhetoric and, 201–2,
        283
    death penalty for, 115
    direct, 83, 86
    disrespect for innocent life in, 178
    doctrinal prohibition of, 281, 282
    indirect, 84, 86
    moral weight of, 155–56, 157n121,
        177
acquired dignity, 64
Adams, Buenka, 220–21, 254n136,
    270–71
Adams, James, 349–52
adultery, 106, 106n10, 124, 174, 295,
    299–300, 311
Against the Donatists (Optatus), 116
Aguilar, Jesus Ledesma, 244n71
Akers, Thomas Wayne, 251n129
Albert the Great, 119
Alix, Franklin DeWayne, 255n143
Allen, Clarence Ray, 245, 245n84
Allen, Gary Thomas, 238n31, 272–73
Allen, Ronald, 330, 331

Alley, Sedley, 244n72, 247n101
"Allocution to Lenten Preachers" (Pius
    XII), 133
Ambrose of Milan, 107–8, 115, 119,
    187, 197
American Law and Economics Review
    (journal), 316, 317
Anderson, Newton Burton, 245n82
anecdotal evidence, for deterrent effects
    of death penalty, 71–72, 198, 379
anger
    collective, 178
    justification for, 106n9
    righteous, 307
    Thomas Aquinas on, 307
Anscombe, Elizabeth, 69
Anselm of Canterbury, 119
appeals process, 72, 346–47, 373–74
Applied Economics (journal), 315–17
Aristotelian categoricals, 23n9
Aristotelian-Thomistic metaphysics
    on creative will of God, 32
    essentialism and teleology in, 22, 37,
        45
    on final causality, 29, 81
    natural law and, 27–28, 43, 86
    rejection of, 35
Aristotle, 12, 18, 21, 33, 54, 86
Athenagoras of Athens, 111–12, 174
attorneys, 368, 369–74
Augustine of Hippo
    The City of God, 115–16
    Contra Faustum, 103–4
    on death penalty, 300
    on deterrence, 174, 313
    as Doctor of the Church, 119
    on power of public authorities, 108,
        115–16

Augustine of Hippo (*continued*)
  on punishment, 103–4, 306
  On the Sermon on the Mount, 115

Baldus, David, 362, 363, 364–65
Baltimore Catechism, 280, 281
Baston, Johnnie Roy, 251n127, 275
Beccaria, Cesare, 76–77
Becker, Gary S., 319–20
Bedau, Hugo, 348–49, 351
Bell, Edward Nathaniel, 243n65
Bellarmine, Robert, 51n64, 119, 120–21
Benedict XVI (pope). *See also*
    Ratzinger, Joseph
  on death penalty, 182–83, 210
  on interpretation of magisterial
      statements, 169
  on punishment, 182
Bentham, Jeremy, 79, 206
Berkley, William Josef, 250n120
Bernardin, Joseph, 285–86, 286n11,
    303n39, 367n191
Berns, Walter, 59, 71, 307
Bertone, Tarcisio, 139–40, 144–45
"best bet" argument, 72
Beuke, Michael Francis, 274
bias. *See* racial discrimination;
    socioeconomic discrimination
Bible. *See* Scripture
Biden, Joseph R., III, 235–36
Bieghler, Marvin, 247n100
Billuart, Charles-Rene, 121
bishops. *See* United States Conference
    of Catholic Bishops
BJS. *See* Bureau of Justice Statistics
Blanton, Reginald Winthrop, 245n85
Blecker, Robert, 323
Boltz, John Albert, 242n53
Bonaventure (saint), 119
Bowles, Carl Cletus, 329
Boyd, Ronald Keith, 247n94
Boyle, Joseph, 81, 83, 84
Bradford, Gayland Charles, 256,
    256n157
Braun, Gregg Francis, 249n114

Brawner, Jan, 235, 235n16, 271
Breyer, Stephen, 353n157
Brooks, Charlie, Jr., 266
Brown, David Jay, 241n50
Brown Simpson, Nicole, 342
Bruce, Kenneth Eugene, 241n49
Brugger, E. Christian
  on abolition of death penalty, 206
  on continuation of traditional
      doctrine by Benedict XVI, 183
  on death penalty, 101, 108–11,
      112–13, 116
  on infallibility, 136–44
  on repentance of offenders, 200
  on reversal of traditional doctrine by
      John Paul II, 163, 164–72
  on statements by Francis, 195
  on Waldensian position of Innocent
      III, 125
brutalization effect, 318
Bryson, William Clifford, 245n80
Budziszewski, J., 99
Bugatti, Giovanni Battista, 9–10, 128
Bundy, Ted, 191, 217, 233
Bureau of Justice Statistics (BJS)
  on felony sentencing, 325n97
  on murder of inmates, 330,
      330–31n111
  recidivism studies by, 328–29,
      329–30n108
Bush, George W., 258–59, 265
Byram, Jason Scott, 247n98

Cain and Abel, 187, 295, 297–98
Cajetan, Thomas, 121, 171
Caldwell, Jeffrey Henry, 242n59
California District Attorneys Association
    (CDAA), 343–44, 344n135
Callan, Charles J., 41–42
Campbell, Ward A., 344n135
Canisius, Peter, 119, 120
Cano, Melchior, 121, 152–53
Cantu, Peter Anthony, 244n76
capital punishment. *See* death penalty
Carter, Clarence, 275

case studies, 215–27
 Adams, 220–21, 254n136, 270–71
 Cook, 224, 271
 Gore, 213, 215–17, 215n2, 233,
  237–38, 270, 306–7
 Harris, 224–25, 368–69
 Hearn, 223, 238n26
 Hernandez, 226–27, 273
 Jackson, 222–23
 Lopez, 223, 235, 235n13, 236, 237,
  271
 Mitchell, 220, 220n6, 240n39
 Moeller, 226, 238n30, 253
 Robert, 225–26, 253, 253n135
 Selsor, 221–22, 237, 237n22, 271
 Stemple, 219–20, 233, 239n33
 Stokley, 227, 273, 337
 Turner, 218
 Waterhouse, 218–19, 233
 Welch, 217–18, 237, 237n21, 238n25
Cassell, Paul, 351, 353, 355, 370, 372
Casti Connubii (Pius XI), 19, 128, 170
The Catechism Explained (Spirago), 171
Catechism of Christian Doctrine, 128
Catechism of the Catholic Church
 on authority of Scripture, 98
 compendium of, 182–83, 188–89,
  188n169
 on death penalty, 158–59, 161–64,
  167–69, 176
 on infliction of punishment by public
  authorities, 253, 305
 interpretations of, 164, 177, 180–81
 on just-war doctrine, 151, 155,
  281–82
 on murder, 266
 on prudential judgments, 380–81
 on punishment, 158–59, 161, 178,
  233, 312, 377
 on retribution, 48, 302
Catechism of the Council of Trent. See
 Roman Catechism
categorical imperatives, 29
Catholic Church. See also Catechism
 of the Catholic Church; Fathers and

Doctors of the Church; papal
 teachings; Scripture; United States
 Conference of Catholic Bishops
 on authority of Scripture, 97–98
 credibility of, 207–11
 on deterrence, 312–13, 331–32
 on economic affairs, 151–52
 historical attitudes toward death
  penalty, 11–12
 just-war doctrine of, 150–51, 155,
  281–82
 natural law in moral theology of,
  17–20
 rejection of NNLT, 196
Catholic Encyclopedia, 125–26
CDAA (California District Attorneys
 Association), 343–44, 344n135
Census Bureau, U.S., 358n166
Centesimus Annus (John Paul II), 151–52
Challoner, Richard, 104, 105
Chamberlain, Karl Eugene, 245n86
Chaput, Charles, 381
children
 murder of, 232
 obligations of parents to, 33
 as offenders, 185
 vaccination of, 77
Christ. See Jesus Christ
"The Church and the Death Penalty"
 (Pontifical Commission for Justice
 and Peace), 134, 301n38
Cicero, 41n43
The City of God (Augustine), 115–16
Clagett, Michael David, 255n144
Clark, Ramsey, 46
Clayton, James Edward, 248n105
Clayton, Robert William, 249, 249n115
Cleary, Norman Richard, 256n154
Clement of Alexandria, 113–14, 174
Code of Canon Law, 14–15
Coleman, Roger, 352–53
collective anger, 178
Colwell, Lawrence, Jr., 243n70
Commentariorum in Isaiam Prophetam
 (Jerome), 116

Commentary on Jeremiah (Jerome), 116

commonsense evidence, for deterrent
effects of death penalty, 71–72, 198,
379

*Compendium of the Catechism of the
Catholic Church*, 182–83, 188–89,
188n169

compensation. *See* restitution

Congregation for the Doctrine of the
Faith, 11, 139, 141, 142, 144

Conner, Kevin Aaron, 255n149

consequentialism, 79–80, 200, 335

Constantine, 114

Contra Faustum (Augustine), 103–4

contraception, 195

contractarian theories, 35–36, 200

Cook, Daniel Wayne, 224, 271

correction. *See* rehabilitation

corruption, 69, 175, 185–86

cosmic justice, 92, 93

Coulson, Robert Otis, 243, 243n62

Councils. *See also* First Vatican Council;
Second Vatican Council

Trent, 117, 125

craniotomy, 83, 84, 86

Crawford, Eddie Albert, 241n51

Crawford, Hilton Lewis, 255n147

crime, defined, 39. *See also* offenders;
punishment; *specific crimes*

Crime in the United States (FBI), 231n10,
358n161

criminal justice system. *See also*
offenders; punishment

appeals process in, 72, 346–47, 373–74

demands of, 203

errors in, 339–46, 342–43nn128–29,
345t

life imprisonment and, 188

objectives of, 283

public defenders in, 370–73

racial discrimination in. *See* racial
discrimination

reintegration and, 192

responsibilities of public authorities
in, 234

selectivity of, 187, 189

socioeconomic discrimination in, 14,
356–57, 367–74

criminals. *See* offenders

Criminology (journal), 317–18, 322–23

Cronin, Michael, 29, 30–31, 32

Crucifixion, 107, 299

A Culture of Life and the Penalty of Death
(USCCB), 185, 292, 295, 314

culture of life rhetoric, 15, 201–2, 283,
292

cycle of violence, 65, 303

Cyprian of Carthage, 114, 174

Cyril of Jerusalem, 297, 298

Dahmer, Jeffrey, 75, 75n102, 77, 233,
327–28

Darrow, Clarence, 369

David (king of Israel), 103, 126

de Lugo, Juan, 121

Dead Man Walking (Prejean), 260

death penalty. *See also* abolition of
death penalty; case studies; criminal
justice system; deterrence; objections
to death penalty; offenders; papal
teachings; punishment

arguments in favor of, 197–200

Catechism of the Catholic Church on,
158–59, 161–64, 167–69, 176

consequentialist and proportionalist
theories on, 79–80

deterrence and, 13–14, 57, 70–73,
174, 180–81, 197–99

families of victims on, 237–43,
249–52

Fathers and Doctors of the Church
on, 111–22, 174, 196, 377

historical attitudes of Catholic
Church toward, 11

individualized determination of
sentencing, 227–30

justice and, 237–43, 249–52

Kant on, 64, 76, 78–79, 81, 86, 93

as leverage in plea negotiations,
323–24, 324n94, 326, 332

methods of execution, 9, 188, 191,
240, 248
NNLT on, 85, 87–95
in Papal States, 9–10, 127–28, 295,
300, 377, 380
proportionality principle and, 52–56,
159
prudential judgments of, 11, 13, 15,
196–97
public authorities on, 234–36
public support for, 383, 383n2
race and. *See* racial discrimination
reassurance of just society through,
234
rehabilitation and, 73–75, 199–200
repentance of offenders and, 74,
199–200, 257–68, 277, 335–38
retribution and, 12–13, 52–56, 88,
171, 174, 197
Roman Catechism on, 103, 126–27,
174, 197, 266, 300, 313, 377
in Scripture. *See* Scripture
social functions of, 57–60, 68–69, 71,
77, 197–98, 333, 355, 381–82
socioeconomic discrimination and,
14, 356–57, 367–74
Thomas Aquinas on, 57–58, 64–65,
108, 108n16
urban-rural differences in, 361
Death Penalty Information Center
(DPIC)
criticisms of, 343–44
on error rates for death sentences,
344–46, 345, 348n140
"Innocence List" from, 341–42, 344,
344n135
mischaracterizations of, 341n127
objectives of, 340
on race of victims, 360
defense attorneys, 324n94, 367, 369–74
Dei Verbum (Second Vatican Council),
98, 166
DeLuna, Carlos, 353–54
desires, correlation with nature's
intentions, 24–25

deterrence, 312–35
"best bet" argument for, 72
Catholic Church on, 312–13, 331–32
consequentialism on, 80
crime rates and, 320–21
criticisms of argument for, 314,
318–19
Dahmer and, 327–28
death penalty and, 13–14, 57, 70–73,
174, 180–81, 197–99
evidence for, 71–72, 198, 314–20,
322–23, 332–34, 379–80
of murder, 315–27, 318n80, 334–35
as purpose of punishment, 46, 47–48,
57, 159, 376
recidivism rates and, 328–30,
329–30n108
secondary deterrent effect, 324, 326,
332, 382
sentencing and, 323–26, 324n94, 332
USCCB on, 313–15, 320, 332, 334
Dictionary of Moral Theology (Roberti &
Palazini), 42–43
Diderot, Denis, 206
dignity of persons. *See* human dignity
Dinkins, Richard Eugene, 251n128
direct abortion, 83, 86
direct appeals, 346
discrimination. *See* racial discrimination;
socioeconomic discrimination
Diuturnum (Leo XIII), 51
divine faith, 122, 138, 139, 145
The Divine Institutes (Lactantius), 112,
113
divine law, 30, 49, 134
Divino Afflante Spiritu (Pius XII), 98
Doctors of the Church. *See* Fathers and
Doctors of the Church
*Donum Veritatis, On the Ecclesial Vocation
of the Theologian* (Congregation for
the Doctrine of the Faith), 142–49,
181, 186
Dostoyevsky, Fyodor, 187, 191
double effect principle, 84, 84n114,
164, 165

Douglass, John C., 324n94, 372
DPIC. *See* Death Penalty Information
　Center
Dulles, Avery
　on abolition of death penalty,
　　206–7
　on authority of church teachings,
　　121–22
　on continuity of church teachings,
　　208
　on Doctors of the Church, 119
　on interpretations of John Paul II's
　　teachings, 163, 167
　on magisterial statements, 144–45,
　　146, 190
　on mercy, 203
　on Papal State executions, 127
　on prudential judgments, 149–50,
　　153, 176, 178
　on reversals of traditional doctrine,
　　166, 173
Duns Scotus, John, 121

economic affairs, church teachings on,
　151–52
Economic Inquiry (journal), 317
Economic Justice for All (USCCB), 288
Ehrhard, Susan, 324n94
Ehrlich, Isaac, 320
Elder, Robert K. (*Last Words of the
　Executed*), 264
Enlightenment, 206
Ephraem of Syria, 115, 119, 174
equality of justice, restoration through
　punishment, 39, 46, 48, 375, 376
Essay on the Development of Doctrine
　(Newman), 175
essentialist metaphysics, 21
eternal law, 29–30, 31, 32, 83
Eusebius, 114, 174
euthanasia
　culture of life rhetoric and, 201–2
　disrespect for innocent life in, 178
　doctrinal prohibition of, 281, 282
　doctrine on illicitness of, 140, 145

moral weight of, 155–56, 157n121,
　177
Evangelium Vitae (John Paul II)
　on death penalty, 159–60, 161n126,
　　162–63, 189
　on human life, 164
　interpretations of, 169, 170, 176, 181
　on punishment, 159–60, 167, 169,
　　178, 200
　on rehabilitation, 168
evil, correlation between pain and, 38,
　44–45
excommunication, 125
executions. *See* death penalty
Exsurge Domine (Leo X), 125
Extraordinary Jubilee of Mercy, 192

fact-value dichotomy, 21–22, 81, 86
Fagothey, Austin, 34
faith, divine, 122, 138, 139, 145
families of victims, 236–52
　closure and healing for, 239–40
　on death penalty, 237–43, 249–52
　on duty to witness executions,
　　246–47
　on forgiveness, 254–56
　on justice, 236–44, 246–47, 249–52,
　　306, 378
　on method of execution, 240, 248–49
　on time between sentencing and
　　execution, 243–45
Fathers and Doctors of the Church. *See
　also specific individuals*
　on absolution of sin through penalty
　　of death, 114
　authority of, 117–18, 119–20, 121–22
　on death penalty, 111–22, 174, 196,
　　377
　on mercy, 114, 115
　rationale of teachings from, 12
Federal Bureau of Investigation (FBI),
　231n10, 232, 357–58, 360, 366
Feinstein, Diane, 322
Fifth World Congress against the Death
　Penalty, 183

finality principle, 19
Finnis, John, 81, 83, 84, 87–88, 135–36
Fiorenza, Joseph A., 292n23
First Vatican Council
   on authority of Scripture, 97–98,
      117, 139
   on Holy Spirit, 165, 191–92
   on interpretation of Scripture, 310
   on natural law, 19
Fluke, Ronald Dunaway, 241n45,
   248n107
Foot, Philippa, 23, 24, 33, 36–37
Ford, John, 170, 181–82
Ford, Prenell, 254n137
forgiveness. *See also* mercy; repentance
      of offenders
   families of victims on, 254–56
   Jesus Christ on, 301
   punishment and, 104, 203, 253–56,
      301–2
   vengeance and, 213–14
Forrester, J. Owen, 363–64, 365
Foster, Cleve, 238, 238n29, 239n37,
   240, 272
Fowler, Mark Andrew, 241n44
Francis (pope)
   on abolition of death penalty,
      183–84, 192–93
   alteration of death penalty doctrine,
      189–92, 195
   on corruption, 185–86
   criticism of statements by, 194–95
   on legitimacy of death penalty,
      184–85, 186–89
   on life imprisonment, 184–85, 188,
      208
   prudential judgments of, 186, 195–96
free will, 89–90, 243, 269
Frye, Robert Wayne, 242n61
Furey, Francis, 209, 286, 289n16
Furman v. Georgia (1972), 266n189, 347,
   348, 354, 357, 362

Gacy, John Wayne, 205, 217, 233
Gallup, 383

Garcia, Frank Martinez, 276
Garza, Juan Raul, 303, 303n45
Gelernter, David, 60, 71, 333
genocide, 53, 282
George, Robert P., 81, 135–36
Getsy, Jason, 242n58
Gibbs, David Earl, 256n153
Gill, Clarence Edward, 244n73
Gilreat, Fred Marion, Jr., 250n123
Glock, Robert Dewey, II, 254n138
Glossip v. Gross (2015), 353n157,
   366n187
God
   creative will of, 32
   Five Ways to demonstrate existence
      of, 31
   natural law and, 18
   in natural Law theory, 82–83
   as ultimate good, 26–27
Goins, Christopher Cornelius,
   251n130
Goldberg, Steven, 70, 71–72, 198
Goldman, Ronald, 342
goodness. *See also* metaphysics of good
   correlation between pleasure and, 38,
      44–45
   natural, 24
   of punishment, 37–43
Gore, David Alan, 213, 215–17, 215n2,
   233, 237–38, 270, 306–7
The Gospel of Life and Capital Punishment
   (California Catholic Conference of
   Bishops), 309–10
Gospels
   John
      8, 300, 304
      8:1–11, 106, 295, 311
      8:7, 299
      8:32, 262
      18 (xviii), 105
   Luke
      23:34, 213, 299, 300
      23:41, 107, 173–74, 377
      23:43, 299
   Mark 12:14–17, 109

Gospels (*continued*)
    Matthew
        4:17, 337
        5:17, 103
        5:38, 105
        5:38–41, 103
        5:38–42, 299
        5:42, 100–101
        5:43–45, 299
        6:12, 299
        18:21–35, 299
government. *See* public authorities
Gravissimas inter (Pius IX), 119
Gregory, Wilton, 155
Gregory of Nazianzus, 114–15, 174
Gregory XVI (pope), 9n1
Grisez, Germain
    on craniotomy, 83
    on death penalty, 135–36, 284
    NNLT and, 81, 172
    opposition to proportionalism, 84
    on prudential judgment, 152, 154
    on statements by Francis, 195,
        195n177
    on Waldensian heresy, 124

habeas corpus appeal, 346, 373
Hall, Michael Wayne, 275
Hampton, James Henry, 248n104
Handbook of Moral Theology (Prümmer),
    41
happiness, role of pleasure in, 37–38
Harjo, Jerald Wayne, 242, 242n60,
    249n116
Harris, Robert Wayne, 224–25, 368–69
Hathaway, Faith, 261, 262, 262n176, 263
Hauptmann, Bruno, 349
Hawkins, Aubrey, 235
Haydock, George, 104–5
healing, promotion through justice,
    239–40
Hearn, Yokamon Laneal, 223, 238n26
Henderson, Jerry Paul, 249n119
heresy, 122, 123–24, 125, 139–40
hermeneutic of continuity, 169, 175, 211

Hernandez, Jesse Joe, 270
Hernandez, Ramon Torres, 226–27,
    273
High, Jose Martinez, 255n146
Hilary of Poitiers, 115
Hobbes, Thomas, 35–36, 50, 51, 86, 93
Hoffman, Morris B., 371, 373
Holy Spirit, 97, 98, 165, 191–92
homicide. *See* murder
Homilies on Leviticus (Origen), 114
Homilies on the Statues (John
    Chrysostom), 114
Hooper, Michael Edward, 239n36,
    271–72
Horne, Tom, 234–35, 236
Hubbard, James Barney, 254n141
human dignity
    acquired dignity, 64
    death penalty as affront to, 63–65,
        187, 294
    NNLT on, 89–90
    USCCB on, 291
human law, 30
Human Life in Our Day (National
    Conference of Catholic Bishops of
    America), 148
Humanae Vitae (Paul VI), 19–20
Humani Generis (Pius XII), 19, 141
Hume, David, 21, 81, 86, 206
Hutcherson, Larry Eugene, 249n113
hypothetical imperatives, 29

Immortale Dei (Leo XIII), 51
immunizations, 77
incapacitation, as purpose of
    punishment, 46, 159, 327–28, 332,
        355, 376, 379, 382
indirect abortion, 84, 86
individualized determination of
    sentencing, 227–30
informal evidence, for deterrent effects
    of death penalty, 71–72, 198
"Innocence List" (DPIC), 341–42, 344,
    344n135
Innocent I (pope), 123, 126, 174, 377

Innocent III (pope), 123–25, 126, 137, 300, 312, 377, 380
International Association of Penal Law, 183
International Commission against the Death Penalty, 186
Iraq war, 155–56

Jackson, Henry "Curtis", 222–23
Jackson, Larry Kenneth, 254n140
Jerome (saint), 116, 119, 174, 181
Jesus Christ
 Crucifixion of, 107, 299
 on mercy and forgiveness, 104, 301
 on punishment, 105–6, 299–300, 304, 311
 Sermon on the Mount by, 103–5, 106, 376
John Chrysostom, 106n9, 114, 174, 297, 298, 307
John Paul II (pope). *See also Evangelium Vitae*
 on abolition of death penalty, 10, 123, 181, 184
 appeal in Tucker case, 258
 on assent required of magisterial statements, 144
 Centesimus Annus, 151–52
 on conditions for forgiveness, 203
 on consequentialism and proportionalism, 80
 development of doctrine on death penalty, 163, 168, 172–75, 179–81
 on economics, 151–52
 on God as supreme good, 83
 on infliction of death penalty by public authorities, 141
 on Iraq war, 155
 on legitimacy of death penalty, 134, 136, 158–63
 magisterial statements of, 169–70
 on natural law, 20, 21
 prudential judgments on death penalty, 163–64, 176–82, 378
 on punishment, 159–61, 297–98

 reversal of doctrine on death penalty, 11, 13, 163, 164–72
 Veritatis Splendor, 20, 80, 83
Johnson, Samuel, 74, 199–200, 337
Johnson, Shannon, 235–36, 236n17
Jones, Dorsie Leslie, Jr., 245n87
Jones, William Robert, Jr., 249n118
Journal of Applied Economics, 316
Journal of Law and Economics, 316
Journal of Legal Studies, 316
judicial error, 77–78, 187, 189
just deserts principle
 death penalty as outlet for, 199, 205, 382
 families of victims and, 238
 in Mosaic Law, 104
 natural law theory on, 45
 offenders and, 267
 Thomas Aquinas on, 252
justice. *See also* criminal justice system; punishment
 cosmic, 92, 93, 94
 death penalty and, 237–43, 249–52
 equality of, 39, 46, 48, 375, 376
 families of victims on, 236–44, 246–47, 249–52, 306, 378
 offenders on, 252–53
 order of, 87–88, 178, 302, 305–6, 307
 political conceptions of, 91, 92, 94
 promotion of healing through, 239–40
 public authorities on, 234–36
 retributive. *See* retribution
 transcendental order of, 178
 vigilante, 68, 199, 205
just-war doctrine, 150–51, 155, 280–82

Kaczor, Christopher, 163, 179–80, 181, 199
Kant, Immanuel, 63, 64, 76, 78–79, 81, 86, 93, 196
Keckler, Charles, 324, 326, 327–28, 333–34
Keeler, William, 291–92
Kelly, Gerald, 170, 181–82

Kemp, Thomas, 236, 236n19
King, Amos Lee, Jr., 247n97
Koons, Robert, 84
Kutzner, Richard William, 248n108
Kuziemko, Ilyana, 324n94

Lactantius, 112, 113, 174
Lafevers, Loyd Winford, 251n132
Lamont, John, 68–69
Last Judgment, 131–32
Last Words of the Executed (Elder), 264
Lateran Treaty of 1929, 295
Laurence, Patrick, 178
lawyers, 368, 369–74
Leavitt, Richard, 235, 235n14
legal representation, 368, 369–74
Leo X (pope), 125, 126, 174, 377
Leo XII (pope), 9n1
Leo XIII (pope), 19, 51–52, 98, 126, 128
Leopold, Nathan, 369
lethal injection, 180, 213, 217, 240, 248, 266, 307
Levada, William J., 157, 157n121, 287–88, 379
Lewis, C. S., 47–48, 80, 204
Lewis, Teresa Wilson Bean, 274–75
lex talionis principle, 54, 102, 103, 104, 105, 174, 295–96, 376
Libertas Praestantissimum (Leo XIII), 19
Licinius, 114
life
  culture of life rhetoric, 15, 201–2, 283, 292
  moral sensitivity regarding value of, 188
  NNLT on, 89–90
  respect for, 65
  right to, 61–63, 62n80, 133, 192
life imprisonment, 66, 72, 184–85, 188, 191, 208, 301, 379
Liguori, Alphonsus, 119, 120
Lindbergh, Charles, 349
Lisska, Anthony, 24

Locke, John, 50, 51, 86, 93
Loeb, Richard, 369
Long, Steven, 64, 163, 169, 178
Lopez, Samuel Villegas, 223, 235, 235n13, 236, 237, 271
Lumen Gentium (Second Vatican Council), 136–37, 138, 141
Lundgren, Jeffrey Don, 242n54, 252n133
Luther, Martin, 125, 169
Lyons, Robbie James, 248, 248n110

magisterial statements, 144–57
  assent required of, 144, 147
  deficiencies of, 149, 186
  definitive declarations of nonrevealed truths (category 2), 145, 149
  disagreements regarding, 146–49
  dogmatic (category 1), 145, 149
  interpretation of, 169–70
  nondefinitive but obligatory teachings (category 3), 145–49
  prudential (category 4), 145, 149–57.
    See also prudential judgments
Mahony, Roger, 291–92
Manicheism, 67
Manual of Moral Theology (Slater), 171
Markman, Stephen, 349–50, 351, 355
Marquette, Richard, 329
Marquis, Joshua, 329, 352, 353, 370–71
marriage
  natural right to, 34
  NNLT on, 91n128
  sexual desire and, 68, 205
Martinez, Johnny Joe, 250n124
mass murder, 53, 54, 178
Massie, Robert, 329
Mathis, Milton Wuzael, 276
May, William, 81, 142–43, 147–48
Mays, Rex Warren, 246n88, 251n131
McCleskey, Warren, 362, 363, 364
McDonald, John F., 135
McDuff, Kenneth, 329
McGinnis, Glen Charles, 244n79

McHugh, John A., 41–42
McInerny, Ralph, 66–67
McNair, Willie, 246n91, 256, 256n156
McVeigh, Timothy, 217, 292, 372–73
McWee, Jerry Bridwell, 243n64
mechanistic view of nature, 21, 22, 25
Medlock, Floyd Allen, 250n122
Megivern, James, 99–100, 101, 112–13
Menninger, Karl, 46
mercy. *See also* forgiveness
    Extraordinary Jubilee of Mercy, 192
    Fathers and Doctors of the Church
        on, 114, 115
    Jesus Christ on, 104
    in punishment, 54, 92, 107, 156, 203
metaphysics of good, 20–27
    Aristotelian-Thomistic, 22, 27–28,
        29, 35, 37, 43, 45, 81, 84
    fact-value dichotomy in, 21–22, 81,
        86
    God as ultimate good, 26–27
    goods inherent in man, 25–27
    natural goodness, 24
    norms and, 23–24
    philosophical foundations of, 21
Miller, J. Michael, 154
Mill, John Stuart, 79
Mitchell, William Gerald, 220, 220n6,
    240n39
Moeller, Donald Eugene, 226, 238n30,
    253
Montour, Edward, 330
Moorman, Robert, 234–35, 235n12,
    268–69, 273
moral hazards, 54–55
moral obligation, 27–32
    creative will of God and, 32
    hypothetical and categorical forces
        of, 29
    natural law and, 27–28, 29–31, 34
    reason and, 28, 32
Moral Theology (McHugh & Callan), 42
Morris, Kenneth Wayne, 256n155
Morrow, Robert Brice, 252n134

Mosaic Law
    adultery under, 106n10
    death penalty under, 102–3, 174, 290
    as divine law, 30
    just deserts principle in, 104
    on murder, 293, 296, 338, 376
    proportionality principle in, 104
Moses (prophet), 101–2, 116, 120, 313
Moss, Tom, 235
Müller, Gerhard, 194, 194n173, 195
murder. *See also* case studies
    Catholic Church on, 126–27, 266
    of children, 232
    communal responses to, 60
    compensation for, 336, 337–38
    death penalty for, 64
    deterrence of, 315–27, 318n80,
        334–35
    genocide, 53, 282
    harm inflicted by, 55
    incidence of, 230–32, 231n10
    by inmates in prisons, 330–31,
        330–31n111
    limitations on quantification of,
        365–66, 366n187
    mass murder, 53, 54, 178
    Mosaic Law on, 293, 296, 338, 376
    Papal State executions for, 9
    racial differences in convictions for,
        357–60, 358–59t, 367
    rape and, 231, 232, 360, 361
    recidivism rates, 328–30, 329–30n108
    robbery and, 232
    sentencing for, 323–26, 325nn96–97,
        332
    in Sermon on the Mount, 105

National Conference of Catholic
    Bishops. *See* United States
    Conference of Catholic Bishops
National Council of Synagogues, 314,
    356–57
National Research Council, 318–19
natural goodness, 24

natural law, 17–95. *See also* New
   Natural Law theory; traditional
   natural law theory
   in Catholic moral theology, 17–20
   death penalty and. *See* death penalty
   defined, 17
   moral obligation and, 27–28, 29–31,
      34
   natural rights and, 32–35, 37, 61–62
   punishment and. *See* punishment
   rival ethical theories, 78–95
natural rights, 32–37
   contractarian theories of, 35–36
   death penalty objections and, 61–63,
      62n80
   foundations of, 35, 62
   limitations of, 34–35, 62
   natural law and, 32–35, 37, 61–62
   obligations and, 32–34
naturalistic fallacy, 21, 24
Neuhaus, Richard John, 176, 208–9
New Natural Law theory (NNLT),
   80–95
   agent-centeredness of, 82
   on basic goods, 82, 87
   challenges posed by, 80–81
   coherency of arguments by, 88–94
   comparison with traditional natural
      law theory, 81–83, 84–85
   compatibility and reconciliation with
      Catholic orthodoxy, 94–95, 136
   criticisms of, 85–87
   on death penalty, 85, 87–95
   irresponsibility of, 172
   moral evaluation of actions in, 83–84
   origins and development of, 81
   practical reason in, 81
   on punishment, 84–85, 90–91n128,
      91–94
   rejection by Catholic Church, 196
   on statements by Francis, 194–95
New Testament. *See also* Gospels
   Acts 23 (xxiii), 105
   Acts 25:11, 107, 174
   authority of, 97

   on death penalty, 103–11, 376–77
   I Peter 2:13–14, 109
   Romans
      1:19–20, 18
      2:14–15, 18
      12:19, 107n11
      12 and 13, 253–54
      13:1–2, 51
      13:1–4, 107–8
      13:1–7, 309–10
      13:4, 254, 300
   Sermon on the Mount, 103–5, 376
   USCCB references to, 298–302
Newman, John Henry, 175
Nicholas I (pope), 123
Nichols, Joseph Bennard, 245n83,
   246n90
Nixon, John B., 246n89
NNLT. *See* New Natural Law theory
Noel, Riley Dobi, 243n63
norms, 23–24, 39
Nuncio, Paul Selso, 245n81

objections to death penalty, 61–78
   affront to human dignity, 63–65, 187,
      294
   arbitrary applications, 189, 201
   criticisms of, 200–3
   culture of life rhetoric and, 201–2,
      283, 292
   erosion of respect for human life, 65
   by families of victims, 250–51
   ineffectiveness of deterrence, 70–73
   lack of authority to take life, 75–77
   motivation of vengeance, 66–70
   race and. *See* racial discrimination
   removal of reform possibilities, 73–75
   by USCCB, 283, 286, 379
   violation of right to life, 61–63,
      62n80
   wrongful executions, 77–78, 189,
      339–40, 348–54
O'Brien, Matthew, 84
O'Brien, T. C., 41n43
Ochoa, George, 236, 236n20

Oderberg, David, 56, 81–82
offenders. *See also* case studies; criminal
   justice system; punishment;
   repentance of offenders; *specific crimes*
   children as, 185
   danger posed by, 12, 13, 57–58
   on justice, 252–53
   legal representation for, 368, 369–74
   life imprisonment for, 66, 72, 184–85,
      188, 191, 208, 301, 379
   overindulgent will of, 39, 40, 375
   poverty of, 368–69
   race of, 357–60, 358–59t, 366, 367
   rational calculation of punishment
      by, 70–71
   recidivism rates for, 328–30,
      329–30n108
Ogan, Craig Neil, Jr., 243n68
Oken, Steven Howard, 248, 248n112
Old Testament. *See also* Mosaic Law
   authority of, 97
   on death penalty, 99–103, 376
   Deuteronomy
      13:6–10, 102
      19:11–13, 102, 173–74, 376
      19:18–21, 102
      19:19–21, 296
      19:20, 174
      19:21, 295
      22:22, 102–3
   Exodus
      21, 174
      21:12–14, 102,
      21:14, 296
      21:15, 103
      21:16, 103
      21:22–25, 102
      21:23–25, 295, 296, 376
      22:19, 103
   Genesis
      1:26, 189
      1:26–27, 291, 295
      2:7, 292, 295
      2:21–23, 292, 295
      4:15, 295, 297

9:1, 5–6, 99
9:4, 100
9:5–6, 101
9:6, 9, 10, 63, 101, 102, 103, 120,
   173–74, 189, 208, 214, 240,
   290, 293, 295, 376, 380, 384
9:7, 100
Jeremiah 29:7, 109
Leviticus
   20:10, 103
   20:11–12, 103
   20:13, 103
   20:15–16, 103
   24, 174
   24:17, 102, 295
   24:19–20, 102, 296
Numbers
   35:31, 338
   35:33, 102, 173–74
   proportionality principle in, 102,
      295–96
Proverbs
   8:15–16, 109
   24:21–22, 109
Psalms
   54:24, 120
   101:8, 103
Ten Commandments, 30
USCCB references to, 290–98
Wisdom 6:1–4, 109
On Crimes and Punishments (Beccaria),
   76
On the Sermon on the Mount (Augustine),
   115
Optatus (saint), 116, 174
order of justice, 87–88, 178, 302, 305–6,
   307
Origen, 107, 114, 174
Original Sin doctrine, 145, 150

pacifism, 69, 104, 206
Page, Elijah, 242, 242n56
pain, natural correlation between evil
   and, 38, 44–45
Palazzini, Pietro, 42

Palmer, Donald L., Jr., 238nn27–28,
     252–53, 272
Papal States, 9–10, 9n1, 127–28, 295,
     300, 377, 380
papal teachings, 122–96. *See also specific
     popes by name*
  on authority of church teachings,
     140–41
  on divine faith, 138, 139
  on heresy, 122, 123–24, 125, 139–40
  infallibility and, 136–44
  on legitimacy of death penalty,
     123–25, 132–35, 158–63, 377
  magisterial statements. *See* magisterial
     statements
  on punishment, 128–33, 158–61
  rationale of, 12
  on retribution, 128–29, 130–32, 308
Pardo, Manuel, 240, 240n42
parents, obligations of children to, 33
Pastoralis Officii (Leo XIII), 128
Patrick, Jessie Joe, 249n117
Paul (saint)
  on death penalty, 107, 179, 203, 300,
     377
  on natural law, 18
  on public authorities as instrument of
     divine authority, 51, 76
  on punishment, 107n11, 108, 109,
     309
  on taxation, 108, 109, 110
Paul VI (pope), 19–20, 134
Perkins, Sammy Crystal, 255n142
Pew Research Center, 383n2
Pius V (pope), 125, 174, 377
Pius VI (pope), 9n1
Pius VII (pope), 9n1
Pius VIII (pope), 9n1
Pius IX (pope)
  on authority of church teachings,
     140–41
  Bugatti and, 9n1
  on death penalty, 10, 11, 128
  on dissent from church teachings, 122
  on divine faith, 138, 139

  Gravissimas inter, 119
  Tuas Libenter, 122, 138, 140–41
Pius X (pope), 126, 128
Pius XI (pope)
  Casti Connubii, 19, 128, 170
  on death penalty, 128
  on natural law, 19
  on sterilization, 170
Pius XII (pope)
  "Allocution to Lenten Preachers",
     133
  on authority of church teachings,
     141
  on death penalty, 132–33, 174, 377
  Divino Afflante Spiritu, 98
  Humani Generis, 19, 141
  importance of teachings of, 133–34
  on natural law, 19
  on pardons, 203
  on punishment, 128–33, 174–75, 190
  on retribution, 128–29, 130–32, 308
  on right to live, 63, 133
  on sterilization, 170
Plato, 12, 18
A Plea for the Christians (Athenagoras of
     Athens), 112
pleasure, natural correlation between
     goodness and, 38, 44–45
Pojman, Louis, 65, 68, 71, 198, 205
Pontifical Biblical Commission,
     149n111
Pontifical Commission for Justice and
     Peace, 134
popes. *See* papal teachings; *specific popes
     by name*
Posner, Richard, 319–20
post-conviction appeals, 346, 373
poverty, 154, 368–69. *See also*
     socioeconomic discrimination
Powell, Eddie Duvall, III, 244n78, 256,
     256n150
practical reason, 81
"A Prayer to End the Use of the Death
     Penalty" (Saint Anthony Catholic
     Church), 279

Prejean, Helen, 200, 260–65, 267, 267n191
"Profession of Faith" (Congregation for the Doctrine of the Faith), 139, 141, 144
proper accidents, 38
proportionalism, 80, 84, 200
proportionality principle
  death penalty and, 52–56, 159
  lex talionis and, 102, 103, 104, 174, 295–96, 376
  natural law and, 43–46
  in Old Testament, 102, 295–96
  punishment and, 43–46, 52–56, 53n65, 376
  qualitative and quantitative nature of, 44–45
  rape and, 52–53, 53n65, 55–56
  retribution and, 43, 44, 52–56
Providentissimus Deus (Leo XIII), 98
prudential judgments
  application of, 150–53
  Catechism of the Catholic Church on, 380–81
  categories of, 153–54, 157
  of death penalty, 11, 13, 15, 196–97
  on economic affairs, 151–52
  features of, 145, 149–50
  of Francis, 186, 195–96
  on Iraq war, 155–56
  of John Paul II, 163–64, 176–82, 378
  nonbinding advisory status of, 154–55
  USCCB on, 288
Prümmer, Dominic M., 41, 42
public authorities
  infliction of punishment by, 50–52, 58–60, 107n11, 108–9, 253, 305
  as instrument of divine authority, 50–52, 51n64, 59, 76, 77
  on justice, 234–36
  responsibilities of, 234
  toleration of vices by, 35
public defenders, 370–73

Puckett, Larry Matthew, 239, 239n35
punishment, 37–52. *See also* criminal justice system; death penalty; justice; offenders
  Catechism of the Catholic Church on, 158–59, 161, 178, 233, 312, 377
  as crime, 46
  equality of justice restored through, 39, 46, 48, 375, 376
  forgiveness and, 104, 203, 253–56, 301–2
  goodness of, 37–43
  Jesus Christ on, 105–6, 299–300, 304, 311
  life imprisonment, 66, 72, 184–85, 188, 191, 208, 301, 379
  mercy in, 54, 92, 107, 156, 203
  NNLT on, 84–85, 90–91n128, 91–94
  papal teachings on, 128–33, 158–61
  proportionality principle and, 43–46, 52–56, 53n65, 376
  by public authorities, 50–52, 58–60, 107n11, 108–9, 253, 305
  purposes of, 40, 46–48, 131, 158, 159, 161, 182, 308, 376
  responsibility for infliction of, 49–52
  USCCB on, 310–11
  vengeance and, 40–42, 41n43

racial discrimination, 355–67
  in criminal justice system, 356–57
  death penalty sentencing data and, 357–60, 358–59t, 367
  limitation of statistical models on, 363–66
  USCCB on, 14, 355–57, 360
  victims and, 360–66
Radelet, Michael, 348–49, 351
Rakoff, Jed, 342, 342–43n129, 344n135
rape
  murder and, 231, 232, 360, 361
  proportionality principle and, 52–53, 53n65, 55–56
Ratcliff, Roy, 75n102

Ratzinger, Joseph. *See also* Benedict XVI
 on application of death penalty, 9, 11, 156, 176–77, 182, 184, 196, 287
 on authority of church teachings, 139–40
 on episcopal conferences, 289–90, 379
 on magisterial statements, 144, 145, 157
 on moral weight of issues, 155–56
 on prudential judgments, 149, 150, 153, 154–55, 282, 378
 "Worthiness to Receive Holy Communion: General Principles", 9, 155–56, 177
Rawls, John, 91
reason
 Catholic teaching grounded in, 12
 moral obligation and, 28, 32
 natural law and, 17, 18, 19
 practical, 81
recidivism rates, 328–30, 329–30n108
reform. *See* rehabilitation
rehabilitation
 consequentialism on, 80
 death penalty and, 73–75, 199–200
 as purpose of punishment, 46, 47–48, 57, 159, 161, 376
repentance of offenders, 257–77
 from 2010 and 2011 executions, 274–76
 from 2012 executions, 268–74
 Brugger on, 200
 Dahmer, 75, 75n102
 death penalty and, 74, 199–200, 257–68, 277, 335–38
 Sonnier, 260, 263–65, 267, 267n191
 Thomas Aquinas on, 13, 73–74, 200, 257, 337, 378
 Tucker, 257–60, 265–66
 USCCB on, 335–38
 Willie, 260–63, 267–68

Responsibility, Rehabilitation, and Restoration: A Catholic Perspective on Crime and Criminal Justice (USCCB), 310–11, 334
restitution
 for murder, 337–338
 as purpose of punishment, 46, 54, 376
retribution
 controversy regarding, 46
 death penalty and, 12–13, 52–56, 88, 171, 174, 197
 defined, 44
 Last Judgment and, 131–32
 natural desire for, 67–68
 papal teachings on, 128–29, 130–32, 308
 primacy of, 48, 56–57
 proportionality principle and, 43, 44, 52–56
 as purpose of punishment, 46–47, 158, 376
 USCCB on, 302, 305–6, 309–12
revenge. *See* vengeance
Revilla, Daniel Juan, 243n69, 247n96
Rice, Charles, 163, 173, 177, 181
Rich, Darrell Keith, 244n75
Richardson, Miguel, 247n95
Rickaby, Joseph, 59–60, 67, 71, 205
righteous anger, 307
rights. *See* natural rights
Rivas, George, 235n15, 269
robbery murders, 232
Robedeaux, James Glenn, 248n106
Robert, Eric Donald, 225–26, 253, 253n135
Roberti, Francesco, 42
Robertson, Pat, 258, 259
Rogers, Kelly Lamont, 243n67
Roman Catechism
 authority of, 125–26
 on death penalty, 103, 126–27, 174, 300, 313, 377
 on murder, 266

Roman Catholic Church. *See* Catholic Church
Rutler, George, 208
Ryan, John, 151

Sacco, Nicola, 348–49
saints. *See specific saints by name*
Scalia, Antonin, 352, 353, 355
Scannell, Thomas B., 118, 119–20
Scheeben, Matthias Joseph, 118, 119–20
Scheidegger, Kent S., 324n94
Scholasticism, 51n64, 122
Scott, Rick, 213, 217
Scripture, 97–111. *See also* Gospels; New Testament; Old Testament
    authority of, 97–99, 117, 139
    infallibility of, 13, 289
    interpretation of, 109, 117, 118, 310
    rationale of teachings from, 12
Second Vatican Council
    on authority of Scripture, 98
    Dei Verbum, 98, 166
    on infallible teachings, 136–37, 138
    on interpretations of Scripture, 166
    Lumen Gentium, 136–37, 138, 141
    magisterial statements by, 146
secondary deterrent effect, 324, 326, 332, 382
self-defense, 128, 164–65, 167–68, 169, 174, 175, 180, 280–81
Selsor, Michael Bascum, 221–22, 237, 237n22, 271
Sermon on the Mount, 103–5, 106, 376
sex and sexuality. *See also* rape
    marriage and, 68, 205
    NNLT on, 91n128
Shamburger, Ron Scott, 254n139
Shavell, Amy, 330, 331
The Shawshank Redemption (film), 233
Shook, Toby, 235
Short, Terry Lyn, 242n57
Simpson, Nicole Brown, 342
Simpson, O.J., 342, 369
Sin, Original, 145, 150

Skylstad, William S., 265
Slater, Thomas, 171
Smith, Charles Edward, 242n55
Smith, Clay King, 255n145
Smith, Lois Nadean, 241n47
social-contract theory, 35, 58, 76–77, 206
socioeconomic discrimination, 14, 356–57, 367–74
Sonnier, Elmo Patrick, 260, 263–65, 267, 267n191
Soria, Juan Salvez, 256n152
Spadaro, Antonio, 195, 195n177
Spirago, Francis, 171
S's are F statements, 23, 23nn9–10
state habeas, 346, 373
statistical evidence, for deterrent effects of death penalty, 71, 72
Stemple, Timothy Shaun, 219–20, 233, 239n33
Stephen, James Fitzjames, 68, 70–71, 198, 205, 333
sterilization, 170
Stevens, Benny Joe, 275–76
Stokley, Richard Dale, 227, 273, 337
Stroman, Mark Anthony, 276
Suarez, Francisco, 51n64, 121
subjective culpability, 124, 125
substantive dignity, 64
Summa Contra Gentiles (Thomas Aquinas), 44
supererogatory virtue, 193
Supreme Court, U.S., 227, 266, 321, 346–47, 362, 384

teleology
    in Aristotelian-Thomistic metaphysics, 22, 37, 45
    moral obligation and, 29
    natural law and, 17, 20, 21
    natural rights and, 35, 62
    norms and, 23
Ten Commandments, 30
Tertullian, 107, 112, 113, 174

Thaxton, Sherod, 324n94

Theodosius, 114

Theologia Moralis (Alphonsus Liguori), 120

"Theological Reflections on Catholics in Political Life and the Reception of Holy Communion" (Levada), 156–57

Thomas, Clarence, 366n187

Thomas Aquinas. *See also* Aristotelian-Thomistic metaphysics
  on anger, 307
  on capacities of human beings, 24
  on death penalty, 57–58, 64–65, 108, 108n16, 120
  on deterrence, 313
  on dignity of persons, 64
  as Doctor of the Church, 119
  on equality of justice, 39, 46, 48, 375
  on eternal law, 29–30, 32, 83
  Five Ways to demonstrate existence of God, 31
  on goods inherent in man, 25–27
  on happiness and unhappiness, 37, 38
  on human law, 30
  on natural law, 12, 17, 18, 21, 27, 35
  on proportionality principle, 43–44
  on public authorities as instrument of divine authority, 50–51
  on punishment, 39–40, 44–45, 49–50, 171, 252, 306
  on rehabilitation, 73
  on repentance of offenders, 13, 73–74, 200, 257, 337, 378
  Summa Contra Gentiles, 44
  on theological arguments, 210
  on vengeance, 40, 41, 42, 308

Thompson, Michael (philosopher), 23n9

Thompson, Michael Eugene (offender), 241n48

tit for tat, 54, 67

Tollefsen, Christopher
  on death penalty, 75, 89, 94
  on good of harmony with God, 82–83
  on human dignity, 89, 90
  NNLT and, 81
  on punishment, 90–91n128, 91–94
  on rape, 55
  on statements by Francis, 194–95

Towery, Robert Charles, 269–70, 273–74

traditional natural law theory, 20–37
  comparison with NNLT, 81–83, 84–85
  on goodness of punishment, 40
  metaphysics of good in, 21–27
  moral obligation in, 27–32
  natural rights in, 32–37, 61
  overview, 20–21
  philosophical foundations of, 12–13, 21
  pleasure and pain in, 37–39
  on punishment, 45–46
  on vengeance, 41
  world-centeredness of, 81–82

transcendental order of justice, 178

Treatise of Human Nature (Hume), 81

Treatise on the Anger of God (Lactantius), 113

Treatise on Civil Government (Robert Bellarmine), 120–21

Treatise on the Soul (Tertullian), 113

Trent, Council of, 117, 125

triangles, objective standards of good and bad for, 22

Tuas Libenter (Pius IX), 122, 138, 140–41

Tucker, Karla Faye, 257–60, 265–66

Turner, Edwin Hart, 218

unhappiness, role of pain in, 37–38

United States Conference of Catholic Bishops (USCCB)
  on abolition of death penalty, 265, 282–84, 285–86, 379
  authority of, 289

A Culture of Life and the Penalty of Death, 185, 292, 295, 314
on deterrence, 313–15, 320, 332, 334
disagreement regarding death penalty, 284–86, 287–88, 378–79
Economic Justice for All, 288
on errors in criminal justice system, 339–41, 346
on human dignity, 291
on Iraq war, 155
on life imprisonment, 185, 301
on McVeigh execution, 292
misrepresentation of teachings of, 294
New Testament references used by, 298–302
objections to death penalty voiced by, 283, 286, 379
Old Testament references used by, 290–98
in political sphere, 282, 283
on prudential judgments, 288
on punishment, 310–11
on racial discrimination, 14, 355–57, 360
on repentance of offenders, 335–38
Responsibility, Rehabilitation, and Restoration: A Catholic Perspective on Crime and Criminal Justice, 310–11, 334
on retribution, 302, 305–6, 309–12
on socioeconomic discrimination, 14, 356–57, 367–68
on vengeance, 302–9
weakness of arguments to oppose death penalty, 14, 288
U.S. Census Bureau, 358n166
U.S. Supreme Court, 227, 266, 321, 346–47, 362, 384
USCCB. *See* United States Conference of Catholic Bishops
utilitarianism, 59, 79, 206, 235

Vaccaro, Joe, 261
vaccinations, 77

Van den Haag, Ernest, 72, 199, 369–70
Van Noort, G., 116–17
Vanzetti, Bartolomeo, 348–49
Varga, Kevin Scott, 274, 277
Vatican Councils. *See* First Vatican Council; Second Vatican Council
vengeance
forgiveness and, 213–14
as objection to capital punishment, 66–70
USCCB on, 302–9
as virtue, 40–42, 41n43, 308
Veritatis Splendor (John Paul II), 20, 80, 83
victims' families. *See* families of victims
vigilante justice, 68, 199, 205
Vincent of Lerins (saint), 175
Vinson, Dexter Lee, 250n125
violence, cycle of, 65, 303
Vitoria, Francisco de, 121, 171
Voltaire, 206
Vrabel, Stephen Allen, 247n99

Waldensian heresy, 123–25
Walker, Gary Alan, 244n74
Walker, Jack Dale, 241, 241n46
Wallace, Donald Ray, Jr., 255n148
warfare
Iraq war, 155–56
just-war doctrine, 150–51, 155, 280–82
NNLT on, 86–87
pacifism and, 69
Waterfield, Fred, 215, 216
Waterhouse, Robert Brian, 218–19, 233
Weeks, Lonnie, Jr., 250n121, 256n151
Welch, Gary Roland, 217–18, 237, 237n21, 238n25
White, Leroy, 250n123
Wiles, Mark Wayne, 270, 273–74
Wilhelm, Joseph, 118, 119–20

Williams, Jason Oric, 247n102
Willie, Robert Lee, 260–63, 267–68
Willingham, Cameron Todd, 353–54, 354n159
Wilson, Daniel E., 244n77
Wilson, Jackie Barron, 246n93
Wilson, Marvin Lee, 271
Wise, Hastings Arthur, 242n52
Witham, Robert, 104
Woodward, Paul Everette, 246n92

"Worthiness to Receive Holy Communion: General Principles" (Ratzinger), 9, 155–56, 177
Wrinkles, Matthew Eric, 251n126
wrongful executions, 77–78, 189, 339–40, 348–54
Wuornos, Aileen Carol, 248n109

Zika virus, 195
Zuern, William G., Jr., 248, 248n111